THE WORKS OF
WILLIAM
SHAKESPEARE

VOLUME FIVE

WILLIAM SHAKESPEARE

THE WORKS OF WILLIAM SHAKESPEARE

VOLUME FIVE

The Tragedy of King Richard II
The Tragedy of King Richard III
Love's Labour Lost
Macbeth
Measure for Measure

THE PEEBLES CLASSIC LIBRARY

Sandy Lesberg, *Editor*

ISBN 0-85690-043-5

Published by Peebles Press International
U.S.A.: 10 Columbus Circle, New York, NY 10019
U.K.: 12 Thayer Street, London W1M 5LD

Distributed by WHS Distributors

PRINTED AND BOUND IN THE U.S.A.

CONTENTS

THE TRAGEDY OF
KING RICHARD THE SECOND

DRAMATIS PERSONÆ

KING RICHARD THE SECOND
JOHN OF GAUNT, *Duke of Lancaster* ⎫
EDMUND OF LANGLEY, *Duke of York* ⎭ *uncles to the King*
HENRY BOLINGBROKE, *Duke of Hereford, son to John of Gaunt; afterwards King Henry IV*
DUKE OF AUMERLE, *son to the Duke of York*
THOMAS MOWBRAY, *Duke of Norfolk*
DUKE OF SURREY
EARL OF SALISBURY
LORD BERKLEY
BUSHY ⎫
BAGOT ⎬ *servants to King Richard*
GREEN ⎭
EARL OF NORTHUMBERLAND
HENRY PERCY, *his son*
LORD ROSS
LORD WILLOUGHBY
LORD FITZWATER
Bishop of Carlisle
Abbot of Westminster
Lord Marshal, and another lord
SIR PIERCE OF EXTON
SIR STEPHEN SCROOP
Captain of a band of Welshmen

Queen to King Richard
DUCHESS OF GLOSTER
DUCHESS OF YORK
Lady attending on the Queen

Lords, Heralds, Officers, Soldiers, two Gardeners, Keeper, Messenger, Groom, and other Attendants.

SCENE.—*Dispersedly in England and Wales*

12

THE TRAGEDY OF

KING RICHARD THE SECOND

ACT ONE

SCENE I.—London. A Room in the Palace

Enter KING RICHARD *and* JOHN OF GAUNT, *with other Nobles, and Attendants*

K. Rich. Old John of Gaunt, time-honoured Lancaster,
Hast thou, according to thy oath and band,
Brought hither Henry Hereford thy bold son
Here to make good the boisterous late appeal,
Which then our leisure would not let us hear,
Against the Duke of Norfolk, Thomas Mowbray?
Gaunt. I have, my liege.
K. Rich. Tell me, moreover, hast thou sounded him
If he appeal the duke on ancient malice,
Or worthily, as a good subject should,
On some known ground of treachery in him?
Gaunt. As near as I could sift him on that argument,
On some apparent danger seen in him,
Aimed at your highness,—no inveterate malice.
K. Rich. Then call them to our presence: face to face,
And frowning brow to brow, ourselves will hear
The accuser and the accuséd freely speak.—
                    [*Exeunt some Attendants*
High-stomached are they both and full of ire,
In rage deaf as the sea, hasty as fire.

Re-enter Attendants, with BOLINGBROKE *and* NORFOLK

Boling. May many years of happy days befall
My gracious sovereign, my most loving liege!
Nor. Each day still better other's happiness;
Until the heavens, envying earth's good hap,
Add an immortal title to your crown!
K. Rich. We thank you both; yet one but flatters us,
As well appeareth by the cause you come;
Namely, to appeal each other of high treason.—
Cousin of Hereford, what dost thou object
Against the Duke of Norfolk, Thomas Mowbray?
Boling. First,—Heaven be the record to my speech!—
In the devotion of a subject's love,
Tendering the precious safety of my prince,
And free from other misbegotten hate,
Come I appellant to this princely presence.—

Now, Thomas Mowbray, do I turn to thee,
And mark my greeting well; for what I speak,
My body shall make good upon this earth,
Or my divine soul answer it in heaven.
Thou art a traitor and a miscreant,
Too good to be so, and too bad to live,
Since the more fair and crystal is the sky
The uglier seem the clouds that in it fly.
Once more, the more to aggravate the note,
With a foul traitor's name stuff I thy throat,
And wish, so please my sovereign, ere I move,
What my tongue speaks my right-drawn sword may prove.
 Nor. Let not my cold words here accuse my zeal:
'T is not the trial of a woman's war,
The bitter clamour of two eager tongues,
Can arbitrate this cause betwixt us twain:
The blood is hot that must be cooled for this.
Yet can I not of such tame patience boast
As to be hushed and nought at all to say.
First, the fair reverence of your highness curbs me
From giving reins and spurs to my free speech,
Which else would post until it had returned
These terms of treason doubled down his throat.
Setting aside his high blood's royalty,
And let him be no kinsman to my liege,
I do defy him, and I spit at him,
Call him a slanderous coward, and a villain:
Which to maintain, I would allow him odds,
And meet him were I tied to run afoot
Even to the frozen ridges of the Alps,
Or any other ground inhabitable
Where ever Englishman durst set his foot.
Meantime, let this defend my loyalty,—
By all my hopes, most falsely doth he lie.
 Boling. Pale trembling coward, there I throw my gage,
Disclaiming here the kindred of the king
And lay aside my high blood's royalty,
Which fear, not reverence, makes thee to except:
If guilty dread have left thee so much strength
As to take up mine honour's pawn, then stoop.
By that and all the rites of knighthood else
Will I make good against thee, arm to arm,
What I have spoke, or thou canst worse devise.
 Nor. I take it up; and by that sword I swear,
Which gently laid my knighthood on my shoulder,
I'll answer thee in any fair degree
Or chivalrous design of knightly trial:
And when I mount, alive may I not light
If I be traitor or unjustly fight!
 K. Rich. What doth our cousin lay to Mowbray's charge?

It must be great that can inherit us
So much as of a thought of ill in him.
   Boling. Look, what I speak, my life shall prove it true:—
That Mowbray hath received eight thousand nobles
In name of lendings for your highness' soldiers,
The which he hath detained for lewd employments,
Like a false traitor and injurious villain.
Besides, I say, and will in battle prove,
Or here, or elsewhere, to the farthest verge
That ever was surveyed by English eye,
That all the treasons for these eighteen years
Complotted and contrivéd in this land
Fetch from false Mowbray their first head and spring.
Further I say, and further will maintain
Upon his bad life to make all this good,
That he did plot the Duke of Gloster's death,
Suggest his soon-believing adversaries,
And consequently, like a traitor coward,
Sluiced out his innocent soul through streams of blood:
Which blood, like sacrificing Abel's, cries,
Even from the tongueless caverns of the earth,
To me for justice and rough chastisement;
And, by the glorious worth of my descent,
This arm shall do it, or this life be spent.
   K. Rich. How high a pitch his resolution soars!
Thomas of Norfolk, what say'st thou to this?
   Nor. O, let my sovereign turn away his face
And bid his ears a little while be deaf,
Till I have told this slander of his blood,
How God and good men hate so foul a liar.
   K. Rich. Mowbray, impartial are our eyes and ears:
Were he my brother, nay, our kingdom's heir,
As he is but my father's brother's son,
Now by my sceptre's awe I make a vow,
Such neighbour nearness to our sacred blood
Should nothing privilege him, nor partialise
The unstooping firmness of my upright soul.
He is our subject, Mowbray, so art thou;
Free speech and fearless I to thee allow.
   Nor. Then, Bolingbroke, as low as to thy heart,
Through the false passage of thy throat, thou liest.
Three parts of that receipt I had for Calais
Disbursed I duly to his highness' soldiers:
The other part resérved I by consent,
For that my sovereign liege was in my debt
Upon remainder of a dear account,
Since last I went to France to fetch his queen.
Now swallow down that lie.—For Gloster's death,—
I slew him not; but to mine own disgrace
Neglected my sworn duty in that case.—

For you, my noble Lord of Lancaster,
The honourable father to my foe,
Once did I lay an ambush for your life,
A trespass that doth vex my grievéd soul;
But, ere I last received the sacrament,
I did confess it, and exactly begged
Your grace's pardon, and I hope I had it.
This is my fault: as for the rest appealed,
It issues from the rancour of a villain,
A recreant and most degenerate traitor:
Which in myself I boldly will defend;
And interchangeably hurl down my gage
Upon this overweening traitor's foot,
To prove myself a loyal gentleman
Even in the best blood chambered in his bosom.
In haste whereof, most heartily I pray
Your highness to assign our trial day.

    K. Rich.   Wrath-kindled gentlemen, be ruled by me.
Let's purge this choler without letting blood:
This we prescribe, though no physician;
Deep malice makes too deep incision:
Forget, forgive; conclude, and be agreed;
Our doctors say this is no month to bleed.—
Good uncle, let this end where it begun;
We'll calm the Duke of Norfolk, you your son.

    Gaunt.   To be a make-peace shall become my age:—
Throw down, my son, the Duke of Norfolk's gage.

    K. Rich.   And, Norfolk, throw down his.

    Gaunt.   When, Harry, when?
Obedience bids I should not bid again.

    K. Rich.   Norfolk, throw down, we bid; there is no boot.

    Nor.   Myself I throw, dread sovereign, at thy foot.
My life thou shalt command, but not my shame:
The one my duty owes; but my fair name,
Despite of death that lives upon my grave,
To dark dishonour's use thou shalt not have.
I am disgraced, impeached, and baffled here;
Pierced to the soul with slander's venomed spear;
The which no balm can cure but his heart-blood
Which breathed this poison.

    K. Rich.   Rage must be withstood.
Give me his gage:—lions make leopards tame.

    Nor.   Yea, but not change his spots: take but my shame,
And I resign my gage.   My dear, dear lord,
The purest treasure mortal times afford
Is spotless reputation; that away,
Men are but gilded loam or painted clay.
A jewel in a ten-times barred-up chest
Is a bold spirit in a loyal breast.
Mine honour is my life, both grow in one:

Take honour from me, and my life is done.
Then, dear my liege, mine honour let me try;
In that I live, and for that will I die.
   K. Rich. Cousin, throw down your gage: do you begin.
   Boling. O, God defend my soul from such deep sin!
Shall I seem crest-fall'n in my father's sight?
Or with pale beggar-fear impeach my height
Before this out-dared dastard? Ere my tongue
Shall wound mine honour with such feeble wrong,
Or sound so base a parle, my teeth shall tear
The slavish motive of recanting fear,
And spit it bleeding, in his high disgrace,
Where shame doth harbour, even in Mowbray's face.

                                      [Exit Gaunt
   K. Rich. We were not born to sue, but to command:
Which since we cannot do to make you friends,
Be ready, as your lives shall answer it,
At Coventry, upon Saint Lambert's day:
There shall your swords and lances arbitrate
The swelling difference of your settled hate.
Since we cannot atone you, we shall see
Justice design the victor's chivalry.—
Marshal, command our officers-at-arms
Be ready to direct these home-alarms.   *[Exeunt*

    Scene II.—The Same. A Room in the Duke of
               Lancaster's Palace

       Enter Gaunt *and* Duchess of Gloster

   Gaunt. Alas! the part I had in Gloster's blood
Doth more solicit me than your exclaims
To stir against the butchers of his life.
But since correction lieth in those hands
Which made the fault that we cannot correct,
Put we our quarrel to the will of Heaven;
Who, when they see the hours ripe on earth,
Will rain hot vengeance on offenders' heads.
   Duch. Finds brotherhood in thee no sharper spur?
Hath love in thy old blood no living fire?
Edward's seven sons, whereof thyself art one,
Were as seven vials of his sacred blood,
Or seven fair branches springing from one root:
Some of those seven are dried by nature's course,
Some of those branches by the Destinies cut;
But Thomas, my dear lord, my life, my Gloster,
One vial full of Edward's sacred blood,
One flourishing branch of his most royal root,
Is cracked, and all the precious liquor spilt;
Is hacked down, and his summer leaves all faded,

By envy's hand and murder's bloody axe.
Ah, Gaunt, his blood was thine! that bed, that womb,
That mettle, that self mould, that fashioned thee,
Made him a man, and though thou liv'st and breath'st
Yet art thou slain in him.   Thou dost consent
In some large measure to thy father's death,
In that thou seest thy wretched brother die,
Who was the model of thy father's life.
Call it not patience, Gaunt, it is despair:
In suffering thus thy brother to be slaughtered
Thou show'st the naked pathway to thy life,
Teaching stern murder how to butcher thee:
That which in mean men we entitle patience
Is pale cold cowardice in noble breasts:
What shall I say? to safeguard thine own life,
The best way is to venge my Gloster's death.
    Gaunt.   God's is the quarrel; for God's substitute,
His deputy anointed in His sight,
Hath caused his death: the which, if wrongfully,
Let Heaven revenge, for I may never lift
An angry arm against His minister.
    Duch.   Where then, alas, may I complain myself?
    Gaunt.   To God, the widow's champion and defence.
    Duch.   Why then, I will.—Farewell, old Gaunt:
Thou go'st to Coventry, there to behold
Our cousin Hereford and fell Mowbray fight.
O, sit my husband's wrongs on Hereford's spear,
That it may enter butcher Mowbray's breast,
Or, if misfortune miss the first career,
Be Mowbray's sins so heavy in his bosom
That they may break his foaming courser's back
And throw the rider headlong in the lists,
A caitiff recreant to my cousin Hereford!
Farewell, old Gaunt: thy sometimes brother's wife
With her companion grief must end her life.
    Gaunt.   Sister, farewell; I must to Coventry:
As much good stay with thee as go with me!
    Duch.   Yet one word more:—grief boundeth where it falls,
Not with the empty hollowness, but weight:
I take my leave before I have begun,
For sorrow ends not when it seemeth done.
Commend me to my brother, Edmund York.
Lo, this is all:—nay, yet depart not so;
Though this be all, do not so quickly go;
I shall remember more.   Bid him—Ah, what?—
With all good speed at Plashy visit me.
Alack, and what shall good old York there see
But empty lodgings and unfurnished walls,
Unpeopled offices, untrodden stones?
And what hear there for welcome, but my groans?

18

Therefore commend me, let him not come there
To seek out sorrow that dwells everywhere.
Desolate, desolate will I hence, and die:
The last leave of thee takes my weeping eye.   *[Exeunt*

SCENE III.—Gosford Green, near Coventry

Lists set out, and a throne. Heralds, etc., attending

Enter the Lord Marshal and AUMERLE

Mar.   My Lord Aumerle, is Harry Hereford armed?
Aum.   Yea, at all points; and longs to enter in.
Mar.   The Duke of Norfolk, sprightfully and bold,
Stays but the summons of the appellant's trumpet.
Aum.   Why then, the champions are prepared, and stay
For nothing but his majesty's approach.

Flourish. Enter KING RICHARD, *who takes his seat on
his throne ;* GAUNT; BUSHY, BAGOT, GREEN, *and
others, who take their places. A trumpet is sounded
and answered by another trumpet within. Then enter*
NORFOLK, *in armour, preceded by a Herald*

K. Rich.   Marshal, demand of yonder champion
The cause of his arrival here in arms:
Ask him his name, and orderly proceed
To swear him in the justice of his cause.
Mar.   In God's name, and the king's say who thou art,
And why thou com'st thus knightly clad in arms,
Against what man thou com'st, and what thy quarrel.
Speak truly, on thy knighthood, and thine oath;
And so defend thee Heaven and thy valour!
Nor.   My name is Thomas Mowbray, Duke of Norfolk:
Who hither come engagéd by my oath,
(Which God defend a knight should violate!)
Both to defend my loyalty and truth
To God, my king, and his succeeding issue,
Against the Duke of Hereford that appeals me,
And, by the grace of God and this mine arm,
To prove him, in defending of myself,
A traitor to my God, my king, and me:
And, as I truly fight, defend me Heaven!

Trumpet sounds. Enter BOLINGBROKE, *in armour,
preceded by a Herald*

K. Rich.   Marshal, ask yonder knight in arms,
Both who he is, and why he cometh hither
Thus plated in habiliments of war;
And formally according to our law
Depose him in the justice of his cause.

19

Mar.   What is thy name, and wherefore com'st thou
          hither,
Before King Richard in his royal lists?
Against whom comest thou? and what 's thy quarrel?
Speak like a true knight, so defend thee Heaven!
  Boling.   Harry of Hereford, Lancaster, and Derby,
Am I; who ready here do stand in arms,
To prove by God's grace, and my body's valour,
In lists, on Thomas Mowbray, Duke of Norfolk,
That he 's a traitor foul and dangerous
To God in heaven, King Richard, and to me:
And, as I truly fight, defend me Heaven!
  Mar.   On pain of death, no person be so bold
Or daring-hardy as to touch the lists,
Except the marshal and such officers
Appointed to direct these fair designs.
  Boling.   Lord marshal, let me kiss my sovereign's hand,
And bow my knee before his majesty.
For Mowbray and myself are like two men
That vow a long and weary pilgrimage;
Then let us take a ceremonious leave
And loving farewell of our several friends.
  Mar.   The appellant in all duty greets your highness,
And craves to kiss your hand and take his leave.
  K. Rich.   We will descend, and fold him in our arms.
Cousin of Hereford, as thy cause is right,
So be thy fortune in this royal fight.
Farewell, my blood; which if to-day thou shed,
Lament we may, but not revenge thee dead.
  Boling.   O, let no noble eye profane a tear
For me, if I be gored with Mowbray's spear.
As confident as is the falcon's flight
Against a bird, do I with Mowbray fight.—
My loving lord, I take my leave of you;
Of you, my noble cousin, Lord Aumerle;—
Not sick, although I have to do with death,
But lusty, young, and cheerly drawing breath.
Lo, as at English feasts, so I regreet
The daintiest last, to make the end most sweet:
O thou, the earthly author of my blood,—
Whose youthful spirit, in me regenerate,
Doth with a two-fold vigour lift me up
To reach at victory above my head,—
Add proof unto mine armour with thy prayers,
And with thy blessings steel my lance's point
That it may enter Mowbray's waxen coat
And furbish new the name of John o' Gaunt
Even in the lusty haviour of his son.
  Gaunt.   God in thy good cause make thee prosperous!
Be swift like lightning in the execution,

And let thy blows, doubly redoubléd,
Fall like amazing thunder on the casque
Of thy adverse pernicious enemy:
Rouse up thy youthful blood, be valiant and live.
    Boling. Mine innocency and Saint George to thrive!
    Nor. However God or fortune cast my lot,
There lives or dies, true to King Richard's throne
A loyal, just, and upright gentleman.
Never did captive with a freer heart
Cast off his chains of bondage and embrace
His golden uncontrolled enfranchisement
More than my dancing soul doth celebrate
This feast of battle with mine adversary.—
Most mighty liege, and my companion peers,
Take from my mouth the wish of happy years;
As gentle and as jocund as to jest
Go I to fight: truth hath a quiet breast.
    K. Rich. Farewell, my lord: securely I espy
Virtue with valour crouchéd in thine eye.—
Order the trial, marshal, and begin.
    Mar. Harry of Hereford, Lancaster, and Derby,
Receive thy lance; and God defend the right!
    Boling. Strong as a tower in hope, I cry Amen.
    Mar. [*To an Officer*] Go bear this lance to Thomas
        Duke of Norfolk.
    First Her. Harry of Hereford, Lancaster, and Derby,
Stands here for God, his sovereign, and himself,
On pain to be found false and recreant
To prove the Duke of Norfolk, Thomas Mowbray,
A traitor to his God, his king, and him;
And dares him to set forward to the fight.
    Sec. Her. Here standeth Thomas Mowbray, Duke of
        Norfolk,
On pain to be found false and recreant,
Both to defend himself, and to approve
Henry of Hereford, Lancaster, and Derby,
To God, his sovereign, and to him, disloyal;
Courageously, and with a free desire,
Attending but the signal to begin.
    Mar. Sound, trumpets; and set forward, combatants.
                         [*A charge sounded*
Stay, stay, the king hath thrown his warder down.
    K. Rich. Let them lay by their helmets and their spears,
And both return back to their chairs again.—
Withdraw with us; and let the trumpets sound,
While we return these dukes what we decree.—
                              [*A long flourish*
Draw near,
And list what with our council we have done.
For that our kingdom's earth should not be soiled

With that dear blood which it hath fosteréd;
And for our eyes do hate the dire aspect
Of civil wounds ploughed up with neighbours' swords;
And for we think the eagle-wingéd pride
Of sky-aspiring and ambitious thoughts,
With rival-hating envy, set on you
To wake our peace, which in our country's cradle
Draws the sweet infant breath of gentle sleep;
Which so roused up with boisterous untuned drums,
With harsh resounding trumpets' dreadful bray
And grating shock of wrathful iron arms,
Might from our quiet confines fright fair peace,
And make us wade even in our kindred's blood;
Therefore, we banish you our territories:—
You, cousin Hereford, upon pain of life,
Till twice five summers have enriched our fields
Shall not regreet our fair dominions,
But tread the stranger paths of banishment.
    Boling.   Your will be done: this must my comfort be,—
The sun that warms you here shall shine on me;
And those his golden beams to you here lent
Shall point on me and gild my banishment.
    K. Rich.   Norfolk, for thee remains a heavier doom,
Which I with some unwillingness pronounce;
The fly-slow hours shall not determinate
The dateless limit of thy dear exile.
The hopeless word of "never to return"
Breathe I against thee, upon pain of life.
    Nor.   A heavy sentence, my most sovereign liege,
And all unlooked for from your highness' mouth.
A dearer merit, not so deep a maim
As to be cast forth in the common air,
Have I deservéd at your highness' hands.
The language I have learned these forty years,
My native English, now I must forego;
And now my tongue's use is to me no more
Than an unstringéd viol, or a harp;
Or like a cunning instrument cased up,
Or, being open, put into his hands
That knows no touch to tune the harmony.
Within my mouth you have engaoled my tongue,
Doubly portcullised with my teeth and lips,
And dull, unfeeling, barren ignorance
Is made my gaoler to attend on me.
I am too old to fawn upon a nurse,
Too far in years to be a pupil now;
What is thy sentence then but speechless death,
Which robs my tongue from breathing native breath?
    K. Rich.   It boots thee not to be compassionate:
After our sentence plaining comes too late.

Nor. Then thus I turn me from my country's light,
To dwell in solemn shades of endless night.   [*Retiring*
   K. Rich. Return again, and take an oath with thee.
Lay on our royal sword your banished hands;
Swear by the duty that ye owe to God,—
Our part therein we banish with yourselves—
To keep the oath that we administer:
You never shall, so help you truth and God,
Embrace each other's love in banishment,
Nor never look upon each other's face,
Nor never write, regreet, nor reconcile
This lowering tempest of your home-bred hate;
Nor never by adviséd purpose meet
To plot, contrive, or complot any ill
'Gainst us, our state, our subjects, or our land.
   Boling. I swear.
   Nor. And I, to keep all this.
   Boling. Norfolk, so far, as to mine enemy:
By this time, had the king permitted us,
One of our souls had wandered in the air,
Banished this frail sepulchre of our flesh,
As now our flesh is banished from this land:—
Confess thy treasons, ere thou fly the realm;
Since thou hast far to go, bear not along
The clogging burden of a guilty soul.
   Nor. No, Bolingbroke; if ever I were traitor,
My name be blotted from the book of life
And I from heaven banished, as from hence.
But what thou art, God, thou, and I do know;
And all too soon, I fear, the king shall rue.—
Farewell, my liege.—Now no way can I stray;
Save back to England, all the world's my way.   [*Exit*
   K. Rich. Uncle, even in the glasses of thine eyes
I see thy grievéd heart: thy sad aspect
Hath from the number of his banished years
Plucked   four   away.—[*To   Bolingbroke*]   Six   frozen
            winters spent,
Return with welcome home from banishment.
   Boling. How long a time lies in one little word!
Four lagging winters and four wanton springs
End in a word: such is the breath of kings.
   Gaunt. I thank my liege, that in regard of me
He shortens four years of my son's exile,
But little vantage shall I reap thereby:
For, ere the six years that he hath to spend
Can change their moons and bring their times about,
My oil-dried lamp and time-bewasted light
Shall be extinct with age and endless night;
My inch of taper will be burnt and done,
And blindfold death not let me see my son.

K. Rich. Why, uncle, thou hast many years to live.
Gaunt. But not a minute, king, that thou canst give:
Shorten my days thou canst with sullen sorrow,
And pluck nights from me, but not lend a morrow!
Thou canst help Time to furrow me with age,
But stop no wrinkle in his pilgrimage;
Thy word is current with him for my death;
But dead, thy kingdom cannot buy me breath.
K. Rich. Thy son is banished upon good advice,
Whereto thy tongue a party-verdict gave.
Why at our justice seem'st thou then to lower?
Gaunt. Things sweet to taste prove in digestion sour.
You urged me as a judge; but I had rather
You would have bid me argue like a father.
O, had it been a stranger, not my child,
To smooth his fault I should have been more mild.
A partial slander sought I to avoid,
And in the sentence my own life destroyed.
Alas, I looked when some of you should say,
I was too strict, to make mine own away;
But you gave leave to my unwilling tongue
Against my will to do myself this wrong.
K. Rich. Cousin, farewell;—and, uncle bid him so:
Six years we banish him; and he shall go.

[*Flourish.   Exeunt King Richard and Train*

Aum. Cousin, farewell: what presence must not know,
From where you do remain let paper show.
Mar. My lord, no leave take I; for I will ride,
As far as land will let me, by your side.
Gaunt. O, to what purpose dost thou hoard thy words,
That thou return'st no greeting to thy friends?
Boling. I have too few to take my leave of you
When the tongue's office should be prodigal
To breathe the abundant dolour of the heart.
Gaunt. Thy grief is but thy absence for a time.
Boling. Joy absent, grief is present for that time.
Gaunt. What is six winters? they are quickly gone.
Boling. To men in joy; but grief makes one hour ten.
Gaunt. Call it a travel that thou tak'st for pleasure.
Boling. My heart will sigh when I miscall it so,
Which finds it an enforcéd pilgrimage.
Gaunt. The sullen passage of thy weary steps
Esteem a foil, wherein thou art to set
The precious jewel of thy home-return.
Boling. Nay rather, every tedious stride I make
Will but remember me what a deal of world
I wander from the jewels that I love.
Must I not serve a long apprenticehood
To foreign passages; and in the end,

24

Having my freedom, boast of nothing else
But that I was a journeyman to grief?
    Gaunt.   All places that the eye of Heaven visits
Are to a wise man ports and happy havens.
Teach thy necessity to reason thus;
There is no virtue like necessity.
Think not, it was the king did banish thee,
But thou the king; woe doth the heavier sit
Where it perceives it is but faintly borne.
Go, say I sent thee forth to purchase honour,
And not the king exiled thee; or suppose,
Devouring pestilence hangs in our air,
And thou art flying to a fresher clime.
Look, what thy soul holds dear, imagine it
To lie that way thou go'st, not whence thou com'st.
Suppose the singing birds musicians,
The grass whereon thou tread'st the presence strewed,
The flowers fair ladies, and thy steps no more
Than a delightful measure, or a dance;
For gnarling sorrow hath less power to bite
The man that mocks at it and sets it light.
    Boling.   O, who can hold a fire in his hand
By thinking on the frosty Caucasus?
Or cloy the hungry edge of appetite
By bare imagination of a feast?
Or wallow naked in December snow
By thinking on fantastic summer's heat?
O, no; the apprehension of the good
Gives but the greater feeling to the worse:
Fell sorrow's tooth doth never rankle more
Than when it bites but lanceth not the sore.
    Gaunt.   Come, come, my son, I'll bring thee on thy way.
Had I thy youth and cause, I would not stay.
    Boling.   Then, England's ground, farewell; sweet soil,
      adieu,
My mother, and my nurse, that bears me yet!
Where'er I wander, boast of this I can,
Though banished, yet a true-born Englishman.   [*Exeunt*

SCENE IV.—The Court

Enter KING RICHARD, BAGOT, *and* GREEN, *at one door :*
AUMERLE *at another*

    K. Rich.   We did observe.—Cousin Aumerle,
How far brought you high Hereford on his way?
    Aum.   I brought high Hereford, if you call him so,
But to the next highway, and there I left him.
    K. Rich.   And, say, what store of parting tears were shed?
    Aum.   'Faith, none for me; except the north-east wind,
Which then blew bitterly against our faces,

Awaked the sleeping rheum and so by chance
Did grace our hollow parting with a tear.
   K. Rich. What said our cousin, when you parted with
     him?
   Aum. "Farewell":
And, for my heart disdainéd that my tongue
Should so profane the word, that taught me craft
To counterfeit oppression of such grief
That words seemed buried in my sorrow's grave.
Marry, would the word "farewell" have lengthened hours
And add years to his short banishment,
He should have had a volume of farewells;
But, since it would not, he had none of me.
   K. Rich. He is our cousin, cousin; but 't is doubt,
When time shall call him home from banishment,
Whether our kinsman come to see his friends.
Ourself, and Bushy, Bagot here, and Green,
Observed his courtship to the common people,
How he did seem to dive into their hearts
With humble and familiar courtesy;
What reverence he did throw away on slaves,
Wooing poor craftsmen with the craft of smiles
And patient underbearing of his fortune,
As 't were to banish their affects with him.
Off goes his bonnet to an oyster-wench;
A brace of draymen bid God speed him well,
And had the tribute of his supple knee,
With—"Thanks, my countrymen, my loving friends;"—
As were our England in reversion his
And he our subjects' next degree in hope.
   Green. Well, he is gone; and with him go these thoughts.
Now for the rebels, which stand out in Ireland,—
Expedient manage must be made, my liege,
Ere further leisure yield them further means
For their advantage and your highness' loss.
   K. Rich. We will ourself in person to this war;
And, for our coffers, with too great a court
And liberal largess, are grown somewhat light,
We are enforced to farm our royal realm;
The revenue whereof shall furnish us
For our affairs in hand. If that come short,
Our substitutes at home shall have blank charters,
Whereto, when they shall know what men are rich,
They shall subscribe them for large sums of gold
And send them after to supply our wants;
For we will make for Ireland presently.

Enter BUSHY

Bushy, what news?
   Bushy. Old John of Gaunt is grievous sick, my lord,

Suddenly taken; and hath sent post-haste
To entreat your majesty to visit him.
  K. Rich. Where lies he?
  Bushy. At Ely House.
  K. Rich. Now put it, God, in his physician's mind,
To help him to his grave immediately!
The lining of his coffers shall make coats
To deck our soldiers for these Irish wars.—
Come, gentlemen, let's all go visit him:
Pray God we may make haste and come too late!

                        [Exeunt

ACT TWO

Scene I.—London.   A Room in Ely House

Gaunt *on a couch; the* Duke of York *and others standing
by him*

  Gaunt. Will the king come, that I may breathe my last
In wholesome counsel to his unstaid youth!
  York. Vex not yourself, nor strive not with your breath;
For all in vain comes counsel to his ear.
  Gaunt. O, but they say the tongues of dying men
Enforce attention like deep harmony:
Where words are scarce they are seldom spent in vain,
For they breathe truth that breathe their words in pain.
He that no more must say is listened more,
  Than they whom youth and ease have taught to glose
More are men's ends marked than their lives before:
  The setting sun, and music at the close,
As the last taste of sweets, is sweetest last.
Writ in remembrance more than things long past.
Though Richard my life's counsel would not hear,
My death's sad tale may yet undeaf his ear.
  York. No; it is stopped with other flattering sounds,
As praises of his state: then there are fond
Lascivious metres, to whose venom sound
The open ear of youth doth always listen:
Report of fashions in proud Italy,
Whose manners still our tardy apish nation
Limps after in base imitation.
Where doth the world thrust forth a vanity,
So it be new, there's no respect how vile,
That is not quickly buzzed into his ears?
Then all too late comes counsel to be heard,
Where will doth mutiny with wit's regard.
Direct not him whose way himself will choose:
'T is breath thou lack'st, and that breath wilt thou lose.
  Gaunt. Methinks, I am a prophet new inspired,
And thus, expiring, do foretell of him:—

His rash fierce blaze of riot cannot last,
For violent fires soon burn out themselves;
Small showers last long, but sudden storms are short;
He tires betimes that spurs too fast betimes;
With eager feeding, food doth choke the feeder:
Light vanity, insatiate cormorant,
Consuming means, soon preys upon itself.
This royal throne of kings, this sceptred isle,
This earth of majesty, this seat of Mars,
This other Eden, demi-paradise;
This fortress built by Nature for herself
Against infection and the hand of war;
This happy breed of men, this little world,
This precious stone set in the silver sea,
Which serves it in the office of a wall,
Or as a moat defensive to a house,
Against the envy of less happier lands:
This blessed plot, this earth, this realm, this England,
This nurse, this teeming womb of royal kings,
Feared by their breed, and famous by their birth,
Renownéd for their deeds as far from home—
For Christian service and true chivalry—
As is the sepulchre in stubborn Jewry
Of the world's ransom, blessed Mary's Son;
This land of such dear souls, this dear, dear land
Dear for her reputation through the world,
Is now leased out, I die pronouncing it,
Like to a tenement or pelting farm.
England, bound in with the triumphant sea,
Whose rocky shore beats back the envious siege
Of watery Neptune, 's now bound in with shame,
With inky blots, and rotten parchment bonds:
That England, that was wont to conquer others,
Hath made a shameful conquest of itself.
Ah, would the scandal vanish with my life,
How happy then were my ensuing death!

     Enter KING RICHARD *and* QUEEN; AUMERLE;
    BUSHY, GREEN, BAGOT; ROSS, *and* WILLOUGHBY

  York. The king is come: deal mildly with his youth;
For young hot colts being reined do rage the more.
  Queen. How fares our noble uncle, Lancaster?
  K. Rich. What comfort, man? how is't with agéd Gaunt?
  Gaunt. O, how that name befits my composition!
Old Gaunt, indeed; and gaunt in being old:
Within me grief hath kept a tedious fast;
And who abstains from meat, that is not gaunt?
For sleeping England long time have I watched;
Watching breeds leanness, leanness is all gaunt.
The pleasure that some fathers feed upon

Is my strict fast, I mean my children's looks;
And therein fasting hast thou made me gaunt.
Gaunt am I for the grave, gaunt as a grave,
Whose hollow womb inherits nought but bones.
 K. Rich. Can sick men play so nicely with their names?
 Gaunt. No, misery makes sport to mock itself.
Since thou dost seek to kill my name in me,
I mock my name, great king, to flatter thee.
 K. Rich. Should dying men flatter with those that live?
 Gaunt. No, no, men living flatter those that die.
 K. Rich. Thou, now a-dying, say'st thou flatter'st me.
 Gaunt. O, no; thou diest, though I the sicker be.
 K. Rich. I am in health, I breathe, and see thee ill.
 Gaunt. Now, He that made me knows I see thee ill;
Ill in myself to see, in thee seeing ill.
Thy death-bed is no lesser than thy land,
Wherein thou liest in reputation sick;
And thou, too careless patient as thou art,
Committ'st thy 'nointed body to the cure
Of those physicians that first wounded thee.
A thousand flatterers sit within thy crown,
Whose compass is no bigger than thy head,
And yet, incagéd in so small a verge,
The waste is no whit lesser than thy land.
O, had thy grandsire, with a prophet's eye,
Seen how his son's son should destroy his sons,
From forth thy reach he would have laid thy shame,
Deposing thee before thou wert possessed,
Which art possessed now to depose thyself.
Why, cousin, wert thou regent of the world,
It were a shame to let this land by lease;
But for thy world enjoying but this land,
Is it not more than shame to shame it so?
Landlord of England art thou now, not king:
Thy state of law is bondslave to the law,
And—
 K. Rich. And thou a lunatic lean-witted fool,
Presuming on an ague's privilege,
Dar'st with thy frozen admonition
Make pale our cheek, chasing the royal blood
With fury from his native residence.
Now, by my seat's right royal majesty,
Wert thou not brother to great Edward's son,
This tongue, that runs so roundly in thy head,
Should run thy head from thy unreverent shoulders.
 Gaunt. O, spare me not, my brother Edward's son,
For that I was his father Edward's son.
That blood already, like the pelican,
Hast thou tapped out, and drunkenly caroused.
My brother Gloster, plain well-meaning soul,—

Whom fair befall in heaven 'mongst happy souls!—
May be a precedent and witness good
That thou respect'st not spilling Edward's blood.
Join with the present sickness that I have;
And thy unkindness be like crookéd age,
To crop at once a too-long withered flower.
Live in thy shame, but die not shame with thee!
These words hereafter thy tormentors be!—
Convey me to my bed, then to my grave:
Love they to live that love and honour have.

       [Exit, borne out by his Attendants
 K. Rich. And let them die that age and sullens have;
For both hast thou, and both become the grave.
 York. Beseech your majesty, impute his words
To wayward sickliness and age in him:
He loves you, on my life, and holds you dear
As Harry, Duke of Hereford, were he here.
 K. Rich. Right, you say true: as Hereford's love, so
  his;
As theirs, so mine; and all be as it is.

     Enter NORTHUMBERLAND

 North. My liege, old Gaunt commends him to your
  majesty
 K. Rich. What says he?
 North.   Nay, nothing: all is said.
His tongue is now a stringless instrument;
Words, life, and all, old Lancaster hath spent.
 York. Be York the next that must be bankrupt so!
Though death be poor, it ends a mortal woe.
 K. Rich. The ripest fruit first falls, and so doth he;
His time is spent, our pilgrimage must be.
So much for that.—Now for our Irish wars:
We must supplant those rough rug-headed kerns,
Which live like venom where no venom else,
But only they, hath privilege to live.
And for these great affairs do ask some charge,
Towards our assistance we do seize to us
The plate, coin, revenues, and movables
Whereof our uncle Gaunt did stand possessed.
 York. How long shall I be patient? Ah, how long
Shall tender duty make me suffer wrong?
Not Gloster's death, nor Hereford's banishment,
Not Gaunt's rebukes, nor England's private wrongs,
Nor the prevention of poor Bolingbroke
About his marriage, nor my own disgrace,
Have ever made me sour my patient cheek,
Or bend one wrinkle on my sovereign's face.
I am the last of noble Edward's sons,
Of whom thy father, Prince of Wales, was first;

In war was never lion raged more fierce,
In peace was never gentle lamb more mild,
Than was that young and princely gentleman.
His face thou hast, for even so looked he,
Accomplished with the number of thy hours;
But when he frowned, it was against the French,
And not against his friends: his noble hand
Did win what he did spend, and spent not that
Which his triumphant father's hand had won:
His hands were guilty of no kindred blood,
But bloody with the enemies of his kin.
O Richard! York is too far gone with grief,
Or else he never would compare between.
   K. Rich. Why, uncle, what's the matter?
   York.   O my liege,
Pardon me, if you please; if not, I, pleased
Not to be pardoned, am content withal:
Seek you to seize and gripe into your hands
The royalties and rights of banished Hereford?
Is not Gaunt dead, and doth not Hereford live?
Was not Gaunt just, and is not Harry true?
Did not the one deserve to have an heir?
Is not his heir a well-deserving son?
Take Hereford's rights away, and take from time
His charters and his customary rights;
Let not to-morrow, then, ensue to-day;
Be not thyself; for how art thou a king
But by fair sequence and succession?
Now, afore God,—God forbid, I say true!—
If you do wrongfully seize Hereford's rights,
Call in the letters-patents that he hath
By his attorneys-general to sue
His livery, and deny his offered homage,
You pluck a thousand dangers on your head,
You lose a thousand well-disposéd hearts,
And prick my tender patience to those thoughts
Which honour and allegiance cannot think.
   K. Rich. Think what you will: we seize into our hands
His plate, his goods, his money, and his lands.
   York. I'll not be by the while. My liege, farewell:
What will ensue hereof, there's none can tell:
But by bad courses may be understood
That their events can never fall out good.   [*Exit*
   K. Rich. Go, Bushy, to the Earl of Wiltshire straight:
Bid him repair to us to Ely House,
To see this business. To-morrow next
We will for Ireland; and 't is time, I trow:
And we create, in absence of ourself,
Our uncle York lord governor of England;
For he is just, and always loved us well.—

Come on, our queen: to-morrow must we part;
Be merry, for our time of stay is short.
      [*Flourish. Exeunt King, Queen, Aumerle, Bushy,*
                              Green, and Bagot
  North.   Well, lords, the Duke of Lancaster is dead.
  Ross.   And living too; for now his son is duke.
  Willo.   Barely in title, not in revenue.
  North.   Richly in both, if justice had her right.
  Ross.   My heart is great; but it must break with silence,
Ere 't be disburdened with a liberal tongue.
  North.   Nay, speak thy mind; and let him ne'er speak
        more
That speaks thy words again to do thee harm!
  Willo.   Tends that thou wouldst speak to the Duke of
        Hereford?
If it be so, out with it boldly, man:
Quick is mine ear to hear of good towards him.
  Ross.   No good at all that I can do for him;
Unless you call it good to pity him,
Bereft and gelded of his patrimony.
  North.   Now, afore God, 't is shame such wrongs are borne
In him, a royal prince, and many more
Of noble blood in this declining land.
The king is not himself, but basely led
By flatterers; and what they will inform,
Merely in hate, 'gainst any of us all,
That will the king severely prosecute
'Gainst us, our lives, our children, and our heirs.
  Ross.   The commons hath he pilled with grievous taxes
And lost their hearts: the nobles hath he fined
For ancient quarrels, and quite lost their hearts.
  Willo.   And daily new exactions are devised,—
As blanks, benevolences, and I wot not what;
But what, o' God's name, doth become of this?
  North.   War hath not wasted it, for warred he hath not,
But basely yielded upon compromise
That which his ancestors achieved with blows:
More hath he spent in peace than they in wars.
  Ross.   The Earl of Wiltshire hath the realm in farm.
  Willo.   The king's grown bankrupt, like a broken man.
  North.   Reproach and dissolution hangeth o'er him.
  Ross.   He hath not money for these Irish wars,
His burdensome taxations notwithstanding,
But by the robbing of the banished duke.
  North.   His noble kinsman:—most degenerate king!
But, lords, we hear this fearful tempest sing,
Yet seek no shelter to avoid the storm;
We see the wind sit sore upon our sails,
And yet we strike not, but securely perish.
  Ross.   We see the very wrack that we must suffer;

And unavoided is the danger now,
For suffering so the causes of our wrack.
    North. Not so: even through the hollow eyes of death
I spy life peering; but I dare not say
How near the tidings of our comfort is.
    Willo. Nay, let us share thy thoughts, as thou dost ours.
    Ross. Be confident to speak, Northumberland:
We three are but thyself; and, speaking so.
Thy words are but as thoughts; therefore, be bold.
    North. Then thus:—I have from Port le Blanc, a bay
In Brittany, received intelligence,
That Harry Duke of Hereford, Rainold Lord Cobham,
That late broke from the Duke of Exeter,
His brother, Archbishop late of Canterbury,
Sir Thomas Erpingham, Sir John Ramston,
Sir John Norbery, Sir Robert Waterton, and Francis Quoint,
All these well furnished by the Duke of Bretagne,
With eight tall ships, three thousand men of war,
Are making hither with all due expedience,
And shortly mean to touch our northern shore:
Perhaps they had ere this, but that they stay
The first departing of the king for Ireland.
If, then, we shall shake off our slavish yoke,
Imp out our drooping country's broken wing,
Redeem from broking pawn the blemished crown,
Wipe off the dust that hides our sceptre's gilt,
And make high majesty look like itself,—
Away with me in post to Ravenspurg;
But if you faint, as fearing to do so,
Stay and be secret, and myself will go.
    Ross. To horse, to horse! urge doubts to them that fear.
    Willo. Hold out my horse, and I will first be there.
                                                    [*Exeunt*

SCENE II.—The Same. An Apartment in the Palace

Enter QUEEN, BUSHY, *and* BAGOT

    Bushy. Madam, your majesty is too much sad:
You promised, when you parted with the king,
To lay aside life-harming heaviness,
And entertain a cheerful disposition.
    Queen. To please the king, I did; to please myself,
I cannot do it; yet I know no cause
Why I should welcome such a guest as grief,
Save bidding farewell to so sweet a guest
As my sweet Richard. Yet, again, methinks,
Some unborn sorrow, ripe in fortune's womb,
Is coming towards me; and my inward soul
With nothing trembles; at some thing it grieves
More than with parting from my lord the king.

Bushy. Each substance of a grief hath twenty shadows,
Which show like grief itself, but are not so.
For sorrow's eye, glazéd with blinding tears,
Divides one thing entire to many objects;
Like pérspectives, which, rightly gazed upon,
Show nothing but confusion,—eyed awry,
Distinguish form: so your sweet majesty,
Looking awry upon your lord's departure,
Finds shapes of grief more than himself to wail;
Which looked on as it is, is nought but shadows
Of what it is not. Then, thrice-gracious queen,
More than your lord's departure weep not,—more's not seen;
Or if it be, 't is with false sorrow's eye,
Which for things true weeps things imaginary.
Queen. It may be so; but yet my inward soul
Persuades me otherwise: howe'er it be,
I cannot but be sad, so heavy sad,
As—though, in thinking, on no thought I think—
Makes me, with heavy nothing, faint and shrink.
Bushy. 'T is nothing but conceit, my gracious lady.
Queen. 'T is nothing less: conceit is still derived
From some forefather grief; mine is not so,
For nothing hath begot my something grief;
Or something hath the nothing that I grieve:
'T is in reversion that I do possess;
But what it is, that is not yet known; what
I cannot name; 't is nameless woe, I wot.

Enter GREEN

Green. God save your majesty!—and well met, gentle-
        men.—
I hope, the king is not yet shipped for Ireland.
Queen. Why hop'st thou so? 't is better hope he is,
For his designs crave haste, his haste good hope:
Then wherefore dost thou hope he is not shipped?
Green. That he, our hope, might have retired his power,
And driven into despair an enemy's hope,
Who strongly hath set footing in this land.
The banished Bolingbroke repeals himself,
And with uplifted arms is safe arrived
At Ravenspurg.
Queen.   Now, God in heaven forbid!
Green. Ah, madam, 't is too true: and that is worse,
The Lord Northumberland, his son, young Henry Percy,
The Lords of Ross, Beaumond, and Willoughby,
With all their powerful friends, are fled to him.
Bushy. Why have you not proclaimed Northumberland
And the rest of the revolted faction traitors?
Green. We have: whereupon the Earl of Worcester
Hath broke his staff, resigned his stewardship,

34

And all the household servants fled with him
To Bolingbroke.
   Queen. So, Green, thou art the midwife to my woe,
And Bolingbroke my sorrow's dismal heir:
Now hath my soul brought forth her prodigy;
And I, a gasping new-delivered mother,
Have woe to woe, sorrow to sorrow joined.
   Bushy. Despair not, madam.
   Queen.   Who shall hinder me?
I will despair, and be at enmity
With cozening hope,—he is a flatterer,
A parasite, a keeper-back of death,
Who gently would dissolve the bands of life
Which false hope lingers in extremity.
   Green. Here comes the Duke of York.
   Queen. With signs of war about his agéd neck.
O, full of careful business are his looks.—

Enter YORK

Uncle, for God's sake, speak comfortable words.
   York. Should I do so, I should belie my thoughts:
Comfort's in heaven; and we are on the earth,
Where nothing lives but crosses, care, and grief.
Your husband, he is gone to save far off
Whilst others come to make him lose at home:
Here am I left to underprop his land,
Who, weak with age, cannot support myself.
Now comes the sick hour that his surfeit made;
Now shall he try his friends that flattered him.

Enter a Servant

   Serv. My lord, your son was gone before I came.
   York. He was?—Why, so.—Go all which way it will!—
The nobles they are fled, the commons cold,
And will, I fear, revolt on Hereford's side.—
Sirrah,
Get thee to Plashy, to my sister Gloster;
Bid her send me presently a thousand pound.—
Hold; take my ring.
   Serv. My lord, I had forgot to tell your lordship:
To-day, as I came by, I calléd there;
But I shall grieve you to report the rest.
   York. What is't, knave?
   Serv. An hour before I came, the duchess died.
   York. God for His mercy! what a tide of woes
Comes rushing on this woful land at once!
I know not what to do:—I would to God,—
So my untruth had not provoked him to it,—
The king had cut off my head with my brother's.—
What! are there no posts despatched for Ireland?—

How shall we do for money for these wars?—
Come, sister,—cousin, I'd say: pray, pardon me.—
[*To the Servant*]   Go, fellow, get thee home; provide some
        carts,
And bring away the armour that is there.—   [*Exit Servant*
Gentlemen, will you go muster men?   If I
Know how, or which way t' order these affairs,
Thus thrust disorderly into my hands,
Never believe me.   Both are my kinsmen:—
The one 's my sovereign, whom both my oath
And duty bids defend; the other again
He is my kinsman, whom the king hath wronged,
Whom conscience and my kindred bids to right.
Well, somewhat we must do.   Come, cousin, I'll
Dispose of you.—Go muster up your men,
And meet me presently at Berkley Castle.—
I should to Plashy too,
But time will not permit.—All is uneven,
And everything is left at six and seven.
                [*Exeunt York and Queen*
  Bushy.   The wind sits fair for news to go to Ireland,
But none returns.   For us to levy power
Proportionable to the enemy
Is all unpossible.
  Green.   Besides, our nearness to the king in love
Is near the hate of those love not the king.
  Bagot.   And that's the wavering commons; for their love
Lies in their purses, whoso empties them,
By so much fills their hearts with deadly hate.
  Bushy.   Wherein the king stands generally condemned.
  Bagot.   If judgment lie in them, then so do we,
Because we ever have been near the king.
  Green.   Well, I'll for refuge straight to Bristol Castle;
The Earl of Wiltshire is already there.
  Bushy.   Thither will I with you; for little office
The hateful commons will perform for us,
Except like curs to tear us all to pieces.—
Will you go along with us?
  Bagot.   No;
I will to Ireland to his majesty.
Farewell: if heart's presages be not vain,
We three here part, that ne'er shall meet again.
  Bushy.   That's as York thrives to beat back Bolingbroke.
  Green.   Alas, poor duke, the task he undertakes
Is numbering sands, and drinking oceans dry:
Where one on his side fights, thousands will fly.
  Bagot.   Farewell at once; for once, for all, and ever.
  Bushy.   Well, we may meet again.   I fear me, never.
  Bagot.
                      [*Exeunt*

SCENE III.—The Wilds in Glostershire

Enter BOLINGBROKE *and* NORTHUMBERLAND, *with Forces*

Boling.   How far is it, my lord, to Berkley now?
North.   Believe me, noble lord,
I am a stranger here in Glostershire.
These high wild hills, and rough uneven ways
Draw out our miles and make them wearisome;
And yet your fair discourse hath been as sugar,
Making the hard way sweet and délectable.
But, I bethink me, what a weary way
From Ravenspurg to Cotswold will be found
In Ross and Willoughby, wanting your company;
Which, I protest, hath very much beguiled
The tediousness and process of my travel:
But theirs is sweetened with the hope to have
The present benefit which I possess;
And hope to joy is little less in joy
Than hope enjoyed: by this the weary lords
Shall make their way seem short, as mine hath done
By sight of what I have, your noble company.
Boling.   Of much less value is my company
Than your good words.   But who comes here?

Enter HARRY PERCY

North.   It is my son, young Harry Percy,
Sent from my brother Worcester, whencesoever.—
Harry, how fares your uncle?
Percy.   I had thought, my lord, to have learned his
health of you.
North.   Why, is he not with the queen?
Percy.   No, my good lord: he hath forsook the court,
Broken his staff of office, and dispersed
The household of the king.
North.   What was his reason?
He was not so resolved when last we spake together.
Percy.   Because your lordship was proclaiméd traitor.
But he, my lord, is gone to Ravenspurg,
To offer service to the Duke of Hereford,
And sent me o'er by Berkley, to discover
What power the Duke of York had levied there;
Then with direction to repair to Ravenspurg.
North.   Have you forgot the Duke of Hereford, boy?
Percy.   No, my good lord; for that is not forgot
Which ne'er I did remember: to my knowledge,
I never in my life did look on him.
North.   Then learn to know him now: this is the duke.
Percy.   My gracious lord, I tender you my service,
Such as it is, being tender, raw, and young,

37

Which elder days shall ripen, and confirm
To more appróvéd service and desert.
   Boling. I thank thee, gentle Percy; and be sure,
I count myself in nothing else so happy
As in a soul remembering my good friends;
And as my fortune ripens with thy love,
It shall be still thy true love's recompense:
My heart this covenant makes, my hand thus seals it.
   North. How far is it to Berkley? and what stir
Keeps good old York there, with his men of war?
   Percy. There stands the castle, by yond tuft of trees,
Manned with three hundred men, as I have heard;
And in't are th' Lords of York, Berkley, and Seymour;
None else of name and noble estimate.

Enter Ross *and* WILLOUGHBY

   North. Here come the Lords of Ross and Willoughby,
Bloody with spurring, fiery-red with haste.
   Boling. Welcome, my lords. I wot, your love pursues
A banished traitor: all my treasury
Is yet but unfelt thanks, which, more enriched,
Shall be your love and labour's recompense.
   Ross. Your presence makes us rich, most noble lord.
   Willo. And far surmounts our labour to attain it.
   Boling. Evermore thanks, the exchequer of the poor;
Which, till my infant fortune comes to years,
Stands for my bounty.—But who comes here?

Enter BERKLEY

   North. It is my Lord of Berkley, as I guess.
   Berk. My Lord of Hereford, my message is to you.
   Boling. My lord, my answer is to Lancaster,
And I am come to seek that name in England;
And I must find that title in your tongue
Before I make reply to aught you say.
   Berk. Mistake me not, my lord: 't is not my meaning
To raze one title of your honour out.
To you, my lord, I come,—what lord you will,—
From the most gracious regent of this land,
The Duke of York, to know what pricks you on
To take advantage of the absent time,
And fright our native peace with self-borne arms.

Enter YORK, *attended*

   Boling. I shall not need transport my words by you:
Here comes his grace in person.—My noble uncle!
                         [*Kneels*
   York. Show me thy humble heart, and not thy knee,
Whose duty is deceivable and false.

Boling.   My gracious uncle—
   York.   Tut, tut!
Grace me no grace, nor uncle me no uncle:
I am no traitor's uncle; and that word "grace"
In an ungracious mouth is but profane.
Why have those banished and forbidden legs
Dared once to touch a dust of England's ground?
But then more, why,—why have they dared to march
So many miles upon her peaceful bosom,
Frighting her pale-faced villages with war,
And ostentation of despisèd arms?
Com'st thou because the anointed king is hence?
Why, foolish boy, the king is left behind,
And in my loyal bosom lies his power.
Were I but now the lord of such hot youth
As when brave Gaunt, thy father, and myself,
Rescued the Black Prince, that young Mars of men,
From forth the ranks of many thousand French,
O, then, how quickly should this arm of mine,
Now prisoner to the palsy, chastise thee,
And minister correction to thy fault!
   Boling.   My gracious uncle, let me know my fault:
On what condition stands it, and wherein?
   York.   Even in condition of the worst degree,
In gross rebellion, and detested treason:
Thou art a banished man, and here art come
Before the expiration of thy time
In braving arms against thy sovereign.
   Boling.   As I was banished, I was banished Hereford;
But as I come, I come for Lancaster.
And, noble uncle, I beseech your grace,
Look on my wrongs with an indifferent eye:
You are my father, for methinks, in you
I see old Gaunt alive: O, then, my father,
Will you permit that I shall stand condemned
A wandering vagabond, my rights and royalties
Plucked from my arms perforce, and given away
To upstart unthrifts?   Wherefore was I born?
If that my cousin king be King of England,
It must be granted I am Duke of Lancaster.
You have a son, Aumerle, my noble kinsman;
Had you first died, and he been thus trod down,
He should have found his uncle Gaunt a father,
To rouse his wrongs and chase them to the bay.
I am denied to sue my livery here,
And yet my letters-patents give me leave:
My father's goods are all distrained and sold;
And these, and all, are all amiss employed.
What would you have me do?   I am a subject,
And challenge law.   Attorneys are denied me,

And therefore personally I lay my claim
To my inheritance of free descent.
    North.   The noble Duke hath been too much abused.
    Ross.   It stands your grace upon, to do him right.
    Willo.   Base men by his endowments are made great.
    York.   My lords of England, let me tell you this:
I have had feelings of my cousin's wrongs,
And laboured all I could to do him right;
But in this kind to come, in braving arms,
Be his own carver, and cut out his way,
To find out right with wrong,—it may not be;
And you that do abet him in this kind
Cherish rebellion, and are rebels all.
    North.   The noble duke hath sworn his coming is
But for his own; and for the right of that
We all have strongly sworn to give him aid;
And let him ne'er see joy that breaks that oath!
    York.   Well, well, I see the issue of these arms;—
I cannot mend it, I must needs confess,
Because my power is weak and all ill left:
But if I could, by him that gave me life,
I would attach you all, and make you stoop
Unto the sovereign mercy of the king;
But, since I cannot, be it known to you
I do remain as neuter. So, fare you well;—
Unless you please to enter in the castle,
And there repose you for this night.
    Boling.   An offer, uncle, that we will accept.
But we must win your grace to go with us
To Bristol Castle, which, they say, is held
By Bushy, Bagot, and their complices,
The caterpillars of the commonwealth,
Which I have sworn to weed and pluck away.
    York.   'T may be I'll go with you;—but yet I'll pause;
For I am loth to break our country's laws.
Nor friends, nor foes, to me welcome you are:
Things past redress are now with me past care.   [*Exeunt*

SCENE IV.—A Camp in Wales

Enter SALISBURY *and a Captain*

    Cap.   My Lord of Salisbury, we have stayed ten days
And hardly kept our countrymen together,
And yet we hear no tidings from the king;
Therefore, we will disperse ourselves: farewell.
    Sal.   Stay yet another day, thou trusty **Welshman**:
The king rests all his confidence in thee.
    Cap.   'T is thought the king is dead: we will not stay.
The bay-trees in our country are all withered,

And meteors fright the fixéd stars of heaven;
The pale-faced moon looks bloody on the earth,
And lean-looked prophets whisper fearful change.
Rich men look sad, and ruffians dance and leap,
The one in fear to lose what they enjoy.
The other to enjoy by rage and war.
These signs forerun the death or fall of kings.
Farewell: our countrymen are gone and fled,
As well assured Richard, their king, is dead.   *[Exit*
  Sal. Ah, Richard, with the eyes of heavy mind
I see thy glory like a shooting star,
Fall to the base earth from the firmament!
Thy sun sets weeping in the lowly west,
Witnessing storms to come, woe, and unrest:
Thy friends are fled, to wait upon thy foes,
And crossly to thy good all fortune goes.   *[Exit*

ACT THREE

SCENE I.—BOLINGBROKE'S Camp at Bristol

Enter BOLINGBROKE, YORK, NORTHUMBERLAND, PERCY,
  WILLOUGHBY, ROSS; *Officers behind, with* BUSHY *and*
  GREEN, *prisoners*

  Boling. Bring forth these men.—
Bushy, and Green, I will not vex your souls—
Since presently your souls must part your bodies—
With too much urging your pernicious lives,
For 't were no charity; yet, to wash your blood
From off my hands, here in the view of men,
I will unfold some causes of your deaths.
You have misled a prince, a royal king,
A happy gentleman in blood and lineaments,
By you unhappied and disfigured clean:
You have in manner with your sinful hours
Made a divorce betwixt his queen and him,
Broke the possession of a royal bed,
And stained the beauty of a fair queen's cheeks
With tears drawn from her eyes by your foul wrongs.
Myself, a prince by fortune of my birth,
Near to the king in blood, and near in love
Till you did make him misinterpret me,
Have stooped my neck under your injuries,
And sighed my English breath in foreign clouds,
Eating the bitter bread of banishment;
Whilst you have fed upon my signories,
Disparked my parks, and felled my forest woods,
From mine own windows torn my household coat,

41

Razed out my impress, leaving me no sign,
Save men's opinions and my living blood,
To show the world I am a gentleman.
This and much more, much more than twice all this,
Condemns you to the death.—See them delivered
To execution and the hand of death.
    Bushy. More welcome is the stroke of death to me
Than Bolingbroke to England.—Lords, farewell.
    Green. My comfort is, that Heaven will take our souls,
And plague injustice with the pains of hell.
    Boling. My Lord Northumberland, see them despatched.
                   [Exeunt Northumberland and others, with
                                  Bushy and Green
Uncle, you say the queen is at your house;
For God's sake, fairly let her be entreated:
Tell her, I send to her my kind commends;
Take special care my greetings be delivered.
    York. A gentleman of mine I have despatched
With letters of your love to her at large.
    Boling. Thanks, gentle uncle.—Come, my lords, away,
To fight with Glendower and his complices:
Awhile to work, and after holiday.   *[Exeunt*

SCENE II.—The Coast of Wales. A Castle in view

Flourish : drums and trumpets. Enter KING RICHARD, *the*
    BISHOP OF CARLISLE, AUMERLE, *and Soldiers, with*
    colours

    K. Rich. Barkloughly Castle call they this at hand?
    Aum. Yea, my good lord. How brooks your grace the
                air,
After late tossing on the breaking seas?
    K. Rich. Needs must I like it well: I weep for joy,
To stand upon my kingdom once again.—
Dear earth, I do salute thee with my hand,
Though rebels wound thee with their horses' hoofs:
As a long parted mother with her child
Plays fondly with her tears and smiles in meeting,
So, weeping, smiling, greet I thee, my earth,
And do thee favour with my royal hands.
Feed not thy sovereign's foe, my gentle earth,
Nor with thy sweets comfort his ravenous sense;
But let thy spiders, that suck up thy venom,
And heavy-gaited toads, lie in their way,
Doing annoyance to the treacherous feet
Which with usurping steps do trample thee.
Yield stinging nettles to mine enemies;
And when they from thy bosom pluck a flower,
Guard it, I pray thee, with a lurking adder,

Whose double tongue may with a mortal touch
Throw death upon thy sovereign's enemies.—
Mock not my senseless conjuration, lords:
This earth shall have a feeling, and these stones
Prove arméd soldiers, ere her native king
Shall falter under foul rebellion's arms.
 Bishop. Fear not, my lord: that power that made you
    king,
Hath power to keep you king, in spite of all.
The means that Heaven yields must be embraced,
And not neglected; else if Heaven would,
And we will not, Heaven's offer we refuse,
The proffered means of succour and redress.
 Aum. He means, my lord, that we are too remiss;
Whilst Bolingbroke, through our security,
Grows strong and great in substance, and in friends.
 K. Rich. Discomfortable cousin! know'st thou not
That when the searching eye of Heaven is hid
Behind the globe, and lights the lower world,
Then thieves and robbers range abroad unseen,
In murders and in outrage bloody here;
But when from under this terrestrial ball
He fires the proud tops of the eastern pines,
And darts his light through every guilty hole,
Then murders, treasons, and detested sins,
The cloak of night being plucked from off their backs,
Stand bare and naked, trembling at themselves?
So when this thief, this traitor, Bolingbroke,—
Who all this while hath revelled in the night,
Whilst we were wandering with the Antipodes,—
Shall see us rising in our throne, the east,
His treasons will sit blushing in his face,
Not able to endure the sight of day,
But self-affrighted, tremble at his sin.
Not all the water in the rough rude sea
Can wash the balm from an anointed king;
The breath of worldly men cannot depose
The deputy elected by the Lord.
For every man that Bolingbroke hath pressed
To lift shrewd steel against our golden crown,
God for his Richard hath in Heavenly pay
A glorious angel; then, if angels fight,
Weak men must fall; for Heaven still guards the right.

    Enter SALISBURY

Welcome, my lord. How far off lies your power?
 Sal. Nor near, nor further off, my gracious lord,
Than this weak arm. Discomfort guides my tongue,
And bids me speak of nothing but despair.
One day too late, I fear, my noble lord,

Hath clouded all thy happy days on earth:
O, call back yesterday, bid time return,
And thou shalt have twelve thousand fighting men:
To-day, to-day, unhappy day, too late,
O'erthrows thy joys, friends, fortune, and thy state;
For all the Welshmen, hearing thou wert dead,
Are gone to Bolingbroke, dispersed, and fled.
 Aum. Comfort, my liege! why looks your grace so pale?
 K. Rich. But now, the blood of twenty thousand men
Did triumph in my face, and they are fled;
And till so much blood thither come again,
 Have I not reason to look pale and dead?
All souls that will be safe fly from my side;
For time hath set a blot upon my pride.
 Aum. Comfort, my liege! remember who you are.
 K. Rich. I had forgot myself. Am I not king?
Awake, thou sluggard majesty! thou sleepest.
Is not the king's name forty thousand names?
Arm, arm, my name! a puny subject strikes
At thy great glory.—Look not to the ground,
Ye favourites of a king: are we not high?
High be our thoughts. I know, my uncle York
Hath power enough to serve our turn. But who comes
  here?

Enter SCROOP

 Scroop. More health and happiness betide my liege,
Than can my care-tuned tongue deliver him!
 K. Rich. Mine ear is open, and my heart prepared:
The worst is worldly loss thou canst unfold.
Say, is my kingdom lost? why, 't was my care;
And what loss is it to be rid of care?
Strives Bolingbroke to be as great as we?
Greater he shall not be; if he serve God,
We'll serve him too, and be his fellow so.
Revolt our subjects? that we cannot mend;
They break their faith to God, as well as us.
Cry woe, destruction, ruin, loss, decay;
The worst is death, and death will have his day.
 Scroop. Glad am I, that your highness is so armed
To bear the tidings of calamity.
Like an unseasonable stormy day,
Which makes the silver rivers drown their shores
As if the world were all dissolved to tears,
So high above his limits swells the rage
Of Bolingbroke, covering your fearful land
With hard bright steel, and hearts harder than steel.
White beards have armed their thin and hairless scalps
Against thy majesty; boys with women's voices
Strive to speak big, and clap their female joints

In stiff unwieldly arms against thy crown;
Thy very beadsmen learn to bend their bows
Of double-fatal yew against thy state;
Yea, distaff women manage rusty bills
Against thy seat; both young and old rebel,
And all goes worse than I have power to tell.
    K. Rich.   Too well, too well thou tell'st a tale so ill.
Where is the Earl of Wiltshire? where is Bagot?
What is become of Bushy? where is Green?
That they have let the dangerous enemy
Measure our confines with such peaceful steps?
If we prevail, their heads shall pay for it,
I warrant they've made peace with Bolingbroke.
    Scroop.   Peace have they made with him, indeed, my
        lord.
    K. Rich.   O villains, vipers, damned without redemp-
        tion!
Dogs, easily won to fawn on any man!
Snakes in my heart-blood warmed, that sting my heart!
Three Judases, each one thrice worse than Judas!
Would they make peace? Terrible hell make war
Upon their spotted souls for this offence!
    Scroop.   Sweet love, I see, changing his property,
Turns to the sourest and most deadly hate.
Again uncurse their souls; their peace is made
With heads, and not with hands: those whom you curse
Have felt the worst of death's destroying wound,
And lie full low, graved in the hollow ground.
    Aum.   Is Bushy, Green, and the Earl of Wiltshire, dead?
    Scroop.   Yea, all of them at Bristol lost their heads.
    Aum.   Where is the duke, my father, with his power?
    K. Rich.   No matter where;—of comfort no man speak:
Let's talk of graves, of worms, and epitaphs:
Make dust our paper, and with rainy eyes
Write sorrow on the bosom of the earth.
Let's choose executors, and talk of wills:
And yet not so—for what can we bequeath,
Save our deposèd bodies to the ground?
Our lands, our lives, and all are Bolingbroke's,
And nothing can we call our own but death,
And that small model of the barren earth
Which serves as paste and cover to our bones.
For God's sake, let us sit upon the ground,
And tell sad stories of the death of kings:—
How some have been deposed, some slain in war,
Some haunted by the ghosts they have deposed,
Some poisoned by their wives, some sleeping killed,
All murdered:—for within the hollow crown
That rounds the mortal temples of a king
Keeps Death his court, and there the antic sits,

Scoffing his state and grinning at his pomp;
Allowing him a breath, a little scene,
To monarchise, be feared, and kill with looks;
Infusing him with self and vain conceit,
As if this flesh which walls about our life
Were brass impregnable; and humoured thus,
Comes at the last, and with a little pin
Bores through his castle wall, and—farewell king!
Cover your heads, and mock not flesh and blood
With solemn reverence; throw away respect,
Tradition, form, and ceremonious duty,
For you have but mistook me all this while:
I live with bread like you, feel want, taste grief,
Need friends,
Subjected thus, how can you say to me,
I am a king?
   Bishop. My lord, wise men ne'er wail their present woes,
But presently prevent the ways to wail.
To fear the foe, since fear oppresseth strength,
Gives, in your weakness, strength unto your foe,
And so your follies fight against yourself.
Fear, and be slain; no worse can come to fight:
And fight and die is death destroying death;
Where fearing dying pays death servile breath.
   Aum. My father hath a power; inquire of him;
And learn to make a body of a limb.
   K. Rich. Thou chid'st me well.—Proud Bolingbroke, I
     come
To change blows with thee for our day of doom.
This ague-fit of fear is over-blown;
An easy task it is to win our own.—
Say, Scroop, where lies our uncle with his power?
Speak sweetly, man, although thy looks be sour.
   Scroop. Men judge by the complexion of the sky
    The state and inclination of the day;
So may you by my dull and heavy eye,
My tongue hath but a heavier tale to say.
I play the torturer, by small and small,
To lengthen out the worst that must be spoken.
Your uncle York is joined with Bolingbroke,
And all your northern castles yielded up,
And all your southern gentlemen in arms
Upon his party.
   K. Rich.   Thou hast said enough.—
Beshrew thee, cousin, which didst lead me forth
Of that sweet way I was in to despair!
What say you now? what comfort have we now?
By Heaven, I'll hate him everlastingly
That bids me be of comfort any more.
Go to Flint Castle: there I'll pine away:

A king, woe's slave, shall kingly woe obey.
That power I have, discharge; and let them go
To ear the land that hath some hope to grow,
For I have none.—Let no man speak again
To alter this, for counsel is but vain.
    Aum.   My liege, one word.
    K. Rich.   He does me double wrong
That wounds me with the flatteries of his tongue.
Discharge my followers; let them hence away,
From Richard's night to Bolingbroke's fair day.   [*Exeunt*

SCENE III.—Wales. A Plain before Flint Castle

Enter, with drum and colours, BOLINGBROKE *and Forces ;*
YORK, NORTHUMBERLAND, *and others*

    Boling.   So that by this intelligence we learn,
The Welshmen are dispersed; and Salisbury
Is gone to meet the king, who lately landed
With some few private friends upon this coast.
    North.   The news is very fair and good, my lord:
Richard not far from hence hath hid his head.
    York.   It would beseem the Lord Northumberland,
To say King Richard:—alack, the heavy day
When such a sacred king should hide his head!
    North.   Your grace mistakes me; only to be brief,
Left I his title out.
    York.   The time hath been,
Would you have been so brief with him, he would
Have been so brief with you to shorten you,
For taking so the head, your whole head's length.
    Boling.   Mistake not, uncle, further than you should.
    York.   Take not, good cousin, further than you should,
Lest you mistake: the heavens are o'er your head.
    Boling.   I know it, uncle; and I not oppose
Myself against their will.—But who comes here?

Enter PERCY

Welcome, Harry: What, will not this castle yield?
    Percy.   The castle royally is manned, my lord,
Against thy entrance.
    Boling.   Royally?
Why, it contains no king?
    Percy.   Yes, my good lord,
It doth contain a king: King Richard lies
Within the limits of yond lime and stone,
And with him are the Lord Aumerle, Lord Salisbury,
Sir Stephen Scroop; besides a clergyman
Of holy reverence, who, I cannot learn.
    North.   O, belike it is the Bishop of Carlisle.

Boling. [*To Northumberland.*]   Noble lord,
Go to the rude ribs of that ancient castle,
Through brazen trumpet send the breath of parle
Into his ruined ears,
And thus deliver:—Henry Bolingbroke
On both his knees doth kiss King Richard's hand,
And sends allegiance and true faith of heart
To his most royal person; hither come
Even at his feet to lay my arms and power,
Provided that my banishment repealed,
And lands restored again, be freely granted.
If not, I'll use the advantage of my power,
And lay the summer's dust with showers of blood
Rained from the wounds of slaughtered Englishmen:
The which, how far off from the mind of Bolingbroke
It is, such crimson tempest should bedrench
The fresh green lap of fair King Richard's land,
My stooping duty tenderly shall show.
Go, signify as much, while here we march
Upon the grassy carpet of this plain.
Let's march without the noise of threatening drum,
That from the castle's tattered battlements
Our fair appointments may be well perused.
Methinks, King Richard and myself should meet
With no less terror than the elements
Of fire and water, when their thundering shock
At meeting tears the cloudy cheeks of heaven.
Be he the fire, I'll be the yielding water:
The rage be his, while on the earth I rain
My waters,—on the earth and not on him.—
March on, and mark King Richard how he looks.

*A   parley sounded, and answered by another trumpet
    within.   Flourish.   Enter on the walls* KING RICHARD,
    the BISHOP OF CARLISLE, AUMERLE, SCROOP, *and*
    SALISBURY

Boling.   See, see, King Richard doth himself appear,
As doth the blushing discontented sun
From out the fiery portal of the east,
When he perceives the envious clouds are bent
To dim his glory and to stain the track
Of his bright passage to the occident.
    York.   Yet looks he like a king: behold his eye,
As bright as is the eagle's, lightens forth
Controlling majesty.   Alack, alack, for woe,
That any harm should stain so fair a show!
    K. Rich.   [*To Northumberland*]   We are amazed; and
        thus long have we stood
To watch the fearful bending of thy knee,
Because we thought ourself thy lawful king:

And if we be, how dare thy joints forget
To pay their awful duty to our presence?
If we be not, show us the hand of God
That hath dismissed us from our stewardship;
For well we know, no hand of blood and bone
Can gripe the sacred handle of our sceptre,
Unless he do profane, steal, or usurp.
And though you think that all, as you have done,
Have torn their souls by turning them from us,
And we are barren and bereft of friends,
Yet know, my master, God omnipotent,
Is mustering in his clouds on our behalf
Armies of pestilence; and they shall strike
Your children yet unborn and unbegot,
That lift your vassal hands against my head,
And threat the glory of my precious crown.
Tell Bolingbroke, for yond, methinks, he stands,
That every stride he makes upon my land
Is dangerous treason: he is come to ope
The purple testament of bleeding war;
But ere the crown he looks for live in peace,
Ten thousand bloody crowns of mothers' sons
Shall ill become the flower of England's face,
Change the complexion of her maid-pale peace
To scarlet indignation, and bedew
Her pastures' grass with faithful English blood.
 North. The King of Heaven forbid our lord the king
Should so with civil and uncivil arms
Be rushed upon! Thy thrice-noble cousin
Harry Bolingbroke doth humbly kiss thy hand;
And by the honourable tomb he swears
That stands upon your royal grandsire's bones,
And by the royalties of both your bloods,
Currents that spring from one most gracious head,
And by the buried hand of warlike Gaunt,
And by the worth and honour of himself,
Comprising all that may be sworn and said,—
His coming hither hath no further scope,
Than for his lineal royalties, and to beg
Enfranchisement immediate on his knees:
Which on thy royal party granted once,
His glittering arms he will commend to rust,
His barbéd steeds to stables, and his heart
To faithful service of your majesty.
This swears he, as he is a prince, is just;
And, as I am a gentleman, I credit him.
 K. Rich. Northumberland, say thus the king returns:—
His noble cousin is right welcome hither;
And all the number of his fair demands
Shall be accomplished without contradiction.

With all the gracious utterance thou hast,
Speak to his gentle hearing kind commends.—
           [*Northumberland retires to Bolingbroke*
[*To Aumerle*] We do debase ourself, cousin, do we not,
To look so poorly, and to speak so fair?
Shall we call back Northumberland, and send
Defiance to the traitor, and so die?
   Aum. No, good my Lord: let's fight with gentle words,
Till time lend friends, and friends their helpful swords.
   K. Rich. O God, O God! that e'er this tongue of mine,
That laid the sentence of dread banishment
On yon proud man, should take it off again
With words of sooth? O, that I were as great
As is my grief, or lesser than my name,
Or that I could forget what I have been,
Or not remember what I must be now!
Swell'st thou, proud heart? I'll give thee scope to beat,
Since foes have scope to beat both thee and me.
   Aum. Northumberland comes back from Bolingbroke.
   K. Rich. What must the king do now? Must he submit?
The king shall do it. Must he be deposed?
The king shall be contented. Must he lose
The name of king? o' God's name, let it go:
I'll give my jewels for a set of beads,
My gorgeous palace for a hermitage,
My gay apparel for an alms-man's gown,
My figured goblets for a dish of wood,
My sceptre for a palmer's walking-staff,
My subjects for a pair of carvéd saints,
And my large kingdom for a little grave,
A little little grave, an obscure grave;
Or I'll be buried in the king's highway,
Some way of common trade, where subjects' feet
May hourly trample on their sovereign's head;
For on my heart they tread, now whilst I live,
And buried once, why not upon my head?—
Aumerle, thou weep'st; my tender-hearted cousin!—
We'll make foul weather with despiséd tears;
Our sighs and they shall lodge the summer corn,
And make a dearth in this revolting land.
Or shall we play the wantons with our woes,
And make some pretty match with shedding tears?
As thus;—to drop them still upon one place,
Till they have fretted us a pair of graves
Within the earth; and, therein laid,—"There lies
Two kinsmen, digged their graves with weeping eyes."
Would not this ill do well?—Well, well, I see
I talk but idly, and you mock at me.
Most mighty prince, my Lord Northumberland,
What says King Bolingbroke? will his majesty

Give Richard leave to live till Richard die?
You make a leg, and Bolingbroke says—ay.
   North. My lord, in the base court he doth attend
To speak with you; may'st please you to come down?
   K. Rich. Down, down, I come; like glistering Phaeton,
Wanting the manage of unruly jades.
In the base court? Base court, where kings grow base,
To come at traitors' calls, and do them grace.
In the base court? Come down? Down, court! down,
      king!
For night-owls shriek where mounting larks should sing.
                              [Exeunt from above
   Boling. What says his majesty?
   North.   Sorrow and grief of heart
Makes him speak fondly, like a frantic man:
Yet he is come.

     Enter KING RICHARD, *and his Attendants, below*

   Boling.   Stand all apart,
And show fair duty to his majesty.—
My gracious lord,—   [*Kneeling*
   K. Rich. Fair cousin, you debase your princely knee,
To make the base earth proud with kissing it:
Me rather had my heart might feel your love
Than my unpleased eye see your courtesy.
Up, cousin, up; your heart is up, I know,
Thus high at least, although your knee be low.
   Boling. My gracious lord, I come but for mine own.
   K. Rich. Your own is yours; and I am yours, and all.
   Boling. So far be mine, my most redoubted lord,
As my true service shall deserve your love.
   K. Rich. Well you deserve: they well deserve to have
That know the strong'st and surest way to get.—
Uncle, give me your hand: nay, dry your eyes;
Tears show their love, but want their remedies.—
Cousin, I am too young to be your father,
Though you are old enough to be my heir.
What you will have, I'll give, and willing too;
For do we must what force will have us do.—
Set on towards London:—Cousin, is it so?
   Boling. Yea, my good lord.
   K. Rich.   Then I must not say no.
                     [*Flourish. Exeunt*

   SCENE IV.—Langley. The DUKE OF YORK's Garden

        Enter the QUEEN *and two Ladies*

   Queen. What sport shall we devise here in this garden,
To drive away the heavy thought of care?
   First Lady. Madam, we'll play at bowls.

Queen. 'T will make me think the world is full of rubs,
And that my fortune runs against the bias.
  First Lady. Madam, we'll dance.
  Queen. My legs can keep no measure in delight,
When my poor heart no measure keeps in grief:
Therefore, no dancing, girl; some other sport.
  First Lady. Madam, we will tell tales.
  Queen. Of sorrow, or of joy?
  First Lady. Of either, madam.
  Queen. No, of neither, girl;
For if of joy, being altogether wanting,
It doth remember me the more of sorrow;
Or if of grief, being altogether had,
It adds more sorrow to my want of joy;
For what I have, I need not to repeat,
And what I want, it boots not to complain.
  First Lady. Madam, I'll sing.
  Queen.   'T is well that thou hast cause;
But thou shouldst please me better, wouldst thou weep.
  First Lady. I could weep, madam, would it do you
              good.
  Queen. And I could sing, would weeping do me good,
And never borrow any tear of thee.
But stay, here come the gardeners:
Let's step into the shadow of these trees.
My wretchedness unto a row of pins,
They'll talk of state; for every one doth so
Against a change: woe is forerun with woe.
                              [*Queen and Ladies retire*

Enter a Gardener and two Servants

  Gard. Go, bind thou up yond dangling apricocks,
Which, like unruly children, make their sire
Stoop with oppression of their prodigal weight:
Give some supportance to the bending twigs.—
Go thou, and like an executioner
Cut off the heads of too-fast-growing sprays,
That look too lofty in our commonwealth:
All must be even in our government.—
You thus employed, I will go root away
The noisome weeds, that without profit suck
The soil's fertility from wholesome flowers.
  First Serv. Why should we, in the compass of a pale,
Keep law, and form, and due proportion,
Showing, as in a model, our firm state,
When our sea-walléd garden, the whole land,
Is full of weeds, her fairest flowers choked up,
Her fruit-trees all unpruned, her hedges ruined,
Her knots disordered, and her wholesome herbs
Swarming with caterpillars?

Gard.   Hold thy peace.
He that hath suffered this disordered spring,
Hath now himself met with the fall of leaf:
The weeds that his broad-spreading leaves did shelter,
That seemed in eating him to hold him up,
Are plucked up, root and all, by Bolingbroke;
I mean, the Earl of Wiltshire, Bushy, Green.
  First Serv. What, are they dead?
  Gard.   They are; and Bolingbroke
Hath seized the wasteful king.—O, what pity is it
That he hath not so trimmed and dressed his land
As we this garden! We at time of year
Do wound the bark, the skin of our fruit-trees,
Lest, being over-proud in sap and blood,
With too much riches it confound itself:
Had he done so to great and growing men,
They might have lived to bear, and he to taste,
Their fruits of duty. All superfluous branches
We lop away, that bearing boughs may live:
Had he done so, himself had borne the crown,
Which waste of idle hours hath quite thrown down.
  First Serv. What, think you then, the king shall be
          deposed?
  Gard. Depressed he is already; and deposed,
'T is doubt, he will be. Letters came last night
To a dear friend of the good Duke of York's,
That tell black tidings.
  Queen. O, I am pressed to death through want of
          speaking.   [*Coming forward*
Thou, old Adam's likeness, set to dress this garden,
How dares thy harsh-rude tongue sound this unpleasing
          news?
What Eve, what serpent hath suggested thee
To make a second fall of curséd man?
Why dost thou say King Richard is deposed?
Dar'st thou, thou little better thing than earth,
Divine his downfall? Say, where, when, and how
Cam'st thou by these ill tidings? Speak, thou wretch.
  Gard. Pardon me, madam: little joy have I
To breathe these news, yet what I say is true.
King Richard, he is in the mighty hold
Of Bolingbroke; their fortunes both are weighed:
In your lord's scale is nothing but himself,
And some few vanities that make him light:
But in the balance of great Bolingbroke,
Besides himself, are all the English peers,
And with that odds he weighs King Richard down.
Post you to London, and you'll find it so;
I speak no more than every one doth know.
  Queen. Nimble mischance that art so light of foot,

Doth not thy embassage belong to me,
And am I last that knows it?   O, thou think'st
To serve me last, that I may longest keep
Thy sorrow in my breast.—Come, ladies, go
To meet at London London's king in woe.—
What! was I born to this, that my sad look
Should grace the triumph of great Bolingbroke?—
Gardener, for telling me this news of woe,
Pray God the plants thou graft'st may never grow.
                        [*Exeunt Queen and Ladies*
   Gard.   Poor Queen! so that thy state might be no worse
I would my skill were subject to thy curse.—
Here did she fall a tear; here, in this place,
I'll set a bank of rue, sour herb of grace;
Rue, even for ruth, here shortly shall be seen,
In the remembrance of a weeping queen.

                                      [*Exeunt*

ACT FOUR

SCENE I.—London.   Westminster Hall

*The Lords Spiritual on the right side of the throne; the Lords
    Temporal on the left; the Commons below*

Enter BOLINGBROKE, AUMERLE, SURREY, NORTHUMBER-
    LAND, PERCY, FITZWATER, *another Lord, the* BISHOP
    OF CARLISLE, *the* ABBOT OF WESTMINSTER, *and Attend-
    ants.   Officers behind with* BAGOT

   Boling.   Call forth Bagot.—
Now, Bagot, freely speak thy mind,
What thou dost know of noble Gloster's death,
Who wrought it with the king, and who performed
The bloody office of his timeless end.
   Bagot.   Then set before my face the Lord Aumerle.
   Boling.   Cousin, stand forth, and look upon that man.
   Bagot.   My Lord Aumerle, I know your daring tongue
Scorns to unsay what once it hath delivered.
In that dead time when Gloster's death was plotted,
I heard you say,—" Is not my arm of length,
That reacheth from the restful English court
As far as Calais, to mine uncle's head?"
Amongst much other talk, that very time,
I heard you say that you had rather refuse
The offer of an hundred thousand crowns
Than Bolingbroke's return to England;
Adding withal, how blest this land would be
In this your cousin's death.
   Aum.   Princes, and noble lords,
What answer shall I make to this base man?

Shall I so much dishonour my fair stars,
On equal terms to give him chastisement?
Either I must, or have mine honour soiled
With the attainder of his slanderous lips.—
There is my gage, the manual seal of death,
That marks thee out for hell: I say, thou liest,
And will maintain what thou hast said is false,
In thy heart-blood, though being all too base
To stain the temper of my knightly sword.
    Boling.   Bagot, forbear; thou shalt not take it up.
    Aum.   Excepting one, I would he were the best
In all this presence that hath moved me so.
    Fitz.   If that thy valour stand on sympathies,
There is my gage, Aumerle, in gage to thine.
By that fair sun which shows me where thou stand'st,
I heard thee say, and vauntingly thou spak'st it,
That thou wert cause of noble Gloster's death.
If thou deny'st it twenty times, thou liest;
And I will turn thy falsehood to thy heart,
Where it was forgéd, with my rapier's point.
    Aum.   Thou dar'st not, coward, live to see that day.
    Fitz.   Now, by my soul, I would it were this hour.
    Aum.   Fitzwater, thou art damned to hell for this.
    Percy.   Aumerle, thou liest; his honour is as true
In this appeal as thou art all unjust;
And, that thou art so, there I throw my gage,
To prove it on thee to the extremest point
Of mortal breathing. Seize it, if thou dar'st.
    Aum.   An if I do not may my hands rot off
And never brandish more revengeful steel
Over the glittering helmet of my foe!
    Lord.   I task the earth to the like, forsworn Aumerle;
And spur thee on with full as many lies
As may be holla'd in thy treacherous ear
From sun to sun. There is my honour's pawn:
Engage it to the trial, if thou dar'st.
    Aum.   Who sets me else? by Heaven, I'll throw at all.
I have a thousand spirits in one breast,
To answer twenty thousand such as you.
    Surrey.   My Lord Fitzwater, I do remember well
The very time Aumerle and you did talk.
    Fitz.   'T is very true: you were in presence then;
And you can witness with me, this is true.
    Surrey.   As false, by Heaven, as Heaven itself is true.
    Fitz.   Surrey, thou liest.
    Surrey.   Dishonourable boy!
That lie shall lie so heavy on my sword,
That it shall render vengeance and revenge
Till thou the lie-giver and that lie, do lie
In earth as quiet as thy father's skull.

In proof whereof, there is my honour's pawn:
Engage it to the trial, if thou dar'st.
   Fitz.   How fondly dost thou spur a forward horse!
If I dare eat, or drink, or breathe, or live,
I dare meet Surrey in a wilderness,
And spit upon him, whilst I say, he lies,
And lies, and lies.   There is my bond of faith,
To tie thee to my strong correction.
As I intend to thrive in this new world,
Aumerle is guilty of my true appeal.
Besides, I heard the banished Norfolk say,
That thou, Aumerle, didst send two of thy men
To execute the noble duke at Calais.
   Aum.   Some honest Christian trust me with a gage.
That Norfolk lies, here do I throw down this,
If he may be repealed to try his honour.
   Boling.   These differences shall all rest under gage,
Till Norfolk be repealed: repealed he shall be,
And, though mine enemy, restored again,
To all his lands and signories; when he's returned,
Against Aumerle we will enforce his trial.
   Bishop.   That honourable day shall ne'er be seen.
Many a time hath banished Norfolk fought
For Jesu Christ in glorious Christian field,
Streaming the ensign of the Christian cross
Against black pagans, Turks, and Saracens;
And, toiled with works of war, retired himself
To Italy, and there at Venice gave
His body to that pleasant country's earth,
And his pure soul unto his captain Christ,
Under whose colours he had fought so long.
   Boling.   Why, bishop, is Norfolk dead?
   Bishop.   As surely as I live, my lord.
   Boling.   Sweet peace conduct his sweet soul to the bosom
Of good old Abraham!—Lords appellants,
Your differences shall all rest under gage
Till we assign you to your days of trial.

Enter YORK, *attended*

   York.   Great Duke of Lancaster, I come to thee
From plume-plucked Richard, who with willing soul
Adopts thee heir, and his high sceptre yields
To the possession of thy royal hand.
Ascend his throne, descending now from him,
And long live Henry, of that name the Fourth!
   Boling.   In God's name, I'll ascend the regal throne.
   Bishop.   Marry, God forbid!—
Worst in this royal presence may I speak,
Yet best beseeming me to speak the truth.
Would God, that any in this noble presence

Were enough noble to be upright judge
Of noble Richard; then true noblesse would
Learn him forbearance from so foul a wrong.
What subject can give sentence on his king?
And who sits here that is not Richard's subject?
Thieves are not judged, but they are by to hear,
Although apparent guilt be seen in them;
And shall the figure of God's majesty,
His captain, steward, deputy elect,
Anointed, crownéd, planted many years,
Be judged by subject and inferior breath,
And he himself not present?   O, forfend it, God,
That, in a Christian climate, souls refined
Should show so heinous, black, obscene a deed!
I speak to subjects, and a subject speaks,
Stirred up by God, thus boldly for his king.
My Lord of Hereford here, whom you call king,
Is a foul traitor to proud Hereford's king;
And if you crown him, let me prophesy,
The blood of English shall manure the ground,
And future ages groan for this foul act;
Peace shall go sleep with Turks and infidels,
And in this seat of peace tumultuous wars
Shall kin with kin and kind with kind confound;
Disorder, horror, fear, and mutiny,
Shall here inhabit, and this land be called
The field of Golgotha and dead men's skulls.
O, if you raise this house against this house,
It will the wofullest division prove,
That ever fell upon this curséd earth.
Prevent it, resist it, let it not be so,
Lest child, child's children, cry against you—woe!
    North.   Well have you argued, sir; and for your pains
Of capital treason, we arrest you here.
My Lord of Westminster, be it your charge
To keep him safely till his day of trial.—
May it please you, lords, to grant the commons' suit?
    Boling.   Fetch hither Richard, that in common view
He may surrender; so we shall proceed
Without suspicion.
    York.   I will be his conduct.   [*Exit*
    Boling.   Lords, you that here are under our arrest,
Procure your sureties for your days of answer.—
[*To the Bishop*] Little are we beholding to your love,
And little looked for at your helping hands.

          Re-enter YORK, *with* KING RICHARD, *and Officers*
                    bearing the crown, etc.

    K. Rich.   Alack, why am I sent for to a king
Before I have shook off the regal thoughts

Wherewith I reigned?   I hardly yet have learned
To insinuate, flatter, bow, and bend my limbs:
Give sorrow leave awhile to tutor me
To this submission.   Yet I well remember
The favours of these men: were they not mine?
Did they not sometime cry, All hail! to me?
So Judas did to Christ: but he, in twelve,
Found truth in all but one; I, in twelve thousand, none.
God save the king!—Will no man say, amen?
Am I both priest and clerk? well then, amen.
God save the king! although I be not he;
And yet, amen, if Heaven do think him me.—
To do what service am I sent for hither?
 York.   To do that office, of thine own good will,
Which tired majesty did make thee offer,
The resignation of thy state and crown
To Harry Bolingbroke.
 K. Rich.   Give me the crown.—Here, cousin, seize the
    crown;
Here, cousin,
On this side my hand, and on that side, thine.
Now is this golden crown like a deep well
That owes two buckets filling one another;
The emptier ever dancing in the air,
The other down, unseen, and full of water:
That bucket down, and full of tears, am I,
Drinking my griefs, whilst you mount up on high.
 Boling.   I thought you had been willing to resign.
 K. Rich.   My crown, I am; but still my griefs are mine.
You may my glories and my state depose,
But not my griefs; still am I king of those.
 Boling.   Part of your cares you give me with your crown.
 K. Rich.   Your cares set up do not pluck my cares down.
My care is loss of care, by old care done:
Your care is gain of care, by new care won:
The cares I give, I have, though given away;
They tend the crown, yet still with me they stay.
 Boling.   Are you contented to resign the crown?
 K. Rich.   Ay, no;—no, ay;—for I must nothing be;
Therefore no no, for I resign to thee.
Now mark me how I will undo myself:—
I give this heavy weight from off my head,
And this unwieldly sceptre from my hand,
The pride of kingly sway from out my heart;
With mine own tears I wash away my balm,
With mine own hands I give away my crown,
With mine own tongue deny my sacred state,
With mine own breath release all duty's rites:
All pomp and majesty I do forswear;
My manors, rents, revenues, I forego;

My acts, decrees and statutes, I deny:
God pardon all oaths that are broke to me!
God keep all vows unbroke, that swear to thee!
Make me, that nothing have, with nothing grieved,
And thou with all pleased, that hast all achieved!
Long may'st thou live in Richard's seat to sit,
And soon lie Richard in an earthly pit!
God save King Henry, unkinged Richard says,
And send him many years of sunshine days!—
What more remains?
    North.   [*Offering a paper*]   No more, but that you read
These accusations, and these grievous crimes
Committed by your person and your followers
Against the state and profit of this land;
That, by confessing them, the souls of men
May deem that you are worthily deposed.
    K. Rich.   Must I do so? and must I ravel out
My weaved-up follies?   Gentle Northumberland,
If thy offences were upon record,
Would it not shame thee, in so fair a troop,
To read a lecture of them?   If thou wouldst,
There shouldst thou find one heinous article,—
Containing the deposing of a king,
And cracking the strong warrant of an oath,—
Marked with a blot, damned in the book of Heaven.—
Nay, all of you, that stand and look upon me
Whilst that my wretchedness doth bait myself,
Though some of you, with Pilate, wash your hands,
Showing an outward pity, yet you Pilates
Have here delivered me to my sour cross,
And water cannot wash away your sin.
    North.   My lord, despatch: read o'er these articles.
    K. Rich.   Mine eyes are full of tears, I cannot see;
And yet salt water blinds them not so much
But they can see a sort of traitors here.
Nay, if I turn mine eyes upon myself,
I find myself a traitor with the rest;
For I have given here my soul's consent,
To undeck the pompous body of a king;
Made glory base, and sovereignty a slave,
Proud majesty a subject, state a peasant.
    North.   My lord,—
    K. Rich.   No lord of thine, thou haught insulting man,
Nor no man's lord: I have no name, no title,—
No, not that name was given me at the font,—
But 't is usurped—Alack, the heavy day!
That I have worn so many winters out
And know not now what name to call myself.
O, that I were a mockery king of snow
Standing before the sun of Bolingbroke

To melt myself away in water drops!—
Good king,—great king,—and yet not greatly good,
An if my word be sterling yet in England,
Let it command a mirror hither straight,
That it may show me what a face I have
Since it is bankrupt of his majesty.
   Boling. Go some of you and fetch a looking-glass.
                               [Exit an Attendant
   North. Read o'er this paper, while the glass doth come.
   K. Rich. Fiend! thou torment'st me ere I come to hell.
   Boling. Urge it no more, my lord Northumberland.
   North. The commons will not then be satisfied.
   K. Rich. They shall be satisfied: I'll read enough,
When I do see the very book indeed
Where all my sins are writ, and that's myself.

       Re-enter Attendant with a glass

Give me that glass, and therein will I read.—
No deeper wrinkles yet? Hath sorrow struck
So many blows upon this face of mine,
And made no deeper wounds?—O flattering glass,
Like to my followers in prosperity,
Thou dost beguile me. Was this face the face
That every day under his household roof
Did keep ten thousand men? Was this the face
That like the sun did make beholders wink?
Was this the face that faced so many follies
And was at last outfaced by Bolingbroke?
A brittle glory shineth in this face:
As brittle as the glory is the face;
             [Dashes the glass against the ground
For there it is, cracked in a hundred shivers.—
Mark, silent king, the moral of this sport,
How soon my sorrow hath destroyed my face.
   Boling. The shadow of your sorrow hath destroyed
The shadow of your face.
   K. Rich.   Say that again.
The shadow of my sorrow? Ha! let's see:—
'T is very true, my grief lies all within;
And these external manners of lament
Are merely shadows to the unseen grief
That swells with silence in the tortured soul;
There lies the substance: and I thank thee, king,
For thy great bounty, that not only giv'st
Me cause to wail, but teachest me the way
How to lament the cause. I'll beg one boon,
And then be gone and trouble you no more.
Shall I obtain it?
   Boling.   Name it, fair cousin.
   K. Rich. 'Fair cousin'? I am greater than a king:

For, when I was a king my flatterers
Were then but subjects; being now a subject,
I have a king here to my flatterer.
Being so great, I have no need to beg.
   Boling.   Yet ask.
   K. Rich.   And shall I have it?
   Boling.   You shall.
   K. Rich.   Why then, give me leave to go.
   Boling.   Whither?
   K. Rich.   Whither you will, so I were from your sights.
   Boling.   Go, some of you; convey him to the Tower.
   K. Rich.   O, good! Convey?—Conveyers are you all,
That rise thus nimbly by a true king's fall.
               [Exeunt King Richard and Guard
   Boling.   On Wednesday next we solemnly set down
Our coronation: lords, prepare yourselves.
  Exeunt all but the Abbot, Bishop of Carlisle, and Aumerle
   Abbot.   A woful pageant have we here beheld.
   Bishop.   The woe's to come: the children yet unborn
Shall feel this day as sharp to them as thorn.
   Aum.   You holy clergymen, is there no plot
To rid the realm of this pernicious blot?
   Abbot.   Before I freely speak my mind herein,
You shall not only take the sacrament
To bury mine intents, but also to effect
Whatever I shall happen to devise.
I see your brows are full of discontent,
Your hearts of sorrow, and your eyes of tears:
Come home with me to supper; I will lay
A plot, shall show us all a merry day.   *[Exeunt*

ACT FIVE

Scene I.—London.   A Street leading to the Tower

Enter Queen *and Ladies*

   Queen.   This way the king will come; this is the way
To Julius Cæsar's ill-erected tower
To whose flint bosom my condemnéd lord
Is doomed a prisoner by proud Bolingbroke.
Here let us rest, if this rebellious earth
Have any resting for her true king's queen.

Enter King Richard *and Guards*

But soft, but see, or rather do not see
My fair rose wither: yet look up, behold,
That you in pity may dissolve to dew,

And wash him fresh again with true-love tears,—
Ah, thou, the model where old Troy did stand,
Thou map of honour, thou King Richard's tomb
And not King Richard, thou most beauteous inn,
Why should hard-favoured grief be lodged in thee,
When triumph is become an ale-house guest?
   K. Rich.   Join not with grief, fair woman, do not so,
To make my end too sudden: learn, good soul,
To think our former state a happy dream;
From which awaked, the truth of what we are
Shows us but this: I am sworn brother, sweet,
To grim Necessity; and he and I
Will keep a league till death.   Hie thee to France,
And cloister thee in some religious house:
Our holy lives must win a new world's crown,
Which our profane hours here have stricken down.
   Queen.   What, is my Richard both in shape and mind
Transformed and weakened?   Hath Bolingbroke deposed
Thine intellect?   Hath he been in thy heart?
The lion, dying, thrusteth forth his paw,
And wounds the earth, if nothing else, with rage
To be o'er powered; and wilt thou, pupil-like,
Take thy correction mildly, kiss the rod,
And fawn on rage with base humility,
Which art a lion and a king of beasts?
   K. Rich.   A king of beasts, indeed; if aught but beasts,
I had been still a happy king of men.
Good sometime queen, prepare thee hence for France:
Think I am dead, and that even here thou tak'st,
As from my death-bed, my last living leave.
In winter's tedious nights sit by the fire
With good old folks, and let them tell the tales
Of woful ages long ago betid;
And ere thou bid good night, to quit their grief,
Tell thou the lamentable fall of me,
And send the hearers weeping to their beds:
For why, the senseless brands will sympathise
The heavy accent of thy moving tongue,
And in compassion weep the fire out;
And some will mourn in ashes, some coal-black,
For the deposing of a rightful king.

          Enter NORTHUMBERLAND, *attended*

   North.   My lord, the mind of Bolingbroke is changed:
You must to Pomfret, not unto the Tower.—
And, madam, there is order ta'en for you;
With all swift speed you must away to France.
   K. Rich.   Northumberland, thou ladder wherewithal
The mounting Bolingbroke ascends my throne,

The time shall not be many hours of age
More than it is, ere foul sin gathering head
Shall break into corruption. Thou shalt think,
Though he divide the realm, and give thee half,
It is too little, helping him to all;
And he shall think that thou, which know'st the way
To plant unrightful kings, wilt know again,
Being ne'er so little urged, another way
To pluck him headlong from the usurpéd throne.
The love of wicked friends converts to fear;
That fear to hate; and hate turns one or both
To worthy danger and deservéd death.
    North. My guilt be on my head, and there an end.
Take leave, and part, for you must part forthwith.
    K. Rich. Doubly divorced!—Bad men, ye violate
A two-fold marriage; 'twixt my crown and me,
And then betwixt me and my married wife.—
Let me unkiss the oath 'twixt thee and me;
And yet not so, for with a kiss 't was made.
Part us, Northumberland: I towards the north,
Where shivering cold and sickness pines the clime;
My wife to France,—from whence, set forth in pomp,
She came adornéd hither like sweet May,
Sent back like Hallowmas or short'st of day.
    Queen. And must we be divided? must we part?
    K. Rich. Ay, hand from hand, my love, and heart from
        heart.
    Queen. Banish us both, and send the king with me.
    North. That were some love, but little policy.
    Queen. Then whither he goes, thither let me go.
    K. Rich. So two, together weeping, make one woe.
Weep thou for me in France, I for thee here;
Better far off than near, be ne'er the near.
Go, count thy way with sighs, I mine with groans.
    Queen. So longest way shall have the longest moans.
    K. Rich. Twice for one step I'll groan, the way being
        short,
And piece the way out with a heavy heart.
Come, come, in wooing sorrow let's be brief,
Since, wedding it, there is such length in grief.
One kiss shall stop our mouths, and dumbly part:
Thus give I mine, and thus take I thy heart.   [*They kiss*
    Queen. Give me mine own again; 't were no good part
To take on me, to keep and kill thy heart.
                      [*They kiss again*
So, now I have mine own again, be gone,
That I may strive to kill it with a groan.
    K. Rich. We make woe wanton with this fond delay:
Once more, adieu;—the rest let sorrow say.
                      [*Exeunt*

Scene II.—London. A Room in the Duke of York's Palace

Enter York *and his* Duchess

Duch. My lord, you told me you would tell the rest,
When weeping made you break the story off,
Of our two cousins coming into London.
    York. Where did I leave?
    Duch.   At that sad stop, my lord,
Where rude misgoverned hands, from windows' tops,
Threw dust and rubbish on King Richard's head.
    York. Then, as I said, the duke, great Bolingbroke,
Mounted upon a hot and fiery steed,
Which his aspiring rider seemed to know,
With slow but stately pace kept on his course,
While all tongues cried—"God save thee, Bolingbroke!"
You would have thought the very windows spake,
So many greedy looks of young and old
Through casements darted their desiring eyes
Upon his visage; and that all the walls
With painted imagery had said at once,—
"Jesu preserve thee! welcome, Bolingbroke!"
Whilst he, from one side to the other turning,
Bareheaded, lower than his proud steed's neck,
Bespake them thus,—"I thank you, countrymen:"
And thus still doing, thus he passed along.
    Duch. Alas, poor Richard! where rode he the whilst?
    York. As in a theatre, the eyes of men,
After a well-graced actor leaves the stage,
Are idly bent on him that enters next,
Thinking his prattle to be tedious;
Even so, or with much more contempt, men's eyes
Did scowl on Richard: no man cried, God save him;
No joyful tongue gave him his welcome home;
But dust was thrown upon his sacred head,
Which with such gentle sorrow he shook off,
His face still combating with tears and smiles,
The badges of his grief and patience,
That had not God, for some strong purpose, steeled
The hearts of men, they must perforce have melted,
And barbarism itself have pitied him.
But Heaven hath a hand in these events,
To whose high will we bound our calm contents.
To Bolingbroke are we sworn subjects now,
Whose state and honour I for aye allow.
    Duch. Here comes my son Aumerle.
    York.   Aumerle that was;
But that is lost for being Richard's friend,
And, madam, you must call him Rutland now.

64

I am in parliament pledge for his truth
And lasting fealty to the new-made king.

Enter AUMERLE

   Duch.   Welcome, my son.   Who are the violets now,
That strew the green lap of the new-come spring?
   Aum.   Madam, I know not, nor I greatly care not;
God knows, I had as lief be none, as one.
   York.   Well, bear you well in this new spring of time,
Lest you be cropped before you come to prime.
What news from Oxford? hold those jousts and triumphs?
   Aum.   For ought I know, my lord, they do.
   York.   You will be there, I know.
   Aum.   If God prevent me not, I purpose so.
   York.   What seal is that, that hangs without thy bosom?
Yea, look'st thou pale? let me see the writing. .
   Aum.   My lord, 't is nothing.
   York.   No matter then who sees it:
I will be satisfied, let me see the writing.
   Aum.   I do beseech your grace to pardon me.
It is a matter of small consequence,
Which for some reasons I would not have seen.
   York.   Which for some reasons, sir, I mean to see.
I fear, I fear,—
   Duch.   What should you fear?
'T is nothing but some bond that he is entered into
For gay apparel 'gainst the triumph day.
   York.   Bound to himself? what doth he with a bond
That he is bound to?   Wife, thou art a fool.—
Boy, let me see the writing.
   Aum.   I do beseech you, pardon me: I may not show it.
   York.   I will be satisfied: let me see it, I say.
                       [Snatches it, and reads
Treason! foul treason!—Villain! traitor! slave!
   Duch.   What is the matter, my lord?
   York.   Ho! who is within there?

Enter a Servant

                      Saddle my horse.
God for his mercy! what treachery is here!
   Duch.   Why, what is it, my lord?
   York.   Give me my boots, I say: saddle my horse.—
                         [Exit Servant
Now, by mine honour, by my life, my troth,
I will appeach the villain.
   Duch.   What's the matter?
   York.   Peace, foolish woman.
   Duch.   I will not peace.—What is the matter, Aumerle?
   Aum.   Good mother, be content: it is no more
Than my poor life must answer.

Duch.   Thy life answer?
York.   Bring me my boots; I will unto the king.

Re-enter Servant with boots

Duch.   Strike   him,   Aumerle.—Poor   boy,   thou   art
     amazed,—
Hence villain: never more come in my sight.—
                                        [*Exit Servant*
     York.   Give me my boots, I say.
     Duch.   Why, York, what wilt thou do?
Wilt thou not hide the trespass of thine own?
Have we more sons, or are we like to have?
Is not my teeming date drunk up with time,
And wilt thou pluck my fair son from mine age,
And rob me of a happy mother's name?
Is he not like thee? is he not thine own?
     York.   Thou fond, mad woman,
Wilt thou conceal this dark conspiracy?
A dozen of them here have ta'en the sacrament,
And interchangeably set down their hands
To kill the king at Oxford.
     Duch.   He shall be none;
We'll keep him here: then, what is that to him?
     York.   Away, fond woman! were he twenty times
My son I would appeach him.
     Duch.   Hadst thou groaned for him,
As I have done, thou 'dst be more pitiful.
But now I know thy mind: thou dost suspect
That I have been disloyal to thy bed;
And that he is a bastard, not thy son.
Sweet York, sweet husband, be not of that mind:
He is as like thee as a man may be,
Not like to me, nor any of my kin,
And yet I love him.
     York.   Make way, unruly woman!   [*Exit*
     Duch.   After, Aumerle!   Mount thee upon his horse:
Spur, post, and get before him to the king,
And beg thy pardon ere he do accuse thee.
I'll not be long behind; though I be old,
I doubt not but to ride as fast as York:
And never will I rise up from the ground,
Till Bolingbroke have pardoned thee.   Away! be gone.
                                        [*Exeunt*

SCENE III.—Windsor.   A 'Room in the Castle

Enter BOLINGBROKE *as King;* PERCY, *and other Lords*

Boling.   Can no man tell me of my unthrifty son?
'T is full three months since I did see him last.
If any plague hang over us, 't is he.

I would to God, my lords, he might be found:
Inquire at London, 'mongst the taverns there,
For there, they say, he daily doth frequent,
With unconstrainéd loose companions,
Even such, they say, as stand in narrow lanes
And beat our watch and rob our passengers;
While he, young wanton, and effeminate boy,
Takes on the point of honour, to support
So dissolute a crew.
   Percy.   My lord, some two days since I saw the prince,
And told him of these triumphs held at Oxford.
   Boling.   And what said the gallant?
   Percy.   His answer was,—he would unto the stews,
And from the common'st creature pluck a glove,
And wear it as a favour; and with that
He would unhorse the lustiest challenger.
   Boling.   As dissolute as desperate; yet through both
I see some sparkles of a better hope,
Which elder days may happily bring forth.—
But who comes here?

Enter AUMERLE

   Aum.   Where is the king?
   Boling.   What means
Our cousin, that he stares and looks so wildly?
   Aum.   God save your grace. I do beseech your majesty,
To have some conference with your grace alone.
   Boling.   Withdraw yourselves, and leave us here alone.—
                        [Exeunt Percy and Lords
What is the matter with our cousin now?
   Aum.   For ever may my knees grow to the earth,
                                 [Kneels
My tongue cleave to my roof within my mouth,
Unless a pardon ere I rise or speak.
   Boling.   Intended or committed was this fault?
If on the first, how heinous e'er it be,
To win thy after-love, I pardon thee.
   Aum.   Then give me leave that I may turn the key,
That no man enter till my tale be done.
   Boling.   Have thy desire.
                     [Aumerle locks the door
   York.   [*Within*] My liege, beware! look to thyself:
Thou hast a traitor in thy presence there.
   Boling.   Villain, I'll make thee safe.   *[Drawing*
   Aum.   Stay thy revengeful hand: thou hast no cause to fear.
   York.   [*Within*] Open the door, secure, fool-hardy king:

Shall I for love speak treason to thy face?
Open the door, or I will break it open.
>   [*Bolingbroke unlocks the door, and afterwards locks*
>   *it again*

Enter YORK

   Boling. What is the matter, uncle? speak;
Recover breath: tell us how near is danger,
That we may arm us to encounter it.
   York. Peruse this writing here, and thou shalt know
The treason that my haste forbids me show.
   Aum. Remember, as thou read'st, thy promise past:
I do repent me; read not my name there;
My heart is not confederate with my hand.
   York. 'T was, villain, ere thy hand did set it down.—
I tore it from the traitor's bosom, king:
Fear, and not love, begets his penitence.
Forget to pity him, lest thy pity prove
A serpent that will sting thee to the heart.
   Boling. O heinous, strong, and bold conspiracy!—
O loyal father of a treacherous son!
Thou sheer, immaculate, and silver fountain,
From whence this stream through muddy passages
Hath held his current, and defiled himself!
Thy overflow of good converts to bad;
And thy abundant goodness shall excuse
This deadly blot in thy digressing son.
   York. So shall my virtue be his vice's bawd,
And he shall spend mine honour with his shame,
As thriftless sons their scraping fathers' gold;
Mine honour lives when his dishonour dies,
Or my shamed life in his dishonour lies:
Thou kill'st me in his life; giving him breath,
The traitor lives, the true man's put to death.
   Duch. [*Within*] What, ho! my liege! for God's sake
     let me in.
   Boling. What shrill-voiced suppliant makes this eager
     cry?
   Duch. A woman, and thine aunt, great king; 't is I.
Speak with me, pity me, open the door:
A beggar begs that never begged before.
   Boling. Our scene is altered from a serious thing,
And now changed to "The Beggar and the King."—
My dangerous cousin, let your mother in:
I know she's come to pray for your foul sin.
   York. If thou do pardon, whosoever pray,
More sins for this forgiveness prosper may,
This festered joint cut off, the rest rests sound;
This, let alone, will all the rest confound.

Enter DUCHESS

   Duch. O king, believe not this hard-hearted man:
Love, loving not itself, none other can.
   York. Thou frantic woman, what dost thou make here?
Shall thy old dugs once more a traitor rear?
   Duch. Sweet York, be patient. Hear me, gentle liege.
                                         [Kneels
   Boling. Rise up, good aunt.
   Duch.   Not yet, I thee beseech:
For ever will I walk upon my knees,
And never see day that the happy sees,
Till thou give joy; until thou bid me joy,
By pardoning Rutland, my transgressing boy.
   Aum. Unto my mother's prayers I bend my knee.
                                         [Kneels
   York. Against them both my true joints bended be.
                                       [Kneels—
Ill may'st thou thrive, if you grant any grace!
   Duch. Pleads he in earnest? look upon his face;
His eyes do drop no tears, his prayers are jest;
His words come from his mouth, ours from our breast:
He prays but faintly, and would be denied;
We pray with heart, and soul, and all beside:
His weary joints would gladly rise, I know;
Our knees shall kneel till to the ground they grow:
His prayers are full of false hypocrisy;
Ours of true zeal and deep integrity.
Our prayers do out-pray his; then let them have
That mercy which true prayers ought to have.
   Boling. Good aunt, stand up.
   Duch.   Nay, do not say—stand up;
But "pardon" first, and afterwards "stand up."
An if I were thy nurse, thy tongue to teach,
"Pardon" should be the first word of thy speech.
I never longed to hear a word till now;
Say "pardon," king; let pity teach thee how:
The word is short, but not so short as sweet;
No word like "pardon" for kings' mouths so meet.
   York. Speak it in French, king: say, *pardonnez-moi.*
   Duch. Dost thou teach pardon pardon to destroy?
Ah, my sour husband, my hard-hearted lord,
That sett'st the word itself against the word!
Speak "pardon" as 't is current in our land;
The chopping French we do not understand.
Thine eye begins to speak, set thy tongue there,
Or in thy piteous heart plant thou thine ear,
That hearing how our plaints and prayers do pierce,
Pity may move thee "pardon" to rehearse
   Boling. Good aunt, stand up.

Duch.   I do not sue to stand;
Pardon is all the suit I have in hand.
    Boling.   I pardon him, as God shall pardon me.
    Duch.   O happy vantage of a kneeling knee!
Yet am I sick for fear: speak it again;
Twice saying pardon doth not pardon twain,
But makes one pardon strong.
    Boling.   With all my heart
I pardon him.
    Duch.   A god on earth thou art.
    Boling.   But for our trusty brother-in-law, and the abbot,
With all the rest of that consorted crew,
Destruction straight shall dog them at the heels.—
Good uncle, help to order several powers
To Oxford, or where'er these traitors are:
They shall not live within this world, I swear;
But I will have them, if I once know where.
Uncle, farewell, and cousin too, adieu:
Your mother well hath prayed, and prove you true.
    Duch.   Come, my old son: I pray God make thee new.
                                              [*Exeunt*

SCENE IV

Enter SIR PIERCE OF EXTON *and a Servant*

    Exton.   Didst thou not mark the king, what words he
            spake?
"Have I no friend will rid me of this living fear?"
Was it not so?
    Serv.   Those were his very words.
    Exton.   "Have I no friend?" quoth he; he spake it
            twice,
And urged it twice together, did he not?
    Serv.   He did.
    Exton.   And, speaking it, he wistly looked on me,
As who should say,—I would thou wert the man
That would divorce this terror from my heart;
Meaning, the king at Pomfret. Come, let's go:
I am the king's friend, and will rid his foe.   [*Exeunt*

SCENE V.—Pomfret. The Dungeon of the Castle

Enter KING RICHARD

    K. Rich.   I have been studying how I may compare
This prison where I live unto the world:
And for because the world is populous,
And here is not a creature but myself,
I cannot do it;—yet I'll hammer 't out.
My brain I'll prove the female to my soul;

My soul the father: and these two beget
A generation of still-breeding thoughts,
And these same thoughts people this little world;
In humours like the people of this world,
For no thought is contented.   The better sort,—
As thoughts of things divine,—are intermixed
With scruples, and do set the word itself
Against the word:
As thus,—"Come, little ones;" and then again,—
"It is as hard to come, as for a camel
To thread the postern of a needle's eye."
Thoughts tending to ambition, they do plot
Unlikely wonders: how these vain weak nails
May tear a passage through the flinty ribs
Of this hard world, my ragged prison walls;
And, for they cannot, die in their own pride.
Thoughts tending to content flatter themselves
That they are not the first of fortune's slaves,
Nor shall not be the last; like silly beggars,
Who, sitting in the stocks, refuge their shame,
That many have, and others must sit there:
And in this thought they find a kind of ease,
Bearing their own misfortune on the back
Of such as have before endured the like.
Thus play I, in one person, many people,
And none contented: sometimes am I king;
Then treason makes me wish myself a beggar,—
And so I am: then, crushing penury
Persuades me I was better when a king;
Then am I kinged again, and, by-and-by,
Think that I am unkinged by Bolingbroke,
And straight am nothing.—But whate'er I am,
Nor I, nor any man, that but man is,
With nothing shall be pleased till he be eased
With being nothing.—[*Music*]   Music do I hear?
Ha, ha! keep time:—How sour sweet music is
When time is broke, and no proportion kept!
So is it in the music of men's lives.
And here have I the daintiness of ear
To check time broke in a disordered string;
But, for the concord of my state and time,
Had not an ear to hear my true time broke.
I wasted time, and now doth time waste me;
For now hath time made me his numbering clock:
My thoughts are minutes, and with sighs they jar
Their watches to mine eyes, the outward watch,
Whereto my finger, like a dial's point,
Is pointing still, in cleansing them from tears.
Now for the sound that tells what hour it is
Are clamorous groans that strike upon my heart,

Which is the bell: so sighs, and tears, and groans,
Show minutes, times, and hours; but my time
Runs posting on in Bolingbroke's proud joy,
While I stand fooling here, his Jack o' the clock.—
This music mads me; let it sound no more;
For though it hath holp madmen to their wits,
In me it seems it will make wise men mad.
Yet blessing on his heart that gives it me!
For 't is a sign of love, and love to Richard
Is a strange brooch in this all-hating world.

Enter Groom

   Groom. Hail, royal Prince!
   K. Rich.   Thanks, noble peer;
The cheapest of us is ten groats too dear.
What art thou? and how com'st thou hither now;
Where no man never comes, but that sad dog
That brings me food to make misfortune live?
   Groom. I was a poor groom of thy stable, king,
When thou wert king; who, travelling towards York,
With much ado, at length have gotten leave
To look upon my sometimes master's face.
O, how it yearned my heart, when I beheld
In London streets that coronation day,
When Bolingbroke rode on roan Barbary,—
That horse that thou so often hast bestrid,
That horse that I so carefully have dressed!
   K. Rich. Rode he on Barbary? Tell me, gentle friend,
How went he under him?
   Groom. So proudly, as if he disdained the gound.
   K. Rich. So proud that Bolingbroke was on his back!
That jade hath eat bread from my royal hand;
This hand hath made him proud with clapping him.
Would he not stumble? would he not fall down—
Since pride must have a fall—and break the neck
Of that proud man that did usurp his back?
Forgiveness, horse! why do I rail on thee,
Since thou, created to be awed by man,
Wast born to bear? I was not made a horse,
And yet I bear a burden like an ass,
Spur-galled, and tired, by jauncing Bolingbroke.

Enter Keeper with a dish

   Keep. [*To the Groom*] Fellow, give place, here is no
      longer stay.
   K. Rich. If thou love me, 't is time thou wert away.
   Groom. What my tongues dares not, that my heart shall
      say.   [*Exit*
   Keep. My lord, will 't please you to fall to?
   K. Rich. Taste of it first, as thou art wont to do.

Keep. My lord, I dare not: Sir Pierce of Exton,
Who late came from the king, commands the contrary.
K. Rich. The devil take Henry of Lancaster, and thee!
Patience is stale, and I am weary of it.   [*Beats the Keeper*
Keep. Help, help, help!

Enter SIR PIERCE OF EXTON, *and Servants, armed*

K. Rich. How now! what means death in this rude
        assault?
Villain, thine own hand yields thy death's instrument.
                [*Snatching a weapon, and killing one*
Go thou, and fill another room in hell.
                [*He kills another : then Exton strikes him down*
That hand shall burn in never-quenching fire,
That staggers thus my person.—Exton, thy fierce hand
Hath with the king's blood stained the king's own land.
Mount, mount, my soul! thy seat is up on high;
Whilst my gross flesh sinks downward, here to die.   [*Dies*
Exton. As full of valour as of royal blood:
Both have I spilt;—O, would the deed were good!
For now the devil, that told me I did well,
Says that this deed is chronicled in hell.
This dead king to the living king I'll bear:—
Take hence the rest, and give them burial here.   [*Exeunt*

SCENE VI.—Windsor. An apartment in the Castle

Flourish. Enter BOLINGBROKE *and* YORK, *with Lords
and Attendants*

Boling. Kind uncle York, the latest news we hear
Is that the rebels have consumed with fire
Our town of Cicester in Glostershire;
But whether they be ta'en, or slain, we hear not.

Enter NORTHUMBERLAND

Welcome, my lord: what is the news?
North.   First, to
Thy sacred state wish I all happiness.
The next news is,—I have to London sent
The heads of Salisbury, Spencer, Blunt, and Kent.
The manner of their taking may appear
At large discoursèd in this paper here.
                [*Presenting a paper*
Boling. We thank thee, gentle Percy, for thy pains;
And to thy worth will add right worthy gains.

Enter FITZWATER

Fitz. My lord, I have from Oxford sent to London
The heads of Brocas and Sir Bennet Seely,

Two of the dangerous consorted traitors
That sought at Oxford thy dire overthrow.
  Boling.   Thy pains, Fitzwater, shall not be forgot;
Right noble is thy merit, well I wot.

Enter PERCY, *with the* BISHOP OF CARLISLE

  Percy.   The grand conspirator, Abbot of Westminster,
With clog of conscience and sour melancholy,
Hath yielded up his body to the grave;
But here is Carlisle living, to abide
Thy kingly doom, and sentence of his pride.
  Boling.   Carlisle, this is your doom:—
Choose out some secret place, some reverend room,
More than thou hast, and with it joy thy life;
So, as thou liv'st in peace, die free from strife:
For though mine enemy thou hast ever been,
High sparks of honour in thee have I seen.

Enter EXTON, *with Attendants bearing a coffin*

  Exton.   Great king, within this coffin I present
Thy buried fear; herein all breathless lies
The mightiest of thy greatest enemies,
Richard of Bordeaux, by me hither brought.
  Boling.   Exton, I thank thee not; for thou hast wrought
A deed of slander, with thy fatal hand,
Upon my head and all this famous land.
  Exton.   From your own mouth, my lord, did I this deed.
  Boling.   They love not poison that do poison need,
Nor do I thee: though I did wish him dead,
I hate the murderer, love him murderéd.
The guilt of conscience take thou for thy labour,
But neither my good word, nor princely favour:
With Cain go wander through the shades of night,
And never show thy head by day nor light.—
Lords, I protest, my soul is full of woe
That blood should sprinkle me to make me grow:
Come, mourn with me for that I do lament,
And put on sullen black incontinent.
I'll make a voyage to the Holy Land,
To wash this blood off from my guilty hand.—
March sadly after; grace my mournings here,
In weeping after this untimely bier.   [*Exeunt*

74

THE TRAGEDY OF
KING RICHARD THE THIRD

DRAMATIS PERSONÆ

KING EDWARD THE FOURTH
EDWARD, *Prince of Wales, afterwards King Edward V* ⎱ *sons to the*
RICHARD, *Duke of York* ⎰ *King*
GEORGE, *Duke of Clarence* ⎱ *brothers*
RICHARD, *Duke of Gloster, afterwards King Richard III* ⎰ *to the King*
A young son of Clarence
HENRY, *Earl of Richmond, afterwards King Henry VII*
CARDINAL BOURCHIER, *Archbishop of Canterbury*
THOMAS ROTHERHAM, *Archbishop of York*
JOHN MORTON, *Bishop of Ely*
DUKE OF BUCKINGHAM
DUKE OF NORFOLK
EARL OF SURREY, *his son*
EARL RIVERS, *brother to Elizabeth*
MARQUIS OF DORSET, *and* LORD GREY, *sons to Elizabeth*
EARL OF OXFORD
LORD HASTINGS
LORD STANLEY
LORD LOVEL
SIR RICHARD RATCLIFF
SIR JAMES TYRREL
SIR THOMAS VAUGHAN
SIR WILLIAM CATESBY
SIR JAMES BLOUNT
SIR WALTER HERBERT
SIR ROBERT BRAKENBURY, *Lieutenant of the Tower*
CHRISTOPHER URSWICK, *a priest.   Another priest*
TRESSEL *and* BERKELEY, *attending on Lady Anne*
Lord Mayor of London
Sheriff of Wiltshire

ELIZABETH, *queen to King Edward IV*
MARGARET, *widow of King Henry VI*
DUCHESS OF YORK, *mother to King Edward IV*
LADY ANNE, *widow of Edward, Prince of Wales, son to King Henry VI, afterwards married to Richard*
A young Daughter of Clarence (MARGARET PLANTAGENET)

Ghosts of those murdered by Richard III, Lords, and other Attendants; a Pursuivant, Scrivener, Citizens, Murderers, Messengers, Soldiers, etc.

SCENE.—*England*

THE TRAGEDY OF

KING RICHARD THE THIRD

ACT ONE

Scene I.—London.　A Street

Enter Richard, Duke of Gloster, *solus*

　Glo.　Now is the winter of our discontent
Made glorious summer by this sun of York;
'And all the clouds that loured upon our house
In the deep bosom of the ocean buried.
Now are our brows bound with victorious wreaths;
Our bruiséd arms hung up for monuments;
Our stern alarums changed to merry meetings,
Our dreadful marches to delightful measures.
Grim-visaged War hath smoothed his wrinkled front;
And now, instead of mounting barbéd steeds
To fright the souls of fearful adversaries,
He capers nimbly in a lady's chamber
To the lascivious pleasing of a lute.
But I, that am not shaped for sportive tricks,
Nor made to court an amorous looking-glass;
I, that am rudely stamped, and want love's majesty
To strut before a wanton ambling nymph;
I, that am curtailed of this fair proportion,
Cheated of feature by dissembling nature,
Deformed, unfinished, sent before my time
Into this breathing world, scarce half made up,
And that so lamely and unfashionable
That dogs bark at me as I halt by them; —
Why, I, in this weak piping time of peace,
Have no delight to pass away the time,
Unless to spy my shadow in the sun
And descant on mine own deformity:
And therefore, since I cannot prove a lover,
To entertain these fair well-spoken days,
I am determinéd to prove a villain
And hate the idle pleasures of these days.
Plots have I laid, inductions dangerous,
By drunken prophecies, libels and dreams,
To set my brother Clarence and the king
In deadly hate the one against the other:
And if King Edward be as true and just
As I am subtle, false and treacherous,
This day should Clarence closely be mewed up,
About a prophecy, which says that G

77

Of Edward's heirs the murderer shall be.—
Dive, thoughts, down to my soul: here Clarence comes.

Enter CLARENCE, *guarded, and* BRAKENBURY

Brother, good day: what means this arméd guard
That waits upon your grace?
 Clar.   His majesty,
Tendering my person's safety, hath appointed
This conduct to convey me to the Tower.
 Glo. Upon what cause?
 Clar.   Because my name is George.
 Glo. Alack, my lord, that fault is none of yours;
He should, for that, commit your godfathers:
O, belike his majesty hath some intent
That you shall be new-christened in the Tower.
But what's the matter, Clarence? may I know?
 Clar. Yea, Richard, when I know; for I protest
As yet I do not: but, as I can learn,
He hearkens after prophecies and dreams;
And from the cross-row plucks the letter G
And says a wizard told him that by G
His issue disinherited should be;
And, for my name of George begins with G,
It follows in his thought that I am he.
These, as I learn, and such like toys as these
Have moved his highness to commit me now.
 Glo. Why, this it is, when men are ruled by women.—
'T is not the king that sends you to the Tower;
My Lady Grey his wife, Clarence, 't is she
That tempts him to this harsh extremity.
Was it not she and that good man of worship,
Anthony Woodville, her brother there,
That made him send Lord Hastings to the Tower,
From whence this present day he is delivered?
We are not safe, Clarence; we are not safe.
 Clar. By heaven, I think, there 's no man is secure
But the queen's kindred and night-walking heralds
That trudge betwixt the king and Mistress Shore.
Heard ye not what an humble suppliant
Lord Hastings was to her for his delivery?
 Glo. Humbly complaining to her deity
Got my lord chamberlain his liberty.
I'll tell you what, I think it is our way,
If we will keep in favour with the king,
To be her men and wear her livery:
The jealous o'erworn widow and herself,
Since that our brother dubbed them gentlewomen,
Are mighty gossips in this monarchy.
 Brak. Beseech your graces both to pardon me;
His majesty hath straitly given in charge

That no man shall have private conference,
Of what degree soever, with his brother.
    Glo.   Even so; an 't please your worship, Brakenbury.
You may partake of anything we say:
We speak no treason, man;—we say the king
Is wise and virtuous, and his noble queen
Well struck in years, fair, and not jealous;—
We say that Shore's wife hath a pretty foot,
A cherry lip, a bonny eye, a passing pleasing tongue;
And the queen's kindred are made gentlefolks:
How say you, sir? can you deny all this?
    Brak.   With this, my lord, myself have naught to do.
    Glo.   Naught to do with Mistress Shore! I tell thee, fellow,
He that doth naught with her, excepting one,
Were best he do it secretly, alone.
    Brak.   What one, my lord?
    Glo.   Her husband, knave: wouldst thou betray me?
    Brak.   I beseech your grace to pardon me, and withal
Forbear your conference with the noble duke.
    Clar.   We know thy charge, Brakenbury, and will obey.
    Glo.   We are the queen's abjects, and must obey.
Brother, farewell: I will unto the king:
And whatsoe'er you will employ me in,
Were it to call King Edward's widow sister,
I will perform it to enfranchise you.
Meantime, this deep disgrace in brotherhood
Touches me deeper than you can imagine.
    Clar.   I know it pleaseth neither of us well.
    Glo.   Well, your imprisonment shall not be long;
I will deliver you, or else lie for you:
Meantime, have patience.
    Clar.   I must perforce.   Farewell.
              [Exeunt Clarence, Brakenbury, and Guard
    Glo.   Go, tread the path that thou shalt ne'er return.
Simple, plain Clarence! I do love thee so,
That I will shortly send thy soul to heaven,
If heaven will take the present at our hands.
But who comes here? the new-delivered Hastings?

Enter Lord Hastings

    Hast.   Good time of day unto my gracious lord!
    Glo.   As much unto my good lord chamberlain!
Well are you welcome to the open air.
How hath your lordship brooked imprisonment?
    Hast.   With patience, noble lord, as prisoners must:
But I shall live, my lord, to give them thanks
That were the cause of my imprisonment.
    Glo.   No doubt, no doubt; and so shall Clarence too;
For they that were your enemies are his,
And have prevailed as much on him as you.

    Hast.   More pity that the eagle should be mewed,
While kites and buzzards prey at liberty.
    Glo.   What news abroad?
    Hast.   No news so bad abroad as this at home;
The king is sickly, weak and melancholy,
And his physicians fear him mightily.
    Glo.   Now, by Saint Paul, this news is bad indeed.
O, he hath kept an evil diet long,
And overmuch consumed his royal person:
'T is very grievous to be thought upon.
What, is he in his bed?
    Hast.   He is.
    Glo.   Go you before, and I will follow you.
                                  [Exit Hastings
He cannot live, I hope; and must not die
Till George be packed with post-horse up to heaven.
I'll in, to urge his hatred more to Clarence,
With lies well steeled with weighty arguments;
And, if I fail not in my deep intent,
Clarence hath not another day to live:
Which done, God take King Edward to his mercy,
And leave the world for me to bustle in!
For then I'll marry Warwick's youngest daughter.
What though I killed her husband and her father?
The readiest way to make the wench amends
Is to become her husband and her father:
The which will I; not all so much for love
As for another secret close intent,
By marrying her which I must reach unto.
But yet I run before my horse to market:
Clarence still breathes; Edward still lives and reigns:
When they are gone, then must I count my gains.   *[Exit*

SCENE II.—The Same. Another Street

Enter the corpse of KING HENRY THE SIXTH, *borne in an
    open coffin, Gentlemen with halberds to guard it, among
    them* TRESSEL *and* BERKELEY; LADY ANNE *being the
    mourner*

    Anne.   Set down, set down your honourable load,—
If honour may be shrouded in a hearse,—
Whilst I awhile obsequiously lament
The untimely fall of virtuous Lancaster.
                      [The bearers set down the coffin
Poor key-cold figure of a holy king!
Pale ashes of the house of Lancaster!
Thou bloodless remnant of that royal blood!
Be 't lawful that I invocate thy ghost,
To hear the lamentations of poor Anne,

Wife to thy Edward, to thy slaughtered son,
Stabbed by the selfsame hand that made these wounds!
Lo, in these windows that let forth thy life,
I pour the helpless balm of my poor eyes.
O, cursèd be the hand that made these holes!
Cursèd the heart that had the heart to do it!
Cursèd the blood that let this blood from hence!
More direful hap betide that hated wretch,
That makes us wretched by the death of thee,
Than I can wish to adders, spiders, toads,
Or any creeping venomed thing that lives!
If ever he have child, abortive be it,
Prodigious, and untimely brought to light,
Whose ugly and unnatural aspéct
May fright the hopeful mother at the view;
And that be heir to his unhappiness!
If ever he have wife, let her be made
As miserable by the death of him
As I am made by my poor lord and thee!
Come, now towards Chertsey with your holy load,
Taken from Paul's to be interréd there;
And still, as you are weary of the weight,
Rest you, whiles I lament King Henry's corse.

Enter GLOSTER

Glo.   Stay, you that bear the corse, and set it down.
Anne.   What black magician conjures up this fiend,
To stop devoted charitable deeds?
Glo.   Villains, set down the corse; or, by Saint Paul,
I'll make a corse of him that disobeys.
Gent.   My lord, stand back, and let the coffin pass.
Glo.   Unmannered dog! stand thou, when I command:
Advance thy halberd higher than my breast,
Or, by Saint Paul, I'll strike thee to my foot,
And spurn upon thee, beggar, for thy boldness.
                    [*The bearers set down the coffin*
Anne.   What, do you tremble? are you all afraid?
Alas, I blame you not; for you are mortal,
And mortal eyes cannot endure the devil.—
Avaunt, thou dreadful minister of hell!
Thou hadst but power o'er his mortal body,
His soul thou canst not have; therefore, be gone.
Glo.   Sweet saint, for charity, be not so curst.
Anne.   Foul devil, for God's sake, hence, and trouble
        us not;
For thou hast made the happy earth thy hell,
Filled it with cursing cries and deep exclaims.
If thou delight to view thy heinous deeds,
Behold this pattern of thy butcheries.
O, gentlemen, see, see! dead Henry's wounds

Open their congealed mouths and bleed afresh!—
Blush, blush, thou lump of foul deformity;
For 't is thy presence that exhales this blood
From cold and empty veins, where no blood dwells;
Thy deed, inhuman and unnatural,
Provokes this deluge most unnatural.—
O God, which this blood mad'st, revenge his death!
O earth, which this blood drink'st, revenge his death!
Either heaven with lightning strike the murderer dead,
Or earth, gape open wide, and eat him quick,
As thou dost swallow up this good king's blood,
Which his hell-governed arm hath butcheréd!
   Glo.   Lady, you know no rules of charity,
Which renders good for bad, blessings for curses.
   Anne.   Villain, thou know'st no law of God nor man:
No beast so fierce but knows some touch of pity.
   Glo.   But I know none, and therefore am no beast.
   Anne.   O wonderful, when devils tell the truth!
   Glo.   More wonderful, when angels are so angry
Vouchsafe, divine perfection of a woman,
Of these supposéd evils to give me leave
By circumstance but to acquit myself.
   Anne.   Vouchsafe, defused infection of a man,
By these known evils, but to give me leave,
By circumstance, to curse thy curséd self.
   Glo.   Fairer than tongue can name thee, let me have
Some patient leisure to excuse myself.
   Anne.   Fouler than heart can think thee, thou canst make
No excuse current, but to hang thyself.
   Glo.   By such despair, I should accuse myself.
   Anne.   And, by despairing, shouldst thou stand excused
For doing worthy vengeance on thyself,
Which didst unworthy slaughter upon others.
   Glo.   Say that I slew them not?
   Anne.   Why, then they are not dead:
But dead they are, and, devilish slave, by thee.
   Glo.   I did not kill your husband.
   Anne.   Why, then he is alive.
   Glo.   Nay, he is dead; and slain by Edward's hand.
   Anne.   In thy foul throat thou liest: Queen Margaret saw
Thy murderous falchion smoking in his blood;
The which thou once didst bend against her breast,
But that thy brothers beat aside the point.
   Glo.   I was provokéd by her slanderous tongue,
Which laid their guilt upon my guiltless shoulders.
   Anne.   Thou wast provokéd by thy bloody mind,
Which never dreamt on aught but butcheries:
Didst thou not kill this king?
   Glo.   I grant ye.
   Anne.   Dost grant me, hedgehog? then, God grant me too

Thou mayst be damnéd for that wicked deed!—
O, he was gentle, mild, and virtuous!
   Glo.   The fitter for the King of heaven, that hath him.
   Anne.   He is in heaven, where thou shalt never come.
   Glo.   Let him thank me, that holp to send him thither;
For he was fitter for that place than earth.
   Anne.   And thou unfit for any place but hell.
   Glo.   Yes, one place else, if you will hear me name it.
   Anne.   Some dungeon.
   Glo.   Your bed-chamber.
   Anne.   Ill rest betide the chamber where thou liest!
   Glo.   So will it, madam, till I lie with you.
   Anne.   I hope so.
   Glo.   I know so.   But gentle Lady Anne,
To leave this keen encounter of our wits,
And fall somewhat into a slower method,—
Is not the causer of the timeless deaths
Of these Plantagenets, Henry and Edward,
As blameful as the executioner?
   Anne.   Thou art the cause, and most accursed effect.
   Glo.   Your beauty was the cause of that effect;
Your beauty, which did haunt me in my sleep
To undertake the death of all the world,
So I might live one hour in your sweet bosom.
   Anne.   If I thought that, I tell thee, homicide,
These nails should rend that beauty from my cheeks.
   Glo.   These eyes could not endure that beauty's wreck;
You should not blemish it, if I stood by:
As all the world is cheeréd by the sun,
So I by that; it is my day, my life.
   Anne. Black night o'ershade thy day, and death thy life!
   Glo.   Curse not thyself, fair creature; thou art both.
   Anne.   I would I were, to be revenged on thee.
   Glo.   It is a quarrel most unnatural,
To be revenged on him that loveth you.
   Anne.   It is a quarrel just and reasonable,
To be revenged on him that slew my husband.
   Glo.   He that bereft thee, lady, of thy husband,
Did it to help thee to a better husband.
   Anne.   His better doth not breathe upon the earth.
   Glo.   He lives that loves thee better than he could.
   Anne.   Name him.
   Glo.   Plantagenet.
   Anne.   Why, that was he.
   Glo.   The selfsame name, but one of better nature.
   Anne.   Where is he?
   Glo.   Here.   *[She spits at him*
Why dost thou spit at me?
   Anne.   Would it were mortal poison, for thy sake!
   Glo.   Never came poison from so sweet a place.

Anne.   Never hung poison on a fouler toad.
Out of my sight! thou dost infect my eyes.
　　Glo.   Thine eyes, sweet lady, have infected mine.
　　Anne.   Would they were basilisks, to strike thee dead!
　　Glo.   I would they were, that I might die at once;
For now they kill me with a living death.
Those eyes of thine from mine have drawn salt tears,
Shamed their aspéct with store of childish drops:
These eyes, which never shed remorseful tear,
No, when my father York and Edward wept,
To hear the piteous moan that Rutland made
When black-faced Clifford shook his sword at him;
Nor when thy warlike father, like a child,
Told the sad story of my father's death,
And twenty times made pause to sob and weep
That all the standers-by had wet their cheeks,
Like trees bedashed with rain: in that sad time
My manly eyes did scorn an humble tear;
And what these sorrows could not thence exhale,
Thy beauty hath, and made them blind with weeping.
I never sued to friend nor enemy;
My tongue could never learn sweet smoothing words;
But, now thy beauty is proposed my fee,
My proud heart sues and prompts my tongue to speak.
　　　　　　　　　　[She looks scornfully at him
Teach not thy lips such scorn, for they were made
For kissing, lady, not for such contempt.
If thy revengeful heart cannot forgive,
Lo, here I lend thee this sharp-pointed sword;
Which if thou please to hide in this true bosom,
And let the soul forth that adoreth thee,
I lay it naked to the deadly stroke,
And humbly beg the death upon my knee.
　　　　[He lays his breast open : she offers at it with his sword
Nay, do not pause; for I did kill King Henry,—
But 't was thy beauty that provokéd me.
Nay, now dispatch; 't was I that stabbed young Edward,—
But 't was thy heavenly face that set me on.
　　　　　　　　　　　　[She lets fall the sword
Take up the sword again, or take up me.
　　Anne.   Arise, dissembler: though I wish thy death,
I will not be thy executioner.
　　Glo.   Then bid me kill myself, and I will do it.
　　Anne.   I have already.
　　Glo.　　　　　　　Tush, that was in thy rage:
Speak it again, and, even with the word,
This hand, which for thy love did kill thy love,
Shall for thy love kill a far truer love;
To both their deaths shalt thou be accessary.
　　Anne.   I would I knew thy heart.

Glo.   'T is figured in my tongue.
Anne.   I fear me both are false.
Glo.   Then never man was true.
Anne.   Well, well, put up your sword.
Glo.   Say, then, my peace is made.
Anne.   That shall you know hereafter.
Glo.   But shall I live in hope?
Anne.   All men, I hope, live so.
Glo.   Vouchsafe to wear this ring.
Anne.   To take is not to give.
Glo.   Look, how this ring encompasseth thy finger,
Even so thy breast encloseth my poor heart;
Wear both of them, for both of them are thine.
And if thy poor devoted suppliant may
But beg one favour at thy gracious hand,
Thou dost confirm his happiness for ever.
Anne.   What is it?
Glo.   That it would please thee leave these sad designs
To him that hath more cause to be a mourner,
And presently repair to Crosby Place;
Where, after I have solemnly interred,
At Chertsey monastery this noble king,
And wet his grave with my repentant tears,
I will with all expedient duty see you:
For divers unknown reasons, I beseech you,
Grant me this boon.
Anne.   With all my heart; and much it joys me too,
To see you are become so penitent.
Tressel and Berkeley, go along with me.
Glo.   Bid me farewell.
Anne.   'T is more than you deserve;
But since you teach me how to flatter you,
Imagine I have said farewell already.
            [*Exeunt Lady Anne, Tressel, and Berkeley*
Glo.   Sirs, take up the corse.
Gent.   Towards Chertsey, noble lord?
Glo.   No, to Whitefriars; there attend my coming.
                [*Exeunt all but Gloster*
Was ever woman in this humour woo'd?
Was ever woman in this humour won?
I'll have her;—but I will not keep her long.
What! I, that killed her husband and his father,
To take her in her heart's extremest hate,
With curses in her mouth, tears in her eyes,
The bleeding witness of her hatred by;
Having God, her conscience, and these bars against me,
And I no thing to back my suit withal
But the plain devil and dissembling looks,
And yet to win her,—all the world to nothing!
Ha!

Hath she forgot already that brave prince,
Edward, her lord, whom I, some three months since,
Stabbed in my angry mood at Tewksbury?
A sweeter and a lovelier gentleman,
Framed in the prodigality of nature,
Young, valiant, wise, and, no doubt, right royal,
The spacious world cannot again afford:
And will she yet debase her eyes on me,
That cropped the golden prime of this sweet prince,
And made her widow to a woful bed?
On me, whose all not equals Edward's moiety!
On me, that halt and am unshapen thus?
My dukedom to a beggarly denier,
I do mistake my person all this while:
Upon my life, she finds, although I cannot,
Myself to be a marvellous proper man.
I'll be at charges for a looking-glass,
And entertain some score or two of tailors
To study fashions to adorn my body:
Since I am crept in favour with myself,
I will maintain it with some little cost.
But first I'll turn yon fellow in his grave;
And then return lamenting to my love.—
Shine out, fair sun, till I have bought a glass,
That I may see my shadow as I pass.   [*Exit*

Scene III.—The Palace

Enter Queen Elizabeth, Lord Rivers, *and* Lord Grey

    Riv.   Have patience, madam: there 's no doubt his
      majesty
Will soon recover his accustomed health.
    Grey.   In that you brook it ill, it makes him worse:
Therefore, for God's sake, entertain good comfort,
And cheer his grace with quick and merry words.
    Q. Eliz.   If he were dead, what would betide of me?
    Riv.   No other harm but loss of such a lord.
    Q. Eliz.   The loss of such a lord includes all harm.
    Grey.   The heavens have blessed you with a goodly son
To be your comforter when he is gone.
    Q. Eliz.   Oh, he is young, and his minority
Is put into the trust of Richard Gloster,
A man that loves not me, nor none of you.
    Riv.   Is it concluded he shall be protector?
    Q. Eliz.   It is determined, not concluded yet:
But so it must be, if the king miscarry.

Enter Buckingham *and* Stanley

    Grey.   Here come the lords of Buckingham and Stanley.
    Buck.   Good time of day unto your royal grace!

Stan.   God make your majesty joyful as you have been!
Q. Eliz.   The Countess Richmond, good my Lord of Stanley,
To your good prayers will scarcely say amen.
Yet, Stanley, notwithstanding she 's your wife,
And loves not me, be you, good lord, assured
I hate not you for her proud arrogance.
Stan.   I do beseech you, either not believe
The envious slanders of her false accusers;
Or, if she be accused in true report,
Bear with her weakness, which, I think, proceeds
From wayward sickness, and no grounded malice.
Riv.   Saw you the king to-day, my Lord of Stanley?
Stan.   But now the Duke of Buckingham and I
Are come from visiting his majesty.
Q. Eliz.   What likelihood of his amendment, lords?
Buck.   Madam, good hope; his grace speaks cheerfully.
Q. Eliz.   God grant him health! Did you confer with him?
Buck.   Ay, madam: he desires to make atonement
Betwixt the Duke of Gloster and your brothers,
And betwixt them and my lord chamberlain;
And sent to warn them to his royal presence.
Q. Eliz.   Would all were well!—but that will never be:
I fear our happiness is at the height.

Enter GLOSTER, HASTINGS, *and* DORSET

Glo.   They do me wrong, and I will not endure 't:
Who are they that complain unto the king
That I, forsooth, am stern and love them not?
By holy Paul, they love his grace but lightly
That fill his ears with such dissentious rumours.
Because I cannot flatter and speak fair,
Smile in men's faces, smooth, deceive and cog,
Duck with French nods and apish courtesy,
I must be held a rancorous enemy.
Cannot a plain man live and think no harm,
But thus his simple truth must be abused
By silken, sly, insinuating Jacks?
Riv.   To whom in all this presence speaks your grace?
Glo.   To thee, that hast nor honesty nor grace.
When have I injured thee? when done thee wrong?
Or thee? or thee? or any of your faction?
A plague upon you all! His royal person,—
Whom God preserve better than you would wish!—
Cannot be quiet scarce a breathing-while,
But you must trouble him with lewd complaints.
Q. Eliz.   Brother of Gloster, you mistake the matter.
The king, of his own royal disposition,
And not provoked by any suitor else,
Aiming, belike, at your interior hatred
Which in your outward actions shows itself

Against my kindred, brothers, and myself,
Makes him to send; that thereby he may gather
The ground of your ill-will, and so remove it.
    Glo.   I cannot tell: the world is grown so bad,
That wrens make prey where eagles dare not perch:
Since every Jack became a gentleman,
There's many a gentle person made a Jack.
    Q. Eliz.   Come, come, we know your meaning, brother
        Gloster;
You envy my advancement, and my friends':
God grant we never may have need of you!
    Glo.   Meantime, God grants that we have need of you:
Our brother is imprisoned by your means,
Myself disgraced, and the nobility
Held in contempt; whilst many fair promotions
Are daily given to ennoble those
That scarce, some two days since, were worth a noble.
    Q. Eliz.   By him that raised me to this careful height
From that contented hap which I enjoyed,
I never did incense his majesty
Against the Duke of Clarence, but have been
An earnest advocate to plead for him.
My lord, you do me shameful injury,
Falsely to draw me in these vile suspects.
    Glo.   You may deny that you were not the cause
Of my Lord Hastings' late imprisonment.
    Riv.   She may, my lord, for—
    Glo.   She may, Lord Rivers! why, who knows not so?
She may do more, sir, than denying that:
She may help you to many fair preferments,
And then deny her aiding hand therein
And lay those honours on your high deserts.
What may she not? She may, yea, marry, may she,—
    Riv.   What, marry, may she?
    Glo.   What, marry, may she! marry with a king,
A bachelor, a handsome stripling too:
I wis your grandam had a worser match.
    Q. Eliz.   My Lord of Gloster, I have too long borne
Your blunt upbraidings and your bitter scoffs:
By heaven, I will acquaint his majesty
With those gross taunts I often have endured.
I had rather be a country servant-maid
Than a great queen, with this condition,
To be thus taunted, scorned, and stormed at:

Enter QUEEN MARGARET, behind

Small joy have I in being England's queen.—
    Q. Mar.   [*Aside*] And lessened be that small, God, I
        beseech thee!
Thy honour, state and seat is due to me.—

Glo. What! threat you me with telling of the king?
Tell him, and spare not: look, what I have said
I will avouch in presence of the king:
I dare adventure to be sent to the Tower.
'T is time to speak,—my pains are quite forgot.—

Q. Mar. [*Aside*] Out, devil! I remember them too well:
Thou slew'st my husband Henry in the Tower,
And Edward, my poor son, at Tewksbury.—

Glo. Ere you were queen, yea, or your husband king,
I was a pack-horse in his great affairs;
A weeder-out of his proud adversaries,
A liberal rewarder of his friends:
To royalise his blood I spilt mine own.—

Q. Mar. [*Aside*] Ay, and much better blood than his
    or thine.

Glo. In all which time you and your husband Grey
Were factious for the house of Lancaster:
And, Rivers, so were you. Was not your husband
In Margaret's battle at Saint Alban's slain?
Let me put in your minds, if you forget,
What you have been ere now, and what you are;
Withal, what I have been, and what I am.—

Q. Mar. [*Aside*] A murderous villain, and so still thou art.—

Glo. Poor Clarence did forsake his father, Warwick;
Yea, and forswore himself,—which Jesu pardon!—

Q. Mar. [*Aside*] Which God revenge!—

Glo. To fight on Edward's party for the crown;
And for his meed, poor lord, he is mewed up.
I would to God my heart were flint, like Edward's;
Or Edward's soft and pitiful, like mine:
I am too childish-foolish for this world.—

Q. Mar. [*Aside*] Hie thee to hell for shame, and leave
    the world,
Thou cacodemon! There thy kingdom is.

Riv. My Lord of Gloster, in those busy days
Which here you urge to prove us enemies,
We followed then our lord, our lawful king:
So should we you, if you should be our king.

Glo. If I should be! I had rather be a pedlar:
Far be it from my heart, the thought of it!

Q. Eliz. As little joy, my lord, as you suppose
You should enjoy, were you this country's king,
As little joy may you suppose in me,
That I enjoy, being the queen thereof.—

Q. Mar. [*Aside*] As little joy enjoys the queen thereof;
For I am she, and altogether joyless.
I can no longer hold me patient.   [*Advancing*
Hear me, you wrangling pirates, that fall out
In sharing that which you have pilled from me!
Which of you trembles not that looks on me?

If not, that, I being queen, you bow like subjects,
Yet that, by you deposed, you quake like rebels?
O gentle villain, do not turn away!
    Glo. Foul wrinkled witch, what mak'st thou in my sight?
    Q. Mar. But repetition of what thou hast marred;
That will I make, before I let thee go.
    Glo. Wert thou not banishéd on pain of death?
    Q. Mar. I was;
But I do find more pain in banishment
Than death can yield me here by my abode.
A husband and a son thou ow'st to me;—
And thou a kingdom;—all of you allegiance:
The sorrow that I have, by right is yours,
And all the pleasures you usurp are mine.
    Glo. The curse my noble father laid on thee,
When thou didst crown his warlike brows with paper
And with thy scorns drew'st rivers from his eyes,
And then, to dry them, gav'st the duke a clout
Steeped in the faultless blood of pretty Rutland,—
His curses, then from bitterness of soul
Denounced against thee, are all fall'n upon thee;
And God, not we, hath plagued thy bloody deed.
    Q. Eliz. So just is God, to right the innocent.
    Hast. O, 't was the foulest deed to slay that babe,
And the most merciless that e'er was heard of!
    Riv. Tyrants themselves wept when it was reported.
    Dor. No man but prophesied revenge for it.
    Buck. Northumberland, then present, wept to see it.
    Q. Mar. What! were you snarling all before I came,
Ready to catch each other by the throat,
And turn you all your hatred now on me?
Did York's dread curse prevail so much with heaven
That Henry's death, my lovely Edward's death,
Their kingdom's loss, my woful banishment,
Could all but answer for that peevish brat?
Can curses pierce the clouds and enter heaven?
Why, then, give way, dull clouds, to my quick curses!
If not by war, by surfeit die your king,
As ours by murder, to make him a king!
Edward thy son, which now is Prince of Wales,
For Edward my son, which was Prince of Wales,
Die in his youth by like untimely violence!
Thyself a queen, for me that was a queen,
Outlive thy glory, like my wretched self!
Long mayst thou live to wail thy children's loss;
And see another, as I see thee now,
Decked in thy rights, as thou art stalled in mine!
Long die thy happy days before thy death;
And, after many lengthened hours of grief
Die, neither mother, wife, nor England's queen!—

Rivers and Dorset, you were standers by,—
And so wast thou, Lord Hastings,—when my son
Was stabbed with bloody daggers: God, I pray him,
That none of you may live your natural age,
But by some unlooked accident cut off!
   Glo. Have done thy charm, thou hateful withered hag!
   Q. Mar. And leave out thee? stay, dog, for thou shalt
      hear me.
If heaven have any grievous plague in store
Exceeding those that I can wish upon thee,
O, let them keep it till thy sins be ripe,
And then hurl down their indignation
On thee, the troubler of the poor world's peace!
The worm of conscience still begnaw thy soul!
Thy friends suspect for traitors while thou liv'st,
And take deep traitors for thy dearest friends!
No sleep close up that deadly eye of thine,
Unless it be whilst some tormenting dream
Affrights thee with a hell of ugly devils!
Thou elvish-marked, abortive, rooting hog!
Thou that was sealed in thy nativity
The slave of nature and the son of hell!
Thou slander of thy mother's heavy womb!
Thou loathéd issue of thy father's loins!
Thou rag of honour! thou detested—
   Glo. Margaret.
   Q. Mar.   Richard!
   Glo.   Ha!
   Q. Mar.   I call thee not.
   Glo. I cry thee mercy then, for I had thought
That thou hadst called me all these bitter names.
   Q. Mar. Why, so I did; but looked for no reply.
O, let me make the period to my curse!
   Glo. 'T is done by me, and ends in "Margaret."
   Q. Eliz. Thus have you breathed your curse against
      yourself.
   Q. Mar. Poor painted queen, vain flourish of my fortune!
Why strew'st thou sugar on that bottled spider
Whose deadly web ensnareth thee about?
Fool, fool! thou whet'st a knife to kill thyself.
The time will come when thou shalt wish for me
To help thee curse that poisonous bunch-backed toad.
   Hast. False-boding woman, end thy frantic curse,
Lest to thy harm thou move our patience.
   Q. Mar. Foul shame upon you! you have all moved mine.
   Riv. Were you well served, you would be taught your duty.
   Q. Mar. To serve me well, you all should do me duty,
Teach me to be your queen, and you my subjects:
O, serve me well, and teach yourselves that duty!
   Dor. Dispute not with her; she is lunatic.

   Q. Mar.   Peace, master marquess, you are malapert:
Your fire-new stamp of honour is scarce current.
O, that your young nobility could judge
What 't were to lose it and be miserable!
They that stand high have many blasts to shake them;
And if they fall, they dash themselves to pieces.
   Glo.   Good counsel, marry: learn it, learn it, marquess.
   Dor.   It toucheth you, my lord, as much as me.
   Glo.   Yea, and much more: but I was born so high,
Our aery buildeth in the cedar's top,
And dallies with the wind and scorns the sun.
   Q. Mar.   And turns the sun to shade; alas! alas!
Witness my son, now in the shade of death;
Whose bright out-shining beams thy cloudy wrath
Hath in eternal darkness folded up.
Your aery buildeth in our aery's nest.
O God, that seest it, do not suffer it;
As it was won with blood, lost be it so!
   Buck.   Peace, peace! for shame, if not for charity.
   Q. Mar.   Urge neither charity nor shame to me:
Uncharitably with me have you dealt,
And shamefully by you my hopes are butchered.
My charity is outrage, life my shame;
And in that shame still live my sorrow's rage!
   Buck.   Have done, have done.
   Q. Mar.   O princely Buckingham, I'll kiss thy hand,
In sign of league and amity with thee:
Now fair befall thee and thy noble house
Thy garments are not spotted with our blood,
Nor thou within the compass of my curse.
   Buck.   Nor no one here; for curses never pass
The lips of those that breathe them in the air.
   Q. Mar.   I'll not believe but they ascend the sky,
And there awake God's gentle-sleeping peace.
O Buckingham, take heed of yonder dog!
Look, when he fawns, he bites; and when he bites,
His venom tooth will rankle to the death:
Have not to do with him, beware of him;
Sin, death, and hell have set their marks on him,
And all their ministers attend on him.
   Glo.   What doth she say, my Lord of Buckingham?
   Buck.   Nothing that I respect, my gracious lord.
   Q. Mar.   What, dost thou scorn me for my gentle
       counsel?
And soothe the devil that I warn thee from?
O, but remember this another day,
When he shall split thy very heart with sorrow.
And say poor Margaret was a prophetess!—
Live each of you the subjects to his hate,
And he to yours, and all of you to God's!   *[Exit*

Hast.   My hair doth stand on end to hear her curses.
Riv.   And so doth mine: I muse why she's at liberty.
Glo.   I cannot blame her: by God's holy mother,
She hath had too much wrong; and I repent
My part thereof that I have done to her.
Q. Eliz.   I never did her any, to my knowledge
Glo.   But you have all the vantage of her wrong.
I was too hot to do somebody good,
That is too cold in thinking of it now.
Marry, as for Clarence, he is well repaid;
He is franked up to fatting for his pains;
God pardon them that are the cause of it!
Riv.   A virtuous and a Christian-like conclusion,
To pray for them that have done scathe to us.
Glo.   So do I ever: [*Aside*] being well advised,
For had I cursed now, I had cursed myself.

Enter CATESBY

Cates.   Madam, his Majesty doth call for you,—
And for your grace,—and you, my noble lords.
Q. Eliz.   Catesby, we come. Lords, will you go with us?
Riv.   We wait upon your grace.
                                        [*Exeunt all but Gloster*
Glo.   I do the wrong, and first begin to brawl.
The secret mischiefs that I set abroach
I lay unto the grievous charge of others.
Clarence, whom I, indeed, have laid in darkness,
I do beweep to many simple gulls;
Namely, to Hastings, Stanley, Buckingham;
And say it is the queen and her allies
That stir the king against the duke my brother.
Now, they believe it; and withal whet me
To be revenged on Rivers, Vaughan, Grey:
But then I sigh; and, with a piece of scripture,
Tell them that God bids us do good for evil.
And thus I clothe my naked villainy
With old odd ends stolen out of holy writ;
And seem a saint, when most I play the devil.
But, soft! here come my executioners.

Enter two Murderers

How now, my hardy, stout, resolvéd mates!
Are you now going to dispatch this deed?
First Murd.   We are, my lord; and come to have the
        warrant,
That we may be admitted where he is.
Glo.   Well thought upon;—I have it here about me.
                                        [*Gives the warrant*
When you have done, repair to Crosby Place.
But, sirs, be sudden in the execution,

Withal obdurate, do not hear him plead;
For Clarence is well-spoken, and perhaps
May move your hearts to pity, if you mark him.
   First Murd. Tut, tut, my lord, we will not stand to prate;
Talkers are no good doers: be assured
We come to use our hands and not our tongues.
   Glo. Your eyes drop millstones, when fools' eyes drop
     tears:
I like you, lads;—about your business straight;
Go, go, dispatch.
   First Murd. We will, my noble lord.   *[Exeunt*

SCENE IV.—London. A Room in the Tower

Enter CLARENCE *and* BRAKENBURY

   Brak. Why looks your grace so heavily to-day?
   Clar. O, I have passed a miserable night,
So full of ugly sights, of ghastly dreams,
That, as I am a Christian faithful man,
I would not spend another such a night,
Though 't were to buy a world of happy days,—
So full of dismal terror was the time!
   Brak. What was your dream, my lord? I pray you
     tell me.
   Clar. Methought that I had broken from the Tower,
And was embarked to cross to Burgundy;
And, in my company, my brother Gloster,
Who from my cabin tempted me to walk
Upon the hatches: thence we looked toward England,
And cited up a thousand fearful times,
During the wars of York and Lancaster
That had befall'n us. As we paced along
Upon the giddy footing of the hatches,
Methought that Gloster stumbled; and, in falling,
Struck me, that thought to stay him, overboard
Into the tumbling billows of the main.
Lord, Lord, methought, what pain it was to drown!
What dreadful noise of waters in mine ears!
What ugly sights of death within mine eyes!
Methought I saw a thousand fearful wrecks;
Ten thousand men that fishes gnawed upon;
Wedges of gold, great anchors, heaps of pearl,
Inestimable stones, unvalued jewels,
All scattered in the bottom of the sea:
Some lay in dead men's skulls; and, in those holes
Where eyes did once inhabit, there were crept,—
As 't were in scorn of eyes,—reflecting gems,

That wooed the slimy bottom of the deep,
And mocked the dead bones that lay scattered by.
    Brak.   Had you such leisure in the time of death
To gaze upon the secrets of the deep?
    Clar.   Methought I had; and often did I strive
To yield the ghost: but still the envious flood
Kept in my soul, and would not let it forth
To seek the empty, vast and wandering air,
But smothered it within my panting bulk,
Which almost burst to belch it in the sea.
    Brak.   Awaked you not with this sore agony?
    Clar.   O, no, my dream was lengthened after life;
O, then began the tempest to my soul,
Who passed, methought, the melancholy flood,
With that grim ferryman which poets write of,
Unto the kingdom of perpetual night.
The first that there did greet my stranger soul
Was my great father-in-law, renownéd Warwick;
Who cried aloud, "What scourge for perjury
Can this dark monarchy afford false Clarence?"
And so he vanished: then came wandering by
A shadow like an angel, with bright hair
Dabbled in blood; and he shrieked out aloud,
"Clarence is come,—false, fleeting, perjured Clarence;
That stabbed me in the field by Tewksbury;—
Seize on him, Furies, take him to your torments!"
With that, methought, a legion of foul fiends
Environed me, and howléd in mine ears
Such hideous cries, that with the very noise
I trembling waked, and for a season after
Could not believe but that I was in hell,—
Such terrible impression made the dream.
    Brak.   No marvel, lord, though it affrighted you;
I am afraid methinks to hear you tell it.
    Clar.   O Brakenbury, I have done those things
Which now bear evidence against my soul,
For Edward's sake; and see how he requites me!—
O God! if my deep prayers cannot appease thee,
But thou wilt be avenged on my misdeeds,
Yet execute thy wrath in me alone,
O, spare my guiltless wife and my poor children!—
Keeper, I prithee, sit by me awhile;
My soul is heavy, and I fain would sleep.
    Brak.   I will, my lord: God give your grace good rest!—
                                        [*Clarence sleeps*
Sorrow breaks seasons and reposing hours,
Makes the night morning, and the noon-tide night.
Princes have but their titles for their glories,
An outward honour for an inward toil;
And, for unfelt imaginations,

They often feel a world of restless cares:
So that, between their titles and low name
There's nothing differs but the outward fame.

Enter the two Murderers

First Murd. Ho! who's here?
Brak. What would'st thou, fellow? and how cam'st
thou hither?
First Murd. I would speak with Clarence and I came
hither on my legs.
Brak. What, so brief?
Sec. Murd. 'T is better, sir, than to be tedious. Let
him see our commission; talk no more.
                                        [*Brakenbury reads it*
Brak. I am, in this, commanded to deliver
The noble Duke of Clarence to your hands:
I will not reason what is meant hereby,
Because I will be guiltless of the meaning.
Here are the keys,—there sits the duke asleep:
I'll to the king; and signify to him
That thus I have resigned my charge to you.
First Murd. You may, sir, 't is a point of wisdom: fare
you well.   [*Exit Brakenbury*
Sec. Murd. What, shall we stab him as he sleeps?
First Murd. No; then he will say 't was done cowardly,
when he wakes.
Sec. Murd. When he wakes! why, fool, he shall never
wake till the judgment-day.
First Murd. Why, then he'll say we stabbed him sleeping.
Sec. Murd. The urging of that word "judgment" hath
bred a kind of remorse in me.
First. Murd. What, art thou afraid?
Sec. Murd. Not to kill him, having a warrant for it;
but to be damned for killing him, from the which no
warrant can defend us.
First Murd. I thought thou hadst been resolute.
Sec. Murd. So I am, to let him live.
First Murd. I'll back to the Duke of Gloster, and tell
him so.
Sec. Murd. Nay, I prithee, stay a little; I hope my
holy humour will change; 't was wont to hold me but
while one tells twenty.
First Murd. How dost thou feel thyself now?
Sec. Murd. Faith, some certain dregs of conscience are
yet within me.
First Murd. Remember our reward when the deed's
done.
Sec. Murd. Zounds, he dies: I had forgot the reward.
First Murd. Where 's thy conscience now?
Sec. Murd. In the Duke of Gloster's purse.

First Murd. So when he opens his purse to give us our reward, thy conscience flies out.

Sec. Murd. 'T is no matter, let it go; there 's few or none will entertain it.

First Murd. What if it come to thee again?

Sec. Murd. I 'll not meddle with it:—it is a dangerous thing: it makes a man a coward: a man cannot steal, but it accuseth him; a man cannot swear, but it checks him; a man cannot lie with his neighbour's wife, but it detects him: 't is a blushing shamefast spirit that mutinies in a man's bosom; it fills one full of obstacles: it made me once restore a purse of gold that by chance I found; it beggars any man that keeps it: it is turned out of all towns and cities for a dangerous thing; and every man that means to live well endeavours to trust to himself and to live without it.

First Murd. Zounds, it is even now at my elbow, persuading me not to kill the duke.

Sec. Murd. Take the devil in thy mind, and believe him not: he would insinuate with thee but to make thee sigh.

First Murd. I am strong-framed, he cannot prevail with me.

Sec. Murd. Spoke like a tall fellow that respects his reputation. Come, shall we fall to work?

First Murd. Take him over the costard with the hilts of thy sword, and then throw him into the malmsey-butt in the next room.

Sec. Murd. O excellent device! make a sop of him.

First Murd. Soft, he wakes.

Sec. Mur. Strike!

First Murd. No, we 'll reason with him.

Clar. [*waking*]. Where art thou, keeper? give me a cup of wine.

Sec. Murd. You shall have wine enough, my lord, anon.

Clar. In God's name, what art thou?

Sec. Murd. A man, as you are.

Clar. But not, as I am, royal.

Sec. Murd. Nor you, as we are, loyal.

Clar. Thy voice is thunder, but thy looks are humble.

Sec. Murd. My voice is now the king's, my looks mine own.

Clar. How darkly and how deadly dost thou speak!
Your eyes do menace me: why look you pale?
Who sent you hither? Wherefore do you come?

Both. To, to, to—

Clar. To murder me?

Both. Ay, ay.

Clar. You scarcely have the hearts to tell me so,
And therefore cannot have the hearts to do it.
Wherein, my friends, have I offended you?

First Murd. Offended us you have not, but the king.

    Clar.   I shall be reconciled to him again.
    Sec. Murd.   Never, my lord; therefore prepare to die.
    Clar.   Are you called forth from out a world of men
To slay the innocent? What's my offence?
Where is the evidence that doth accuse me?
What lawful quest have given their verdict up
Unto the frowning judge? or who pronounced
The bitter sentence of poor Clarence' death?
Before I be convict by course of law,
To threaten me with death is most unlawful.
I charge you, as you hope to have redemption
By Christ's dear blood shed for our grievous sins,
That you depart, and lay no hands on me:
The deed you undertake is damnable.
    First Murd.   What we will do, we do upon command.
    Sec. Murd.   And he that hath commanded is our king.
    Clar.   Erroneous vassals! the great King of kings
Hath in the table of his law commanded
That thou shalt do no murder: will you, then,
Spurn at his edict and fulfil a man's?
Take heed: for he holds vengeance in his hands
To hurl upon their heads that break his law.
    Sec. Murd.   And that same vengeance doth he hurl on
      thee
For false forswearing, and for murder too:
Thou didst receive the sacrament to fight
In quarrel of the house of Lancaster.
    First Murd.   And, like a traitor to the name of God,
Didst break that vow; and with thy treacherous blade
Unripp'dst the bowels of thy sovereign's son.
    Sec. Murd.   Whom thou wert sworn to cherish and defend.
    First Murd.   How canst thou urge God's dreadful law to us,
When thou hast broke it in such dear degree?
    Clar.   Alas! for whose sake did I that ill deed?
For Edward, for my brother, for his sake:
He sends you not to murder me for this;
For in that sin he is as deep as I.
If God will be revengéd for this deed,
O, know you yet, he doth it publicly:
Take not the quarrel from his powerful arm;
He needs no indirect nor lawless course
To cut off those that have offended him.
    First Murd.   Who made thee, then, a bloody minister,
When gallant-springing brave Plantagenet,
That princely novice, was struck dead by thee?
    Clar.   My brother's love, the devil, and my rage.
    First Murd.   Thy brother's love, our duty, and thy fault,
Provoke us hither now to slaughter thee.
    Clar.   If you do love my brother, hate not me;
I am his brother, and I love him well.

If you be hired for meed, go back again,
And I will send you to my brother Gloster,
Who shall reward you better for my life
Than Edward will for tidings of my death.
    Sec. Murd.   You are deceived, your brother Gloster
        hates you.
    Clar.   O, no, he loves me, and he holds me dear:
Go you to him from me.
    Both.   Ay, so we will.
    Clar.   Tell him, when that our princely father York
Blessed his three sons with his victorious arm,
And charged us from his soul to love each other,
He little thought of this divided friendship:
Bid Gloster think of this, and he will weep.
    First Murd.   Ay, millstones; as he lessoned us to weep.
    Clar.   O, do not slander him, for he is kind.
    First Murd.   Right.
As snow in harvest.—Come, you deceive yourself:
'T is he that sends us to destroy you here.
    Clar.   It cannot be; for he bewept my fortune,
And hugged me in his arms, and swore, with sobs,
That he would labour my delivery.
    Sec. Murd.   Why, so he doth, when he delivers you
From this earth's thraldom to the joys of heaven.
    First Murd.   Make peace with God, for you must die,
        my lord.
    Clar.   Hast thou that holy feeling in thy soul.
To counsel me to make my peace with God,
And art thou yet to thy own soul so blind,
That thou wilt war with God by murdering me?
Ah, sirs, consider, ne that set you on
To do this deed will hate you for the deed.
    Sec. Murd.   What shall we do?
    Clar.   Relent, and save your souls.
Which of you, if you were a prince's son,
Being pent from liberty, as I am now,
If two such murderers as yourselves came to you,
Would not entreat for life?
    First Murd.   Relent! 't is cowardly and womanish.
    Clar.   Not to relent is beastly, savage, devilish,—
My friend, I spy some pity in thy looks;
O, if thine eye be not a flatterer,
Come thou on my side, and entreat for me,
As you would beg, were you in my distress:
A begging prince what beggar pities not?
    Sec. Murd.   Look behind you, my lord.
    First Murd.   Take that, and that; if all this will not
        do,   [*Stabs him*
I 'll drown you in the malmsey-butt within.
                                  [*Exit with the body*

Sec. Murd. A bloody deed, and desperately dispatched!
How fain, like Pilate, would I wash my hands
Of this most grievous guilty murder done!

Re-enter First Murderer

First Murd. How now! what mean'st thou, that thou
          help'st me not?
By heavens, the duke shall know how slack thou art!
Sec. Murd. I would he knew that I had saved his brother!
Take thou the fee, and tell him what I say;
For I repent me that the duke is slain.   [*Exit*
First Murd. So do not I: go, coward as thou art!
Now must I hide his body in some hole,
Until the duke take order for his burial:
And when I have my meed, I will away;
For this will out, and here I must not stay.   [*Exit*

ACT TWO

Scene I.—London. A Room in the Palace

Enter King Edward *led in sick,* Queen Elizabeth,
Dorset, Rivers, Hastings, Buckingham, Grey, *and others*

K. Edw. Why, so; now have I done a good day's
          work:—
You peers, continue this united league:
I every day expect an embassage
From my Redeemer to redeem me hence;
And now in peace my soul shall part to heaven,
Since I have set my friends at peace on earth.
Rivers and Hastings, take each other's hand;
Dissemble not your hatred, swear your love.
Riv. By heaven, my heart is purged from grudging hate;
And with my hand I seal my true heart's love.
Hast. So thrive I, as I truly swear the like!
K. Edw. Take heed you dally not before your king;
Lest he that is the supreme King of kings
Confound your hidden falsehood, and award
Either of you to be the other's end.
Hast. So prosper I, as I swear perfect love!
Riv. And I, as I love Hastings with my heart!
K. Edw. Madam, yourself are not exempt in this,
Nor your son Dorset,—Buckingham, nor you;—
You have been factious one against the other.
Wife, love Lord Hastings, let him kiss your hand;
And what you do, do it unfeignedly.
Q. Eliz. There, Hastings; I will never more remember
Our former hatred, so thrive I and mine!

K. Edw. Dorset, embrace him;—Hastings, love lord
  marquess.
Dor. This interchange of love, I here protest,
Upon my part shall be unviolable.
Hast. And so swear I.   [*They embrace*
K. Edw. Now, princely Buckingham, seal thou this league
With thy embracements to my wife's allies,
And make me happy in your unity.
Buck. [*To the Queen*] Whenever Buckingham doth turn
  his hate
Upon your grace, but with all duteous love
Doth cherish you and yours, God punish me
With hate in those where I expect most love!
When I have most need to employ a friend,
And most assuréd that he is a friend,
Deep, hollow, treacherous, and full of guile,
Be he unto me!—this do I beg of God,
When I am cold in zeal to you or yours.   [*They embrace*
K. Edw. A pleasing cordial, princely Buckingham,
Is this thy vow unto my sickly heart.
There wanteth now our brother Gloster here,
To make the perfect period of this peace.
Buck. And, in good time, here comes the noble duke.

Enter GLOSTER

Glo. Good morrow to my sovereign king and queen;
And, princely peers, a happy time of day!
K. Edw. Happy, indeed, as we have spent the day.
Brother, we have done deeds of charity;
Made peace of enmity, fair love of hate,
Between these swelling wrong-incenséd peers.
Glo. A blesséd labour, my most sovereign liege.—
Amongst this princely heap, if any here,
By false intelligence, or wrong surmise,
Hold me a foe;
If I unwittingly, or in my rage,
Have aught committed that is hardly borne
By any in this presence, I desire
To reconcile me to his friendly peace:
'T is death to me to be at enmity;
I hate it, and desire all good men's love.—
First, madam, I entreat true peace of you,
Which I will purchase with my duteous service,—
Of you, my noble cousin Buckingham,
If ever any grudge were lodged between us;—
Of you, Lord Rivers,—and Lord Grey, of you,—
That all without desert have frowned on me;—
Dukes, earls, lords, gentlemen;—indeed, of all
I do not know that Englishman alive
With whom my soul is any jot at odds

101

More than the infant that is born to-night:
I thank my God for my humility.
   Q. Eliz. A holy day shall this be kept hereafter:—
I would to God all strifes were well compounded.—
My sovereign lord, I do beseech your highness
To take our brother Clarence to your grace.
   Glo. Why, madam, have I offered love for this,
To be so flouted in this royal presence?
Who knows not that the noble duke is dead?
                               [They all start
You do him injury to scorn his corse.
   Riv. Who knows not he is dead! Who knows he is?
   Q. Eliz. All-seeing heaven, what a world is this!
   Buck. Look I so pale, Lord Dorset, as the rest?
   Dor. Ay, my good lord; and no one in this presence
But his red colour hath forsook his cheeks.
   K. Edw. Is Clarence dead? The order was reversed.
   Glo. But he, poor soul, by your first order died,
And that a wingéd Mercury did bear;
Some tardy cripple bore the countermand,
That came too lag to see him buriéd.
God grant that some, less noble, and less loyal,
Nearer in bloody thoughts, but not in blood,
Deserve not worse than wretched Clarence did,
And yet go current from suspicion!

Enter STANLEY

   Stan. A boon, my sovereign, for my service done!
   K. Edw. I pray thee, peace: my soul is full of sorrow.
   Stan. I will not rise, unless your highness grant.
   K. Edw. Then speak at once what is it thou demand'st.
   Stan. The forfeit, sovereign, of my servant's life;
Who slew to-day a riotous gentleman
Lately attendant on the Duke of Norfolk.
   K. Edw. Have I a tongue to doom my brother's death,
And shall that tongue give pardon to a slave?
My brother killed no man, his fault was thought,
And yet his punishment was bitter death.
Who sued to me for him? who, in my rage,
Kneeled at my feet, and bade me be advised?
Who spoke of brotherhood? who spoke of love?
Who told me how the poor soul did forsake
The mighty Warwick, and did fight for me?
Who told me, in the field by Tewksbury,
When Oxford had me down, he rescued me,
And said, "Dear brother, live, and be a king"?
Who told me, when we both lay in the field
Frozen almost to death, how he did lap me
Even in his garments, and did give himself,
All thin and naked, to the numb cold night?

All this from my remembrance brutish wrath
Sinfully plucked, and not a man of you
Had so much grace to put it in my mind.
But when your carters or your waiting-vassals
Have done a drunken slaughter, and defaced
The precious image of our dear Redeemer,
You straight are on your knees for pardon, pardon;
And I, unjustly too, must grant it you:—
But for my brother not a man would speak,—
Nor I, ungracious, speak unto myself
For him, poor soul.   The proudest of you all
Have been beholding to him in his life;
Yet none of you would once plead for his life.
O God, I fear thy justice will take hold
On me and you, and mine and yours for this!
Come, Hastings, help me to my closet.   Ah!
Poor Clarence!

               [Exeunt King and Queen, Hastings, Rivers,
                              Dorset and Grey

    Glo.   This is the fruit of rashness!—Marked you not
How that the guilty kindred of the queen
Looked pale when they did hear of Clarence' death?
O, they did urge it still unto the king!
God will revenge it.—But come, let us in,
To comfort Edward with our company.
    Buck.   We wait upon your grace.   *[Exeunt*

    Scene II.—Another Room in the Palace

Enter the Duchess of York, *with a Son and Daughter of*
Clarence

    Boy.   Tell me, good grandam, is our father dead?
    Duch.   No, boy.
    Boy.   Why do you wring your hands, and beat your breast,
And cry "O Clarence, my unhappy son!"
    Girl.   Why do you look on us, and shake your head,
And call us wretches, orphans, castaways,
If that our noble father be alive?
    Duch.   My pretty cousins, you mistake me both;
I do lament the sickness of the king,
As loth to lose him, not your father's death;
It were lost sorrow to wail one that's lost.
    Boy.   Then, grandam, you conclude that he is dead.
The king my uncle is to blame for this:
God will revenge it; whom I will importune
With daily prayers all to that effect.
    Girl.   And so will I.
    Duch.   Peace, children, peace! the king doth love you well;
Incapable and shallow innocents,
You cannot guess who caused your father's death.

Boy.   Grandam, we can; for my good uncle Gloster
Told me, the king, provoked to 't by the queen,
Devised impeachments to imprison him:
And when my uncle told me so, he wept,
And pitied me, and kindly kissed my cheek;
Bade me rely on him as on my father,
And he would love me dearly as his child.
   Duch.   Ah, that deceit should steal such gentle shapes,
And with a virtuous vizor hide foul guile!
He is my son; yea, and therein my shame;
Yet from my dugs he drew not this deceit.
   Son.   Think you my uncle did dissemble, grandam?
   Duch.   Ay, boy.
   Son.   I cannot think it.—Hark! what noise is this?

Enter QUEEN ELIZABETH, *with her hair about her ears ;*
RIVERS *and* DORSET *after her*

   Q. Eliz.   O, who shall hinder me to wail and weep,
To chide my fortune, and torment myself?
I 'll join with black despair against my soul,
And to myself become an enemy.
   Duch.   What means this scene of rude impatience?
   Q. Eliz.   To make an act of tragic violence:
Edward, my lord, your son, our king, is dead.
Why grow the branches when the root is gone?
Why wither not the leaves that want their sap?
If you will live, lament; if die, be brief,
That our swift-wingéd souls may catch the king's;
Or, like obedient subjects, follow him
To his new kingdom of perpetual rest.
   Duch.   Ah, so much interest have I in thy sorrow
As I had title in thy noble husband!
I have bewept a worthy husband's death,
And lived by looking on his images:
But now two mirrors of his princely semblance
Are cracked in pieces by malignant death,
And I for comfort have but one false glass,
That grieves me when I see my shame in him.
Thou art a widow; yet thou art a mother,
And hast the comfort of thy children left thee:
But death hath snatched my husband from mine arms,
And plucked two crutches from my feeble hands,—
Edward and Clarence.   O, what cause have I,—
Thine being but a moiety of my grief,—
To overgo thy plaints and drown thy cries!
   Son.   Good aunt, you wept not for our father's death!
How can we aid you with our kindred tears?
   Daughter.   Our fatherless distress we left unmoaned;
Your widow-dolour likewise be unwept!
   Q. Eliz.   Give me no help in lamentation;

I am not barren to bring forth complaints:
All springs reduce their currents to mine eyes,
That I, being governed by the watery moon,
May send forth plenteous tears to drown the world!
Ah for my husband, for my dear lord Edward!
    Chil. Ah for our father, for our dear lord Clarence!
    Duch. Alas for both, both mine, Edward and Clarence!
    Q. Eliz. What stay had I but Edward? and he's gone.
    Chil. What stay had we but Clarence? and he's gone.
    Duch. What stays had I but they? and they are gone.
    Q. Eliz Was never widow had so dear a loss!
    Chil. Were never orphans had so dear a loss!
    Duch. Was never mother had so dear a loss!
Alas, I am the mother of these moans!
Their woes are parcelled, mine are general.
She for an Edward weeps, and so do I;
I for a Clarence weep, so doth not she:
These babes for Clarence weep, and so do I;
I for an Edward weep, so do not they;
Alas, you three, on me, threefold distressed,
Pour all your tears?   I am your sorrow's nurse,
And I will pamper it with lamentations.
    Dor. Comfort, dear mother: God is much displeased
That you take with unthankfulness his doing:
In common worldly things, 't is called ungrateful,
With dull unwillingness to repay a debt
Which with a bounteous hand was kindly lent;
Much more to be thus opposite with heaven
For it requires the royal debt it lent you.
    Riv. Madam, bethink you, like a careful mother,
Of the young prince your son: send straight for him;
Let him be crowned; in him your comfort lives:
Drown desperate sorrow in dead Edward's grave,
And plant your joys in living Edward's throne.

    Enter GLOSTER, BUCKINGHAM, STANLEY, HASTINGS,
            RATCLIFF, *and others*

    Glo. Madam, have comfort; all of us have cause
To wail the dimming of our shining star;
But none can cure their harms by wailing them.—
Madam, my mother, I do cry you mercy;
I did not see your grace:—humbly on my knee
I crave your blessing.
    Duch. God bless thee; and put meekness in thy mind,
Love, charity, obedience, and true duty!
    Glo. Amen; [*Aside*] and make me die a good old man!—
That is the butt-end of a mother's blessing:
I marvel that her grace did leave it out.
    Buck. You cloudy princes and heart-sorrowing peers,
That bear this mutual heavy load of moan,

Now cheer each other in each other's love:
Though we have spent our harvest of this king,
We are to reap the harvest of his son.
The broken rancour of your high-swoln hearts,
But lately splintered, knit, and joined together,
Must gently be preserved, cherished, and kept:
Me seemeth good, that, with some little train,
Forthwith from Ludlow the young prince be fetched
Hither to London, to be crowned our king.
    Riv. Why with some little train, my Lord of Buckingham?
    Buck. Marry, my lord, lest, by a multitude,
The new-healed wound of malice should break out;
Which would be so much the more dangerous,
By how much the state's green and yet ungoverned;
Where every horse bears his commanding rein,
And may direct his course as please himself,
As well the fear of harm as harm apparent,
In my opinion, ought to be prevented.
    Glo. I hope the king made peace with all of us;
And the compáct is firm and true in me.
    Riv. And so in me; and so, I think, in all:
Yet, since it is but green, it should be put
To no apparent likelihood of breach,
Which haply by much company might be urged:
Therefore I say with noble Buckingham,
That it is meet so few should fetch the prince.
    Hast. And so say I.
    Glo. Then be it so; and go we to determine
Who they shall be that straight shall post to Ludlow.
Madam,—and you, my mother,—will you go
To give your censures in this business?
                 [Exeunt all but Buckingham and Gloster
    Buck. My lord, whoever journeys to the prince,
For God's sake, let not us two stay at home;
For, by the way, I'll sort occasion,
As index to the story we late talked of,
To part the queen's proud kindred from the prince.
    Glo. My other self, my counsel's consistory,
My oracle, my prophet!—My dear cousin,
I, like a child, will go by thy direction.
Towards Ludlow then, for we'll not stay behind.
                                [Exeunt

Scene III.—London. A Street

Enter two Citizens, meeting

    First Cit. Good morrow, neighbour, well met: whither
        away so fast?
    Sec. Cit. I promise you, I scarcely know myself:
Hear you the news abroad?

First Cit.   Ay,—that the king is dead.
Sec. Cit.   Ill news, by'r lady; seldom comes the better:
I fear, I fear 't will prove a giddy world.

Enter another Citizen

Third Cit.   Neighbours, God speed!
First Cit.   Give you good morrow, sir.
Third Cit.   Doth the news hold of good King Edward's
     death?
Sec. Cit.   Ay, sir, it is too true; God help, the while!
Third Cit.   Then, masters, look to see a troublous world.
First Cit.   No, no; by God's good grace his son shall reign.
Third Cit.   Woe to that land that's governed by a child!
Sec. Cit.   In him there is a hope of government,
That, in his nonage, Council under him,
And in his full and ripened years himself,
No doubt, shall then, and till then, govern well.
First. Cit.   So stood the state when Henry the Sixth
Was crowned in Paris but at nine months old.
Third Cit.   Stood the state so? No, no good friends,
     God wot;
For then this land was famously enriched
With politic grave counsel; then the king
Had virtuous uncles to protect his grace.
First Cit.   Why, so hath this, both by his father and
     mother.
Third. Cit.   Better it were they all came by his father,
Or by his father there were none at all;
For emulation now, who shall be nearest,
Will touch us all too near, if God prevent not.
O, full of danger is the Duke of Gloster!
And the queen's sons and brothers haught and proud:
And were they to be ruled, and not to rule,
This sickly land might solace as before.
First Cit.   Come, come, we fear the worst: all will be well.
Third Cit.   When clouds are seen, wise men put on their
     cloaks;
When great leaves fall, then winter is at hand;
When the sun sets, who doth not look for night?
Untimely storms make men expect a dearth.
All may be well; but, if God sort it so,
'T is more than we deserve, or I expect.
Sec. Cit.   Truly, the hearts of men are full of fear;
Ye cannot reason almost with a man
That looks not heavily and full of dread.
Third Cit.   Before the days of change, still is it so:
By a divine instinct men's minds mistrust
Ensuing danger; as, by proof, we see
The waters swell before a boisterous storm.
But leave it all to God.—Whither away?

Sec. Cit.   Marry, we were sent for to the justices.
Third Cit.   And so was I: I'll bear you company.
[*Exeunt*

SCENE IV.—London.   A Room in the Palace

Enter the ARCHBISHOP OF YORK, *the young* DUKE OF YORK,
QUEEN ELIZABETH, *and the* DUCHESS OF YORK

Arch.   Last night, I hear, they lay at Northampton;
At Stony-Stratford will they be to-night:
To-morrow, or next day, they will be here.
Duch.   I long with all my heart to see the prince:
I hope he is much grown since last I saw him.
Q. Eliz.   But I hear, no; they say my son of York
Hath almost overta'en him in his growth.
York.   Ay, mother; but I would not have it so.
Duch.   Why, my young cousin, it is good to grow.
York.   Grandam, one night, as we did sit at supper,
My uncle Rivers talked how I did grow
More than my brother: "Ay," quoth my uncle Gloster,
"Small herbs have grace, great weeds do grow apace:"
And since, methinks I would not grow so fast,
Because sweet flowers are slow, and weeds make haste.
Duch.   Good faith, good faith, the saying did not hold
In him that did object the same to thee:
He was the wretched'st thing when he was young,
So long a-growing and so leisurely,
That, if his rule were true, he should be gracious.
Arch.   Why, madam, so, no doubt, he is.
Duch.   I hope he is; but yet let mothers doubt.
York.   Now, by my troth, if I had been remembered,
I could have given my uncle's grace a flout,
To touch his growth nearer than he touched mine.
Duch.   How, my pretty York?   I prithee, let me hear it.
York.   Marry, they say my uncle grew so fast
That he could gnaw a crust at two hours old:
'T was full two years ere I could get a tooth:
Grandam, this would have been a biting jest.
Duch.   I prithee, pretty York, who told thee this?
York.   Grandam, his nurse.
Duch.   His nurse! why, she was dead ere thou wert born.
York.   If 't were not she, I cannot tell who told me.
Q. Eliz.   A parlous boy:—go to, you are too shrewd.
Arch.   Good madam, be not angry with the child.
Q. Eliz.   Pitchers have ears.
Arch.   Here comes a messenger.

Enter a Messenger

What news?
Mess.   Such news, my lord, as grieves me to report.

108

Q. Eliz.   How doth the prince?
Mess.   Well, madam, and in health.
Duch.   What is thy news then?
Mess.   Lord Rivers and Lord Grey are sent to Pomfret,
With them Sir Thomas Vaughan, prisoners.
Duch.   Who hath committed them?
Mess.   The mighty Dukes
Gloster and Buckingham.
Q. Eliz.   For what offence?
Mess.   The sum of all I can, I have disclosed;
Why or for what these nobles were committed
Is all unknown to me, my gracious lady.
Q. Eliz.   Ay me, I see the downfall of our house!
The tiger now hath seized the gentle hind;
Insulting tyranny begins to jet
Upon the innocent and aweless throne:—
Welcome, destruction, blood, and massacre!
I see, as in a map, the end of all.
Duch.   Accursèd and unquiet wrangling days,
How many of you have mine eyes beheld!
My husband lost his life to get the crown;
And often up and down my sons were tossed,
For me to joy and weep their gain and loss:
And being seated, and domestic broils
Clean over-blown, themselves, the conquerors,
Make war upon themselves; brother to brother,
Blood to blood, self against self: O preposterous
And frantic outrage, end thy damnèd spleen;
Or let me die, to look on death no more!
Q. Eliz.   Come, come, my boy; we will to sanctuary.—
Madam, farewell.
Duch.   Stay, I will go with you.
Q. Eliz.   You have no cause.
Arch.   My gracious lady, go;
And thither bear your treasure and your goods.
For my part, I 'll resign unto your grace
The seal I keep; and so betide to me
As well I tender you and all of yours!
Come, I'll conduct you to the sanctuary.   [*Exeunt*

ACT THREE

SCENE I.—London.   A Street

The trumpets sound.   Enter the young PRINCE, *the* DUKES
OF GLOSTER, *and* BUCKINGHAM, CARDINAL BOURCHIER,
CATESBY, *and others*

Buck.   Welcome, sweet prince, to London, to your chamber.
Glo.   Welcome, dear cousin, my thoughts' sovereign:
The weary way hath made you melancholy.

Prince.   No, uncle; but our crosses on the way
Have made it tedious, wearisome, and heavy:
I want more uncles here to welcome me.
  Glo.   Sweet prince, the untainted virtue of your years
Hath not yet dived into the world's deceit;
Nor more can you distinguish of a man
Than of his outward show, which, God he knows,
Seldom or never jumpeth with the heart.
Those uncles which you want were dangerous;
Your grace attended to their sugared words,
But looked not on the poison of their hearts:
God keep you from them, and from such false friends!
  Prince.   God keep me from false friends! but they were
      none.
  Glo.   My lord, the mayor of London comes to greet you.

Enter the Lord Mayor, and his train

  May.   God bless your grace with health and happy days!
  Prince.   I thank you, good my lord;—and thank you all.
I thought my mother, and my brother York,
Would long ere this have met us on the way:
Fie, what a slug is Hastings, that he comes not
To tell us whether they will come or no!
  Buck.   And, in good time, here comes the sweating lord.

Enter LORD HASTINGS

  Prince.   Welcome, my lord: what, will our mother
      come?
  Hast.   On what occasion, God he knows, not I,
The queen your mother, and your brother York,
Have taken sanctuary: the tender Prince
Would fain have come with me to meet your grace,
But by his mother was perforce withheld.
  Buck.   Fie, what an indirect and peevish course
Is this of hers!   Lord cardinal, will your grace
Persuade the queen to send the Duke of York
Unto his princely brother presently?
If she deny,—Lord Hastings, go with him,
And from her jealous arms pluck him perforce.
  Card.   My Lord of Buckingham if my weak oratory
Can from his mother win the Duke of York,
Expect him here; but if she be obdurate
To mild entreaties, God in heaven forbid
We should infringe the holy privilege
Of blesséd sanctuary! not for all this land
Would I be guilty of so deep a sin.
  Buck.   You are too senseless-obstinate, my lord,
Too ceremonious and traditional:
Weigh it but with the grossness of this age,
You break not sanctuary in seizing him.

The benefit thereof is always granted
To those whose dealings have deserved the place,
And those who have the wit to claim the place:
This prince hath neither claimed it nor deserved it;
Therefore, in mine opinion, cannot have it:
Then, taking him from thence that is not there,
You break no privilege nor charter there.
Oft have I heard of sanctuary men;
But sanctuary children ne'er till now.
    Card. My lord, you shall o'er-rule my mind for once.
Come on, Lord Hastings, will you go with me?
    Hast. I go, my lord.
    Prince. Good lords, make all the speedy haste you may.
                       [*Exeunt Cardinal and Hastings*
Say, uncle Gloster, if our brother come,
Where shall we sojourn till our coronation?
    Glo. Where it seems best unto your royal self.
If I may counsel you, some day or two
Your highness shall repose you at the Tower:
Then where you please and shall be thought most fit
For your best health and recreation.
    Prince. I do not like the Tower, of any place.
Did Julius Cæsar build that place, my lord?
    Buck. He did, my gracious lord, begin that place;
Which, since, succeeding ages have re-edified.
    Prince. Is it upon record, or else reported
Successively from age to age, he built it?
    Buck. Upon record, my gracious lord.
    Prince. But say, my lord, it were not registered,
Methinks the truth should live from age to age,
As 't were retailed to all posterity,
Even to the general all-ending day.
    Glo. [*Aside*] So wise so young, they say, do ne'er live
        long.
    Prince. What say you, uncle?
    Glo. I say, without characters fame lives long.
[*Aside*] Thus, like the formal vice, Iniquity,
I moralise two meanings in one word.
    Prince. That Julius Cæsar was a famous man;
With what his valour did enrich his wit,
His wit set down to make his valour live;
Death makes no conquest of this conqueror;
For now he lives in fame, though not in life.—
I'll tell you what, my cousin Buckingham,—
    Buck. What, my gracious lord?
    Prince. An if I live until I be a man,
I'll win our ancient right in France again,
Or die a soldier, as I lived a king.
    Glo. [*Aside*] Short summers lightly have a forward
        spring.

Buck.   Now, in good time, here comes the Duke of York.

Enter YORK, HASTINGS, *and the* CARDINAL

Prince.   Richard of York! how fares our loving brother?
York.   Well, my dread lord; so must I call you now.
Prince.   Ay, brother,—to our grief, as it is yours:
Too late he died that might have kept that title,
Which by his death hath lost much majesty.
Glo.   How fares our cousin, noble Lord of York?
York.   I thank you, gentle uncle. O, my lord,
You said that idle weeds are fast in growth:
The prince my brother hath outgrown me far.
Glo.   He hath, my lord.
York.   And therefore is he idle?
Glo.   O, my fair cousin, I must not say so.
York.   Then is he more beholding to you than I.
Glo.   He may command me as my sovereign;
But you have power in me as in a kinsman.
York.   I pray you, uncle, give me this dagger.
Glo.   My dagger, little cousin? with all my heart.
Prince.   A beggar, brother?
York.   Of my kind uncle, that I know will give;
Being but a toy, which is no grief to give.
Glo.   A greater gift than that I'll give my cousin.
York.   A greater gift! O, that 's the sword to it.
Glo.   Ay, gentle cousin, were it light enough.
York.   O, then, I see, you'll part but with light gifts;
In weightier things you'll say a beggar nay.
Glo.   It is too heavy for your grace to wear.
York.   I weigh it lightly, were it heavier.
Glo.   What, would you have my weapon, little lord?
York.   I would, that I might thank you as you call me.
Glo.   How?
York.   Little.
Prince.   My Lord of York will still be cross in talk:
Uncle, your grace knows how to bear with him.
York.   You mean, to bear me, not to bear with me:
Uncle, my brother mocks both you and me;
Because that I am little, like an ape,
He thinks that you should bear me on your shoulders.
Buck.   [*Aside to Hastings*]   With what a sharp-provided
        wit he reasons!
To mitigate the scorn he gives his uncle,
He prettily and aptly taunts himself:
So cunning and so young is wonderful.
Glo.   My lord, will 't please you pass along!
Myself and my good cousin Buckingham
Will to your mother, to entreat of her
To meet you at the Tower, and welcome you.
York.   What, will you go unto the Tower, my lord?

Prince.   My lord protector needs will have it so.
York.   I shall not sleep in quiet at the Tower.
Glo.   Why, what should you fear?
York.   Marry, my uncle Clarence' angry ghost:
My grandam told me he was murdered there.
Prince.   I fear no uncles dead.
Glo.   Nor none that live, I hope.
Prince.   An if they live, I hope I need not fear.
But come, my lord; and with a heavy heart,
Thinking on them, go I unto the Tower.
      [*A Sennet. Exeunt all but Gloster, Buckingham,
             and Catesby*
    Buck.   Think you, my lord, this little prating York
Was not incensèd by his subtle mother
To taunt and scorn you thus opprobriously?
    Glo.   No doubt, no doubt: O, 't is a parlous boy:
Bold, quick, ingenious, forward, capable:
He 's all the mother's, from the top to toe.
    Buck.   Well, let them rest.—Come hither, Catesby.
Thou 'rt sworn as deep to effect what we intend
As closely to conceal what we impart:
Thou know'st our reasons urged upon the way;
What think'st thou? is it not an easy matter
To make William Lord Hastings of our mind,
For the instalment of this noble duke
In the seat royal of this famous isle?
    Cate.   He for his father's sake so loves the prince,
That he will not be won to aught against him.
    Buck.   What think'st thou, then, of Stanley? will not he?
    Cate.   He will do all in all as Hastings doth.
    Buck.   Well, then, no more but this: go, gentle Catesby,
And, as it were far off, sound thou Lord Hastings,
How he doth stand affected to our purpose;
And summon him to-morrow to the Tower,
To sit about the coronation.
If thou dost find him tractable to us,
Encourage him, and show him all our reasons·
If he be leaden, icy-cold, unwilling,
Be thou so too; and so break off your talk,
And give us notice of his inclination:
For we to-morrow hold divided councils,
Wherein thyself shalt highly be employed.
    Glo.   Commend me to Lord William: tell him, Catesby,
His ancient knot of dangerous adversaries
To-morrow are let blood at Pomfret Castle;
And bid my friend, for joy of this good news,
Give Mistress Shore one gentle kiss the more.
    Buck.   Good Catesby, go, effect this business soundly.
    Cate.   My good lords both, with all the heed I can.
    Glo.   Shall we hear from you, Catesby, ere we sleep?

Cate.   You shall, my lord.
Glo.   At Crosby Place, there shall you find us both.
                                              [*Exit Catesby*
    Buck.   Now, my lord, what shall we do, if we perceive
Lord Hastings will not yield to our complots?
    Glo.   Chop off his head, man—somewhat we will do:—
And, look, when I am king, claim thou of me
The earldom of Hereford, and the movables
Whereof the king my brother stood possessed.
    Buck.   I 'll claim that promise at your grace's hands.
    Glo.   And look to have it yielded with all kindness.
Come, let us sup betimes, that afterwards
We may digest our complots in some form.   [*Exeunt*

SCENE II.—Before LORD HASTINGS' HOUSE

Enter a Messenger

Mess.   My lord! my lord!
Hast.   [*Within*] Who knocks?
Mess.   One from the Lord Stanley.
Hast.   What is 't o'clock?
Mess.   Upon the stroke of four.

Enter HASTINGS

    Hast.   Cannot thy master sleep these tedious nights?
    Mess.   So it appears by that I have to say.
First, he commends him to your noble self.
    Hast.   What then?
    Mess.   Then certifies your lordship that this night
He dreamt the boar had razéd off his helm:
Besides he says there are two councils held;
And that may be determined at the one
Which may make you and him to rue at the other.
Therefore he sends to know your lordship's pleasure,—
If presently you will take horse with him
And with all speed post with him towards the north,
To shun the danger that his soul divines.
    Hast.   Go, fellow, go, return unto thy lord;
Bid him not fear the separated councils:
His honour and myself are at the one,
And at the other is my good friend Catesby;
Where nothing can proceed that toucheth us
Whereof I shall not have intelligence.
Tell him his fears are shallow, wanting instance:
And for his dreams, I wonder he's so fond
To trust the mockery of unquiet slumbers:
To fly the boar before the boar pursues
Were to incense the boar to follow us
And make pursuit where he did mean no chase.

Go, bid thy master rise and come to me;
And we will both together to the Tower,
Where, he shall see, the boar will use us kindly.
　　Mess.　I 'll go, my lord, and tell him what you say.
　　　　　　　　　　　　　　　　　　　　　　[Exit

　　　　　　　Enter CATESBY

　　Cate.　Many good morrows to my noble lord!
　　Hast.　Good morrow, Catesby; you are early stirring:
What news, what news, in this our tottering state?
　　Cate.　It is a reeling world, indeed, my lord;
And I believe 't will never stand upright.
Till Richard wear the garland of the realm.
　　Hast.　How! wear the garland! dost thou mean the
　　　　　　crown?
　　Cate.　Ay, my good lord.
　　Hast.　I 'll have this crown of mine cut from my shoulders
Ere I will see the crown so foul misplaced.
But canst thou guess that he doth aim at it?
　　Cate.　Ay, on my life; and hopes to find you forward
Upon his party for the gain thereof:
And thereupon he sends you this good news,—
That this same very day your enemies,
The kindred of the queen, must die at Pomfret.
　　Hast.　Indeed, I am no mourner for that news,
Because they have been still my adversaries:
But, that I 'll give my voice on Richard's side
To bar my master's heirs in true descent,
God knows I will not do it, to the death.
　　Cate.　God keep your lordship in that gracious mind!
　　Hast.　But I shall laugh at this a twelve-month hence,
That they who brought me in my master's hate
I live to look upon their tragedy.
I tell thee, Catesby,—
　　Cate.　What, my lord?
　　Hast.　Ere a fortnight make me older,
I 'll send some packing that yet think not on it.
　　Cate.　'T is a vile thing to die, my gracious lord,
When men are unprepared and look not for it.
　　Hast.　O monstrous, monstrous! and so falls it out
With Rivers, Vaughan, Grey: and so 't will do
With some men else, who think themselves as safe
As thou and I, who, as thou know'st, are dear
To princely Richard and to Buckingham.
　　Cate.　The princes both make high account of you;—
[*Aside*] For they account his head upon the bridge.
　　Hast.　I know they do; and I have well deserved it.

　　　　　　　Enter LORD STANLEY
Come on, come on; where is your boar-spear, man!
Fear you the boar and go so unprovided?

Stan. My lord, good morrow;—good morrow, Catesby:—
You may jest on, but, by the holy rood,
I do not like these several councils, I.
    Hast. My lord,
I hold my life as dear as you do yours;
And never in my life I do protest,
Was it more precious to me than 't is now:
Think you, but that I know our state secure,
I would be so triumphant as I am?
    Stan. The lords at Pomfret, when they rode from London,
Were jocund, and supposed their state were sure,—
And they indeed had no cause to mistrust;
But yet, you see, how soon the day o'ercast.
This sudden stab of rancour I misdoubt:
Pray God, I say, I prove a needless coward!—
What, shall we toward the Tower? the day is spent.
    Hast. Come, come, have with you. Wot you what, my
            lord?
To-day the lords you talk of are beheaded.
    Stan. They, for their truth, might better wear their
            heads
Than some that have accused them wear their hats.
But come, my lord, let us away.

Enter a Pursuivant

    Hast. Go on before; I 'll talk with this good fellow.
                            [*Exeunt Stanley and Catesby*
How now, sirrah! how goes the world with thee?
    Purs. The better that your lordship please to ask.
    Hast. I tell thee, man, 't is better with me now
Than when I met thee last where now we meet:
Then was I going prisoner to the Tower,
By the suggestion of the queen's allies;
But now, I tell thee—keep it to thyself—
This day those enemies are put to death,
And I in better state than e'er I was.
    Purs. God hold it, to your honour's good content!
    Hast. Gramercy, fellow: there, drink that for me.
                            [*Throws him his purse*
    Purs. God save your lordship!   [*Exit*

Enter a Priest

    Priest. Well met, my lord; I am glad to see your honour.
    Hast. I thank thee, good Sir John, with all my heart.
I'm in your debt for your last exercise;
Come the next Sabbath, and I will content you.
                            [*He whispers in his ear*

Enter BUCKINGHAM

    Buck. What, talking with a priest, lord chamberlain?

116

Your friends at Pomfret, they do need the priest;
Your honour hath no shriving work in hand.
   Hast.   Good faith, and when I met this holy man,
Those men you talk of came into my mind.—
What, go you toward the Tower?
   Buck.   I do, my lord; but long I cannot stay there:
I shall return before your lordship thence.
   Hast.   'T is like enough, for I stay dinner there.
   Buck.   [*Aside*]   And supper too, although thou know'st
      it not.—
Come, will you go?
   Hast.   I 'll wait upon your lordship.   [*Exeunt*

SCENE III.—Pomfret Castle

Enter SIR RICHARD RATCLIFF, *with halberds, carrying*
RIVERS, GREY, *and* VAUGHAN *to death*

   Riv.   Sir Richard Ratcliff, let me tell thee this:
To-day shalt thou behold a subject die
For truth, for duty, and for loyalty.
   Grey.   God keep the prince from all the pack of you!
A knot you are of damnéd blood-suckers.
   Vaugh.   You live that shall cry woe for this hereafter.
   Rat.   Dispatch; the limit of your lives is out.
   Riv.   O Pomfret, Pomfret!   O thou bloody prison,
Fatal and ominous to noble peers!
Within the guilty closure of thy walls
Richard the Second here was hacked to death;
And, for more slander to thy dismal seat,
We give thee up our guiltless blood to drink.
   Grey.   Now Margaret's curse is fallen upon our heads,
For standing by when Richard stabbed her son.
   Riv.   Then cursed she Hastings, then cursed she
      Buckingham,
Then cursed she Richard.   O, remember, God,
To hear her prayers for them, as now for us!
And for my sister and her princely sons,
Be satisfied, dear God, with our true blood,
Which, as thou know'st, unjustly must be spilt.
   Rat.   Make haste; the hour of death is expiate.
   Riv.   Come, Grey,—come, Vaughan,—let us all embrace:
Farewell, until we meet again in heaven.   [*Exeunt*

SCENE IV.—London. A Room in the Tower

BUCKINGHAM, STANLEY, HASTINGS, *the* BISHOP OF ELY,
RATCLIFF, LOVEL, *with others, at a table*

   Hast.   My lords, at once: the cause why we are met
Is, to determine of the coronation.
In God's name, speak:—when is the royal day?

Buck.   Are all things fitting for that royal time?
Stan.   It is, and wants but nomination.
Ely.   To-morrow, then, I judge a happy day.
Buck.   Who knows the lord protector's mind herein?
Who is most inward with the noble duke?
    Ely.   Your grace, we think, should soonest know his mind.
    Buck.   We know each other's faces; for our hearts,
He knows no more of mine than I of yours,
Nor I of his, my lord, than you of mine.
Lord Hastings, you and he are near in love.
    Hast.   I thank his grace, I know he loves me well;
But, for his purpose in the coronation,
I have not sounded him, nor he delivered
His gracious pleasure any way therein:
But you, my noble lords, may name the time;
And in the duke's behalf I 'll give my voice,
Which, I presume, he 'll take in gentle part.
    Ely.   In happy time, here comes the duke himself.

Enter GLOSTER

Glo.   My noble lords and cousins all, good morrow.
I have been long a sleeper; but, I trust,
My absence doth neglect no great design,
Which by my presence might have been concluded.
    Buck.   Had not you come upon your cue, my lord,
William Lord Hastings had pronounced your part,—
I mean, your voice,—for crowning of the king.
    Glo.   Than my Lord Hastings no man might be bolder;
His lordship knows me well, and loves me well.
My lord of Ely, when I was last in Holborn,
I saw good strawberries in your garden there:
I do beseech you send for some of them.
    Ely.   Marry, and will, my lord, with all my heart. [*Exit*
    Glo.   Cousin of Buckingham, a word with you.
                                        [*Drawing him aside*
Catesby hath sounded Hastings in our business,
And finds the testy gentleman so hot,
As he will lose his head ere give consent
His master's son, as worshipful he terms it,
Shall lose the royalty of England's throne.
    Buck.   Withdraw you hence, my lord, I 'll follow you.
                         [*Exit Gloster, Buckingham following*
    Stan.   We have not yet set down this day of triumph.
To-morrow, in mine opinion, is too sudden;
For I myself am not so well provided
As else I would be were the day prolonged.

Re-enter BISHOP OF ELY

Ely.   Where is my lord the Duke of Gloster?
I have sent for these strawberries.

118

Hast. His grace looks cheerfully and smooth to-day;
There 's some conceit or other likes him well
When he doth bid good morrow with such spirit.
I think there 's ne'er a man in Christendom
That can less hide his love or hate than he;
For by his face straight shall you know his heart.
    Stan. What of his heart perceive you in his face
By any likelihood he showed to-day?
    Hast. Marry, that with no man here he is offended;
For, were he, he had shown it in his looks.

Re-enter GLOSTER and BUCKINGHAM

    Glo. I pray you all, tell me what they deserve
That do conspire my death with devilish plots
Of damnéd witchcraft, and that have prevailed
Upon my body with their hellish charms?
    Hast. The tender love I bear your grace, my lord.
Makes me most forward in this noble presence
To doom the offenders, whatsoe'er they be:
I say, my lord, they have deservéd death.
    Glo. Then be your eyes the witness of this ill:
See how I am bewitched; behold mine arm
Is, like a blasted sapling, withered up:
And this is Edward's wife, that monstrous witch,
Consorted with that harlot strumpet Shore,
That by their witchcraft thus have markéd me.
    Hast. If they have done this thing, my gracious lord,—
    Glo. If! thou protector of this damnéd strumpet,
Tellest thou me of "ifs"? Thou art a traitor:
Off with his head! Now, by Saint Paul I swear
I will not dine until I see the same.
Lovel and Ratcliff, look that it be done:
The rest, that love me, rise and follow me.
        [*Exeunt all but Hastings, Ratcliff, and Lovel*
    Hast. Woe, woe for England! not a whit for me;
For I, too fond, might have prevented this.
Stanley did dream the boar did raze his helm;
But I disdained it, and did scorn to fly:
Three times to-day my foot-cloth horse did stumble,
And startled, when he looked upon the Tower,
As loth to bear me to the slaughter-house.
O, now I want the priest that spake to me:
I now repent I told the pursuivant,
As 't were triúmphing at mine enemies,
How they at Pomfret bloodily were butchered,
And I myself secure in grace and favour.
O Margaret, Margaret, now thy heavy curse
Is lighted on poor Hastings' wretched head!
    Rat. Dispatch, my lord; the duke would be at dinner:
Make a short shrift; he longs to see your head.

119

Hast.   O momentary grace of mortal men,
Which we more hunt for than the grace of God!
Who builds his hopes in air of your fair looks,
Lives like a drunken sailor on a mast,
Ready, with every nod, to tumble down
Into the fatal bowels of the deep.
   Lov.   Come, come, dispatch; 't is bootless to exclaim.
   Hast.   O bloody Richard! miserable England!
I prophesy the fearfull'st time to thee
That ever wretched age hath looked upon.
Come, lead me to the block; bear him my head:
They smile at me who shortly shall be dead.   [*Exeunt*

SCENE V.—The Tower-walls

Enter GLOSTER *and* BUCKINGHAM, *in rotten armour,*
marvellous ill-favoured

   Glo.   Come cousin, canst thou quake and change thy
      colour,
Murder thy breath in middle of a word,
And then begin again, and stop again,
As if thou wert distraught and mad with terror?
   Buck.   Tut, I can counterfeit the deep tragedian;
Speak and look back, and pry on every side.
Tremble and start at wagging of a straw,
Intending deep suspicion: ghastly looks
Are at my service, like enforcèd smiles;
And both are ready in their offices,
At any time, to grace my stratagems.
But what, is Catesby gone?
   Glo.   He is; and, see, he brings the mayor along.
   Buck.   Let me alone to entertain him.

Enter the Mayor and CATESBY

Lord Mayor,—
   Glo.   Look to the drawbridge there!
   Buck.   Hark! a drum.
   Glo.   Catesby, o'erlook the walls.
   Buck.   Lord mayor, the reason we have sent for you—
   Glo.   Look back, defend thee,—here are enemies.
   Buck.   God and our innocence defend and guard us!
   Glo.   Be patient, they are friends,—Ratcliff, and Lovel.

Enter LOVEL *and* RATCLIFF, *with* HASTINGS' *head*

   Lov.   Here is the head of that ignoble traitor,
The dangerous and unsuspected Hastings.
   Glo.   So dear I loved the man; that I must weep.
I took him for the plainest harmless creature
That breathed upon this earth a Christian;
Made him my book, wherein my soul recorded

The history of all her secret thoughts:
To smooth he daubed his vice with show of virtue,
That, his apparent open guilt omitted,—
I mean, his conversation with Shore's wife,—
He lived from all attainder of suspect.
 Buck. Well, well, he was the covert'st sheltered traitor
That ever lived.
Would you imagine, or almost believe,—
Were 't not that, by great preservation,
We live to tell it you,—the subtle traitor
This day had plotted, in the council-house
To murder me and my good Lord of Gloster?
 May. What, had he so?
 Glo. What, think you we are Turks or infidels?
Or that we would, against the form of law,
Proceed thus rashly to the villain's death,
But that the extreme peril of the case,
The peace of England and our persons' safety,
Enforced us to this execution?
 May. Now, fair befall you! he deserved his death;
And you, my good lords, both have well proceeded,
To warn false traitors from the like attempts.
I never looked for better at his hands,
After he once fell in with Mistress Shore.
 Glo. Yet had not we determined he should die
Until your lordship came to see his end;
Which now the loving haste of these our friends,
Somewhat against our meaning, have prevented:
Because, my lord, we would have had you hear
The traitor speak, and timorously confess
The manner and the purpose of his treason;
That you might well have signified the same
Unto the citizens, who haply may
Misconstrue us in him and wail his death.
 May. But, my good lord your grace's word shall serve,
As well as I had seen and heard him speak:
And doubt you not, right noble princes both,
But I' ll acquaint our duteous citizens
With all your just proceedings in this case.
 Glo. And to that end we wished your lordship here,
To avoid the censures of the carping world.
 Buck. But since you come too late of our intent,
Yet witness what you hear we did intend:
And so, my good lord mayor, we bid farewell.
         [Exit Lord Mayor
 Glo. Go, after, after, cousin Buckingham.
The mayor towards Guildhall hies him in all post:—
There, at your meetest vantage of the time,
Infer the bastardy of Edward's children:
Tell them how Edward put to death a citizen,

Only for saying he would make his son
Heir to the crown; meaning indeed his house,
Which, by the sign thereof, was terméd so.
Moreover, urge his hateful luxury,
And bestial appetite in change of lust;
Which stretchéd to their servants, daughters, wives,
Even where his lustful eye or savage heart,
Without control, listed, to make a prey.
Nay, for a need, thus far come near my person:—
Tell them, when that my mother went with child
Of that unsatiate Edward, noble York
My princely father then had wars in France;
And, by just computation of the time,
Found that the issue was not his begot;
Which well appearéd in his lineaments,
Being nothing like the noble duke my father:
But touch this sparingly, as 't were far off;
Because you know, my lord, my mother lives.
   Buck. Fear not, my lord, I 'll play the orator
As if the golden fee for which I plead
Were for myself: and so, my lord, adieu.
   Glo. If you thrive well, bring them to Baynard's Castle,
Where you shall find me well accompanied
With reverend fathers and well-learnéd bishops.
   Buck. I go; and towards three or four o'clock
Look for the news that the Guildhall affords.   [*Exit*
   Glo. Go, Lovel, with all speed to Doctor Shaw,—
[*To Cate.*] Go thou to Friar Penker;—bid them both
Meet me within this hour at Baynard's Castle.
                   [*Exeunt all but Gloster*
Now will I in, to take some privy order,
To draw the brats of Clarence out of sight;
And to give notice, that no manner person
Have any time recourse unto the princes.   [*Exit*

Scene VI.—The Same.   A Street

Enter a Scrivener with a paper in his hand

   Scriv. This is the indictment of the good Lord Hastings;
Which in a set hand fairly is engrossed,
That it may be this day read o'er in Paul's.
And mark how well the sequel hangs together:—
Eleven hours I spent to write it over,
For yesternight by Catesby was it brought me;
The precedent was full as long a-doing:
And yet within these five hours Hastings lived,
Untainted, unexamined, free, at liberty.
Here 's a good world the while!   Why who 's so gross,
That cannot see this palpable device?
Yet who 's bold, but says he sees it not?

Bad is the world; and all will come to naught,
When such ill dealing must be seen in thought.   [*Exit*

SCENE VII.—Court of Baynard's Castle

Enter GLOSTER *and* BUCKINGHAM, *at several doors*

Glo. How now, how now! what say the citizens?
  Buck. Now, by the holy mother of our Lord,
The citizens are mum, say not a word.
  Glo. Touched you the bastardy of Edward's children?
  Buck. I did; with this contráct with Lady Lucy,
And his contract by deputy in France;
The insatiate greediness of his desires,
And his enforcement of the city wives;
His tyranny for trifles; his own bastardy,—
As being got, your father then in France,
And his resemblance, being not like the duke:
Withal I did infer your lineaments,—
Being the right idea of your father,
Both in your form and nobleness of mind;
Laid open all your victories in Scotland,
Your discipline in war, wisdom in peace,
Your bounty, virtue, fair humility;
Indeed, left nothing fitting for the purpose
Untouched, or slightly handled, in discourse:
And when mine oratory grew toward end,
I bid them that did love their country's good
Cry "God save Richard, England's royal king!"
  Glo. And did they so?
  Buck. No, so God help me, they spake not a word;
But, like dumb statuas or breathing stones,
Stared each on other, and looked deadly pale.
Which when I saw, I reprehended them;
And asked the mayor what meant this wilful silence:
His answer was, the people were not wont
To be spoke to but by the récorder.
Then he was urged to tell my tale again,
"Thus saith the duke, thus hath the duke inferred;"
But nothing spake in warrant from himself.
When he had done, some followers of mine own,
At lower end of the hall, hurled up their caps,
And some ten voices cried "God save King Richard!"
And thus I took the vantage of those few,
"Thanks, gentle citizens and friends," quoth I;
"This general applause and loving shout
Argues your wisdoms and your love to Richard:"
And even here brake off, and came away.
  Glo. What tongueless blocks were they! would they not
        speak?

   Buck. No, by my troth, my lord.
   Glo. Will not the mayor then and his brethren come?
   Buck. The mayor is here at hand: intend some fear;
Be not you spoke with, but by mighty suit:
And look you get a prayer-book in your hand,
And stand betwixt two churchmen, good my lord;
For on that ground I 'll build a holy descant:
And be not easily won to our request:
Play the maid's part,—still answer nay, and take it.
   Glo. I go; and if you plead as well for them
As I can say nay to thee for myself,
No doubt we'll bring it to a happy issue.
   Buck. Go, go, up to the leads; the lord mayor knocks.
                           [Exit Gloster

Enter the Lord Mayor, Aldermen, and Citizens

Welcome, my lord: I dance attendance here;
I think the duke will not be spoke withal.

Enter from the Castle CATESBY

Here comes his servant: how now, Catesby,
What says he?
   Cate. My lord, he doth entreat your grace
To visit him to-morrow or next day:
He is within, with two right reverend fathers,
Divinely bent to meditation;
And in no worldly suit would he be moved
To draw him from his holy exercise.
   Buck. Return, good Catesby, to the gracious duke;
Tell him, myself, the mayor and aldermen,
In deep designs and matters of great moment,
No less importing than our general good,
Are come to have some conference with his grace.
   Cate. I 'll signify so much unto him straight.   *[Exit*
   Buck. Ah, ah, my lord, this prince is not an Edward!
He is not lolling on a lewd day-bed,
But on his knees at meditation;
Not dallying with a brace of courtesans,
But meditating with two deep divines;
Not sleeping, to engross his idle body,
But praying, to enrich his watchful soul:
Happy were England, would this gracious prince
Take on himself the sovereignty thereof:
But, sure, I fear, we shall not win him to 't.
   May. Marry, God forbid his grace should say us nay!
   Buck. I fear he will. Here Catesby comes again.

Re-enter CATESBY

Now, Catesby, what says his grace?
   Cate. He wonders to what end you have assembled

Such troops of citizens to come to him,
His grace not being warned thereof before:
He fears, my lord, you mean no good to him.
    Buck.   Sorry I am my noble cousin should
Suspect me, that I mean no good to him;
By heaven, we come to him in perfect love;
And so once more return and tell his grace.   [*Exit Catesby*
When holy and devout religious men
Are at their beads, 't is hard to draw them thence,—
So sweet is zealous contemplation.

Enter GLOSTER *aloft, between two Bishops.* CATESBY *returns*

    May.   See, where he stands between two clergymen!
    Buck.   Two props of virtue for a Christian prince,
To stay him from the fall of vanity:
And, see, a book of prayer in his hand,
True ornament to know a holy man.—
Famous Plantagenet, most gracious prince,
Lend favourable ears to our request;
And pardon us the interruption
Of thy devotion and right Christian zeal.
    Glo.   My lord, there needs no such apology:
I rather do beseech you pardon me,
Who, earnest in the service of my God,
Neglect the visitation of my friends.
But leaving this, what is your grace's pleasure?
    Buck.   Even that, I hope, which pleaseth God above,
And all good men of this ungoverned isle.
    Glo.   I do suspect I have done some offence
That seems disgracious in the city's eyes,
And that you come to reprehend my ignorance.
    Buck.   You have, my lord: would it might please your grace
At our entreaties, to amend that fault!
    Glo.   Else wherefore breathe I in a Christian land?
    Buck.   Know then, it is your fault that you resign
The supreme seat, the throne majestical,
The sceptered office of your ancestors,
Your state of fortune and your due of birth,
The lineal glory of your royal house,
To the corruption of a blemished stock:
Whilst, in the mildness of your sleepy thoughts—
Which here we waken to our country's good—
This noble isle doth want her proper limbs;
Her face defaced with scars of infamy,
Her royal stock graft with ignoble plants,
And almost shouldered in the swallowing gulf
Of dark forgetfulness and deep oblivion.
Which to recure, we heartily solicit
Your gracious self to take on you the charge
And kingly government of this your land;—

Not as protector, steward, substitute,
Or lowly factor for another's gain;
But as successively from blood to blood,
Your right of birth, your empery, your own.
For this, consorted with the citizens,
Your very worshipful and loving friends,
And by their vehement instigation,
In this just suit come I to move your grace.
　Glo.　I cannot tell if to depart in silence
Or bitterly to speak in your reproof
Best fitteth my degree or your condition:
If not to answer, you might haply think
Tongue-tied ambition, nor replying, yielded
To bear the golden yoke of sovereignty,
Which fondly you would here impose on me;
If to reprove you for this suit of yours,
Be seasoned with your faithful love to me,
Then, on the other side, I checked my friends.
Therefore, to speak, and to avoid the first,
And then, in speaking, not to incur the last,
Definitively thus I answer you.
Your love deserves my thanks; but my desert
Unmeritable shuns your high request.
First, if all obstacles were cut away,
And that my path were even to the crown,
As the ripe revenue and due by birth;
Yet so much is my poverty of spirit,
So mighty and so many my defects,
As I had rather hide me from my greatness,—
Being a bark to brook no mighty sea,
Than in my greatness covet to be hid,
And in the vapour of my glory smothered.
But, God be thanked, there is no need of me,
And much I need to help you, if need were;—
The royal tree hath left us royal fruit,
Which, mellowed by the stealing hours of time,
Will well become the seat of majesty,
And make, no doubt, us happy by his reign.
On him I lay what you would lay on me,—
The right and fortune of his happy stars;
Which God defend that I should wring from him!
　Buck.　My lord, this argues conscience in your grace;
But the respects thereof are nice and trivial,
All circumstances well consideréd.
You say that Edward is your brother's son:
So say we too, but not by Edward's wife;
For first he was contract to Lady Lucy—
Your mother lives a witness to his vow,—
And afterwards by substitute betrothed
To Bona, sister to the King of France.

These both put by, a poor petitioner,
A care-crazed mother of a many children,
A beauty-waning and distresséd widow,
Even in the afternoon of her best days,
Made prize and purchase of his wanton eye,
Seduced the pitch and height of his degree
To base declension and loathed bigamy:
By her, in his unlawful bed, he got
This Edward, whom our manners call the prince.
More bitterly could I expostulate,
Save that, for reverence to some alive,
I give a sparing limit to my tongue.
Then, good my lord, take to your royal self
This proffered benefit of dignity;
If not to bless us and the land withal,
Yet to draw forth your noble ancestry
From the corruption of abusing time,
Unto a lineal true-derivéd course.

   May. Do, good, my lord; your citizens entreat
     you.
   Buck. Refuse not, mighty lord, this proffered love.
   Cate. O, make them joyful, grant their lawful suit!
   Glo. Alas, why would you heap these cares on me?
I am unfit for state and majesty:—
I do beseech you, take it not amiss;
I cannot nor I will not yield to you.
   Buck. If you refuse it,—as, in love and zeal,
Loth to depose the child, your brother's son;
As well we know your tenderness of heart,
And gentle, kind, effeminate remorse,
Which we have noted in you to your kin,
And equally indeed to all estates,—
Yet whether you accept our suit or no,
Your brother's son shall never reign our king:
But we will plant some other in the throne,
To the disgrace and downfall of your house:
And in this resolution here we leave you.—
Come, citizens; zounds, I'll entreat no more.
   Glo. O, do not swear, my lord of Buckingham.
            [Exit Buckingham with some of the Citizens
   Cate. Call them again, sweet prince, accept their suit.
If you deny them all the land will rue it.
   Glo. Would you enforce me to a world of care?
Call them again. *[Catesby goes to the Mayor, etc., and then
     exit.]* I am not made of stones,
But penetrable to your kind entreats,
Albeit against my conscience and my soul.

Re-enter Buckingham *and* Catesby, *the Mayor, etc., coming
       forward*

Cousin of Buckingham, and you sage, grave men,
Since you will buckle fortune on my back,
To bear her burden, whether I will or no,
I must have patience to endure the load:
But if black scandal or foul-faced reproach
Attend the sequel of your imposition,
Your mere enforcement shall acquittance me
From all the impure blots and stains thereof;
For God He knows, and you may partly see,
How far I am from the desire of this.
    May. God bless your grace! we see it, and will say it.
    Glo. In saying so, you shall but say the truth.
    Buck. Then I salute you with this kingly title:
Long live King Richard, England's worthy king!
    May. and Cit. Amen.
    Buck. To-morrow may it please you to be crowned?
    Glo. Even when you please, since you will have it so.
    Buck. To-morrow, then, we will attend your grace:
And so most joyfully we take our leave.
    Glo. Come, let us to our holy task again.—
Farewell, good cousin;—farewell, gentle friends.   [*Exeunt*

ACT FOUR

SCENE I.—London. Before the Tower

Enter, on one side, QUEEN ELIZABETH, DUCHESS OF YORK,
and MARQUESS OF DORSET; *on the other,* ANNE, DUCHESS
OF GLOSTER, *leading* LADY MARGARET PLANTAGENET,
CLARENCE'S *young Daughter*

    Duch. Who meets us here? my niece Plantagenet.
Led in the hand of her kind aunt of Gloster?
Now, for my life, she 's wandering to the Tower,
On pure heart's love, to greet the tender princes.
Daughter, well met.
    Anne.   God give your graces both
A happy and a joyful time of day!
    Q. Eliz. As much to you, good sister! Whither away?
    Anne. No farther than the Tower; and, as I guess,
Upon the like devotion as yourselves,
To gratulate the gentle princes there.
    Q. Eliz. Kind sister, thanks: we 'll enter all together.
And, in good time, here the lieutenant comes.

Enter BRAKENBURY

Master lieutenant, pray you, by your leave,
How doth the prince, and my young son of York?
    Brak. Right well, dear madam. By your patience,
I may not suffer you to visit them;
The king hath straitly charged the contrary.
    Q. Eliz. The king! who 's that?

Brak.   I mean the lord protector.

Q. Eliz.   The Lord protect him from that kingly title!
Hath he set bounds between their love and me?
I am their mother; who shall bar me from them?

Duch.   I am their father's mother; I will see them.

Anne.   Their aunt I am in law, in love their mother:
Then bring me to their sights; I 'll bear thy blame
And take thy office from thee, on my peril.

Brak.   No, madam, no,—I may not leave it so:
I 'm bound by oath, and therefore pardon me.   [*Exit*

Enter STANLEY

Stan.   Let me but meet you, ladies, one hour hence,
And I 'll salute your grace of York as mother,
And reverend looker on, of two fair queens.
[*To Anne*] Come, madam, you must straight to West-
          minster,
There to be crownéd Richard's royal queen.

Q. Eliz.   Ah, cut my lace in sunder,
That my pent heart may have some scope to beat,
Or else I swoon with this dead-killing news!

Anne.   Despiteful tidings! O unpleasing news!

Dor.   Be of good cheer:—mother, how fares your grace?

Q. Eliz.   O Dorset, speak not to me, get thee hence!
Death and destruction dog thee at the heels;
Thy mother's name is ominous to children.
If thou wilt outstrip death, go cross the seas,
And live with Richmond, from the reach of hell:
Go, hie thee, hie thee, from this slaughter-house,
Lest thou increase the number of the dead,
And make me die the thrall of Margaret's curse,—
Nor mother, wife, nor England's counted queen.

Stan.   Full of wise care is this your counsel, madam.—
Take all the swift advantage of the hours;
You shall have letters from me to my son
In your behalf, to meet you on the way:
Be not ta'en tardy by unwise delay.

Duch.   O ill-dispersing wind of misery!—
O my acccurséd womb, the bed of death!
A cockatrice hast thou hatched to the world,
Whose unavoided eye is murderous.

Stan.   Come, madam, come; I in all haste was sent.

Anne.   And I in all unwillingness will go.—
I would to God that the inclusive verge
Of golden metal that must round my brow
Were red-hot steel, to sear me to the brain!
Anointed let me be with deadly venom,
And die, ere men can say, God save the queen!

Q. Eliz.   Go, go, poor soul, I envy not thy glory;
To feed my humour, wish thyself no harm.

Anne. No! why?—When he that is my husband now
Came to me, as I followed Henry's corse,
When scarce the blood was well washed from his hands
Which issued from my other angel husband
And that dead saint which then I weeping followed;
O, when, I say, I looked on Richard's face,
This was my wish,—"Be thou," quoth I, "accursed,
For making me, so young, so old a widow!
And, when thou wed'st, let sorrow haunt thy bed;
And be thy wife—if any be so mad—
As miserable by the life of thee
As thou hast made me by my dear lord's death!"
Lo, ere I can repeat this curse again,
Even in so short a space, my woman's heart
Grossly grew captive to his honey words,
And proved the subject of mine own soul's curse,
Which ever since hath kept mine eyes from rest;
For never yet one hour in his bed
Have I enjoyed the golden dew of sleep,
But have been wakéd by his timorous dreams.
Besides, he hates me for my father Warwick;
And will, no doubt, shortly be rid of me.
    Q. Eliz. Poor heart, adieu! I pity thy complaining.
    Anne. No more than from my soul I mourn for yours.
    Q. Eliz. Farewell, thou woful welcomer of glory!
    Anne. Adieu, poor soul, that tak'st thy leave of it!
    Duch. [*To Dorset*] Go thou to Richmond, and good
        fortune guide thee!
[*To Anne*] Go thou to Richard, and good angels guard thee!
[*To Queen Eliz.*] Go thou to sanctuary, and good thoughts
        possess thee!
I to my grave, where peace and rest lie with me!
Eighty odd years of sorrow have I seen,
And each hour's joy wrecked with a week of teen.
    Q. Eliz. Stay, yet look back with me unto the Tower.—
Pity, you ancient stones, those tender babes
Whom envy hath immured within your walls,
Rough cradle for such little pretty ones!
Rude ragged nurse, old sullen playfellow
For tender princes, use my babies well!
So foolish sorrow bids your stones farewell.   [*Exeunt*

SCENE II.—London. A Room of State in the Palace

Sennet.   Enter RICHARD, *crowned ;* BUCKINGHAM,
CATESBY, *a Page, and others*

K. Rich. Stand all apart.—Cousin of Buckingham,—
Buck. My gracious sovereign?
K. Rich. Give me thy hand. [*Ascendeth the throne.*]
    Thus high, by thy advice

And thy assistance, is King Richard seated:
But shall we wear these honours for a day?
Or shall they last, and we rejoice in them?
   Buck.   Still live they and for ever let them last!
   K. Rich.   O Buckingham, now do I play the touch,
To try if thou be current gold indeed:—
Young Edward lives:—think now what I would speak.
   Buck.   Say on, my loving lord.
   K. Rich.   Why, Buckingham, I say, I would be king.
   Buck.   Why, so you are, my thrice renownéd liege.
   K. Rich.   Ha! am I king? 't is so:—but Edward lives.
   Buck.   True, noble prince.
   K. Rich.   O bitter consequence,
That Edward still should live! "True, noble prince!"—
Cousin, thou wert not wont to be so dull:
Shall I be plain?—I wish the bastards dead;
And I would have it suddenly performed.
What say'st thou now? speak suddenly; be brief.
   Buck.   Your grace may do your pleasure.
   K. Rich.   Tut, tut, thou art all ice, thy kindness freezes:
Say, have I thy consent that they shall die?
   Buck.   Give me some breath, some little pause, my lord,
Before I positively speak herein:
I will resolve your grace immediately.   *[Exit*
   Cate.   *[Aside to a stander-by]* The king is angry: see, he
        bites the lip.
   K. Rich.   I will converse with iron-witted fools
                  [Descends from his throne
And unrespective boys: none are for me
That look into me with considerate eyes:
High-reaching Buckingham grows circumspect.—
Boy!—
   Page.   My lord?
   K. Rich.   Know'st thou not any whom corrupting gold
Would tempt unto a close exploit of death?
   Page.   My lord, I know a discontented gentleman,
Whose humble means match not his haughty mind:
Gold were as good as twenty orators,
And will, no doubt, tempt him to any thing.
   K. Rich.   What is his name?
   Page.   His name, my lord, is Tyrrel.
   K. Rich.   I partly know the man: go, call him hither.
                           [Exit Page
The deep-revolving witty Buckingham
No more shall be the neighbour to my counsels:
Hath he so long held out with me untired,
And stops he now for breath?—Well, be it so.

           Enter STANLEY

How now! what news with you?

Stan.   My lord, I hear the Marquis Dorset 's fled
To Richmond, in those parts beyond the seas
Where he abides.   [*Stands apart*
   K. Rich.   Come hither, Catesby!   Rumour it abroad
That Anne, my wife, is very grievous sick;
I will take order for her keeping close.
Inquire me out some mean-born gentleman,
Whom I will marry straight to Clarence' daughter;—
The boy is foolish, and I fear not him.—
Look, how thou dream'st!—I say again, give out
That Anne, my wife, is sick and like to die:
About it; for it stands me much upon,
To stop all hopes whose growth may damage me.
                              [*Exit Catesby*
I must be married to my brother's daughter,
Or else my kingdom stands on brittle glass.—
Murder her brothers, and then marry her!
Uncertain way of gain!   But I am in
So far in blood, that sin will pluck on sin:
Tear-falling pity dwells not in this eye.

Re-enter Page, with TYRREL

Is thy name Tyrrel?
   Tyr.   James Tyrrel, and your most obedient subject.
   K. Rich.   Art thou, indeed?
   Tyr.   Prove me, my gracious sovereign.
   K. Rich.   Dar'st thou resolve to kill a friend of mine?
   Tyr.   Ay, my lord;
But I rather kill two enemies.
   K. Rich.   Why, there thou hast it: two deep enemies,
Foes to my rest and my sweet sleep's disturbers,
Are they that I would have thee deal up:—
Tyrrel, I mean those bastards in the Tower.
   Tyr.   Let me have open means to come to them,
And soon I 'll rid you from the fear of them.
   K. Rich.   Thou sing'st sweet music.   Hark, come hither,
      Tyrrel:
Go, by this token:—rise, and lend thine ear: [*Whispers*
There is no more but so:—say it is done,
And I will love thee, and prefer thee for it.
   Tyr.   'T is done, my gracious lord.
   K. Rich.   Shall we hear from thee, Tyrrel, ere we sleep?
   Tyr.   Ye shall, my lord.   [*Exit*

Re-enter BUCKINGHAM

   Buck.   My lord, I have considered in my mind
The late demand that you sound in me.
   K. Rich.   Well, let that pass.   Dorset is fled to Richmond.
   Buck.   I hear that news, my lord.
   K. Rich.   Stanley, he is your wife's son:—well, look to it.

Buck. My lord, I claim the gift, my due by promise,
For which your honour and your faith is pawned;
Th' earldom of Hereford and the moveables
The which you promiséd I should possess.
  K. Rich. Stanley, look to your wife: if she convey
Letters to Richmond, you shall answer it.
  Buck. What says your highness to my just demand?
  K. Rich. As I remember, Henry the Sixth
Did prophesy that Richmond should be king,
When Richmond was a little peevish boy.
A king!—perhaps,—
  Buck. My lord!—
  K. Rich. How chance the prophet could not at that time
Have told me, I being by, that I should kill him?
  Buck. My lord, your promise for the earldom,—
  K. Rich. Richmond!—when last I was at Exeter,
The mayor in courtesy showed me the castle,
And called it Rougemont: at which name I started,
Because a bard of Ireland told me once
I should not live long after I saw Richmond.
  Buck. My lord!—
  K. Rich. Ay, what's o'clock?
  Buck. I am thus bold to put your grace in mind
Of what you promised me.
  K. Rich.   Well, but what's o'clock?
  Buck. Upon the stroke of ten.
  K. Rich.   Well, let it strike.
  Buck. Why let it strike?
  K. Rich. Because that, like a Jack, thou keep'st the
        stroke
Betwixt thy begging and my meditation.
I am not in the giving vein to-day.
  Buck. Why, then resolve me whether you will or no.
  K. Rich. Thou troublest me; I am not in the vein.
                            [*Exeunt all but Buckingham*
  Buck. Is it even so? rewards he my true service
With such contempt? made I him king for this?
O, let me think on Hastings, and be gone
To Brecknock, while my fearful head is on.   [*Exit*

SCENE III.—Another Room in the Palace

Enter TYRREL

  Tyr. The tyrannous and bloody deed is done;
The most arch act of piteous massacre
That ever yet this land was guilt of.
Dighton and Forrest, whom I did suborn
To do this ruthless piece of butchery,
Although they were fleshed villains, bloody dogs,

133

Melting with tenderness and kind compassion,
Wept like two children in their deaths' sad story.
"Lo thus," quoth Dighton, "lay those tender babes:"
"Thus, thus," quoth Forrest, "girdling one another
Within their innocent alabaster arms:
Their lips were four red roses on a stalk,
Which in their summer beauty kissed each other.
A book of prayers on their pillow lay;
Which once," quoth Forrest, "almost changed my mind;
But O! the devil"—there the villain stopped;
Whilst Dighton thus told on:—"We smotheréd
The most replenishéd sweet work of nature
That from the prime creation e'er she framed."
Hence both are gone with conscience and remorse;
They could not speak; and so I left them both,
To bring this tidings to the bloody king:—
And here he comes.

Enter KING RICHARD

                    All health, my sovereign liege!
K. Rich. Kind Tyrrel, am I happy in thy news?
Tyr. If to have done the thing you gave in charge
Beget your happiness, be happy then,
For it is done.
K. Rich.   But didst thou see them dead?
Tyr. I did, my lord.
K. Rich.   And buried, gentle Tyrrel?
Tyr. The chaplain of the Tower hath buried them;
But where, to say the truth, I do not know.
K. Rich. Come to me, Tyrrel, soon at after supper,
When thou shalt tell the process of their death.
Meantime, but think how I may do thee good,
And be inheritor of thy desire.
Farewell till then.   [*Exit Tyrrel*
The son of Clarence have I pent up close;
His daughter meanly have I matched in marriage;
The sons of Edward sleep in Abraham's bosom,
And Anne my wife hath bid the world good night.
Now, for I know the Breton Richmond aims
At young Elizabeth, my brother's daughter,
And, by that knot, looks proudly on the crown,
To her I go, a jolly thriving wooer.

Enter CATESBY

Cate. My lord,—
K. Rich. Good news or bad, that thou com'st in so
        bluntly?
Cate. Bad news, my lord: Ely is fled to Richmond;
And Buckingham, backed with the hardy Welshmen,
Is in the field, and still his power increaseth.

K. Rich. Ely with Richmond troubles me more near
Than Buckingham and his rash-levied strength.
Come,—I have learned that fearful commenting
Is leaden servitor to dull delay;
Delay leads impotent and snail-paced beggary:
Then fiery expedition be my wing,
Jove's Mercury, and herald for a king!
Come, muster men: my counsel is my shield;
We must be brief when traitors brave the field.   [*Exeunt*

SCENE IV.—Before the Palace

Enter QUEEN MARGARET

Q. Mar. So, now prosperity begins to mellow
And drop into the rotten mouth of death.
Here in these confines slily have I lurked,
To watch the waning of mine enemies.
A dire induction am I witness to,
And will to France; hoping the consequence
Will prove as bitter, black, and tragical.—
Withdraw thee, wretched Margaret: who comes here?

Enter QUEEN ELIZABETH *and the* DUCHESS OF YORK

Q. Eliz. Ah, my young princes! ah, my tender babes!
My unblown flowers, new-appearing sweets!
If yet your gentle souls fly in the air
And be not fixed in doom perpetual,
Hover about me with your airy wings
And hear your mother's lamentation!
Q. Mar. [*Aside*] Hover about her; say, that right for right
Hath dimmed your infant morn to agèd night.
Duch. So many miseries have crazed my voice,
That my woe-wearied tongue is still and mute.
Edward Plantagenet, why art thou dead?
Q. Mar. [*Aside*] Plantagenet doth quit Plantagenet,
Edward for Edward pays a dying debt.
Q. Eliz. Wilt Thou, O God, fly from such gentle lambs,
And throw them in the entrails of the wolf?
When didst Thou sleep, when such a deed was done?
Q. Mar. [*Aside*] When holy Harry died, and my sweet son.
Duch. Blind sight, dead life, poor mortal living ghost,
Woe's scene, world's shame, grave's due by life usurped,
Brief abstract and record of tedious days,
Rest thy unrest on England's lawful earth,   [*Sitting down*
Unlawfully made drunk with innocents' blood!
Q. Eliz. Ah, that thou wouldst as well afford a grave
As thou canst yield a melancholy seat!
Then would I hide my bones, not rest them here.
Ah, who hath any cause to mourn but I?
[*Sitting down by her*

 Q. Mar. [*Coming forward*] If ancient sorrow be most
   reverend,
Give mine the benefit of seniory,
And let my griefs frown on the upper hand.
If sorrow can admit society,   [*Sitting down with them*
Tell o'er your woes again by viewing mine:—
I had an Edward, till a Richard killed him;
I had a Harry, till a Richard killed him:
Thou hadst an Edward, till a Richard killed him;
Thou hadst a Richard, till a Richard killed him.
 Duch. I had a Richard too, and thou didst kill him;
I had a Rutland too, thou holp'st to kill him.
 Q. Mar. Thou hadst a Clarence too, and Richard killed
   him.
From forth the kennel of thy womb hath crept
A hell-hound that doth hunt us all to death:
That dog, that had his teeth before his eyes,
To worry lambs and lap their gentle blood;
That foul defacer of God's handiwork;
That excellent grand tyrant of the earth,
That reigns in gallèd eyes of weeping souls,—
Thy womb let loose, to chase us to our graves.—
O upright, just, and true-disposing God,
How do I thank Thee, that this carnal cur
Preys on the issue of his mother's body,
And makes her pew-fellow with others' moan!
 Duch. O Harry's wife, triumph not in my woes!
God witness with me, I have wept for thine.
 Q. Mar. Bear with me; I am hungry for revenge,
And now I cloy me with beholding it.
Thy Edward he is dead, that stabbed my Edward;
Thy other Edward dead, to quit my Edward;
Young York he is but boot, because both they
Match not the high perfection of my loss:
Thy Clarence he is dead that killed my Edward;
And the beholders of this tragic play,
The adulterate Hastings, Rivers, Vaughan, Grey,
Untimely smothered in their dusky graves.
Richard yet lives, hell's black intelligencer,
Only reserved their factor, to buy souls
And send them thither:—but at hand, at hand,
Ensues his piteous and unpitied end:
Earth gapes, hell burns, fiends roar, saints pray,
To have him suddenly conveyed away.
Cancel his bond of life, dear God, I pray,
That I may live to say, The dog is dead!
 Q. Eliz. O, thou didst prophesy the time would
   come
That I should wish for thee to help me curse
That bottled spider, that foul bunch-backed toad!

Q. Mar.   I called thee then, vain flourish of my fortune,
I called thee then poor shadow, painted queen;
The presentation of but what I was,
The flattering index of a direful pageant;
One heaved a-high, to be hurled down below;
A mother only mocked with two sweet babes;
A dream of what thou wert; a breath, a bubble;
A sign of dignity, a garish flag
To be the aim of every dangerous shot;
A queen in jest, only to fill the scene.
Where is thy husband now? where be thy brothers?
Where be thy two sons? wherein dost thou joy?
Who sues to thee, and cries, "God save the queen"?
Where be the bending peers that flattered thee?
Where be the thronging troops that followed thee?
Decline all this, and see what now thou art:
For happy wife, a most distresséd widow;
For joyful mother, one that wails the name;
For queen, a very caitiff crowned with care;
For one being sued to, one that humbly sues;
For one that scorned at me, now scorned of me;
For one being feared of all, now fearing one;
For one commanding all, obeyed of none.
Thus hath the course of justice wheeled about,
And left thee but a very prey to time;
Having no more but thought of what thou wert,
To torture thee the more, being what thou art.
Thou didst usurp my place, and dost thou not
Usurp the just proportion of my sorrow?
Now thy proud neck bears half my burdened yoke:
From which even here I slip my weary neck,
And leave the burden of it all on thee.
Farewell, York's wife, and queen of sad mischance:—
These English woes will make me smile in France.
    Q. Eliz.   O thou well skilled in curses, stay awhile,
And teach me how to curse mine enemies!
    Q. Mar.   Forbear to sleep the night, and fast the day;
Compare dead happiness with living woe;
Think that thy babes were fairer than they were,
And he that slew them fouler than he is:
Bettering thy loss makes the bad causer worse:
Revolving this will teach thee how to curse.
    Q. Eliz.   My words are dull; O, quicken them with thine!
    Q. Mar.   Thy woes will make them sharp, and pierce
        like mine.   [*Exit*
    Duch.   Why should calamity be full of words?
    Q. Eliz.   Windy attorneys to their client woes,
Airy succeeders of intestate joys,
Poor breathing orators of miseries!
Let them have scope: though what they do impart

137

Help nothing else, yet do they ease the heart.
   Duch. If so, then be not tongue-tied: go with me,
And in the breath of bitter words let's smother
My damnéd son, that thy two sweet sons smothered.
I hear his drum:—be copious in exclaims.

Enter KING RICHARD, *marching, with drums and trumpets*

   K. Rich. Who intercepts me in my expedition?
   Duch. O, she that might have intercepted thee,
By strangling thee in her accurséd womb,
From all the slaughters, wretch, that thou has done!
   Q. Eliz. Hid'st thou that forehead with a golden crown,
Where should be branded, if that right were right,
The slaughter of the prince that owed that crown,
And the dire death of my poor sons and brothers?
Tell me, thou villain slave, where are my children?
   Duch. Thou toad, thou toad, where is thy brother
      Clarence?
And little Ned Plantagenet, his son?
   Q. Eliz. Where is the gentle Rivers, Vaughan, Grey?
   Duch. Where is kind Hastings?
   K. Rich. A flourish, trumpets! strike alarum, drums!
Let not the heavens hear these tell-tale women
Rail on the Lord's anointed: strike, I say!—
                    [*Flourish. Alarums*
Either be patient, and entreat me fair,
Or with the clamorous report of war
Thus will I drown your exclamations.
   Duch. Art thou my son?
   K. Rich. Ay, I thank God, my father, and yourself.
   Duch. Then patiently hear my impatience.
   K. Rich. Madam, I have a touch of your condition,
Which cannot brook the accent of reproof.
   Duch. O let me speak!
   K. Rich.   Do then; but I'll not hear.
   Duch. I will be mild and gentle in my words.
   K. Rich. And brief, good mother; for I am in haste.
   Duch. Art thou so hasty? I have stayed for thee,
God knows, in torment and in agony.
   K. Rich. And came I not at last to comfort you?
   Duch. No, by the holy rood, thou know'st it well,
Thou cam'st on earth to make the earth my hell.
A grievous burthen was thy birth to me;
Tetchy and wayward was thy infancy;
Thy school-days frightful, desperate, wild, and furious;
Thy prime of manhood daring, bold, and venturous,
Thy age confirmed, proud, subtle, bloody, treacherous,
More mild, but yet more harmful,—kind in hatred:
What comfortable hour canst thou name,
That every graced me in thy company?

    K. Rich. Faith, none, but Humphrey Hour, that
      called your grace
To breakfast once forth of my company.
If I be so disgracious in your eye,
Let me march on, and not offend you, madam.
Strike up the drum.
    Duch.   I prithee, hear me speak.
    K. Rich. You speak too bitterly.
    Duch.   Hear me a word;
For I shall never speak to thee again.
    K. Rich. So.
    Duch. Either thou'lt die, by God's just ordinance,
Ere from this war thou turn a conqueror;
Or I with grief and extreme age shall perish,
And never look upon thy face again.
Therefore take with thee my most heavy curse;
Which, in the day of battle, tire thee more
Than all the complete armour that thou wear'st!
My prayers on the adverse party fight;
And there the little souls of Edward's children
Whispers the spirits of thine enemies,
And promise them success and victory,
Bloody thou art, bloody will be thy end;
Shame serves thy life, and doth thy death attend.   [*Exit*
    Q. Eliz. Though far more cause, yet much less spirit to
      curse
Abides in me; I say amen to all.   [*Going*
    K. Rich. Stay, madam; I must speak a word with you.
    Q. Eliz. I have no more sons of the royal blood
For thee to murder: for my daughters, Richard,—
They shall be praying nuns, not weeping queens;
And therefore level not to hit their lives.
    K. Rich. You have a daughter called Elizabeth,
Virtuous and fair, royal and gracious.
    Q. Eliz. And must she die for this?   O, let her live,
And I'll corrupt her manners, stain her beauty;
Slander myself as false to Edward's bed;
Throw over her the veil of infamy:
So she may live unscarred of bleeding slaughter,
I will confess she was not Edward's daughter.
    K. Rich. Wrong not her birth, she is of royal blood.
    Q. Eliz. To save her life, I'll say she is not so.
    K. Rich. Her life is safest only in her birth.
    Q. Eliz. And only in that safety died her brothers.
    K. Rich. Lo, at their births good stars were opposite.
    Q. Eliz. No, to their lives bad friends were contrary.
    K. Rich. All unavoided is the doom of destiny.
    Q. Eliz. True, when avoided grace makes destiny:
My babes were destined to a fairer death,
If grace had blessed thee with a fairer life.

K. Rich.   You speak as if that I had slain my cousins.
  Q. Eliz.   Cousins, indeed; and by their uncle cozened
Of comfort, kingdom, kindred, freedom, life.
Whose hand soever lanced their tender hearts,
Thy head, all indirectly, gave direction:
No doubt the murderous knife was dull and blunt
Till it was whetted on thy stone-hard heart,
To revel in the entrails of my lambs.
But that still use of grief makes wild grief tame,
My tongue should to thy ears not name my boys
Till that my nails were anchored in thine eyes;
And I, in such a desperate bay of death,
Like a poor bark of sails and tackling reft,
Rush all to pieces on thy rocky bosom.
  K. Rich.   Madam, so thrive I in my enterprise
And dangerous success of bloody wars,
As I intend more good to you and yours
Than ever you or yours were by me wronged!
  Q. Eliz.   What good is covered with the face of heaven,
To be discovered, that can do me good?
  K. Rich.   The advancement of your children, gentle lady.
  Q. Eliz.   Up to some scaffold, there to lose their heads?
  K. Rich.   No, to the dignity and height of honour,
The high imperial type of this earth's glory.
  Q. Eliz.   Flatter my sorrows with report of it;
Tell me what state, what dignity, what honour,
Canst thou demise to any child of mine?
  K. Rich.   Even all I have; yea, and myself and all,
Will I withal endow a child of thine;
So in the Lethe of thy angry soul
Thou drown the sad remembrance of those wrongs
Which thou supposest I have done to thee.
  Q. Eliz.   Be brief, lest that the process of thy kindness
Last longer telling than thy kindness' date.
  K. Rich.   Then know, that from my soul I love thy
        daughter.
  Q. Eliz.   My daughter's mother thinks it with her soul.
  K. Rich.   What do you think?
  Q. Eliz.   That thou dost love my daughter from thy soul:
So from thy soul's love didst thou love her brothers;
And from my heart's love I do thank thee for it.
  K. Rich.   Be not so hasty to confound my meaning:
I mean, that with my soul I love thy daughter,
And do intend to make her queen of England.
  Q. Eliz.   Say then, who dost thou mean shall be her king?
  K. Rich.   Even he that makes her queen: who else
        should be?
  Q. Eliz.   What, thou?
  K. Rich.   Even I: what think you of it, madam?
  Q. Eliz.   How can'st thou woo her?

K. Rich.   That would I learn of you,
As one being best acquainted with her humour.
Q. Eliz.   And wilt thou learn of me?
K. Rich.   Madam, with all my heart.
Q. Eliz.   Send to her, by the man that slew her brothers,
A pair of bleeding hearts; thereon engraven
"Edward and York;" then haply will she weep:
Therefore present to her,—as sometime Margaret
Did to thy father, steeped in Rutland's blood,—
A handkerchief; which, say to her, did drain
The purple sap from her sweet brothers' bodies,
And bid her dry her weeping eyes withal.
If this inducement force her not to love,
Send her a story of thy noble deeds;
Tell her thou mad'st away her uncle Clarence,
Her uncle Rivers; yea, and, for her sake,
Mad'st quick conveyance with her good aunt Anne.
K. Rich.   You mock me, madam; this is not the way
To win your daughter.
Q. Eliz.   There 's no other way;
Unless thou couldst put on some other shape,
And not be Richard that hath done all this.
K. Rich.   Say that I did all this for love of her.
Q. Eliz.   Nay, then indeed she cannot choose but hate
      thee,
Having bought love with such a bloody spoil.
K. Rich.   Look, what is done cannot be now amended:
Men shall deal unadvisedly sometimes,
Which after hours give leisure to repent.
If I did take the kingdom from your sons,
To make amends, I'll give it to your daughter.
If I have killed the issue of your womb,
To quicken your increase, I will beget
Mine issue of your blood upon your daughter:
A grandam's name is little less in love
Than is the doting title of a mother;
They are as children but one step below,
Even of your mettle, of your very blood;
Of all one pain,—save for a night of groans
Endured of her, for whom you bid like sorrow.
Your children were vexation to your youth,
But mine shall be a comfort to your age.
The loss you have is but a son being king,
And by that loss your daughter is made queen.
I cannot make you what amends I would,
Therefore accept such kindness as I can.
Dorset, your son, that with a fearful soul
Leads discontented steps in foreign soil,
This fair alliance quickly shall call home
To high promotions and great dignity:

The king, that calls your beauteous daughter wife,
Familiarly shall call thy Dorset brother;
Again shall you be mother to a king,
And all the ruins of distressful times
Repaired with double riches of content.
What! we have many goodly days to see:
The liquid drops of tears that you have shed
Shall come again, transformed to orient pearl,
Advantaging their loan with interest
Of ten times double gain of happiness.
Go, then, my mother, to thy daughter go;
Make bold her bashful years with your experience;
Prepare her ears to hear a wooer's tale;
Put in her tender heart the aspiring flame
Of golden sovereignty; acquaint the princess
With the sweet silent hours of marriage joys:
And when this arm of mine hath chastisèd
The petty rebel, dull-brained Buckingham,
Bound with triumphant garlands will I come
And lead thy daughter to a conqueror's bed;
To whom I will retail my conquest won,
And she shall be sole victress, Cæsar's Cæsar.
  Q. Eliz.   What were I best to say? her father's brother
Would be her lord? or shall I say, her uncle?
Or, he that slew her brothers and her uncles?
Under what title shall I woo for thee,
That God, the law, my honour and her love,
Can make seem pleasing to her tender years?
  K. Rich.   Infer fair England's peace by this alliance.
  Q. Eliz.   Which she shall purchase with still lasting war.
  K. Rich.   Tell her the king, that may command, entreats.
  Q. Eliz.   That at her hands which the king's King
      forbids.
  K. Rich.   Say, she shall be a high and mighty queen.
  Q. Eliz.   To wail the title, as her mother doth.
  K. Rich.   Say, I will love her everlastingly.
  Q. Eliz.   But how long shall that title "ever" last?
  K. Rich.   Sweetly in force unto her fair life's end.
  Q. Eliz.   But how long fairly shall her sweet life last?
  K. Rich.   So long as heaven and nature lengthen it.
  Q. Eliz.   So long as hell and Richard like of it.
  K. Rich.   Say I, her sovereign, am her subject love.
  Q. Eliz.   But she, your subject, loathes such sovereignty.
  K. Rich.   Be eloquent in my behalf to her.
  Q. Eliz.   An honest tale speeds best being plainly told.
  K. Rich.   Then in plain terms tell her my loving tale.
  Q. Eliz.   Plain and not honest is too harsh a style.
  K. Rich.   Your reasons are too shallow and too quick.
  Q. Eliz.   O no, my reasons are too deep and dead;
Too deep and dead, poor infants, in their grave.

K. Rich. Harp not on that string, madam; that is past.
Q. Eliz. Harp on it still shall I till heart-strings break.
K. Rich. Now, by my George, my garter, and my
    crown,—
Q. Eliz. Profaned, dishonoured, and the third usurped.
K. Rich. I swear—
Q. Eliz.   By nothing; for this is no oath:
The George, profaned, hath lost his holy honour;
The garter, blemished, pawned his knightly virtue;
The crown, usurped, disgraced his kingly glory.
If something thou wilt swear to be believed,
Swear then by something that thou hast not wronged.
K. Rich. Now, by the world—
Q. Eliz.   'T is full of thy foul wrongs.
K. Rich. My father's death—
Q. Eliz.   Thy life hath that dishonoured.
K. Rich. Then, by myself—
Q. Eliz.   Thyself is self misused.
K. Rich. Why then, by God—
Q. Eliz.   God's wrong is most of all.
If thou hadst feared to break an oath by Him,
The unity the king thy brother made
Had not been broken, nor my brother slain:
If thou hadst feared to break an oath by Him,
The imperial metal, circling now thy brow,
Had graced the tender temples of my child,
And both the princes had been breathing here,
Which now, too tender bedfellows for dust,
Thy broken faith hath made a prey for worms.
What canst thou swear by now?
K. Rich.   The time to come.
Q. Eliz. That thou hast wrongéd in the time o'erpast;
For I myself have many tears to wash
Hereafter time, for time past wronged by thee.
The children live, whose parents thou hast slaughtered,
Ungoverned youth, to wail it in their age;
The parents live, whose children thou hast butchered,
Old withered plants, to wail it with their age.
Swear not by time to come; for that thou hast
Misused ere used, by time misused o'erpast.
  K. Rich. As I intend to prosper and repent,
So thrive I in my dangerous attempt
Of hostile arms! myself myself confound!
Heaven and fortune bar me happy hours!
Day, yield me not thy light; nor night, thy rest!
Be opposite all planets of good luck
To my proceeding, if, with pure heart's love,
Immaculate devotion, holy thoughts,
I tender not thy beauteous princely daughter!
In her consists my happiness and thine;

143

Without her, follows to this land and me,
To thee, herself, and many a Christian soul,
Death, desolation, ruin and decay:
It cannot be avoided but by this;
It will not be avoided but by this.
Therefore, dear mother,—I must call you so,—
Be the attorney of my love to her:
Plead what I will be, not what I have been;
Not my deserts, but what I will deserve:
Urge the necessity and state of times,
And be not peevish-fond in great designs.
    Q. Eliz.   Shall I be tempted of the devil thus?
    K. Rich.   Ay, if the devil tempt thee to do good.
    Q. Eliz.   Shall I forget myself to be myself?
    K. Rich.   Ay, if your self's remembrance wrong yourself.
    Q. Eliz.   But thou didst kill my children.
    K. Rich.   But in your daughter's womb I'll bury them:
Where in that nest of spicery they shall breed
Selves of themselves, to your recomforture.
    Q. Eliz.   Shall I go win my daughter to thy will?
    K. Rich.   And be a happy mother by the deed.
    Q. Eliz.   I go.—Write to me very shortly,
And you shall understand from me her mind.
    K. Rich.   Bear her my true love's kiss, and so farewell.
                                  [Exit Queen Elizabeth
Relenting fool, and shallow, changing woman!

            Enter RATCLIFF; CATESBY *following*

How now! what news?
    Rat.   My gracious sovereign, on the western coast
Rideth a puissant navy; to the shore
Throng many doubtful hollow-hearted friends,
Unarmed, and unresolved to beat them back:
'T is thought that Richmond is their admiral;
And there they hull, expecting but the aid
Of Buckingham to welcome them ashore.
    K. Rich.   Some light-foot friend post to the Duke of
        Norfolk:—
Ratcliff, thyself,—or Catesby; where is he?
    Cate.   Here, my good lord.
    K. Rich.   Fly to the duke:—[*To Ratcliff*] Post thou to
        Salisbury:
When thou com'st thither,—[*To Catesby*] Dull, unmindful
    villain,
Why stand'st thou still, and go'st not to the duke?
    Cate.   First, mighty liege, tell me your highness' plea-
    sure,
What from your grace I shall deliver to him.
    K. Rich.   O true, good Catesby: bid him levy straight
The greatest strength and power he can make,

And meet me suddenly at Salisbury.
 Cate. I go.   *[Exit*
 Rat. What may it please you I shall do at Salisbury?
 K. Rich. Why, what wouldst thou do there before I go?
 Rat. Your highness told me I should post before.
 K. Rich. My mind is changed.

Enter STANLEY

Stanley, what news with you?
 Stan. None good, my lord, to please you with the hearing;
Nor none so bad, but it may be told.
 K. Rich. Hoyday, a riddle! neither good nor bad!
What need'st thou run so many miles about,
When thou mayest tell thy tale the nearest way?
Once more, what news?
 Stan.   Richmond is on the seas.
 K. Rich. There let him sink, and be the seas on him!
White-livered runagate, what doth he there?
 Stan. I know not, mighty sovereign, but by guess.
 K. Rich. Well, as you guess?
 Stan. Stirred up by Dorset, Buckingham, and Ely,
He makes for England, here to claim the crown.
 K. Rich. Is the chair empty? is the sword unswayed?
Is the king dead? the empire unpossessed?
What heir of York is there alive but we?
And who is England's king but great York's heir?
Then, tell me, what makes he upon the seas?
 Stan. Unless for that, my liege, I cannot guess.
 K. Rich. Unless for that he comes to be your liege,
You cannot guess wherefore the Welshman comes.
Thou wilt revolt, and fly to him, I fear.
 Stan. No, mighty liege; therefore mistrust me not.
 K. Rich. Where is thy power, then, to beat him back?
Where are thy tenants and thy followers?
Are they not now upon the western shore,
Safe-cónducting the rebels from their ships?
 Stan. No, my good lord, my friends are in the north.
 K. Rich. Cold friends to Richard, what do they in the
   north,
When they should serve their sovereign in the west?
 Stan. They have not been commanded, mighty king:
Please it your majesty to give me leave,
I 'll muster up my friends, and meet your grace
Where and what time your majesty shall please.
 K. Rich. Ay, ay, thou wouldst be gone to join with
   Richmond:
I will not trust you, sir.
 Stan.   Most mighty sovereign,
You have no cause to hold my friendship doubtful:
I never was nor never will be false.

K. Rich.   Well,
Go muster men.   But, hear you, leave behind
Your son, George Stanley: look your faith be firm,
Or else his head's assurance is but frail.
    Stan.   So deal with him as I prove true to you.   [*Exit*

Enter a Messenger

Mess.   My gracious sovereign, now in Devonshire,
As I by friends am well advértiséd,
Sir Edward Courtney, and the haughty prelate
Bishop of Exeter, his elder brother,
With many more confederates, are in arms.

Enter a second Messenger

Sec. Mess.   My liege, in Kent the Guildfords are in arms;
And every hour more competitors
Flock to the rebels, and their power grows strong.

Enter a third Messenger

Third Mess.   My lord, the army of great Buckingham—
    K. Rich.   Out on you, owls! nothing but songs of death?
                                            [*He striketh him*
Take that until thou bring me better news.
    Third Mess.   The news I have to tell your majesty
Is, that by sudden floods and fall of waters,
Buckingham's army is dispersed and scattered;
And he himself wandered away alone,
No man knows whither.
    K. Rich.   O, I cry thee mercy:
There is my purse to cure that blow of thine.
Hath any well-advidéd friend proclaimed
Reward to him that brings the traitor in?
    Third Mess.   Such proclamation hath been made, my
        liege.

Enter a fourth Messenger

Fourth Mess.   Sir Thomas Lovel and Lord Marquis
        Dorset,
'T is said, my liege, in Yorkshire are in arms.
Yet this good comfort bring I to your grace,
The Breton navy is dispersed by tempest:
Richmond, in Dorsetshire, sent out a boat
Unto the shore, to ask those on the banks
If they were his assistants, yea or no;
Who answered him they came from Buckingham
Upon his party: he, mistrusting them,
Hoist sail and made away for Brittany.
    K. Rich.   March on, march on, since we are up in arms;
If not to fight with foreign enemies,
Yet to beat down these rebels here at home.

Re-enter CATESBY

Cate.   My liege, the Duke of Buckingham is taken,—
That is the best news: that the Earl of Richmond
Is with a mighty power landed at Milford,
Is colder tidings yet they must be told.
K. Rich.   Away towards Salisbury! while we reason here,
A royal battle might be won and lost:—
Some one take order Buckingham be brought
To Salisbury; the rest march on with me.

                               [*Flourish. Exeunt*

SCENE V.—LORD DERBY'S House

Enter STANLEY *and* SIR CHRISTOPHER URSWICK

Stan.   Sir Christopher, tell Richmond this from me:—
That in the sty of this most bloody boar
My son George Stanley is franked up in hold:
If I revolt, off goes young George's head;
The fear of that withholds my present aid.
But, tell me, where is princely Richmond now?
Chris.   At Pembroke, or at Ha'rford-west in Wales.
Stan.   What men of name resort to him?
Chris.   Sir Walter Herbert, a renownéd soldier;
Sir Gilbert Talbot and Sir William Stanley;
Oxford, redoubted Pembroke, Sir James Blunt,
And Rice ap Thomas, with a valiant crew;
And many more of noble fame and worth:
And towards London they do bend their course,
If by the way they be not fought withal.
Stan.   Return unto thy lord; commend me to him:
Tell him the Queen hath heartily consented
He shall espouse Elizabeth her daughter.
These letters will resolve him of my mind.   [*Giving letters*
Farewell.   [*Exeunt*

ACT FIVE

SCENE I.—Salisbury. An Open Place

Enter the Sheriff, and BUCKINGHAM, *with halberds, led to*
execution

Buck.   Will not King Richard let me speak with him?
Sher.   No, my good lord; therefore be patient.
Buck.   Hastings, and Edward's children, Rivers, Grey,
Holy King Henry, and thy fair son Edward,
Vaughan, and all that have miscarriéd
By underhand corrupted foul injustice,—
If that your moody discontented souls

Do through the clouds behold this present hour,
Even for revenge mock my destruction!—
This is All-Souls' day, fellows, is it not?
   Sher.   It is, my lord.
   Buck.   Why, then All-Souls' day is my body's doomsday.
This is the day that, in King Edward's time,
I wished might fall on me, when I was found
False to his children or his wife's allies;
This is the day wherein I wished to fall
By the false faith of him I trusted most;
This, this All-Souls' day to my fearful soul
Is the determined respite of my wrongs:
That high All-Seer that I dallied with
Hath turned my feignéd prayer on my head
And given in earnest what I begged in jest.
Thus doth he force the swords of wicked men
To turn their own points on their masters' bosoms:
Now Margaret's curse falls heavy on my neck,—
"When he," quoth she, "shall split thy heart with sorrow,
Remember Margaret was a prophetess."—
Come, sirs, convey me to the block of shame;
Wrong hath but wrong, and blame the due of blame.
                             [Exeunt

Scene II.—The Camp near Tamworth

Enter Richmond, Oxford, Sir James Blunt, Sir Walter
   Herbert, *and others, with Forces, marching*

   Richm.   Fellows in arms, and my most loving friends,
Bruised underneath the yoke of tyranny,
Thus far into the bowels of the land
Have we marched on without impediment;
And here receive we from our father Stanley
Lines of fair comfort and encouragement.
The wretched, bloody, and usurping boar,
That spoiled your summer fields and fruitful vines,
Swills your warm blood like wash, and makes his trough
In your embowelled bosoms, this foul swine
Lies now even in the centre of this isle,
Near to the town of Leicester, as we learn:
From Tamworth thither is but one day's march.
In God's name, cheerly on, courageous friends,
To reap the harvest of perpetual peace
By this one bloody trial of sharp war.
   Oxf.   Every man's conscience is a thousand swords,
To fight against this guilty homicide.
   Herb.   I doubt not but his friends will turn to us.
   Blunt.   He hath no friends but what are friends for fear,
Which in his dearest need will shrink from him.

Richm. All for our vantage. Then, in God's name, march:
True hope is swift and flies with swallow's wings:
Kings it makes gods, and meaner creatures kings.

[*Exeunt*

SCENE III.—Bosworth Field

Enter KING RICHARD, *and Forces, the* DUKE OF NORFOLK,
EARL OF SURREY, *and others*

  K. Rich. Here pitch our tents, even here in Bosworth
    field.—
My Lord of Surrey, why look you so sad?
  Sur. My heart is ten times lighter than my looks.
  K. Rich. My Lord of Norfolk,—
  Nor.   Here, most gracious liege.
  K. Rich. Norfolk, we must have knocks; ha! must we
    not?
  Nor. We must both give and take, my loving lord.
  K. Rich. Up with my tent! [*Soldiers begin to set up the
    King's tent.*] Here will I lie to-night;
But where to-morrow? Well, all 's one for that.
Who hath descried the number of the traitors?
  Nor. Six or seven thousand is their utmost power.
  K. Rich. Why, our battalia trebles that account:
Besides, the king's name is a tower of strength,
Which they upon the adverse party want.—
Up with the tent!—Come, noble gentlemen,
Let us survey the vantage of the ground;—
Call for some men of sound direction:—
Let's want no discipline, make no delay;
For, lords, to-morrow is a busy day.   [*Exeunt*

Enter, on the other side of the field, RICHMOND, SIR WILLIAM
BRANDON, OXFORD, *and others. Some of the Soldiers
pitch* RICHMOND'S *tent*

  Richm. The weary sun hath made a golden set,
And, by the bright track of his fiery car,
Gives token of a goodly day to-morrow.—
Sir William Brandon, you shall bear my standard.—
Give me some ink and paper in my tent:
I'll draw the form and model of our battle,
Limit each leader to his several charge,
And part in just proportion our small power.—
My Lord of Oxford,—you, Sir William Brandon,—
And you, Sir Walter Herbert,—stay with me.—
The Earl of Pembroke keeps his regiment:—
Good Captain Blunt, bear my good-night to him,
And by the second hour in the morning
Desire the earl to see me in my tent:
Yet one thing more, good captain, do for me,—

Where is Lord Stanley quartered, do you know?
   Blunt.   Unless I have mista'en his colours much,—
Which well I am assured I have not done,—
His regiment lies half a mile at least
South from the mighty power of the king.
   Richm.   If without peril it be possible,
Sweet Blunt, make some good means to speak with him,
And give him from me this most needful scroll.
   Blunt.   Upon my life, my lord I'll undertake it;
And so, God give you quiet rest to-night!
   Richm.   Good night, good Captain Blunt.   [*Exit Blunt*
       Come, gentlemen,
Let us consult upon to-morrow's business:
In to my tent; the air is raw and cold.
                    [*They withdraw into the tent*

     Re-enter, to his tent, KING RICHARD, NORFOLK,
       RATCLIFF, CATESBY, *and others*

   K. Rich.   What is 't o'clock?
   Cate.   It 's supper-time, my lord;
It 's nine o'clock.
   K. Rich.   I will not sup to-night.
Give me some ink and paper.
What, is my beaver easier than it was?
And all my armour laid into my tent?
   Cate.   It is, my liege; and all things are in readiness.
   K. Rich.   Good Norfolk, hie thee to thy charge;
Use careful watch; choose trusty sentinels.
   Nor.   I go, my lord.
   K. Rich.   Stir with the lark to-morrow, gentle Norfolk.
   Nor.   I warrant you, my lord.   [*Exit*
   K. Rich.   Catesby!
   Cate.   My lord?
   K. Rich.   Send out a pursuivant at arms
To Stanley's regiment; bid him bring his power
Before sunrising, lest his son George fall
Into the blind cave of eternal night.   [*Exit Catesby*
Fill me a bowl of wine.—Give me a watch.—
Saddle white Surrey for the field to-morrow.—
Look that my staves be sound, and not too heavy.—
Ratcliff,—
   Rat.   My lord?
   K. Rich.   Saw'st thou the melancholy Lord Northumber-
       land?
   Rat.   Thomas the Earl of Surrey, and himself,
Much about cock-shut time, from troop to troop
Went through the army, cheering up the soldiers.
   K. Rich.   So, I am satisfied.—Give me a bowl of wine:
I have not that alacrity of spirit,
Nor cheer of mind, that I was wont to have. [*Wine brought*

Set it down. Is ink and paper ready?
   Rat. It is, my lord.
   K. Rich. Bid my guard watch; leave me, Ratcliff,
About the mid of night come to my tent
And help to arm me.—Leave me, I say.
              [Exeunt Ratcliff and the other Attendants

Enter STANLEY *to* RICHMOND *in his tent, Lords and others attending*

   Stan. Fortune and victory sit on thy helm!
   Richm. All comfort that the dark night can afford
Be to thy person, noble father-in-law!
Tell me, how fares our loving mother?
   Stan. I, by attorney, bless thee from thy mother,
Who prays continually for Richmond's good:
So much for that.—The silent hours steal on,
And flaky darkness breaks within the east.
In brief,—for so the season bids us be,—
Prepare thy battle early in the morning,
And put thy fortune to the arbitrement
Of bloody strokes and mortal-staring war.
I, as I may—that which I would I cannot,—
With best advantage will deceive the time,
And aid thee in this doubtful shock of arms:
But on thy side I may not be too forward,
Lest, being seen, thy brother, tender George,
Be executed in his father's sight.
Farewell: the leisure and the fearful time
Cuts off the ceremonious vows of love
And ample interchange of sweet discourse,
Which so long sundered friends should dwell upon:
God give us leisure for these rites of love!
Once more, adieu: be valiant, and speed well!
   Richm. Good lords, conduct him to his regiment:
I 'll strive, with troubled thoughts, to take a nap,
Lest leaden slumber peise me down to-morrow
When I should mount with wings of victory:
Once more, good night, kind lords and gentlemen.
                   [Exeunt all but Richmond
O Thou, whose captain I account myself,
Look on my forces with a gracious eye;
Put in their hands thy bruising irons of wrath,
That they may crush down with a heavy fall
The usurping helmets of our adversaries!
Make us thy ministers of chastisement,
That we may praise Thee in the victory!
To Thee I do commend my watchful soul,
Ere I let fall the windows of mine eyes:
Sleeping and waking, O defend me still!   *[Sleeps*

The Ghost of PRINCE EDWARD, *son to* HENRY VI., *rises
between the two Tents*

Ghost of P. E. [*To Richard*] Let me sit heavy on thy
    soul to-morrow!
Think, how thou stabb'dst me in my prime of youth
At Tewksbury:—despair, therefore, and die!—
[*To Richmond*] Be cheerful, Richmond; for the wrongéd
    souls
Of butchered princes fight in thy behalf:
King Henry's issue, Richmond, comforts thee.

The Ghost of HENRY VI. *rises*

Ghost of K. H. [*To Richard*] When I was mortal, my
    anointed body
By thee was punchéd full of deadly holes:
Think on the Tower and me:—despair, and die!
Harry the Sixth bids thee despair and die!—
[*To Richmond*] Virtuous and holy, be thou conqueror!
Harry, that prophesied thou shouldst be king,
Doth comfort thee in sleep: live thou, and flourish!

The Ghost of CLARENCE *rises*

Ghost of C. [*To Richard*] Let me sit heavy on thy soul
    to-morrow,
I, that was washed to death with fulsome wine,
Poor Clarence, by thy guile betrayed to death!
To-morrow in the battle think on me,
And fall thy edgeless sword:—despair, and die!—
[*To Richmond*] Thou offspring of the house of Lancaster,
The wrongéd heirs of York do pray for thee:
Good angels guard thy battle! live and flourish!

The Ghosts of RIVERS, GREY, *and* VAUGHAN *rise*

Ghost of R. [*To Richard*] Let me sit heavy on thy soul
    to-morrow,
Rivers, that died at Pomfret!—despair, and die!
Ghost of G. [*To Richard*] Think upon Grey, and let thy
    soul despair!
Ghost of V. [*To Richard*] Think upon Vaughan, and,
    with guilty fear,
Let fall thy lance:—despair, and die!
All. [*To Richmond*] Awake, and think our wrongs in
    Richard's bosom
Will conquer him! awake, and win the day!

The Ghost of HASTINGS *rises*

Ghost of H. [*To Richard*] Bloody and guilty, guiltily
    awake,
And in a bloody battle end thy days!
Think on Lord Hastings: so despair, and die!—
[*To Richmond*] Quiet untroubled soul, awake, awake!

Arm, fight, and conquer, for fair England's sake!

The Ghosts of the two young Princes rise

Ghosts of the two P. [*To Richard*] Dream on thy cousins
    smothered in the Tower:
Let us be lead within thy bosom, Richard,
And weigh thee down to ruin, shame, and death!
Thy nephews' souls bid thee despair and die:—
[*To Richmond*] Sleep, Richmond, sleep in peace, and wake
    in joy;
Good angels guard thee from the boar's annoy!
Live, and beget a happy race of kings!
Edward's unhappy sons do bid thee flourish.

The Ghost of QUEEN ANNE *rises*

Ghost of Q. A. [*To Richard*] Richard, thy wife, that
    wretched Anne thy wife,
That never slept a quiet hour with thee,
Now fills thy sleep with perturbations:
To-morrow in the battle think on me,
And fall thy edgeless sword:—despair, and die!
[*To Richmond*] Thou quiet soul, sleep thou a quiet sleep;
Dream of success and happy victory!
Thy adversary's wife doth pray for thee.

The Ghost of BUCKINGHAM *rises*

Ghost of B. [*To Richard*] The first was I that helped
    thee to the crown;
The last was I that felt thy tyranny:
O, in the battle think on Buckingham,
And die in terror of thy guiltiness!
Dream on, dream on, of bloody deeds and death:
Fainting, despair; despairing, yield thy breath!—
[*To Richmond*] I died for hope ere I could lend thee aid:
But cheer thy heart, and be thou not dismayed:
God and good angels fight on Richmond's side;
And Richard falls in height of all his pride.

The Ghosts vanish.   KING RICHARD *starts out of his dream*

K. Rich.   Give me another horse,—bind up my wounds,—
Have mercy, Jesu!—Soft! I did but dream.—
O coward conscience, how dost thou afflict me!—
The lights burn blue.—It is now dead midnight.
Cold fearful drops stand on my trembling flesh.
What do I fear? Myself? There 's none else by:
Richard loves Richard; that is, I am I.
Is there a murderer here? No;—Yes; I am,
Then fly. What, from myself? Great reason why,—
Lest I revenge myself upon myself.
Alack, I love myself. Wherefore? for any good
That I myself have done unto myself?

O, no! alas, I rather hate myself
For hateful deeds committed by myself!
I am a villain: yet I lie, I am not.
Fool, of thyself speak well:—fool, do not flatter.
My conscience hath a thousand several tongues,
And every tongue brings in a several tale,
And every talk condemns me for a villain.
Perjury, perjury, in the high'st degree;
Murder, stern murder, in the dir'st degree;
All several sins, all used in each degree,
Throng to the bar, crying all,—"Guilty! guilty!"—
I shall despair.   There is no creature loves me;
And if I die, no soul shall pity me:
Nay, wherefore should they, since that I myself
Find in myself no pity to myself?

Re-enter RATCLIFF

   Rat. My lord,—
   K. Rich. Who's there?
   Rat. My lord, 't is I.   The early village-cock
Hath twice done salutation to the morn;
Your friends are up, and buckle on their armour.
   K. Rich. O Ratcliff, I have dreamed a fearful dream!
What thinkest thou,—will our friends prove all true?
   Rat. No doubt, my lord.
   K. Rich.   O Ratcliff, I fear, I fear,—
Methought the souls of all that I had murdered
Came to my tent, and every one did threat
To-morrow's vengeance on the head of Richard.
   Rat. Nay, good my lord, be not afraid of shadows.
   K. Rich. By the apostle Paul, shadows to-night
Have struck more terror to the soul of Richard
Than can the substance of ten thousand soldiers
Arméd in proof, and led by shallow Richmond.
It is not yet near day.   Come, go with me;
Under our tents I 'll play the eaves-dropper,
To see if any mean to shrink from me.   [*Exeunt*

Enter the Lords to RICHMOND, sitting in his tent

   Lords. Good morrow, Richmond!
   Richm. Cry mercy, lords and watchful gentlemen,
That you have ta'en a tardy sluggard here.
   Lords. How have you slept, my lord?
   Richm. The sweetest sleep, and fairest-boding dreams
That ever entered in a drowsy head,
Have I since your departure had, my lords.
Methought their souls, whose bodies Richard murdered,
Came to my tent, and cried on victory:
I promise you, my soul is very jocund
In the remembrance of so fair a dream.
How far into the morning is it, lords?

Lords.   Upon the stroke of four.
Richm.   Why, then 't is time to arm and give direc-
        tion.   [*He advances to the troops*
More than I have said, loving countrymen,
The leisure and enforcement of the time
Forbids to dwell on: yet remember this—
God and our good cause fight upon our side;
The prayers of holy saints and wrongéd souls,
Like high-reared bulwarks, stand before our faces;
Richard except, those whom we fight against
Had rather have us win than him they follow.
For what is he they follow? truly, gentlemen,
A bloody tyrant and a homicide;
One raised in blood, and one in blood established;
One that made means to come by what he hath,
And slaughtered those that were the means to help him;
A base foul stone, made precious by the foil
Of England's chair, where he is false set;
One that hath ever been God's enemy:
Then, if you fight against God's enemy,
God will in justice ward you as His soldiers;
If you do sweat to put a tryant down,
You sleep in peace, the tyrant being slain;
If you do fight against your country's foes,
Your country's fat shall pay your pains the hire;
If you do fight in safeguard of your wives,
Your wives shall welcome home the conquerors;
If you do free your children from the sword,
Your children's children quit it in your age
Then, in the name of God and all these rights,
Advance your standards, draw your willing swords.
For me, the ransom of my bold attempt
Shall be this cold corpse on the earth's cold face;
But if I thrive, the gain of my attempt
The least of you shall share his part thereof.
Sound drums and trumpets, boldly, cheerfully;
God and Saint George!   Richmond and victory!   [*Exeunt*

Re-enter KING RICHARD, RATCLIFF, *Attendants and*
Forces

K. Rich.   What said Northumberland as touching
        Richmond?
Rat.   That he was never trainéd up in arms,
K. Rich.   He said the truth: and what said Surrey then?
Rat.   He smiled and said, "The better for our purpose."
K. Rich.   He was in the right; and so indeed it is.
                                        [*Clock striketh*
Tell the clock there.—Give me a calendar.—
Who saw the sun to-day?
Rat.   Not I, my lord.

K. Rich.   Then he disdains to shine; for by the book
He should have braved the east an hour ago:
A black day will it be for somebody.—
Ratcliff,—
   Rat.   My lord?
   K. Rich.   The sun will not be seen to-day;
The sky doth frown and lour upon our army.
I would these dewy tears were from the ground.
Not shine to-day! Why, what is that to me
More than to Richmond? for the selfsame heaven
That frowns on me looks sadly upon him.

Enter NORFOLK

   Nor.   Arm, arm, my lord; the foe vaunts in the field.
   K. Rich.   Come, bustle, bustle;—caparison my horse.—
Call up Lord Stanley, bid him bring his power:
I will lead forth my soldiers to the plain,
And thus my battle shall be orderéd:
My foreword shall be drawn out all in length,
Consisting equally of horse and foot;
Our archers shall be placéd in the midst:
John Duke of Norfolk, Thomas Earl of Surrey,
Shall have the leading of this foot and horse.
They thus directed, we ourself will follow
In the main battle, that on either side
Shall be well wingéd with our chiefest horse.
This, and Saint George to boot!—What think'st thou,
               Norfolk?
   Nor.   A good direction, warlike sovereign.—
This found I on my tent this morning.   [*Giving a scroll*
   K. Rich. [*Reads*] "Jockey of Norfolk, be not too bold,
For Dickon thy master is bought and sold."
A thing deviséd by the enemy.
Go, gentlemen, every man unto his charge:
Let not our babbling dreams affright our souls:
Conscience is but a word that cowards use,
Devised at first to keep the strong in awe:
Our strong arms be our conscience, swords our law.
March on, join bravely, let us to 't pell-mell:
If not to heaven, then hand in hand to hell.—
[*To his soldiers*] What shall I say more than I have inferred?
Remember whom you are to cope withal;—
A sort of vagabonds, rascals, runaways,
A scum of Bretons and base lackey peasants
Whom their o'ercloyéd country vomits forth
To desperate ventures and assured destruction.
You sleeping safe, they bring to you unrest;
You having lands, and blest with beauteous wives,
They would distrain the one, distain the other.
And who doth lead them but a paltry fellow,

156

Long kept in Bretagne at our mother's cost?
A milk-sop, one that never in his life
Felt so much cold as over shoes in snow?
Let 's whip these stragglers o'er the seas again;
Lash hence these overweenming rags of France,
These famished beggars, weary of their lives,
Who, but for dreaming on this fond exploit,
For want of means, poor rats, had hanged themselves.
If we be conquered, let men conquer us,
And not these bastard Bretons; whom our fathers
Have in their own land beaten, bobbed, and thumped,
And on record, left them heirs of shame.
Shall these enjoy our lands? lie with our wives?
Ravish our daughters?—[*Drum afar off*] Hark! I hear
            their drum.—
Fight, gentlemen of England! fight, bold yeomen!
Draw, archers, draw your arrows to the head!
Spur your proud horses hard, and ride in blood;
Amaze the welkin with your broken staves!

Enter a Messenger

What says Lord Stanley? will he bring his power?
  Mess. My lord, he doth deny to come.
  K. Rich. Off with his son George's head!
  Nor. My lord, the enemy is past the marsh:
After the battle let George Stanley die.
  K. Rich. A thousand hearts are great within my bosom:
Advance our standards, set upon our foes;
Our ancient word of courage, fair St. George,
Inspire us with the spleen of fiery dragons!
Upon them! Victory sits on our helms.   [*Exeunt*

SCENE IV.—Another Part of the Field

Alarum: excursions. Enter NORFOLK *and Forces fighting;*
to him CATESBY

  Cate. Rescue, my Lord of Norfolk, rescue, rescue!
The king enacts more wonders than a man,
Daring an opposite to every danger:
His horse is slain, and all on foot he fights,
Seeking for Richmond in the throat of death.
Rescue, fair lord, or else the day is lost!

Alarums. Enter KING RICHARD

  K. Rich. A horse! a horse! my kingdom for a horse!
  Cate. Withdraw, my lord; I 'll help you to a horse.
  K. Rich. Slave, I have set my life upon a cast,
And I will stand the hazard of the die:
I think there be six Richmonds in the field;

Five have I slain to-day instead of him.
A horse! a horse! my kingdom for a horse!   [*Exeunt*

SCENE V.—Another Part of the Field

Alarum. Enter RICHARD *and* RICHMOND ; *they fight.*
RICHARD *is slain. Retreat and flourish. Re-enter*
RICHMOND, STANLEY *bearing the crown, with divers
other Lords, and Forces*

   Richm.   God and your arms be praised, victorious friends;
The day is ours; the bloody dog is dead.
   Stan.   Courageous Richmond, well hast thou acquit thee.
Lo, here, this long-usurpéd royalty
From the dead temples of this bloody wretch
Have I plucked off, to grace thy brows withal:
Wear it, enjoy it, and make much of it.
   Richm.   Great God of heaven, say Amen to all!
But, tell me now, is young George Stanley living?
   Stan.   He is, my lord, and safe in Leicester town;
Whither, if it please you, we may now withdraw us.
   Richm.   What men of name are slain on either side?
   Stan.   John Duke of Norfolk, Walter Lord Ferrers,
Sir Robert Brakenbury, and Sir William Brandon.
   Richm.   Inter their bodies as becomes their births:
Proclaim a pardon to the soldiers fled
That in submission will return to us:
And then, as we have ta'en the sacrament,
We will unite the White Rose and the Red:
Smile heaven upon this fair conjunction,
That long hath frowned upon their enmity!
What traitor hears me, and says not Amen?
England hath long been mad, and scarred herself;
The brother blindly shed the brother's blood,
The father rashly slaughtered his own son,
The son, compelled, been butcher to the sire:
All this divided York and Lancaster,
Divided in their dire division,
O, now, let Richmond and Elizabeth,
The true succeeders of each royal house,
By God's fair ordinance conjoin together!
And let their heirs,—God, if Thy will be so,—
Enrich the time to come with smooth-faced peace,
With smiling plenty and fair prosperous days!
Abate the edge of traitors, gracious Lord,
That would reduce these bloody days again,
And make poor England weep in streams of blood!
Let them not live to taste this land's increase
That would with treason wound this fair land's peace!
Now civil wounds are stopped, peace lives again:
That she may long live here, God say Amen!   [*Exeunt*

LOVE'S LABOUR'S LOST

DRAMATIS PERSONÆ

FERDINAND, *King of Navarre*

BIRON

LONGAVILLE } *lords attending on the King*

DUMAIN

BOYET

MERCADET } *lords attending on the Princess of France*

DON ADRIANO DE ARMADO, *a fantastical Spaniard*

SIR NATHANIEL, *a curate*

HOLOFERNES, *a schoolmaster*

DULL, *a constable*

COSTARD, *a clown*

MOTH, *page to Armado*

A Forester

PRINCESS OF FRANCE

ROSALINE

MARIA } *ladies attending on the Princess*

KATHARINE

JAQUENETTA, *a country wench*

Officers and others, Attendants on the King and Princess

SCENE.—*Navarre*

LOVE'S LABOUR'S LOST

ACT ONE

Scene I.—Navarre. A Park, with a Palace in it

Enter the King, Biron, Longaville, *and* Dumain

King. Let fame, that all hunt after in their lives,
Live registered upon our brazen tombs,
And then grace us in the disgrace of death;
When, spite of cormorant devouring Time,
The endeavour of this present breath may buy
That honour which shall bate his scythe's keen edge,
And make us heirs of all eternity.
Therefore, brave conquerors,—for so you are,
That war against your own affections,
And the huge army of the world's desires,—
Our late edict shall strongly stand in force:
Navarre shall be the wonder of the world;
Our court shall be a little Academe,
Still and contemplative in living art.
You three, Biron, Dumain, and Longaville,
Have sworn for three years' term to live with me,
My fellow-scholars, and to keep those statutes
That are recorded in this schedule here:
Your oaths are passed; and now subscribe your names,
That his own hand may strike his honour down
That violates the smallest branch herein:
If you are armed to do as sworn to do,
Subscribe to your deep oaths, and keep it too.
Long. I am resolved: 't is but a three years' fast:
The mind shall banquet, though the body pine:
Fat paunches have lean pates; and dainty bits
Make rich the ribs, but bankrupt quite the wits.
Dum. My loving lord, Dumain is mortified:
The grosser manner of these world's delights
He throws upon the gross world's baser slaves:
To love, to wealth, to pomp, I pine and die;
With all these living in philosophy.
Biron. I can but say their protestation over:
So much, dear liege, I have already sworn,
That is, to live and study here three years.
But there are other strict observances:
As, not to see a woman in that term,—
Which, I hope well, is not enrolléd there:

And, one day in a week to touch no food,
And but one meal on every day beside,—
The which, I hope, is not enrollèd there;
And then, to sleep but three hours in the night,
And not be seen to wink of all the day,—
When I was wont to think no harm all night,
And make a dark night too of half the day,—
Which, I hope well, is not enrollèd there.
O, these are barren tasks, too hard to keep,—
Not to see ladies, study, fast, not sleep.
 King. Your oath is passed to pass away from these.
 Biron. Let me say no, my liege, an if you please:
I only swore to study with your grace,
And stay here in your court for three years' space.
 Long. You swore to that, Birón, and to the rest.
 Biron. By yea and nay, sir, then I swore in jest.—
What is the end of study? let me know.
 King. Why, that to know which else we should not know.
 Biron. Things hid and barred, you mean, from common
  sense?
 King. Ay, that is study's god-like recompense.
 Biron. Come on, then; I will swear to study so,
To know the thing I am forbid to know;
As thus,—to study where I well may dine,
 When I to feast expressly am forbid;
Or study where to meet some mistress fine,
 When mistresses from common sense are hid;
Or, having sworn too hard-a-keeping oath,
Study to break it, and not break my troth.
If study's gain be thus, and this be so,
Study knows that which yet it doth not know.
Swear me to this, and I will ne'er say no.
 King. These be the stops that hinder study quite,
And train our intellects to vain delight.
 Biron. Why, all delights are vain; but that most vain,
Which, with pain purchased, doth inherit pain;
As, painfully to pore upon a book,
 To seek the light of truth; while truth the while
Doth falsely blind the eyesight of his look.
 Light, seeking light, doth light of light beguile:
So, ere you find where light in darkness lies,
Your light grows dark by losing of your eyes.
Study me how to please the eye indeed,
 By fixing it upon a fairer eye;
Who dazzling so, that eye shall be his heed,
 And give him light that it was blinded by.
Study is like the heaven's glorious sun,
 That will not be deep-searched with saucy looks:
Small have continual plodders ever won,
 Save base authority from others' books.

These earthly godfathers of heaven's lights
    That give a name to every fixéd star,
Have no more profit of their shining nights
    Than those that walk and wot not what they are.
Too much to know is to know nought but fame;
And every godfather can give a name.

   King.   How well he 's read, to reason against reading!
   Dum.   Proceeded well, to stop all good proceeding!
   Long.   He weeds the corn, and still lets grow the weeding.
   Biron.   The spring is near, when green geese are a-
breeding.
   Dum.   How follows that?
   Biron.   Fit in his place and time.
   Dum.   In reason nothing.
   Biron.   Something then in rhyme.
   King.   Birón is like an envious sneaping frost,
That bites the first-born infants of the spring.
   Biron.   Well, say I am: why should proud summer boast,
Before the birds have any cause to sing?
Why should I joy in an abortive birth?
    At Christmas I no more desire a rose,
Than wish a snow in May's new-fangled shows;
But like of each thing that in season grows.
So you, to study now it is too late,
Climb o'er the house to unlock the little gate.
   King.   Well, sit you out; go home, Birón: adieu!
   Biron.   No, my good lord; I have sworn to stay with
         you:
And, though I have for barbarism spoke more
    Than for that angel knowledge you can say,
Yet confident I 'll keep what I have swore,
    And bide the penance of each three years' day.
Give me the paper: let me read the same;
And to the strict'st decrees I 'll write my name.
   King.   How well this yielding rescues thee from shame!
   Biron.   [*Reads*] "*Item, That no woman shall come
within a mile of my court.*"—Hath this been proclaimed?
   Long.   Four days ago.
   Biron.   Let 's see the penalty. [*Reads*] "*On pain of
losing her tongue.*"—Who devised this penalty?
   Long.   Marry, that did I.
   Biron.   Sweet lord, and why?
   Long.   To fright them hence with that dread penalty.
   Biron.   A dangerous law against gentility! [*Reads*] "*Item,
If any man be seen to talk with a woman within the term of
three years, he shall endure such public shame as the rest
of the court can possibly devise.*"—
This article, my liege, yourself must break;
    For, well you know, here comes in embassy
The French king's daughter with yourself to speak,—

A maid of grace, and complete majesty,—
About surrender-up of Aquitain
   To her decrepit, sick, and bed-rid father:
Therefore, this article is made in vain,
   Or vainly comes the admiréd princess hither.
   King. What say you, lords? why, this was quite forgot.
   Biron. So study evermore is overshot:
While it doth study to have what it would,
It doth forget to do the thing it should;
And when it hath the thing it hunteth most,
'T is won as towns with fire,—so won, so lost.
   King. We must of force dispense with this decree:
She must lie here on mere necessity.
   Biron. Necessity will make us all forsworn
   Three thousand times within this three years' space;
For every man with his affects is born,
   Not by might mastered, but by special grace.
If I break faith, this word shall speak for me,
I am forsworn on mere necessity.—
So to the laws at large I write my name;   [*Subscribes*
   And he that breaks them in the least degree,
Stands in attainder of eternal shame.
   Suggestions are to others as to me;
But, I believe, although I seem so loath,
I am the last that will last keep his oath.
But is there no quick recreation granted?
   King. Ay, that there is. Our court, you know, is haunted
   With a refinéd traveller of Spain;
A man in all the world's new fashion planted,
   That hath a mint of phrases in his brain,
One, whom the music of his own vain tongue
   Doth ravish like enchanting harmony:
A man of compliments, whom right and wrong
   Have chose as umpire of their mutiny:
This child of fancy, that Armado hight,
   For interim to our studies, shall relate
In high-born words the worth of many a knight
   From tawny Spain, lost in the world's debate.
How you delight, my lords, I know not, I;
But, I protest, I love to hear him lie,
And I will use him for my minstrelsy.
   Biron. Armado is a most illustrious wight,
A man of fire-new words, fashion's own knight.
   Long. Costard, the swain, and he shall be our sport;
And so to study, three years is but short.

Enter DULL, *with a letter, and* COSTARD

   Dull. Which is the duke's own person?
   Biron. This, fellow. What wouldst?
   Dull. I myself reprehend his own person, for I am his

164

grace's tharborough: but I would see his own person in flesh and blood.

Biron. This is he.

Dull. Signior Arm—Arm—commends you. There 's villainy abroad: this letter will tell you more.

Cost. Sir, the contempts thereof are as touching me.

King. A letter from the magnificent Armado.

Biron. How low soever the matter, I hope in God for high words.

Long. A high hope of a low heaven: God grant us patience!

Biron. To hear? or forbear laughing?

Long. To hear meekly, sir, and to laugh moderately; or to forbear both.

Biron. Well, sir, be it as the style shall give us cause to climb in the merriness.

Cost. The matter is to me, sir, as concerning Jaquenetta. The manner of it is, I was taken with the manner.

Biron. In what manner?

Cost. In manner and form following, sir; all those three: I was seen with her in the manor-house, sitting with her upon the form, and taken following her into the park; which, put together, is in manner and form following. Now, sir, for the manner,—it is the manner of a man to speak to a woman; for the form,—in some form.

Biron. For the following, sir?

Cost. As it shall follow in my correction: and God defend the right!

King. Will you hear this letter with attention?

Biron. As we would hear an oracle.

Cost. Such is the simplicity of man to hearken after the flesh.

King. [*Reads*] "*Great deputy, the welkin's vicegerent, and sole dominator of Navarre, my souls' earth's God, and body's fostering patron,*"—

Cost. Not a word of Costard yet.

King. "*So it is,*"—

Cost. It may be so; but if he say it is so, he is in telling true, but so.—

King. Peace!

Cost. —be to me, and every man that dares not fight.

King. No words!

Cost. —of other men's secrets, I beseech you.

King. "*So it is, besieged with sable-coloured melancholy, I did commend the black-oppressing humour to the most wholesome physic of thy health-giving air; and, as I am a gentleman, betook myself to walk. The time when? About the sixth hour; when beasts most graze, birds best peck, and men sit down to that nourishment which is called supper. So much for the time when. Now for the ground*

*which ; which, I mean, I walked upon : it is ycleped thy
park.   Then for the place where ; where, I mean, I did
encounter that obscene and most preposterous event, that
draweth from my snow-white pen the ebon-coloured ink,
which here thou viewest, beholdest, surveyest, or seest.   But
to the place where ;—it standeth north-north-east and by east
from the west corner of thy curious-knotted garden : there
did I see that low-spirited swain, that base minnow of thy
mirth,"—*

Cost.   Me.

King.   —*"that unlettered small-knowing soul,"*—

Cost.   Me.

King.   —*"that shallow vassal,"*—

Cost.   Still me.

King.   —*"which, as I remember, hight Costard,"*—

Cost.   O, me.

King.   —*"sorted and consorted, contrary to thy established proclaimed edict and continent canon, with—with—
O ! with—but with this I passion to say wherewith,"*—

Cost.   With a wench.

King.   —*"with a child of our grandmother Eve, a female ;
or, for thy more sweet understanding, a woman.   Him I
(as my ever-esteemed duty pricks me on) have sent to thee,
to receive the meed of punishment, by thy sweet grace's officer,
Antony Dull, a man of good repute, carriage-bearing, and
estimation."*

Dull.   Me, an 't shall please you: I am Antony Dull.

King.   —*"For Jaquenetta (so is the weaker vessel called),
which I apprehended with the aforesaid swain, I keep her
as a vessel of thy law's fury ; and shall, at the least of thy
sweet notice, bring her to trial.   Thine, in all compliments
of devoted and heart-burning heat of duty,* Don Adriano
de Armado."

Biron.   This is not so well as I looked for, but the best
that ever I heard.

King.   Ay, the best for the worst.—But, sirrah, what
say you to this?

Cost.   Sir, I confess the wench.

King.   Did you hear the proclamation?

Cost.   I do confess much of the hearing it, but little of
the marking of it.

King.   It was proclaimed a year's imprisonment, to be
taken with a wench.

Cost.   I was taken with none, sir: I was taken with a
damosel.

King.   Well, it was proclaimed damosel.

Cost.   This was no damosel neither, sir: she was a virgin.

King.   It is so varied too, for it was proclaimed virgin.

Cost.   If it were, I deny her virginity: I was taken with
a maid.

King. This maid will not serve your turn, sir.

Cost. This maid will serve my turn, sir.

King. Sir, I will pronounce your sentence: you shall fast a week with bran and water.

Cost. I had rather pray a month with mutton and porridge.

King. And Don Armado shall be your keeper.—
My Lord Biron, see him delivered o'er:
And go we, lords, to put in practice that
Which each to other hath so strongly sworn.

[Exeunt King, Longaville, and Dumain

Biron. I 'll lay my head to any good man's hat
These oaths and laws will prove an idle scorn.—
Sirrah, come on.

Cost. I suffer for the truth, sir: for true it is, I was taken with Jaquenetta, and Jaquenetta is a true girl; and therefore, welcome the sour cup of prosperity! Affliction may one day smile again, and till then, sit thee down, sorrow!   [*Exeunt*

Scene II.—Armado's House in the Park

Enter Armado *and* Moth

Arm. Boy, what sign is it, when a man of great spirit grows melancholy?

Moth. A great sign, sir, that he will look sad.

Arm. Why, sadness is one and the selfsame thing, dear imp.

Moth. No, no; O Lord, sir, no.

Arm. How canst thou part sadness and melancholy, my tender juvenal?

Moth. By a familiar demonstration of the working, my tough senior.

Arm. Why tough senior? why tough senior?

Moth. Why tender juvenal? why tender juvenal?

Arm. I spoke it, tender juvenal, as a congruent epitheton appertaining to thy young days, which we may nominate tender.

Moth. And I, tough senior, as an appertinent title to your old time, which we may name tough.

Arm. Pretty, and apt.

Moth. How mean you, sir? I pretty, and my saying apt? or I apt, and my saying pretty?

Arm. Thou pretty, because little.

Moth. Little pretty, because little. Wherefore apt?

Arm. And therefore apt, because quick.

Moth. Speak you this in my praise, master?

Arm. In thy condign praise.

Moth. I will praise an eel with the same praise.

Arm. What, that an eel is ingenious?

Moth. That an eel is quick.

Arm. I do say, thou art quick in answers. Thou heatest my blood.

Moth. I am answered, sir.

Arm. I love not to be crossed.

Moth. [*Aside*] He speaks the mere contrary: crosses love not him.

Arm. I have promised to study three years with the duke.

Moth. You may do it in an hour, sir.

Arm. Impossible.

Moth. How many is one thrice told?

Arm. I am ill at reckoning: it fitteth the spirit of a tapster.

Moth. You are a gentleman and a gamester, sir.

Arm. I confess both: they are both the varnish of a complete man.

Moth. Then, I am sure, you know how much the gross sum of deuce-ace amounts to.

Arm. It doth amount to one more than two.

Moth. Which the base vulgar do call three.

Arm. True.

Moth. Why, sir, is this such a piece of study? Now, here is three studied, ere you 'll thrice wink; and how easy it is to put years to the word three, and study three years in two words, the dancing horse will tell you.

Arm. A most fine figure!

Moth. [*Aside*] To prove you a cypher.

Arm. I will hereupon confess I am in love; and, as it is base for a soldier to love, so am I in love with a base wench. If drawing my sword against the humour of affection would deliver me from the reprobate thought of it, I would take Desire prisoner, and ransom him to any French courtier for a new-devised courtesy. I think scorn to sigh: methinks, I should outswear Cupid. Comfort me, boy. What great men have been in love?

Moth. Hercules, master.

Arm. Most sweet Hercules!—More authority, dear boy, name more; and, sweet my child, let them be men of good repute and carriage.

Moth. Samson, master: he was a man of good carriage, great carriage, for he carried the town-gates on his back like a porter: and he was in love.

Arm. O well-knit Samson! strong-jointed Samson! I do excel thee in my rapier as much as thou didst me in carrying gates. I am in love too. Who was Samson's love, my dear Moth?

Moth. A woman, master.

Arm. Of what complexion?

Moth. Of all the four, or the three, or the two, or one of the four.

Arm. Tell me precisely of what complexion.

Moth. Of the sea-water green, sir.

Arm. Is that one of the four complexions?

Moth. As I have read, sir; and the best of them too.

Arm. Green, indeed, is the colour of lovers; but to have a love of that colour, methinks Samson had small reason for it. He, surely, affected her for her wit.

Moth. It was so, sir; for she had a green wit.

Arm. My love is most immaculate white and red.

Moth. Most maculate thoughts, master, are masked under such colours.

Arm. Define, define, well-educated infant.

Moth. My father's wit and my mother's tongue assist me!

Arm. Sweet invocation of a child; most pretty, and pathetical!

Moth.   If she be made of white and red,
               Her faults will ne'er be known;
          For blushing cheeks by faults are bred,
               And fears by pale-white shown:
          Then, if she fear, or be to blame,
               By this you shall not know;
          For still her cheeks possess the same,
               Which native she doth owe.

A dangerous rhyme, master, against the reason of white and red.

Arm. Is there not a ballad, boy, of the King and the Beggar?

Moth. The world was very guilty of such a ballad some three ages since; but I think, now 't is not to be found; or, if it were, it would neither serve for the writing nor the tune.

Arm. I will have that subject newly writ o'er, that I may example my digression by some mighty precedent. Boy, I do love that country girl that I took in the park with the rational hind Costard: she deserves well.

Moth. [*Aside*] To be whipped; and yet a better love than my master.

Arm. Sing, boy; my spirit grows heavy in love.

Moth. And that 's great marvel, loving a light wench.

Arm. I say, sing.

Moth. Forbear till this company be past.

Enter DULL, COSTARD, *and* JAQUENETTA

Dull. Sir, the duke's pleasure is, that you keep Costard safe: and you must let him take no delight nor no penance; but 'a must fast three days a week. For this damsel, I must keep her at the park; she is allowed for the day woman. Fare you well.

Arm. I do betray myself with blushing.—Maid,—

Jaq. Man.

Arm. I will visit thee at the lodge.

Jaq. That 's hereby.

Arm. I know where it is situate.

Jaq. Lord, how wise you are!

Arm. I will tell thee wonders.

Jaq. With that face?

Arm. I love thee.

Jaq. So I heard you say.

Arm. And so farewell.

Jaq. Fair weather after you!

Dull. Come, Jaquenetta, away.

                          [*Exeunt Dull and Jaquenetta*

Arm. Villain, thou shalt fast for thy offences, ere thou be pardoned.

Cost. Well, sir, I hope, when I do it, I shall do it on a full stomach.

Arm. Thou shalt be heavily punished.

Cost. I am more bound to you than your fellows, for they are but lightly rewarded.

Arm. Take away this villain; shut him up.

Moth. Come, you transgressing slave; away!

Cost. Let me not be pent up, sir: I will fast, being loose.

Moth. No, sir; that were fast and loose: thou shalt to prison.

Cost. Well, if ever I do see the merry days of desolation that I have seen, some shall see—

Moth. What shall some see?

Cost. Nay, nothing, Master Moth, but what they look upon. It is not for prisoners to be too silent in their words; and therefore I will say nothing: I thank God I have as little patience as another man; and therefore I can be quiet.   [*Exeunt Moth and Costard*

Arm. I do affect the very ground, which is base, where her shoe, which is baser, guided by her foot, which is basest, doth tread. I shall be forsworn—which is a great argument of falsehood—if I love. And how can that be true love which is falsely attempted? Love is a familiar; Love is a devil: there is no evil angel but Love. Yet was Samson so tempted, and he had an excellent strength: yet was Solomon so seduced, and he had a very good wit. Cupid's butt-shaft is too hard for Hercules' club; and therefore too much odds for a Spaniard's rapier. The first and second cause will not serve my turn; the passado he respects not, the duello he regards not: his disgrace is to be called boy; but his glory is to subdue men. Adieu, valour! rust, rapier! be still, drum! for your manager is in love; yea, he loveth. Assist me some extemporal god of rhyme, for I am sure I shall turn sonnet. Devise, wit,—write, pen; for I am for whole volumes in folio.   [*Exit*

ACT TWO

SCENE I.—Outside the Park. A Pavilion and Tents

Enter the PRINCESS OF FRANCE, ROSALINE, MARIA, KATHARINE, BOYET, *Lords, and other Attendants*

Boyet. Now, madam, summon up your dearest spirits:
Consider who the king your father sends;
To whom he sends, and what 's his embassy:
Yourself, held precious in the world's esteem,
To parley with the sole inheritor
Of all perfections that a man may owe,
Matchless Navarre; the plea of no less weight
Than Aquitain,—a dowry for a queen.
Be now as prodigal of all dear grace,
As Nature was in making graces dear
When she did starve the general world beside
And prodigally gave them all to you.
Prin. Good Lord Boyet, my beauty, though but mean,
Needs not the painted flourish of your praise:
Beauty is bought by judgment of the eye,
Not uttered by base sale of chapmen's tongues.
I am less proud to hear you tell my worth
Than you much willing to be counted wise
In spending your wit in the praise of mine.
But now to task the tasker: Good Boyet,
You are not ignorant, all-telling fame
Doth noise abroad, Navarre hath made a vow,
Till painful study shall outwear three years
No woman may approach his silent court:
Therefore to 's seemeth it a needful course,
Before we enter his forbidden gates,
To know his pleasure; and in that behalf,
Bold of your worthiness, we single you
As our best-moving fair solicitor.
Tell him, the daughter of the King of France,
On serious business craving quick despatch,
Impórtunes personal conference with his grace.
Haste, signify so much; while we attend,
Like humble-visaged suitors, his high will.
Boyet. Proud of employment, willingly I go.
Prin. All pride is willing pride, and yours is so.—

                         [*Exit Boyet*

Who are the votaries, my loving lords,
That are vow-fellows with this virtuous duke?
First Lord. Longaville is one.
Prin.   Know you the man?
Mar. I know him, madam: at a marriage-feast

Between Lord Perigort and the beauteous heir
Of Jaques Falconbridge solemniséd
In Normandy, saw I this Longaville.
A man of sovereign parts he is esteemed;
Well fitted in the arts, glorious in arms:
Nothing becomes him ill that he would well.
The only soil of his fair virtue's gloss,
If virtue's gloss still stain with any soil,
Is a sharp wit matched with too blunt a will;
Whose edge hath power to cut, whose will still wills
It should none spare that come within his power.
 Prin. Some merry mocking lord, belike; is 't so?
 Mar. They say so most that most his humours know.
 Prin. Such short-lived wits do wither as they grow.
Who are the rest?
 Kath. The young Dumain, a well-accomplished youth,
Of all that virtue love for virtue loved:
Most power to do most harm, least knowing ill,
For he hath wit to make an ill shape good,
And shape to win grace though he had no wit.
I saw him at the Duke Alençon's once;
And much too little of that good I saw
Is my report to his great worthiness.
 Ros. Another of these students at that time
Was there with him: if I have heard a truth,
Birón they call him; but a merrier man,
Within the limit of becoming mirth,
I never spent an hour's talk withal.
His eye begets occasion for his wit;
For every object that the one doth catch,
The other turns to a mirth-moving jest,
Which his fair tongue, conceit's expositor,
Delivers in such apt and gracious words,
That agéd ears play truant at his tales,
And younger hearings are quite ravishéd,
So sweet and voluble is his discourse.
 Prin. God bless my ladies! are they all in love,
That every one her own hath garnishéd
With such bedecking ornaments of praise?
 Lord. Here comes Boyet.

Re-enter BOYET

 Prin.   Now, what admittance, lord?
 Boyet. Navarre had notice of your fair approach;
And he and his competitors in oath
Were all addressed to meet you, gentle lady
Before I came. Marry, thus much I have learnt,
He rather means to lodge you in the field
Like one that comes here to besiege his court,
Than seek a dispensation for his oath,

To let you enter his unpeopled house.
Here comes Navarre.   *[The Ladies mask*

Enter KING, LONGAVILLE, DUMAIN, BIRON, *and Attendants*

King.   Fair princess, welcome to the court of Navarre.
Prin.   "Fair," I give you back again; and "welcome" I
have not yet: the roof of this court is too high to be yours;
and welcome to the wide fields too base to be mine.
King.   You shall be welcome, madam, to my court.
Prin.   I will be welcome, then.   Conduct me thither.
King.   Hear me, dear lady: I have sworn an oath.
Prin.   Our Lady help my lord! he 'll be forsworn.
King.   Not for the world, fair madam, by my will.
Prin.   Why, will shall break it; will, and nothing else.
King.   Your ladyship is ignorant what it is.
Prin.   Were my lord so, his ignorance were wise,
Where now his knowledge must prove ignorance.
I hear, your grace hath sworn out house-keeping:
'T is deadly sin to keep that oath, my lord,
And sin to break it.
But pardon me, I am too sudden-bold:
To teach a teacher ill beseemeth me.
Vouchsafe to read the purpose of my coming,
And suddenly resolve me in my suit.   *[Gives a paper*
King.   Madam, I will, if suddenly I may.
Prin.   You will the sooner, that I were away,
For you 'll prove perjured, if you make me stay.
Biron.   Did not I dance with you in Brabant once?
Ros.   Did not I dance with you in Brabant once?
Biron.   I know you did.
Ros.   How needless was it then
To ask the question!
Biron.   You must not be so quick.
Ros.   'T is 'long of you, that spur me with such questions.
Biron.   Your wit 's too hot, it speeds too fast, 't will tire.
Ros.   Not till it leave the rider in the mire.
Biron.   What time o' day?
Ros.   The hour that fools should ask.
Biron.   Now fair befall your mask!
Ros.   Fair fall the face it covers!
Biron.   And send you many lovers!
Ros.   Amen, so you be none.
Biron.   Nay, then will I be gone.
King.   Madam, your father here doth intimate
The payment of a hundred thousand crowns;
Being but the one-half of an entire sum
Disbursèd by my father in his wars.
But say that he or we—as neither have—
Received that sum, yet there remains unpaid
A hundred thousand more; in surety of which,

173

One part of Aquitain is bound to us,
Although not valued to the money's worth.
If then the king your father will restore
But that one-half which is unsatisfied,
We will give up our right in Aquitain,
And hold fair friendship with his majesty.
But that, it seems, he little purposeth,
For here he doth demand to have repaid
A hundred thousand crowns; and not demands,
On payment of a hundred thousand crowns,
To have his title live in Aquitain;
Which we much rather had depart withal,
And have the money by our father lent,
Than Aquitain, so gelded as it is.
Dear princess, were not his requests so far
From reason's yielding, your fair self should make
A yielding, 'gainst some reason, in my breast,
And go well satisfied to France again.
   Prin.   You do the king my father too much wrong,
And wrong the reputation of your name,
In so unseeming to confess receipt
Of that which hath so faithfully been paid.
   King.   I do protest, I never heard of it;
And if you prove it, I 'll repay it back,
Or yield up Aquitain.
   Prin.   We arrest your word.
Boyet, you can produce acquittances
For such a sum, from special officers
Of Charles his father.
   King.   Satisfy me so.
   Boyet.   So please your grace, the packet is not come,
Where that and other specialities are bound:
To-morrow you shall have a sight of them.
   King.   It shall suffice me: at which interview,
All liberal reason I will yield unto.
Meantime, receive such welcome at my hand
As honour, without breach of honour, may
Make tender of to thy true worthiness.
You may not come, fair princess, in my gates;
But here without you shall be so received,
As you shall deem yourself lodged in my heart,
Though so denied fair harbour in my house.
Your own good thoughts excuse me, and farewell:
To-morrow shall we visit you again.
   Prin.   Sweet health and fair desires consort your grace!
   King.   Thy own wish wish I thee in every place!
                   [*Exeunt King and his Train*
   Biron.   Lady, I will commend you to mine own heart.
   Ros.   Pray you, do my commendations; I would be
    glad to see it.

Biron.   I would you heard it groan.
Ros.   Is the fool sick?
Biron.   Sick at the heart.
Ros.   Alack, let it blood.
Biron.   Would that do it good?
Ros.   My physic says, ay.
Biron.   Will you prick 't with your eye?
Ros.   *No point*, with my knife.
Biron.   Now, God save thy life!
Ros.   And yours from long living!
Biron.   I cannot stay thanksgiving.   [*Retiring*
Dum.   Sir, I pray you, a word. What lady is that same?
Boyet.   The heir of Alençon, Katharine her name.
Dum.   A gallant lady. Monsieur, fare you well.   [*Exit*
Long.   I beseech you a word. What is she in the white?
Boyet.   A woman sometimes, an you saw her in the light.
Long.   Perchance, light in the light. I desire her name.
Boyet.   She hath but one for herself; to desire that,
were a shame.
Long.   Pray you, sir, whose daughter?
Boyet.   Her mother's, I have heard.
Long.   God's blessing on your beard!
Boyet.   Good sir, be not offended.
She is an heir of Falconbridge.
Long.   Nay, my choler is ended.
She is a most sweet lady.
Boyet.   Not unlike, sir; that may be.   [*Exit Long*
Biron.   What 's her name in the cap?
Boyet.   Rosaline, by good hap.
Biron.   Is she wedded or no?
Boyet.   To her will, sir, or so.
Biron.   O, you are welcome, sir. Adieu.
Boyet.   Farewell to me, sir, and welcome to you.
                [*Exit Biron.—Ladies unmask*
Mar.   That last is Biron, the merry madcap lord:
Not a word with him but a jest.
Boyet.   And every jest but a word.
Prin.   It was well done of you to take him at his word.
Boyet.   I was as willing to grapple as he was to board.
Mar.   Two hot sheeps, marry!
Boyet.   And wherefore not ships?
No sheep, sweet lamb, unless we feed on your lips.
Mar.   You sheep, and I pasture: shall that finish the jest?
Boyet.   So you grant pasture for me.
                [*Offering to kiss her*
Mar.   Not so, gentle beast.
My lips are no common, though several they be.
Boyet.   Belonging to whom?
Mar.   To my fortunes and me.
Prin.   Good wits will be jangling; but, gentles, agree.

The civil war of wits were much better used
On Navarre and his book-men, for here 't is abused.
   Boyet.   If my observation—which very seldom lies—
By the heart's still rhetoric disclosèd with eyes,
Deceive me not now, Navarre is infected.
   Prin.   With what?
   Boyet.   With that which we lovers entitle, affected.
   Prin.   Your reason?
   Boyet.   Why, all his behaviours did make their retire
To the court of his eye, peeping thorough desire:
His heart, like an agate, with your print impressed,
Proud with his form, in his eye pride expressed;
His tongue, all impatient to speak and not see,
Did stumble with haste in his eyesight to be;
All senses to that sense did make their repair,
To feel only looking on fairest of fair.
Methought, all his senses were locked in his eye,
As jewels in crystal for some prince to buy;
Who, tendering their own worth from where they were
     glassed
Did point you to buy them, along as you passed.
His face's own margent did quote such amazes,
That all eyes saw his eyes enchanted with gazes.
I 'll give you Aquitain, and all that is his,
An you give him for my sake but one loving kiss.
   Prin.   Come to our pavilion: Boyet is disposed.
   Boyet.   But to speak that in words, which his eye hath
     disclosed.
I only have made a mouth of his eye,
By adding a tongue which I know will not lie.
   Ros.   Thou art an old love-monger, and speakest skilfully.
   Mar.   He is Cupid's grandfather, and learns news of him.
   Ros.   Then was Venus like her mother, for her father is
     but grim.
   Boyet.   Do you hear, my mad wenches?
   Mar.   No.
   Boyet.   What then, do you see?
   Ros.   Ay, our way to be gone.
   Boyet.   You are too hard for me.
                                       [Exeunt

ACT THREE

Scene I.—In the Park

Enter Armado *and* Moth

   Arm.   Warble, child; make passionate my sense of
hearing.
   Moth.   *[Singing]* Concolinel—
   Arm.   Sweet air!—Go, tenderness of years; take this

key, give enlargement to the swain, bring him festinately
hither: I must employ him in a letter to my love.

Moth. Master, will you win your love with a French brawl?

Arm. How meanest thou? brawling in French?

Moth. No, my complete master; but to jig off a tune
at the tongue's end, canary to it with your feet, humour
it with turning up your eyes, sigh a note, and sing a
note; sometime through the throat, as if you swallowed
love with singing love; sometime through the nose, as
if you snuffed up love by smelling love; with your hat,
penthouse-like, o'er the shop of your eyes; with your
arms crossed on your thin bellydoublet, like a rabbit on
a spit; or your hands in your pocket, like a man after the
old painting; and keep not too long in one tune, but a
snip and away. These are compliments, these are humours,
these betray nice wenches—that would be betrayed without
these; and make them men of note,—do you note me?—that
most are affected to these.

Arm. How hast thou purchased this experience?

Moth. By my penny of observation.

Arm. But O,—but O,—

Moth. —the hobby-horse is forgot.

Arm. Callest thou my love hobby-horse?

Moth. No, master; the hobby-horse is but a colt,
and your love, perhaps, a hackney. But have you forgot
your love?

Arm. Almost I had.

Moth. Negligent student! learn her by heart.

Arm. By heart and in heart, boy.

Moth. And out of heart, master: all those three I
will prove.

Arm. What wilt thou prove?

Moth. A man, if I live; and this, "by," "in," and
"without," upon the instant: by heart you love her, because
your heart cannot come by her; in heart you love her,
because your heart is in love with her; and out of heart
you love her, being out of heart that you cannot enjoy her.

Arm. I am all these three.

Moth. And three times as much more, and yet nothing
at all.

Arm. Fetch hither the swain: he must carry me a letter.

Moth. A message well sympathised; a horse to be
ambassador for an ass.

Arm. Ha, ha! what sayest thou?

Moth. Marry, sir, you must send the ass upon the
horse, for he is very slow-gaited. But I go.

Arm. The way is but short. Away!

Moth. As swift as lead, sir.

Arm. Thy meaning, pretty ingenious?
Is not lead a metal heavy, dull, and slow?

177

Moth.   *Minime,* honest master; or rather, master, no.
Arm.   I say, lead is slow.
Moth.   You are too swift, sir, to say so:
Is that lead slow which is fired from a gun?
Arm.   Sweet smoke of rhetoric!
He reputes me a cannon; and the bullet, that 's he:—
I shoot thee at the swain.
Moth.   Thump, then, and I flee.   [*Exit*
Arm.   A most acute juvenal; voluble and free of grace!—
By thy favour, sweet welkin, I must sigh in thy face:—
Most rude melancholy, valour gives thee place.—
My herald is returned.

Re-enter MOTH *with* COSTARD

Moth.   A wonder, master! here 's a Costard broken in
          a shin.
Arm.   Some enigma, some riddle: come,—thy *l'envoy ;*
          —begin.
Cost.   No egma, no riddle, no *l'envoy !* no salve in the
mail, sir. O, sir, plantain, a plain plantain! no *l'envoy,*
no *l'envoy ;* no salve, sir, but a plantain.
Arm.   By virtue, thou enforcest laughter; thy silly
thought, my spleen; the heaving of my lungs provokes
me to ridiculous smiling: O, pardon me, my stars! Doth
the inconsiderate take salve for *l'envoy,* and the word
l'envoy for a salve?
Moth.   Do the wise think them other? is not *l'envoy*
a salve?
Arm.   No, page: it is an epilogue or discourse, to make
          plain
Some obscure precedence that hath tofore been saint.
I will example it:
          The fox, the ape, and the humble-bee,
          Were still at odds, being but three.
There 's the moral.   Now the *l'envoy.*
Moth.   I will add the *l'envoy.*   Say the moral again.
Arm.   The fox, the ape, and the humble-bee,
          Were still at odds, being but three.
Moth.   Until the goose came out of door,
          And stayed the odds by adding four.
Now will I begin your moral, and do you follow with my
l'envoy.
          The fox, the ape, and the humble-bee,
          Were still at odds, being but three.
Arm.   Until the goose came out of door,
          Staying the odds by adding four.
Moth.   A good *l'envoy,* ending in the goose.   Would
you desire more?
Cost.   The boy hath sold him a bargain, a goose, that 's
flat.—

178

Sir, your pennyworth is good, an your goose be fat.—
To sell a bargain well, is as cunning as fast and loose:
Let me see, a fat *l'envoy*; ay, that 's a fat goose.

Arm. Come hither, come hither. How did this argument begin?

Moth. By saying that a Costard was broken in a shin.
Then call'd you for the *l'envoy*.

Cost. True, and I for a plantain: thus came your
argument in;
Then the boy's fat *l'envoy*, the goose that you bought,
And he ended the market.

Arm. But tell me; how was there a Costard broken
in a shin?

Moth. I will tell you sensibly.

Cost. Thou hast no feeling of it, Moth: I will speak
that *l'envoy*.
    I, Costard, running out, that was safely within,
    Fell over the threshold, and broke my shin.

Arm. We will talk no more of this matter.

Cost. Till there be more matter in the shin.

Arm. Sirrah Costard, I will enfranchise thee.

Cost. O! marry me to one Frances?—I smell some
l'envoy, some goose in this.

Arm. By my sweet soul, I mean, setting thee at liberty,
enfreedoming thy person: thou wert immured, restrained,
captivated, bound.

Cost. True, true; and now you will be my purgation,
and let me loose.

Arm. I give thee thy liberty, set thee from durance;
and, in lieu thereof, impose on thee nothing but this:—
bear this significant [*giving a letter*] to the country maid
Jaquenetta. There is remuneration [*giving three farthings*];
for the best ward of mine honour is rewarding my
dependents. Moth, follow.   [*Exit*

Moth. Like the sequel, I.—Signior Costard, adieu.

Cost. My sweet ounce of man's flesh! my incony Jew!—
                                        [*Exit Moth*
Now will I look to his remuneration. Remuneration! O!
that 's the Latin word for three farthings: three farthings
—remuneration.—"What 's the price of this inkle?"   "A
penny."—"No, I 'll give you a remuneration:" why, it
carries it.—Remuneration!—why, it is a fairer name than
French crown. I will never buy and sell out of this word.

Enter BIRON

Biron. O, my good knave Costard! exceedingly well met.

Cost. Pray you, sir, how much carnation ribbon may
a man buy for a remuneration?

Biron. What is a remuneration?

Cost. Marry, sir, halfpenny farthing.

Biron.   O, why then, three-farthing-worth of silk.
Cost.   I thank your worship.   God be wi' you.
Biron.   O, stay, slave; I must employ thee:
As thou wilt win my favour, good my knave,
Do one thing for me that I shall entreat.
Cost.   When would you have it done, sir?
Biron.   O, this afternoon.
Cost.   Well, I will do it, sir.   Fare you well.
Biron.   O, thou knowest not what it is.
Cost.   I shall know, sir, when I have done it.
Biron.   Why, villain, thou must know first.
Cost.   I will come to your worship to-morrow morning.
Biron.   It must be done this afternoon.   Hark, slave,
it is but this:—
The princess comes to hunt here in the park,
And in her train there is a gentle lady;
When tongues speak sweetly, then they name her name,
And Rosaline they call her: ask for her,
And to her white hand see thou do commend
This sealed-up counsel.   There 's thy guerdon: go.
                  [*Gives him a shilling*
Cost.   Gardon.—O, sweet gardon! better than remuneration; eleven-pence farthing better.   Most sweet gardon!—I
will do it, sir, in print.—Gardon—remuneration!   [*Exit*
Biron.   O,—and I, forsooth, in love!   I, that have
been love's whip;
A very beadle to a humorous sigh;
A critic, nay, a night-watch constable;
A domineering pedant o'er the boy,
Than whom no mortal so magnificent!
This wimpled, whining, purblind, wayward boy;
This senior-junior, giant-dwarf, Dan Cupid,
Regent of love-rhymes, lord of folded arms,
The anointed sovereign of sighs and groans,
Liege of all loiterers and malcontents,
Dread prince of plackets, king of codpieces,
Sole imperator, and great general
Of trotting paritors:—O my little heart!—
And I to be a corporal of his field,
And wear his colours like a tumbler's hoop!
What, I love,—I!   I sue!   I seek a wife;
A woman, that is like a German clock,
Still a repairing, ever out of frame,
And never going aright, being a watch,
But being watched that it may still go right!
Nay, to be perjured, which is worst of all;
And, among three, to love the worst of all;
A whitely wanton with a velvet brow,
With two pitch-balls stuck in her face for eyes;
Ay, and, by heaven, one that will do the deed,

Though Argus were her eunuch and her guard;
And I to sigh for her! to watch for her!
To pray for her! Go to; it is a plague
That Cupid will impose for my neglect
Of his almighty dreadful little might.
Well, I will love, write, sigh, pray, sue, and groan:
Some men must love my lady, and some Joan.   [*Exit*

ACT FOUR

Scene I.—In the Park

Enter the Princess, Rosaline, Maria, Katharine, Boyet,
Lords, Attendants, and a Forester

   Prin.   Was that the king, that spurred his horse so hard
Against the steep up-rising of the hill?
   Boyet.   I know not; but I think it was not he.
   Prin.   Whoe'er he was, he showed a mounting mind.
Well, lords, to-day we shall have our despatch;
On Saturday we will return to France.—
Then, forester, my friend, where is the bush
That we must stand and play the murderer in?
   For.   Hereby, upon the edge of yonder coppice;
A stand where you may make the fairest shoot.
   Prin.   I thank my beauty, I am fair that shoot,
And thereupon thou speak'st the fairest shoot.
   For.   Pardon me, madam, for I meant not so.
   Prin.   What, what? first praise me, and again say, no?
O short-lived pride! Not fair? alack for woe!
   For.   Yes, madam, fair.
   Prin.   Nay, never paint me now:
Where fair is not, praise cannot mend the brow.
Here, good my glass, take this for telling true.
                     [*Giving him money*
Fair payment for foul words is more than due.
   For.   Nothing but fair is that which you inherit.
   Prin.   See, see, my beauty will be saved by merit.
O heresy in fair, fit for these days!
A giving hand, though foul, shall have fair praise.—
But come, the bow:—now mercy goes to kill,
And shooting well is then accounted ill.
Thus will I save my credit in the shoot:
Not wounding, pity would not let me do 't;
If wounding, then it was to show my skill,
That more for praise than purpose meant to kill.
And, out of question, so it is sometimes:
Glory grows guilty of detested crimes,
When, for fame's sake, for praise, an outward part,

We bend to that the working of the heart;
As I for praise alone now seek to spill
The poor deer's blood, that my heart means no ill.
    Boyet. Do not curst wives hold that self-sovereignty
Only for praise' sake, when they strive to be
Lords o'er their lords?
    Prin. Only for praise; and praise we may afford
To any lady that subdues a lord.
    Boyet. Here comes a member of the commonwealth.

Enter COSTARD

    Cost. God dig-you-den all. Pray you, which is the head lady?
    Prin. Thou shalt know her, fellow, by the rest that have no heads.
    Cost. Which is the greatest lady, the highest?
    Prin. The thickest, and the tallest.
    Cost. The thickest, and the tallest? it is so; truth is truth.
An your waist, mistress, were as slender as my wit,
One o' these maids' girdles for your waist should be fit.
Are you not the chief woman? you are the thickest here.
    Prin. What 's your will, sir? what 's your will?
    Cost. I have a letter from Monsieur Biron to one Lady Rosaline.
    Prin. O, thy letter, thy letter! he 's a good friend of mine.
Stand aside, good bearer.—Boyet, you can carve;
Break up this capon.
    Boyet.   I am bound to serve.—
This letter is mistook; it importeth none here:
It is writ to Jaquenetta.
    Prin.   We will read it, I swear.
Break the neck of the wax, and every one give ear.
    Boyet. [*Reads*] "*By heaven, that thou art fair, is most infallible ; true, that thou art beauteous ; truth itself, that thou art lovely. More fairer than fair, beautiful than beauteous, truer than truth itself, have commiseration on thy heroical vassal ! The magnanimous and most illustrate King Cophetua set eye upon the pernicious and indubitate beggar Penelophon, and he it was that might rightly say, Veni, vidi, vici ; which to anatomise in the vulgar (O base and obscure vulgar !) videlicet, he came, saw, and overcame : he came, one ; saw, two ; overcame, three. Who came? the king ; why did he come? to see ; why did he see? to overcome. To whom came he? to the beggar ; what saw he? the beggar ; who overcame he? the beggar. The conclusion is victory : on whose side? the king's. The captive is enriched : on whose side? the beggar's. The catastrophe is a nuptial : on whose side? the king's?—no, on both in one, or one in both. I am the king, for so stands the com-*"

parison; thou the beggar, for so witnesseth thy lowliness.
Shall I command thy love? I may. Shall I enforce thy
love? I could. Shall I entreat thy love? I will. What
shalt thou exchange for rags? robes; for tittles? titles;
for thyself? me. Thus, expecting thy reply, I profane my
lips on thy foot, my eyes on thy picture, and my heart on
thy every part.

              " Thine, in the dearest design of industry,
                     "Don Adriano de Armado?

" Thus dost thou hear the Nemean lion roar
  'Gainst thee, thou lamb, that standest as his prey;
Submissive fall his princely feet before,
  And he from forage will incline to play.
But if thou strive, poor soul, what art thou then?
  Food for his rage, repasture for his den."

    Prin.   What plume of feathers is he that indited this
      letter?
What vane? what weathercock? did you ever hear better?
    Boyet.   I am much deceived, but I remember the style.
    Prin.   Else your memory is bad, going o'er it erewhile.
    Boyet.   This Armado is a Spaniard, that keeps here in
      court;
A phantasm, a Monarcho, and one that makes sport
To the prince, and his book-mates.
    Prin.   Thou, fellow, a word.
Who gave thee this letter?
    Cost.   I told you; my lord.
    Prin.   To whom shouldst thou give it?
    Cost.   From my lord to my lady.
    Prin.   From which lord to which lady?
    Cost.   From my Lord Biron, a good master of mine,
To a lady of France, that he called Rosaline.
    Prin.   Thou hast mistaken his letter.—Come, lords,
      away.
Here, sweet, put up this: 't will be thine another day.
                         [Exeunt Princess and Train
    Boyet.   Who is the suitor? who is the suitor?
    Ros.   Shall I teach you to know?
    Boyet.   Ay, my continent of beauty.
    Ros.   Why, she that bears the bow.
Finely put off!
    Boyet.   My lady goes to kill horns; but if thou marry,
Hang me by the neck, if horns that year miscarry.
Finely put on!
    Ros.   Well then, I am the shooter.
    Boyet.   And who is your deer?
    Ros.   If we choose by the horns, yourself: come not near.
Finely put on, indeed!—
    Mar.   You still wrangle with her, Boyet, and she strikes
      at the brow.

Boyet. But she herself is hit lower. Have I hit her now?
Ros. Shall I come upon thee with an old saying, that
was a man when King Pepin of France was a little boy, as
touching the hit it?
Boyet. So I may answer thee with one as old, that was
a woman when Queen Guinever of Britain was a little wench,
as touching the hit it.
Ros.   *Thou canst not hit it, hit it, hit it,*
            Thou canst not hit it, my good man,
Boyet.   *An I cannot, cannot, cannot,*
            An I cannot, another can.
                                        [*Exeunt Ros. and Kath.*
Cost. By my troth, most pleasant: how both did fit it!
Mar. A mark marvellous well shot, for they both did
    hit it.
Boyet. A mark! O, mark but that mark: a mark says
    my lady.
Let the mark have a prick in't to mete at, if it may be.
Mar. Wide o' the bow-hand: i' faith, your hand is out.
Cost. Indeed, 'a must shoot nearer, or he'll ne'er hit the
    clout.
Boyet. An if my hand be out, then belike your hand is in.
Cost. Then will she get the upshot by cleaving the pin.
Mar. Come, come, you talk greasily; your lips grow foul.
Cost. She's too hard for you at pricks, sir: challenge
    her to bowl.
Boyet. I fear too much rubbing. Good night, my good
    owl.   [*Exeunt Boyet and Maria*
Cost. By my soul, a swain! a most simple clown!
Lord, Lord! how the ladies and I have put him down!
O' my truth, most sweet jests! most incony vulgar wit!
When it comes so smoothly off, so obscenely, as it were, so
    fit.
Armado o' the one side,—O, a most dainty man!
To see him walk before a lady, and to bear her fan!
To see him kiss his hand! and how most sweetly 'a will
    swear!—
And his page o' t' other side, that handful of wit!
Ah, heavens, it is a most pathetical nit!
Sola, sola!   [*Shouting within*
                                          [*Exit Costard*

SCENE II.—The Same

Enter HOLOFERNES, SIR NATHANIEL, *and* DULL

Nath. Very reverend sport, truly: and done in the
testimony of a good conscience.
Hol. The deer was, as you know, *in sanguis,*—blood;
ripe as a pomewater, who now hangeth like a jewel in the

ear of *coelum*,—the sky, the welkin, the heaven; and anon falleth like a crab on the face of *terra*,—the soil, the land, the earth.

Nath. Truly, Master Holofernes, the epithets are sweetly varied, like a scholar at the least; but, sir, I assure ye, it was a buck of the first head.

Hol. Sir Nathaniel, *haud credo*.

Dull. 'T was not a *haud credo*, 't was a pricket.

Hol. Most barbarous intimation! yet a kind of insinuation, as it were, *in via*, in way, of explication; *facere*, as it were, replication, or, rather, *ostentare*, to show, as it were, his inclination,—after his undressed, unpolished, uneducated, unpruned, untrained, or rather unlettered, or, ratherest, unconfirmed fashion,—to insert again my *haud credo* for a deer.

Dull. I said, the deer was not a *haud credo :* 't was a pricket.

Hol. Twice-sod simplicity, *bis coctus !*—

O, thou monster Ignorance, how deforméd dost thou look!

  Nath. Sir, he hath never fed of the dainties that are
      bred in a book;
He hath not eat paper, as it were; he hath not drunk ink:
His intellect is not replenished; he is only an animal, only
      sensible in the duller parts, can't think;
And such barren plants are set before us, that we thankful
      should be—
Which we of taste and feeling are—for those parts that do
      fructify in us more than he;
For as it would ill become me to be vain, indiscreet, or a
      fool,
So, were there a patch set on learning, to see him in a
      school:—
But, *omne bene*, say I; being of an old father's mind,
Many can brook the weather, that love not the wind.

Dull. You two are book-men: can you tell by your wit, What was a month old at Cain's birth, that 's not five weeks old as yet?

  Hol. Dictynna, goodman Dull; Dictynna, goodman Dull.

Dull. What is Dictynna?

Nath. A title to Phœbe, to Luna, to the moon.

Hol. The moon was a month old when Adam was no
      more;
And raught not to five weeks, when he came to five-score.
The allusion holds in the exchange.

Dull. 'T is true indeed; the collusion holds in the exchange.

Hol. God comfort thy capacity! I say, the allusion holds in the exchange.

Dull. And I say, the pollution holds in the exchange,

for the moon is never but a month old; and I say beside,
that 't was a pricket that the princess killed.

Hol. Sir Nathaniel, will you hear an extemporal epitaph
on the death of the deer? and, to humour the ignorant, I
have called the deer the princess killed, a pricket.

Nath. *Perge,* good Master Holofernes, *perge;* so it shall
please you to abrogate scurrility.

Hol. I will something affect the letter; for it argues
facility.

*The preyful princess pierced and pricked a pretty pleasing
pricket ;*
    *Some say, a sore ; but not a sore, till now made sore with
shooting.*
The dogs did yell ; put l to sore, then sorel jumps from thicket ;
    Or pricket sore, or else sorel; the people fall a-hooting.
If sore be sore, then l to sore makes fifty sores ; O sore l !
Of one sore I an hundred make, by adding but one more l.

Nath. A rare talent!

Dull. If a talent be a claw, look how he claws him with
a talent.

Hol. This is a gift that I have, simple, simple; a foolish,
extravagant spirit, full of forms, figures, shapes, objects,
ideas, apprehensions, motions, revolutions! these are begot in the ventricle of memory, nourished in the womb of
pia mater, and delivered upon the mellowing of occasion.
But the gift is good in those in whom it is acute, and I am
thankful for it.

Nath. Sir, I praise the Lord for you, and so may my
parishioners; for their sons are well tutored by you, and
their daughters profit very greatly under you: you are a
good member of the commonwealth.

Hol. *Mehercle !* if their sons be ingenious, they shall
want no instruction; if their daughters be capable, I will
put it to them. But, *vir sapit qui pauca loquitur.* A soul
feminine saluteth us.

Enter JAQUENETTA *and* COSTARD

Jaq. God give you good morrow, master person.

Hol. Master person,—*quasi* pers-on. An if one should
be pierced: which is the one?

Cost. Marry, master schoolmaster, he that is likest to
a hogshead.

Hol. Of piercing a hogshead! a good lustre of conceit
in a turf of earth; fire enough for a flint, pearl enough for
a swine: 't is pretty; it is well.

Jaq. Good master person, be so good as read me this
letter. It was given me by Costard, and sent me from Don
Armado: I beseech you, read it.

Hol. *Fauste, precor, gelidâ quando pecus omne sub umbrâ*

*Ruminat,** and so forth. Ah, good old Mantuan! I may speak of thee as the traveller doth of Venice:

Venetia, Venetia,
Chi non ti vede, non ti pretia.

Old Mantuan! old Mantuan! who understandeth thee not loves thee not.—*Ut, re, sol, la, mi, fa.*—Under pardon, sir, what are the contents? or, rather, as Horace says in his—What, my soul, verses?

Nath. Ay, sir, and very learned.

Hol. Let me hear a staff, a stanza, a verse: *lege, domine.*

Nath. *If love make me forsworn, how shall I swear to love?*
Ah, never faith could hold, if not to beauty vowed!
Though to myself forsworn, to thee I'll faithful prove;
Those thoughts to me were oaks, to thee like osiers bowed.
Study his bias leaves and makes his book thine eyes,
Where all those pleasures live that art would comprehend:
If knowledge be the mark, to know thee shall suffice.
Well learnèd is that tongue that well can thee commend;
All ignorant that soul that sees thee without wonder;
Which is to me some praise, that I thy parts admire.
Thy eye Jove's lightning bears, thy voice his dreadful thunder,
Which, not to anger bent, is music, and sweet fire.
Celestial as thou art, O, pardon love this wrong,
That sings the heavens' praise with such an earthly tongue!

Hol. You find not the apostrophes, and so miss the accent: let me supervise the canzonet. Here are only numbers ratified; but, for the elegancy, facility, and golden cadence of poesy, *caret.* Ovidius Naso was the man: and why, indeed, Naso, but for smelling out the odoriferous flowers of fancy, the jerks of invention? *Imitari* is nothing, so doth the hound his master, the ape his keeper, the tired horse his rider. But, damosella virgin, was this directed to you?

Jaq. Ay, sir, from one Monsieur Biron, one of the strange queen's lords.

Hol. I will overglance the superscript. "To the snow-white hand of the most beauteous Lady Rosaline." I will look again on the intellect of the letter, for the nomination of the party writing to the person written unto: "Your ladyship's in all desired employment, BIRON." Sir Nathaniel, this Biron is one of the votaries with the king; and here he hath framed a letter to a sequent of the stranger queen's, which, accidentally, or by the way of progression,

* The beginning of the first Eclogue of Mantuan, in which the speakers were Faustus and Fortunatus. The Latin poems of the Carmelite Baptista Spagnolo of Mantua—Mantuanus—were used as a schoolbook in Shakespeare's time, and their first words, "*Fauste, precor, gelidâ*," were used by Farnaby to be dearer to pedants than Virgil's "*Arma virumque cano.*"

hath miscarried.—Trip and go, my sweet; deliver this paper into the royal hand of the king: it may concern much. Stay not thy compliment; I forgive thy duty: adieu.

Jaq.   Good Costard, go with me.—Sir, God save your life!

Cost.   Have with thee, my girl. [*Exeunt Cost. and Jaq.*

Nath.   Sir, you have done this in the fear of God, very religiously, and, as a certain Father saith—

Hol.   Sir, tell not me of the father; I do fear colourable colours. But, to return to the verses: did they please you, Sir Nathaniel?

Nath.   Marvellous well for the pen.

Hol.   I do dine to-day at the father's of a certain pupil of mine; where if before repast it shall please you to gratify the table with a grace, I will, on my privilege I have with the parents of the foresaid child or pupil, undertake your *ben venuto ;* where I will prove those verses to be very unlearned, neither savouring of poetry, wit, nor invention. I beseech your society.

Nath.   And thank you too; for society, saith the text, is the happiness of life.

Hol.   And, certes, the text most infallibly concludes it.— [*To Dull*] Sir, I do invite you too; you shall not say me nay: *pauca verba.* Away! the gentles are at their game, and we will to our recreation.   [*Exeunt*

SCENE III.—Another Part of the Park

Enter BIRON, *with a paper*

Biron.   The king he is hunting the deer; I am coursing myself: they have pitched a toil; I am toiling in a pitch,— pitch that defiles. Defile! a foul word. Well, sit thee down, sorrow! for so, they say, the fool said, and so say I,— and I the fool. Well proved, wit! By the Lord, this love is as mad as Ajax: it kills sheep; it kills me;—I a sheep. Well proved again o' my side! I will not love; if I do, hang me: i' faith, I will not. O, but her eye,—by this light, but for her eye, I would not love her! yes, for her two eyes. Well, I do nothing in the world but lie, and lie in my throat. By heaven, I do love, and it hath taught me to rhyme, and to be melancholy; and here is part of my rhyme, and here my melancholy. Well, she hath one o' my sonnets already: the clown bore it, the fool sent it, and the lady hath it: sweet clown, sweeter fool, sweetest lady! By the world, I would not care a pin if the other three were in.—Here comes one with a paper: God give him grace to groan!   [*Gets up into a tree*

Enter the KING, *with a paper*

King.   Ay me!

Biron. [*Aside*] Shot, by heaven!—Proceed, sweet
Cupid; thou hast thumped him with thy bird-bolt under
the left pap.—In faith, secrets!—
    King. [*Reads*] *So sweet a kiss the golden sun gives not*
        To those fresh morning drops upon the rose,
    As thy eyebeams, when their fresh rays have smote
        The night of dew that on my cheeks down flows :
    Nor shines the silver moon one half so bright
        Through the transparent bosom of the deep,
    As doth thy face through tears of mine give light ;
        Thou shin'st in every tear that I do weep :
    No drop but as a coach doth carry thee,
        So ridest thou triumphing in my woe.
    Do but behold the tears that swell in me,
        And they thy glory through my grief will show :
    But do not love thyself ; then thou wilt keep
    My tears for glasses, and still make me weep.
    O queen of queens ! how far thou dost excel,
    No thought can think, nor tongue of mortal tell.

How shall she know my griefs?   I 'll drop the paper:—
Sweet leaves, shade folly.—Who is he comes here?
                           [*Steps aside*
What, Longaville! and reading! listen, ear.
    Biron. [*Aside*] Now, in thy likeness, one more fool
    appear!

Enter LONGAVILLE, *with a paper*

    Long. Ay me! I am forsworn.
    Biron. [*Aside*] Why, he comes in like a perjure, wearing
    papers.
    King. [*Aside*] In love, I hope: sweet fellowship in shame!
    Biron. [*Aside*] One drunkard loves another of the name.
    Long. Am I the first that have been perjured so?
    Biron. [*Aside*] I could put thee in comfort: not by two
    that I know.
Thou mak'st the triumviry, the corner-cap of society,
The shape of Love's Tyburn that hangs up simplicity.
    Long. I feat these stubborn lines lack power to move:—
O sweet Maria, empress of my love!
These numbers will I tear, and write in prose.
    Biron. [*Aside*] O, rhymes are guards on wanton Cupid's
    hose:
Disfigure not his slop.
    Long.   This same shall go.   [*Reads*
    Did not the heavenly rhetoric of thine eye,
        'Gainst whom the world cannot hold argument,
    Persuade my heart to this false perjury?
        Vows for thee broke deserve not punishment.

A woman I forswore ; but I will prove,
  Thou being a goddess, I forswore not thee :
My vow was earthly, thou a heavenly love ;
  Thy grace being gained cures all disgrace in me.
Vows are but breath, and breath a vapour is :
  Then thou, fair sun, which on my earth dost shine,
Exhal'st this vapour-vow ; in thee it is :
  If broken, then it is no fault of mine
If by me broke.   What fool is not so wise
To lose an oath to win a paradise ?

  Biron. [*Aside*] This is the liver-vein, which makes flesh
    a deity,
A green goose a goddess: pure, pure idolatry.
God amend us, God amend! we are much out o' the way.
  Long. By whom shall I send this?—Company! stay.
                              [*Steps aside*
  Biron. [*Aside*] All hid, all hid; an old infant play.
Like a demi-god here sit I in the sky,
And wretched fools' secrets heedfully o'er-eye.
More sacks to the mill!   O heavens! I have my wish:
Dumain transformed: four woodcocks in a dish!

         Enter DUMAIN, *with a paper*

  Dum. O most divine Kate!
  Biron. [*Aside*] O most profane coxcomb!
  Dum. By heaven, the wonder of a mortal eye!
  Biron. [*Aside*] By earth, she is but corporal; there
    you lie.
  Dum. Her amber hairs for foul have amber quoted.
  Biron. [*Aside*] An amber-colour'd raven was well noted.
  Dum. As upright as the cedar.
  Biron. [*Aside*]   Stoops, I say:
Her shoulder is with child.
  Dum.   As fair as day.
  Biron. [*Aside*] Ay, as some days; but then no sun
    must shine.
  Dum. O, that I had my wish!
  Long. [*Aside*]   And I had mine!
  King. [*Aside*] And I mine too, good Lord!
  Biron. [*Aside*] Amen, so I had mine. Is not that a
    good word?
  Dum. I would forget her; but a fever she
Reigns in my blood, and will remembered be.
  Biron. [*Aside*] A fever in your blood? why, then
    incision
Would let her out in saucers: sweet misprision!
  Dum. Once more I 'll read the ode that I have writ.
  Biron. [*Aside*] Once more I 'll mark how love can vary
    wit.

Dum.   *On a day, alack the day !*
   Love, whose month is ever May,
   Spied a blossom passing fair
   Playing in the wanton air :
   Through the velvet leaves the wind,
   All unseen, 'gan passage find ;
   That the lover, sick to death,
   Wished himself the heaven's breath.
   Air, quoth he, thy cheeks may blow ;
   Air, would I might triumph so !
   But alack ! my hand is sworn
   Ne'er to pluck thee from thy thorn :
   Vow, alack ! for youth unmeet,
   Youth so apt to pluck a sweet.
   Do not call it sin in me
   That I am forsworn for thee ;
   Thou for whom e'en Jove would swear
   Juno but an Ethiop were ;
   And deny himself for Jove,
   Turning mortal for thy love.

This will I send, and something else more plain
That shall express my true love's fasting pain.
O, would the king, Biron, and Longaville,
Were lovers too! Ill to example ill,
Would from my forehead wipe a perjured note;
For none offend where all alike do dote.
  Long. [*Advancing*] Dumain, thy love is far from
    charity,
That in love's grief desir'st society:
You may look pale; but I should blush, I know,
To be o'erheard, and taken napping so.
  King. [*Advancing*] Come, sir, your blush.
As his your case is such;
You chide at him, offending twice as much:
You do not love Maria; Longaville
Did never sonnet for her sake compile,
Nor never lay his wreathéd arms athwart
His loving bosom, to keep down his heart.
I have been closely shrouded in this bush,
And marked you both, and for you both did blush.
I heard your guilty rhymes, observed your fashion,
Saw sighs reek from you, noted well your passion;
Ay me! says one; O Jove! the other cries;
One's hairs were gold, crystal the other's eyes:
[*To Longaville*] You would for paradise break faith and
    troth;
[*To Dumain*] And Jove for your love would infringe an oath.
What will Biron say, when that he shall hear
The faith infringéd, which such zeal did swear?

How will he scorn! how will he spend his wit!
How will he triumph, leap, and laugh at it!
For all the wealth that ever I did see,
I would not have him know so much by me.
   Biron.   Now step I forth to whip hypocrisy.—
                                       [Descends from the tree
Ah, good my liege, I pray thee, pardon me.
Good heart! what grace hast thou, thus to reprove
These worms for loving, that art most in love?
Your eyes do make no coaches; in your tears
There is no certain princess that appears:
You 'll not be perjured, 't is a hateful thing:
Tush, none but minstrels like of sonneting.
But are you not ashamed? nay, are you not,
All three of you, to be thus much o'ershot?
You found his mote; the king your mote did see;
But I a beam do find in each of three.
O, what a scene of foolery have I seen,
Of sighs, of groans, or sorrow, and of teen!
O me! with what strict patience have I sat,
To see a king transforméd to a gnat!
To see great Hercules whipping a gig,
And profound Solomon tuning a jig,
And Nestor play at push-pin with the boys,
And critic Timon laugh at idle toys!
Where lies thy grief? O, tell me, good Dumain:
And, gentle Longaville, where lies thy pain?
And where my liege's? all about the breast;—
A caudle, ho!
   King.   Too bitter is thy jest.
Are we betrayed thus to thy over-view?
   Biron.   Not you to me, but I betrayed by you:
I, that am honest; I, that hold it sin
To break the vow I am engagéd in:
I am betrayed, by keeping company
With men like you, men of inconstancy.
When shall you see me write a thing in rhyme?
Or groan for Joan? or spend a minute's time
In pruning me? When shall you hear that I
Will praise a hand, a foot, a face, an eye,
A gait, a state, a brow, a breast, a waist,
A leg, a limb?—
   King.   Soft! Whither away so fast?
A true man or a thief that gallops so?
   Biron.   I post from love;—good lover, let me go.

Enter JAQUENETTA *and* COSTARD

   Jaq.   God bless the king!
   King.   What present hast thou there?
   Cost.   Some certain treason.

    King.   What makes treason here?
    Cost.   Nay, it makes nothing, sir.
    King.   If it mar nothing neither,
The treason and you go in peace away together.
    Jaq.   I beseech your grace, let this letter be read:
Our person misdoubts it; it was treason, he said.
    King.   Biron, read it over.   [*Biron reads the letter*
Where hadst thou it?
    Jaq.   Of Costard.
    King.   Where hadst thou it?
    Cost.   Of Dun Adramadio, Dun Adramadio.
    King.   How now! what is in you? why dost thou tear it?
    Biron.   A toy, my liege, a toy: your grace needs. not
        fear it.
    Long.   It did move him to passion, and therefore let 's
        hear it.
    Dum.   [*Picking up the pieces*] It is Biron's writing, and
        here is his name.
    Biron.   [*To Costard*] Ah, you whoreson loggerhead! you
        were born to do me shame.—
Guilty, my lord, guilty! I confess, I confess.
    King.   What?
    Biron.   That you three fools lacked me, fool, to make
        up the mess;
He, he, and you, and you, my liege, and I,
Are pick-purses in love, and we deserve to die.
O, dismiss this audience, and I shall tell you more.
    Dum.   Now the number is even.
    Biron.   True, true; we are four.—
Will these turtles be gone?
    King.   Hence, sirs; away!
    Cost.   Walk aside the true folk, and let the traitors stay.
                [*Exeunt Costard and Jaqueneita*
    Biron.   Sweet lords, sweet lovers, O, let us embrace.
As true we are as flesh and blood can be;
The sea will ebb and flow, heaven show his face;
Young blood doth not obey an old decree:
We cannot cross the cause why we are born;
Therefore, of all hands must we be forsworn.
    King.   What, did these rent lines show some love of
        thine?
    Biron.   Did they? quoth you. Who sees the heavenly
        Rosaline,
That, like a rude and savage man of Inde,
   At the first opening of the gorgeous east,
Bows not his vassal head, and, stricken blind,
   Kisses the base ground with obedient breast?
What peremptory, eagle-sighted eye
   Dares look upon the heaven of her brow,
That is not blinded by her majesty?

King.   What zeal, what fury hath inspired thee now?
My love, her mistress, is a gracious moon,
  She an attending star, scarce seen a light.
Biron.   My eyes are then no eyes, nor I Biron.
O, but for my love, day would turn to night.
Of all complexions the culled sovereignty
  Do meet, as at a fair, in her fair cheek;
Where several worthies make one dignity,
  Where nothing wants that want itself doth seek.
Lend me the flourish of all gentle tongues,—
  Fie, painted rhetoric! O, she needs it not:
To things of sale a seller's praise belongs,
  She passes praise; then praise too short doth blot.
A withered hermit, five-score winters worn,
  Might shake off fifty, looking in her eye:
Beauty doth vanish age, as if new-born,
  And gives the crutch the cradle's infancy.
O, 't is the sun, that maketh all things shine!
  King.   By heaven, thy love is black as ebony.
Biron.   Is ebony like her? O wood divine!
  A wife of such wood were felicity.
O, who can give an oath? where is a book?
  That I may swear beauty doth beauty lack,
If that she learn not of her eye to look:
  No face is fair, that is not full so black.
King.   O, paradox! Black is the badge of hell,
  The hue of dungeons, and the scowl of night:
And beauty's crest becomes the heavens well.
  Biron.   Devils soonest tempt, resembling spirits of light.
O, if in black my lady's brows be decked,
  It mourns, that painting, and usurping hair,
Should ravish doters with a false aspect;
  And therefore is she born to make black fair.
Her favours turns the fashion of the days;
  For native blood is counted painting now,
And therefore red, that would avoid dispraise,
  Paints itself black, to imitate her brow.
Dum.   To look like her are chimney-sweepers black.
Long.   And since her time are colliers counted bright.
King.   And Ethiops of their sweet complexion crack.
Dum.   Dark needs no candles now, for dark is light.
Biron.   Your mistresses dare never come in rain,
For fear their colours should be washed away.
King.   'T were good, yours did; for, sir, to tell you plain,
I'll find a fairer face not washed to-day.
Biron.   I 'll prove her fair, or talk till doomsday here.
King.   No devil will fright thee then so much as she.
Dum.   I never knew man hold vile stuff so dear.
Long.   [*Showing his shoe*] Look, here 's thy love: my
  foot and her face see.

Biron. O, if the streets were pavéd with thine eyes,
Her feet were much too dainty for such tread.
Dum. O vile! then, as she goes, what upward lies
The streets should see, as she walked overhead.
King. But what of this? Are we not all in love?
Biron. O, nothing so sure; and thereby all forsworn.
King. Then leave this chat: and, good Biron, now prove
Our loving lawful, and our faith not torn.
Dum. Ay, marry, there; some flattery for this evil.
Long. O, some authority how to proceed;
Some tricks, some quillets, how to cheat the devil.
Dum. Some salve for perjury.
Biron.   O, 't is more than need.—
Have at you then, affection's men-at-arms:
Consider, what you first did swear unto,—
To fast,—to study,—and to see no woman:
Flat treason 'gainst the kingly state of youth.
Say, can you fast? your stomachs are too young,
And abstinence engenders maladies.
And where that you have vowed to study, lords,
In that each of you have forsworn his book,
Can you still dream, and pore, and thereon look?
For when would you, my lord, or you, or you,
Have found the ground of study's excellence,
Without the beauty of a woman's face?
From women's eyes this doctrine I derive:
They are the ground, the books, the academies,
From whence doth spring the true Promethean fire.
Why, universal plodding prisons up
The nimble spirits in the arteries,
As motion and long-during action tires
The sinewy vigour of the traveller.
Now, for not looking on a woman's face,
You have in that forsworn the use of eyes,
And study too, the causer of your vow;
For where is any author in the world
Teaches such beauty as a woman's eye?
Learning is but an adjunct to ourself,
And where we are, our learning likewise is:
Then, when ourselves we see in ladies' eyes,
Do we not likewise see our learning there?
O, we have made a vow to study, lords,
And in that vow we have forsworn our books:
For when would you, my liege, or you, or you,
In leaden contemplation have found out
Such fiery numbers, as the prompting eyes
Of beauty's tutors have enriched you with?
Other slow arts entirely keep the brain,
And therefore, finding barren practisers,

Scarce show a harvest of their heavy toil;
But love, first learnéd in a lady's eyes,
Lives not alone immuréd in the brain,
But, with the motion of all elements,
Courses as swift as thought in every power,
And gives to every power a double power
Above their functions and their offices.
It adds a precious seeing to the eye;
A lover's eyes will gaze an eagle blind:
A lover's ear will hear the lowest sound,
When the suspicious head of theft is stopped:
Love's feeling is more soft, and sensible,
Than are the tender horns of cockled snails:
Love's tongue proves dainty Bacchus gross in taste.
For valour, is not Love a Hercules,
Still climbing trees in the Hesperides?
Subtle as Sphinx; as sweet and musical,
As bright Apollo's lute, strung with his hair;
And, when Love speaks, the voice of all the gods
Makes heaven drowsy with the harmony.
Never durst poet touch a pen to write,
Until his love were tempered with Love's sighs;
O, then his lines would ravish savage ears,
And plant in tyrants mild humility.
From women's eyes this doctrine I derive:
They sparkle still the right Promethean fire;
They are the books, the arts, the academies,
That show, contain, and nourish all the world;
Else none at all in aught proves excellent.
Then, fools you were these women to forswear,
Or, keeping what is sworn, you will prove fools.
For wisdom's sake, a word that all men love,
Or for love's sake, a word that loves all men,
Or for men's sake, the authors of these women,
Or women's sake, by whom we men are men,
Let us once lose our oaths, to find ourselves,
Or else we lose ourselves, to keep our oaths.
It is religion to be thus forsworn;
For charity itself fulfils the law;
And who can sever love from charity?
    King. Saint Cupid, then! and soldiers, to the field!
    Biron. Advance your standards, and upon them, lords!
Pell-mell, down with them! but be first advised,
In conflict that you get the sun of them.
    Long. Now to plain-dealing: lay these glozes by.
Shall we resolve to woo these girls of France?
    King. And win them too: therefore, let us devise
Some entertainment for them in their tents.
    Biron. First, from the park let us conduct them thither;
Then, homeward, every man attach the hand

Of his fair mistress.   In the afternoon
We will with some strange pastime solace them,
Such as the shortness of the time can shape;
For revels, dances, masks, and merry hours,
Forerun fair Love, strewing her way with flowers.
    King.   Away, away! no time shall be omitted,
That will be time and may by us be fitted.
    Biron.   *Allons ! Allons !*—Sowed cockle reaped no corn;
And justice always whirls in equal measure:
Light wenches may prove plagues to men forsworn;
If so, our copper buys no better treasure.   [*Exeunt*

ACT FIVE

Scene I.—In the Park

Enter Holofernes, Sir Nathaniel, *and* Dull

Hol.   *Satis quod sufficit.*
Nath.   I praise God for you, sir: your reasons at dinner
have been sharp and sententious; pleasant without scurrility, witty without affection, audacious without impudency,
learned without opinion, and strange without heresy.   I
did converse this *quondam* day with a companion of the
king's, who is intituled, nominated, or called, Don Adriano
de Armado.
    Hol.   *Novi hominem tanquam te :* his humour is lofty,
his discourse peremptory, his tongue filed, his eye ambitious,
his gait majestical, and his general behaviour vain, ridiculous and thrasonical.   He is too picked, too spruce, too
affected, too odd, as it were, too peregrinate, as I may
call it.
    Nath.   A most singular and choice epithet.
                          [*Takes out his table-book*
    Hol.   He draweth out the thread of his verbosity finer
than the staple of his argument.   I abhor such fanatical
phantasms, such insociable and point-device companions;
such rackers of orthography, as to speak dout, fine, when
we should say doubt; det, when he should pronounce
debt,—d, e, b, t, not d, e, t; he clepeth a calf, cauIf; half,
hauIf; neighbour *vocatur* nebour; neigh abbreviated ne.
This is abhominable (which he would call abominable), it
insinuateth me of *insanire : ne intelligis, domine*? to make
frantic, lunatic.
    Nath.   *Laus Deo, bone intelligo.*
    Hol.   *Bone ?*—*bone* for *bene:* Priscian a little scratched;
't will serve.

Enter ARMADO, MOTH, *and* COSTARD

Nath.   *Videsne quis venit ?*
Hol.   *Video, et gaudeo.*
Arm.   [*To Moth*] Chirrah!
Hol.   *Quare* chirrah, not sirrah?
Arm.   Men of peace, well encountered.
Hol.   Most military, sir, salutation.
Moth.   They have been at a great feast of languages, and stolen the scraps.
Cost.   O, they have lived long on the alms-basket of words. I marvel thy master hath not eaten thee for a word; for thou art not so long by the head as *honorificabilitudinitatibus :* thou art easier swallowed than a flap-dragon.
Moth.   Peace! the peal begins.
Arm.   [*To Hol.*] Monsieur, are you not lettered?
Moth.   Yes, yes, he teaches boys the horn-book.—What is a, b, spelt backward with the horn on his head?
Hol.   Ba, *pueritia*, with a horn added.
Moth.   Ba! most silly sheep, with a horn.—You hear his learning.
Hol.   *Quis, quis*, thou consonant?
Moth.   The third of the five vowels, if you repeat them; or the fifth, if I.
Hol.   I will repeat them,—a, e, i.
Moth.   The sheep! the other two concludes it;—o,—u.
Arm.   Now, by the salt wave of the Mediterranean, a sweet touch, a quick venue of wit! snip, snap, quick and home: it rejoiceth my intellect; true wit!
Moth.   Offered by a child to an old man; which is wit-old.
Hol.   What is the figure? what is the figure?
Moth.   Horns.
Hol.   Thou disputeth like an infant: go, whip thy gig.
Moth.   Lend me your horn to make one, and I will whip about your infamy *circum circa.* A gig of a cuckold's horn!
Cost.   An I had but one penny in the world, thou shouldst have it to buy gingerbread. Hold, there is the very Remuneration I had of thy master, thou halfpenny purse of wit, thou pigeon-egg of discretion. O, and the heavens were so pleased that thou wert but my bastard, what a joyful father wouldst thou make me! Go to; thou hast it *ad dunghill*, at the fingers' ends, as they say.
Hol.   O! I smell false Latin; dunghill for *unguem.*
Arm.   Arts-man, *præambula :* we will be singled from the barbarous. Do you not educate youth at the charge-house on the top of the mountain?
Hol.   Or *mons*, the hills.

Arm. At your sweet pleasure, for the mountain.

Hol. I do, *sans* question.

Arm. Sir, it is the king's most sweet pleasure and affection, to congratulate the princess at her pavilion in the posteriors of this day, which the rude multitude call the afternoon.

Hol. The posterior of the day, most generous sir, is liable, congruent, and measurable for the afternoon: the word is well culled, chose; sweet and apt, I do assure you, sir; I do assure.

Arm. Sir, the king is a noble gentleman, and my familiar, I do assure you, very good friend,—For what is inward between us, let it pass. I do beseech thee, remember thy courtesy,—I beseech thee, apparel thy head:—and among other importunate and most serious designs,—and of great import indeed, too,—but let that pass.—For I must tell thee, it will please his grace, by the world, sometime to lean upon my poor shoulder, and with his royal finger, thus, dally with my excrement, with my mustachio: but, sweet heart, let that pass. By the world, I recount no fable: some certain special honours it pleaseth his greatness to impart to Armado, a soldier, a man of travel, that hath seen the world: but let that pass.—The very all of all is,—but, sweet heart, I do implore secrecy,—that the king would have me present the princess, sweet chuck, with some delightful ostentation, or show, or pageant, or antick, or fire-work. Now, understanding that the curate and your sweet self are good at such eruptions and sudden breaking out of mirth, as it were, I have acquainted you withal, to the end to crave your assistance.

Hol. Sir, you shall present before her the Nine Worthies. —Sir Nathaniel, as concerning some entertainment of time, some show in the posterior of this day, to be rendered by our assistance,—at the king's command, and this most gallant, illustrate, and learned gentleman,—before the princess; I say, none so fit as to present the Nine Worthies.

Nath. Where will you find men worthy enough to present them?

Hol. Joshua, yourself; myself, or this gallant gentleman, Judas Maccabæus; this swain (because of his great limb or joint) shall pass Pompey the Great; the page, Hercules.

Arm. Pardon, sir; error: he is not quantity enough for that Worthy's thumb: he is not so big as the end of his club.

Hol. Shall I have audience? he shall present Hercules in minority: his *enter* and *exit* shall be strangling a snake; and I will have an apology for that purpose.

Moth. An excellent device: so, if any of the audience hiss, you may cry, "Well done, Hercules! now thou

crushest the snake!" that is the way to make an offence
gracious, though few have the grace to do it.

Arm. For the rest of the Worthies?

Hol. I will play three myself.

Moth. Thrice-worthy gentleman!

Arm. Shall I tell you a thing?

Hol. We attend.

Arm. We will have, if this fadge not, an antick, I
beseech you, follow.

Hol. Via !—Goodman Dull, thou hast spoken no word
all this while.

Dull. Nor understood none neither, sir.

Hol. Allons ! we will employ thee.

Dull. I 'll make one in a dance, or so! or I will play
On the tabor to the Worthies, and let them dance the hay.

Hol. Most dull, honest Dull.—To our sport, away!

[*Exeunt*

SCENE II.—Outside the Park.   Before the PRINCESS'S
Pavilion

Enter the PRINCESS, KATHARINE, ROSALINE, *and* MARIA

Prin. Sweet hearts, we shall be rich ere we depart,
If fairings come thus plentifully in:
A lady walled about with diamonds!
Look you, what I have from the loving king.

Ros. Madam, came nothing else along with that?

Prin. Nothing but this? yes, as much love in rhyme,
As would be crammed up in a sheet of paper,
Writ on both sides the leaf, margin and all,
That he was fain to seal on Cupid's name.

Ros. That was the way to make his godhead wax;
For he hath been five thousand years a boy.

Kath. Ay, and a shrewd unhappy gallows too.

Ros. You 'll ne'er be friends with him: he killed your
sister.

Kath. He made her melancholy, sad, and heavy;
And so she died: had she been light, like you,
Of such a merry, nimble, stirring spirit,
She might have been a grandam ere she died;
And so may you, for a light heart lives long.

Ros. What 's your dark meaning, mouse, of this light
word?

Kath. A light condition in a beauty dark.

Ros. We need more light to find your meaning out.

Kath. You'll mar the light by taking it in snuff;
Therefore I'll darkly end the argument.

Ros. Look, what you do, you do it still i' the dark.

Kath. So do not you, for you are a light wench.

Ros.   Indeed, I weigh not you, and therefore light.
Kath.   You weigh me not?—O! that 's you care not
   for me.
Ros.   Great reason; for, past cure is still past care.
Prin.   Well bandied both; a set of wit well played.
But, Rosaline, you have a favour too:
Who sent it? and what is 't?
   Ros.   I would you knew:
An if my face were but as fair as yours,
My favour were as great: be witness this.
Nay, I have verses too, I thank Biron.
The numbers true; and, were the numbering too,
I were the fairest goddess on the ground:
I am compared to twenty thousand fairs.
O, he hath drawn my picture in his letter.
   Prin.   Anything like?
   Ros.   Much in the letters; nothing in the praise.
   Prin.   Beauteous as ink: a good conclusion.
   Kath.   Fair as a text B in a copy-book.
   Ros.   Ware pencils, ho! let me not die your debtor,
My red dominical, my golden letter:
O, that your face were not so full of O's!
   Kath.   A pox of that jest! and beshrew all shrows!
   Prin.   But, what was sent to you from fair Dumain?
   Kath.   Madam, this glove.
   Prin.   Did he not send you twain?
   Kath.   Yes, madam; and moreover,
Some thousand verses of a faithful lover:
A huge translation of hypocrisy,
Vilely compiled, profound simplicity.
   Mar.   This, and these pearls to me sent Longaville:
The letter is too long by half a mile.
   Prin.   I think no less.   Dost thou not wish in heart,
The chain were longer, and the letter short!
   Mar.   Ay, or I would these hands might never part.
   Prin.   We are wise girls to mock our lovers so.
   Ros.   They are worse fools to purchase mocking so.
That same Biron I 'll torture ere I go.
O, that I knew he were but in by the week!
How I would make him fawn, and beg, and seek,
And wait the season, and observe the times,
And spend his prodigal wits in bootless rhymes,
And shape his service wholly to my hests,
And make him proud to make me proud that jests!
So portent-like would I o'ersway his state,
That he should be my fool, and I his fate.
   Prin.   None are so surely caught, when they are catched,
As wit turned fool: folly, in wisdom hatched,
Hath wisdom's warrant and the help of school,
And wit's own grace to grace a learnéd fool.

Ros. The blood of youth burns not with such excess
As gravity's revolt to wantonness.
    Mar. Folly in fools bears not so strong a note
As foolery in the wise, when wit doth dote;
Since all the power thereof it doth apply,
To prove, by wit, worth in simplicity.
    Prin. Here comes Boyet, and mirth is in his face.

Enter BOYET

    Boyet. O, I am stabbed with laughter. Where 's her
      grace?
    Prin. Thy news, Boyet?
    Boyet.   Prepare, madam, prepare!
Arm, wenches, arm! encounters mounted are
Against your peace. Love doth approach disguised,
Arméd in arguments: you 'll be surprised.
Muster your wits; stand in your own defence;
Or hide your heads like cowards, and fly hence.
    Prin. Saint Denis to Saint Cupid! What are they
That charge their breath against us? say, scout, say.
    Boyet. Under the cool shade of a sycamore
I thought to close mine eyes some half an hour,
When, lo! to interrupt my purposed rest,
Toward that shade I might behold addrest
The king and his companions: warily
I stole into a neighbour thicket by,
And overheard what you shall overhear;
That by-and-by disguised they will be here.
Their herald is a pretty knavish page,
That well by heart hath conned his embassage:
Action and accent did they teach him there;
"Thus must thou speak, and thus thy body bear:"
And ever and anon they made a doubt
Presence majestical would put him out;
"For," quoth the king, "an angel shalt thou see;
Yet fear not thou, but speak audaciously."
The boy replied, "An angel is not evil;
I should have feared her, had she been a devil."
With that all laughed, and clapped him on the shoulder,
Making the bold wag by their praises bolder.
One rubbed his elbow thus, and fleered, and swore
A better speech was never spoke before;
Another with his finger and his thumb,
Cried " *Via!* we will do 't, come what will come;"
The third he capered, and cried, "All goes well;"
The fourth turned on the toe, and down he fell.
With that they all did tumble on the ground,
With such a zealous laughter, so profound,
That in this spleen ridiculous appears,
To check their folly, passion's solemn tears.

Prin. But what, but what, come they to visit us?
Boyet. They do, they do; and are apparelled thus,—
Like Muscovites, or Russians: as I guess,
Their purpose is, to parle, to court, and dance;
And every one his love-feat will advance
Unto his several mistress; which they 'll know
By favours several which they did bestow.
Prin. And will they so? the gallants shall be tasked;
For, ladies, we will every one be masked,
And not a man of them shall have the grace,
Despite of suit, to see a lady's face.—
Hold, Rosaline, this favour thou shalt wear,
And then the king will court thee for his dear:
Hold, take thou this, my sweet, and give me thine,
So shall Biron take me for Rosaline.—
And change you favours, too; so shall your loves
Woo contrary, deceived by these removes.
Ros. Come on, then; wear the favours most in sight.
Kath. But in this changing what is your intent?
Prin. The effect of my intent is, to cross theirs:
They do it but in mocking merriment;
And mock for mock is only my intent.
Their several counsels they unbosom shall,
To loves mistook; and so be mocked withal,
Upon the next occasion that we meet
With visages displayed, to talk and greet.
Ros. But shall we dance, if they desire us to 't?
Prin. No; to the death, we will not move a foot:
Nor to their penned speech render we no grace;
But, while 't is spoke, each turn away her face.
Boyet. Why, that contempt will kill the speaker's heart
And quite divorce his memory from his part.
Prin. Therefore I do it; and, I make no doubt,
The rest will ne'er come in, if he be out.
There 's no such sport, as sport by sport o'erthrown;
To make theirs ours, and ours none but our own:
So shall we stay, mocking intended game,
And they, well mocked, depart away with shame.
                              [*Trumpets sound within*
Boyet. The trumpet sounds: be masked, the maskers
        come.   [*The Ladies mask*

Enter the KING, BIRON, LONGAVILLE, *and* DUMAIN, *in
    Russian habits, and masked ;* MOTH, *Musicians, and
    Attendants*

Moth. "*All hail, the richest beauties on the earth !*"
Boyet. Beauties no richer than rich taffata.
Moth. "*A holy parcel of the fairest dames,*
                    [*The Ladies turn their backs to him*
That ever turned their—backs—to mortal views !"

    Biron.   "Their eyes," villain, "their eyes."
    Moth.   "*That ever turned their eyes to mortal views!*
Out"—
    Boyet.   True; "out," indeed.
    Moth.   "*Out of your favours, heavenly spirits, vouch-*
        safe
Not to behold"—
    Biron.   "Once to behold," rogue.
    Moth.   "*Once to behold with your sunbeaméd eyes*
    —*with your sunbeamed eyes*"—
    Boyet.   They will not answer to that epithet:
You were best to call it daughter-beaméd eyes.
    Moth.   They do not mark me, and that brings me out.
    Biron.   Is this your perfectness? be gone, you rogue.
    Ros.   What would these strangers? know their minds,
        Boyet.
If they do speak our language, 't is our will
That some plain man recount their purposes.
Know what they would.
    Boyet.   What would you with the princess?
    Biron.   Nothing but peace, and gentle visitation.
    Ros.   What would they, say they?
    Boyet.   Nothing but peace, and gentle visitation.
    Ros.   Why, that they have; and bid them so be gone.
    Boyet.   She says, you have it, and you may be gone.
    King.   Say to her, we have measured many miles
To tread a measure with her on this grass.
    Boyet.   They say, that they have measured many a
        mile
To tread a measure with you on this grass.
    Ros.   It is not so. Ask them how many inches
Is in one mile; if they have measured many
The measure then of one is easily told.
    Boyet.   If, to come hither, you have measured miles,
And many miles, the princess bids you tell
How many inches do fill up one mile.
    Biron.   Tell her, we measure them by weary steps.
    Boyet.   She hears herself.
    Ros.   How many weary steps,
Of many weary miles you have o'ergone,
Are numbered in the travel of one mile?
    Biron.   We number nothing that we spend for you:
Our duty is so rich, so infinite,
That we may do it still without accompt.
Vouchsafe to show the sunshine of your face,
That we, like savages, may worship it.
    Ros.   My face is but a moon, and clouded too.
    King.   Blesséd are clouds, to do as such clouds do!
Vouchsafe, bright moon, and these thy stars, to shine—
Those clouds removed—upon our watery eyne.

Ros.   O vain petitioner, beg a greater matter;
Thou now request'st but moonshine in the water.
   King.   Then, in our measure vouchsafe but one change.
Thou bidd'st me beg; this begging is not strange.
   Ros.   Play, music, then! nay, you must do it soon.
                                        [*Music plays*
Not yet;—no dance.—Thus change I like the moon.
   King.   Will you not dance?   How come you thus
      estranged?
   Ros.   You took the moon at full, but now she's changed.
   King.   Yet still she is the moon, and I the man:
Yet music plays; vouchsafe some motion to it.
   Ros.   Our ears vouchsafe it.
   King.   But your legs should do it.
   Ros.   Since you are strangers, and come here by chance,
We'll not be nice: take hands:—we will not dance.
   King.   Why take we hands then?
   Ros.   Only to part friends.—
Court'sy, sweet hearts; and so the measure ends.
   King.   More measure of this measure: be not nice.
   Ros.   We can afford no more at such a price.
   King.   Prize you yourselves?   What buys your com-
      pany?
   Ros.   Your absence only.
   King.   That can never be.
   Ros.   Then cannot we be bought; and so adieu.
Twice to your visor, and half once to you!
   King.   If you deny to dance, let's hold more chat.
   Ros.   In private then.
   King.   I am best pleased with that.
                                  [*They converse apart*
   Biron.   White-handed mistress, one sweet word with
      thee.
   Prin.   Honey, and milk, and sugar: there are three.
   Biron.   Nay then, two treys, as if you grow so nice,—
Metheglin, wort, and malmsey.—Well run, dice!
There's half a dozen sweets.
   Prin.   Seventh sweet, adieu.
Since you can cog, I'll play no more with you.
   Biron.   One word in secret.
   Prin.   Let it not be sweet.
   Biron.   Thou griev'st my gall.
   Prin.   Gall? bitter.
   Biron.   Therefore meet.
                                  [*They converse apart*
   Dum.   Will you vouchsafe with me to change a word?
   Mar.   Name it.
   Dum.   Fair lady.—
   Mar   Say you so?   Fair lord.—
Take that for your fair lady.

Dum.   Please it you,
As much in private, and I'll bid adieu.
                               [They converse apart

Kath. What, was your visard made without a tongue?
Long. I know the reason, lady, why you ask.
Kath. O, for your reason! quickly, sir; I long.
Long. You have a double tongue within your mask,
And would afford my speechless visard half.
Kath. Veal, quoth the Dutchman:—Is not veal a calf?
Long. A calf, fair lady?
Kath.   No, a fair lord calf.
Long. Let's part the word.
Kath.   No, I'll not be your half:
Take all, and wean it: it may prove an ox.
Long. Look, how you butt yourself in these sharp
    mocks.
Will you give horns, chaste lady? do not so.
Kath. Then die a calf, before your horns do grow.
Long. One word in private with you, ere I die.
Kath. Bleat softly then: the butcher hears you cry.
                               [They converse apart

Boyet. The tongues of mocking wenches are as keen
As is the razor's edge invisible,
Cutting a smaller hair than may be seen;
Above the sense of sense, so sensible
Seemeth their conference; their conceits have wings
Fleeter than arrows, bullets, wind, thought, swifter things.
Ros. Not one word more, my maids: break off, break
    off.
Biron. By heaven, all dry-beaten with pure scoff!
King. Farewell, mad wenches: you have simple wits.
      [Exeunt King, Lords, Moth, Music and Attendants
Prin. Twenty adieus, my frozen Muscovites.—
Are these the breed of wits so wondered at?
Boyet. Tapers they are, with your sweet breaths puffed
    out.
Ros. Well-liking wits they have; gross, gross; fat, fat.
Prin. O poverty in wit, kingly-poor flout!
Will they not, think you, hang themselves to-night,
Or ever, but in visards, show their faces?
This pert Biron was out of countenance quite.
Ros. O, they were all in lamentable cases!
The king was weeping-ripe for a good word.
Prin. Biron did swear himself out of all suit.
Mar. Dumain was at my service, and his sword:
No point, quoth I: my servant straight was mute.
Kath. Lord Longaville said, I came o'er his heart;
And trow you, what he called me?
Prin.   Qualm, perhaps.
Kath. Yes, in good faith.

Prin.   Go, sickness, as thou art!
Ros.   Well, better wits have worn plain statute-caps.
But will you hear? the king is my love sworn.
Prin.   And quick Biron have plighted faith to me.
Kath.   And Longaville was for my service born.
Mar.   Dumain is mine, as sure as bark on tree.
Boyet.   Madam, and pretty mistresses, give ear.
Immediately they will again be here
In their own shapes: for it can never be,
They will digest this harsh indignity.
Prin.   Will they return?
Boyet.   They will, they will, God knows;
And leap for joy, though they are lame with blows:
Therefore, change favours; and, when they repair,
Blow like sweet roses in this summer air.
Prin.   How blow? how blow? speak to be understood.
Boyet.   Fair ladies masked are roses in their bud:
Dismasked, their damask sweet commixture shown,
Are angels vailing clouds, or roses blown.
Prin.   Avaunt, perplexity! What shall we do,
If they return in their own shapes to woo?
Ros.   Good madam, if by me you 'll be advised,
Let 's mock them still, as well known as disguised.
Let us complain to them what fools were here,
Disguised like Muscovites, in shapeless gear;
And wonder what they were, and to what end
Their shallow shows and prologue vilely penned,
And their rough carriage so ridiculous,
Should be presented at our tents to us.
Boyet.   Ladies, withdraw; the gallants are at hand.
Prin.   Whip to our tents, as roes run over land.
                [Exeunt Prin., Rosaline, Katherine, and Maria

Enter the KING, BIRON, LONGAVILLE, *and* DUMAIN, *in
their proper habits*

King.   Fair sir, God save you! Where is the princess?
Boyet.   Gone to her tent. Please it your majesty
Command me any service to her thither?
King.   That she vouchsafe me audience for one word.
Boyet.   I will; and so will she, I know, my lord.   *[Exit*
Biron.   This fellow pecks up wit, as pigeons peas,
And utters it again when God doth please.
He is wit's pedlar, and retails his wares
At wakes and wassails, meetings, markets, fairs;
And we that sell by gross, the Lord doth know,
Have not the grace to grace it with such show.
This gallant pins the wenches on his sleeve:
Had he been Adam, he had tempted Eve.
He can carve too, and lisp: why, this is he,
That kissed away his hand in courtesy;

This is the ape of form, monsieur the nice,
That, when he plays at tables, chides the dice
In honourable terms: nay, he can sing
A mean most meanly; and, in ushering,
Mend him who can: the ladies call him, sweet;
The stairs, as he treads on them, kiss his feet.
This is the flower that smiles on every one,
To show his teeth as white as whalés-bone;
And consciences, that will not die in debt,
Pay him the due of honey-tongued Boyet.
    King. A blister on his sweet tongue, with my heart,
That put Armado's page out of his part!
    Biron. See where it comes!—Behaviour, what wert thou,
Till this man showed thee? and what art thou now?

Enter the PRINCESS, *ushered by* BOYET; ROSALINE, MARIA,
           KATHARINE, *and Attendants*

    King. All hail, sweet madam, and fair time of day!
    Prin. Fair, in all hail, is foul, as I conceive.
    King. Construe my speeches better, if you may.
    Prin. Then wish me better: I will give you leave.
    King. We came to visit you, and purpose now
To lead you to our court; vouchsafe it, then.
    Prin. This field shall hold me, and so hold your vow:
Nor God, nor I, delights in perjured men.
    King. Rebuke me not for that which you provoke;
The virtue of your eye must break my oath.
    Prin. You nickname virtue; vice you should have
      spoke;
For virtue's office never breaks men's troth.
Now, by my maiden honour, yet as pure
As the unsullied lily, I protest,
A world of torments though I should endure,
I would not yield to be your house's guest;
So much I hate a breaking cause to be
Of heavenly oaths, vowed with integrity.
    King. O, you have lived in desolation here,
Unseen, unvisited, much to our shame.
    Prin. Not so, my lord; it is not so, I swear:
We have had pastimes here, and pleasant game.
A mess of Russians left us but of late.
    King. How, madam? Russians?
    Prin.   Ay, in truth, my lord;
Trim gallants, full of courtship and of state.
    Ros. Madam, speak true. It is not so, my lord:
My lady—to the manner of the days—
In courtesy gives undeserving praise.
We four, indeed, confronted were with four
In Russian habit: here they stayed an hour,
And talked apace; and in that hour, my lord,

They did not bless us with one happy word.
I dare not call them fools; but this I think,
When they are thirsty fools would fain have drink.
    Biron.   This jest is dry to me.—Fair, gentle sweet,
Your wit makes wise things foolish: when we greet
With eyes best seeing heaven's fiery eye,
By light we lose light: your capacity
Is of that nature, that to your huge store
Wise things seem foolish, and rich things but poor.
    Ros.   This proves you wise and rich, for in my eye,—
    Biron.   I am a fool, and full of poverty.
    Ros.   But that you take what doth to you belong,
It were a fault to snatch words from my tongue.
    Biron.   O, I am yours, and all that I possess.
    Ros.   All the fool mine?
    Biron.   I cannot give you less.
    Ros.   Which of the visards was it that you wore?
    Biron.   Where? when? what visard? why demand you
      this?
    Ros.   There, then, that visard; that superfluous case
That hid the worse and showed the better face.
    King.   We are descried: they'll mock us now down-
      right.
    Dum.   Let us confess, and turn it to a jest.
    Prin.   Amazed, my lord? Why looks your highness sad?
    Ros.   Help, hold his brows! he'll swoon. Why look
      you pale?—
Sea-sick, I think, coming from Muscovy.
    Biron.   Thus pour the stars down plagues for perjury.
Can any face of brass hold longer out?—
Here stand I, lady; dart thy skill at me;
    Bruise me with scorn, confound me with a flout;
Thrust thy sharp wit quite through my ignorance;
    Cut me to pieces with thy keen conceit:
And I will wish thee never more to dance,
    Nor never more in Russian habit wait.
O, never will I trust to speeches penned,
    Nor to the motion of a school-boy's tongue;
Nor never come in visard to my friend;
    Nor woo in rhyme, like a blind harper's song;
Taffeta phrases, silken terms precise,
    Three-piled hyperboles, spruce affectation,
Figures pedantical: these summer-flies
    Have blown me full of maggot ostentation.
I do forswear them; and I here protest,
    By this white glove,—how white the hand, God knows—
Henceforth my wooing mind shall be expressed
    In russet yeas, and honest kersey noes:
And, to begin,—wench, so God help me, la!
My love to thee is sound, *sans* crack or flaw.

Ros.   Sans "*sans*," I pray you.
Biron.   Yet I have a trick
Of the old rage:—bear with me, I am sick;
I'll leave it by degrees. Soft, let us see:—
Write "Lord have mercy on us" on those three;
They are infected, in their hearts it lies;
They have the plague, and caught it of your eyes:
These lords are visited; you are not free,
For the lords' tokens on you do I see.
     Prin.   No, they are free that gave these tokens to us.
     Biron.   Our states are forfeit: seek not to undo us.
     Ros.   It is not so; for how can this be true,
That you stand forfeit, being those that sue?
     Biron.   Peace! for I will not have to do with you.
     Ros.   Nor shall not, if I do as I intend.
     Biron.   Speak for yourselves: my wit is at an end.
     King.   Teach us, sweet madam, for our rude transgression
Some fair excuse.
     Prin.   The fairest is confession.
Were you not here, but even now, disguised?
     King.   Madam, I was.
     Prin.   And were you well advised?
     King.   I was, fair madam.
     Prin.   When you then were here,
What did you whisper in your lady's ear?
     King.   That more than all the world I did respect her.
     Prin.   When she shall challenge this, you will reject her.
     King.   Upon mine honour, no.
     Prin.   Peace! peace, forbear:
Your oath once broke, you force not to forswear.
     King.   Despise me, when I break this oath of mine.
     Prin.   I will; and therefore keep it.—Rosaline,
What did the Russian whisper in your ear?
     Ros.   Madam, he swore, that he did hold me dear
As precious eyesight, and did value me
Above this world; adding thereto, moreover,
That he would wed me, or else die my lover.
     Prin.   God give thee joy of him! the noble lord
Most honourably doth uphold his word.
     King.   What mean you, madam? by my life, my troth,
I never swore this lady such an oath.
     Ros.   By heaven, you did; and to confirm it plain,
You gave me this: but take it, sir, again.
     King.   My faith, and this, the princess I did give:
I knew her by this jewel on her sleeve.
     Prin.   Pardon me, sir, this jewel did she wear;
And Lord Biron, I thank him, is my dear.—
What! will you have me, or your pearl again?
     Biron.   Neither of either; I remit both twain.—

I see the trick on 't:—here was a consent,
Knowing aforehand of our merriment,
To dash it like a Christmas comedy.
Some carry-tale, some please-man, some slight zany,
Some mumble-news, some trencher-knight, some Dick,
That smiles his cheek in years, and knows the trick
To make my lady laugh when she 's disposed,
Told our intents before; which once disclosed,
The ladies did change favours, and then we,
Following the signs, wooed but the sign of she.
Now, to our perjury to add more terror,
We are again forsworn,—in will and error.
Much upon this it is;—[*to Boyet*] and might not you
Forestall our sport, to make us thus untrue?
Do not you know my lady's foot by the squire,
   And laugh upon the apple of her eye?
And stand between her back, sir, and the fire,
   Holding a trencher, jesting merrily?
You put our page out: go, you are allowed;
Die when you will, a smock shall be your shroud.
You leer upon me, do you? there's an eye
Wounds like a leaden sword.
   Boyet.   Full merrily
Hath this brave managed, this career, been run.
   Biron.   Lo, he is tilting straight!—Peace! I have done.

Enter COSTARD

Welcome, pure wit! thou partest a fair fray.
   Cost.   O Lord, sir, they would know,
Whether the three Worthies shall come in, or no.
   Biron.   What, are there but three?
   Cost.   No, sir; but it is vara fine,
For every one pursents three.
   Biron.   And three times thrice is nine.
   Cost.   Not so, sir; under correction, sir, I hope, it is
     not so.
You cannot beg us, sir, I can assure you, sir; we know
     what we know:
I hope sire, three times thrice, sir,—
   Biron.   Is not nine.
   Cost.   Under correction, sir, we know whereuntil it
doth amount.
   Biron.   By Jove, I always took three threes for nine.
   Cost.   O Lord! sir, it were pity you should get your
living by reckoning, sir.
   Biron.   How much is it?
   Cost.   O Lord, sir, the parties themselves, the actors,
sir, will show whereuntil it doth amount: for mine own
part, I am, as they say, but to perfect one man,—e'en one
poor man,—Pompion the Great, sir.

Biron. Art thou one of the Worthies?

Cost. It pleased them to think me worthy of Pompion the Great: for mine own part, I know not the degree of the Worthy: but I am to stand for him.

Biron. Go, bid them prepare.

Cost. We will turn it finely off, sir: we will take some care.   [*Exit*

King. Biron, they will shame us; let them not approach.

Biron. We are shame-proof, my lord; and 't is some policy

To have one show worse than the king's and his company.

King. I say, they shall not come.

Prin. Nay, my good lord, let me o'errule you now.

That sport best pleases that doth least know how:

Where zeal strives to content, and the contents

Die in the zeal of them which it presents,

Their form confounded makes most form in mirth,

When great things labouring perish in their birth.

Biron. A right description of our sport, my lord.

Enter ARMADO

Arm. Anointed, I implore so much expense of thy royal sweet breath, as will utter a brace of words.

[*Armado converses with the King, and delivers a paper to him*

Prin. Doth this man serve God?

Biron. Why ask you?

Prin. He speaks not like a man of God's making.

Arm. That's all one, my fair, sweet, honey monarch; for, I protest, the schoolmaster is exceeding fantastical; too, too vain; too, too vain: but we will put it, as they say, to *fortuna della guerra.* I wish you the peace of mind, most royal couplement!   [*Exit*

King. Here is like to be a good presence of Worthies. He presents Hector of Troy; the swain, Pompey the Great; the parish curate, Alexander; Armado's page, Hercules; the pedant, Judas Maccabæus.

And if these four Worthies in their first show thrive,

These four will change habits, and present the other five.

Biron. There is five in the first show.

King. You are deceived, 't is not so.

Biron. The pedant, the braggart, the hedge-priest, the fool, and the boy:—

Abate throw at novum, and the whole world again

Cannot pick out five such, take each one in his vein.

King. The ship is under sail, and here she comes amain.

Enter COSTARD *armed, for Pompey*

Cost. "I Pompey am,"—

Boyet.   You lie, you are not he.
Cost.   "*I Pompey am,*"—
Boyet.   With libbard's head on knee.
Biron.   Well said, old mocker: I must needs be friends
  with thee.
Cost.   "*I Pompey am, Pompey surnamed the Big,*"—
Dum.   The Great.
Cost.   It is "*Great,*" sir;—"*Pompey surnamed the Great ;*
*That oft in field, with targe and shield, did make my foe to
  sweat :*
And travelling along this coast, I here am come by chance,
*And lay my arms before the legs of this sweet lass of
  France.*"
If your ladyship would say, "*Thanks, Pompey,*" I had
  done.
Prin.   Great thanks, great Pompey.
Cost.   'T is not so much worth; but I hope, I was per-
fect.   I made a little fault in "*Great.*"
  Biron.   My hat to a halfpenny, Pompey proves the best
  Worthy.

Enter SIR NATHANIEL *armed, for Alexander*

Nath.   "*When in the world I lived, I was the world's
  commander ;*
*By east, west, north, and south, I spread my conquering
  might :*
My 'scutcheon plain declares that I am Alisander."
  Boyet.   Your nose says, no, you are not; for it stands
  too right.
  Biron.   Your nose smells, no, in this, most tender-
  smelling knight.
  Prin.   The conqueror is dismayed.   Proceed, good
  Alexander.
  Nath.   "*When in the world I lived, I was the world's
  commander ;*"
  Boyet.   Most true: 't is right: you were so, Alisander.
  Biron.   Pompey the Great,—
  Cost.   Your servant, and Costard.
  Biron.   Take away the conqueror, take away Alisander
  Cost.   [*To Nath.*]   O, sir, you have overthrown
Alisander the conqueror.   You will be scraped out of the
painted cloth for this: your lion, that holds his poll-axe
sitting on a close-stool, will be given to Ajax: he will be
the ninth Worthy.   A conqueror, and afeard to speak?
run away for shame, Alisander.   [*Nath. retires*]   There,
an 't shall please you: a foolish mild man; an honest man,
look you, and soon dashed!   He is a marvellous neighbour,
faith, and a very good bowler; but, for Alisander, alas!
you see, how 't is;—a little o'erparted.—But there are

Worthies a-coming will speak their mind in some other
sort.
    Prin.   Stand aside, good Pompey.

    Enter HOLOFERNES *armed, for Judas, and* MOTH
           armed, for Hercules

    Hol.   *"Great Hercules is presented by this imp,*
    Whose club killed Cerberus, that three-headed canus;
And, when he was a babe, a child, a shrimp,
    Thus did he strangle serpents in his manus.
Quoniam *he seemeth in minority,*
Ergo *I come with this apology."*
Keep some state in thy *exit,* and vanish.—   [*Moth retires*
" Judas I am,"—
    Dum.   A Judas!
    Hol.   Not Iscariot, sir.—
" Judas I am, ycleped *Maccabæus."*
    Dum.   Judas Maccabæus clipt, 'is plain Judas.
    Biron.   A kissing traitor.—How art thou proved Judas?
    Hol.   *"Judas I am,"*—
    Dum.   The more shame for you, Judas.
    Hol.   What mean you, sir?
    Boyet.   To make Judas hang himself.
    Hol.   Begin, sir: you are my elder.
    Biron.   Well followed: Judas was hanged on an elder.
    Hol.   I will not be put out of countenance.
    Biron.   Because thou hast no face.
    Hol.   What is this?
    Boyet.   A cittern-head.
    Dum.   The head of a bodkin.
    Biron.   A death's face in a ring.
    Long.   The face of an old Roman coin, scarce seen.
    Boyet.   The pummel of Cæsar's falchion.
    Dum.   The carved-bone face on a flask.
    Biron.   St. George's half-cheek in a brooch.
    Dum.   Ay, and in a brooch of lead.
    Biron.   Ay, and worn in the cap of a tooth-drawer.
And now, forward; for we have put thee in countenance.
    Hol.   You have put me out of countenance.
    Biron.   False: we have given thee faces.
    Hol.   But you have out-faced them all.
    Biron.   An thou wert a lion, we would do so.
    Boyet.   Therefore, as he is an ass, let him go.
And so adieu, sweet Jude! nay, why dost thou stay?
    Dum.   For the latter end of his name.
    Biron.   For the ass to the Jude? give it him:—Jud-as
    away.
    Hol.   This is not generous, not gentle, not humble.
    Boyet.   A light for Monsieur Judas! it grows dark, he
    may stumble.

Prin. Alas, poor Maccabæus, how hath he been baited

Enter ARMADO *armed, for Hector*

Biron. Hide thy head, Achilles: here comes Hector in arms.

Dum. Though my mocks come home by me, I will now be merry.

King. Hector was but a Trojan in respect of this.

Boyet. But is this Hector?

King. I think Hector was not so clean-timbered.

Long. His leg is too big for Hector's.

Dum. More calf, certain.

Boyet. No; he is best indued in the small.

Biron. This cannot be Hector.

Dum. He 's a god or a painter; for he makes faces.

Arm. " *The armipotent Mars, of lances the almighty,*
Gave Hector a gift,"—

Dum. A gilt nutmeg.

Biron. A lemon.

Long. Stuck with cloves.

Dum. No, cloven.

Arm. Peace!

" *The armipotent Mars, of lances the almighty,*
Gave Hector a gift, the heir of Ilion ;
A man so breathed, that certain he would fight ye,
From morn till night, out of his pavilion
I am that flower,"—

Dum.   That mint.

Long.   That columbine.

Arm. Sweet Lord Longaville, rein thy tongue.

Long. I must rather give it the rein, for it runs against Hector.

Dum. Ay, and Hector's a greyhound.

Arm. The sweet war-man is dead and rotten: sweet chucks, beat not the bones of the buried: when he breathed, he was a man.—But I will forward with my device. Sweet royalty, bestow on me the sense of hearing.

                              [*Biron whispers Costard*

Prin. Speak, brave Hector: we are much delighted.

Arm. I do adore thy sweet grace's slipper.

Boyet. Loves her by the foot.

Dum. He may not by the yard.

Arm. " *This Hector far surmounted Hannibal,"*—

Cost. The party is gone: fellow Hector, she is gone; she is two months on her way.

Arm. What meanest thou?

Cost. Faith, unless you play the honest Trojan, the poor wench is cast away: she's quick; the child brags in her belly already: 't is yours.

Arm. Dost thou infamonise me among potentates? Thou shalt die.

Cost. Then shall Hector be whipped for Jaquenetta that is quick by him, and hanged for Pompey that is dead by him.

Dum. Most rare Pompey!

Boyet. Renowned Pompey!

Biron. Greater than great;—great, great, great Pompey! Pompey the Huge!

Dum. Hector trembles.

Biron. Pompey is moved.—More Atés, more Atés! stir them on! stir them on!

Dum. Hector will challenge him.

Biron. Ay, if he have no more man's blood in 's belly than will sup a flea.

Arm. By the north pole, I do challenge thee.

Cost. I will not fight with a pole, like a northern man: I'll slash; I'll do it by the sword.—I pray you, let me borrow my arms again.

Dum. Room for the incensed Worthies!

Cost. I'll do it in my shirt.

Dum. Most resolute Pompey!

Moth. Master, let me take you a buttonhole lower. Do you not see, Pompey, is uncasing for the combat? What mean you? you will lose your reputation.

Arm. Gentlemen, and soldiers, pardon me; I will not combat in my shirt.

Dum. You may not deny it: Pompey hath made the challenge.

Arm. Sweet bloods, I both may and will.

Biron. What reason have you for 't?

Arm. The naked truth of it is, I have no shirt.   I go woolward for penance.

Boyet. True, and it was enjoined him in Rome for want of linen; since when, I 'll be sworn, he wore none but a dishclout of Jaquenetta's, and that he wears next his heart for a favour.

Enter MONSIEUR MERCADET, *a Messenger*

Mer. God save you, madam.

Prin. Welcome, Mercadet,
But that thou interrupt'st our merriment.

Mer. I am sorry, madam; for the news I bring
Is heavy in my tongue.—The king your father—

Prin. Dead, for my life!

Mer. Even so; my tale is told.

Biron. Worthies, away! The scene begins to cloud.

Arm. For mine own part, I breathe free breath. I have seen the day of wrong through the little hole of discretion, and I will right myself like a soldier.   [*Exeunt Worthies*

King.   How fares your majesty?
Prin.   Boyet, prepare: I will away to-night.
King.   Madam, not so; I do beseech you, stay.
Prin.   Prepare, I say.—I thank you, gracious lords,
For all your fair endeavours; and entreat,
Out of a new-sad soul, that you vouchsafe
In your rich wisdom to excuse, or hide,
The liberal opposition of our spirits:
If over-boldly we have borne ourselves
In the converse of breath, your gentleness
Was guilty of it.   Farewell, worthy lord!
A heavy heart bears not a humble tongue.
Excuse me so, coming so short of thanks
For my great suit so easily obtained.
   King.   The extreme part of time extremely forms
All causes to the purpose of his speed;
And often, at his very loose, decides
That which long process could not arbitrate:
And though the mourning brow of progeny
Forbid the smiling courtesy of love
The holy suit which fain it would convince;
Yet, since love's argument was first on foot,
Let not the cloud of sorrow justle it
From what it purposed; since, to wail friends lost
Is not by much so wholesome, profitable,
As to rejoice at friends but newly found.
   Prin.   I understand you not: my griefs are dull.
   Biron.   Honest plain words best pierce the ear of
      grief;
And by these badges understand the king.
For your fair sakes have we neglected time,
Played foul play with our oaths.   Your beauty, ladies
Hath much deformed us, fashioning our humours
Even to the opposéd end of our intents;
And what in us hath seemed ridiculous,
As love is full of unbefitting strains;
All wanton as a child, skipping, and vain;
Formed by the eye, and, therefore, like the eye,
Full of strange shapes, of habits, and of forms,
Varying in subjects as the eye doth roll
To every varied object in his glance:
Which party-coated presence of loose love
Put on by us, if, in your heavenly eyes,
Have misbecomed our oaths and gravities,
Those heavenly eyes, that look into these faults,
Suggested us to make them.   Therefore, ladies,
Our love being yours, the error that love makes
Is likewise yours: we to ourselves prove false,
By being once false for ever to be true
To those that make us both,—fair ladies, you:

And even that falsehood, in itself a sin,
Thus purifies itself, and turns to grace.
 Prin. We have received your letters full of love;
Your favours, the ambassadors of love;
And, in our maiden council, rated them
At courtship, pleasant jest, and courtesy,
As bombast and as lining to the time.
But more devout than this in our respects
Have we not been; and therefore met your loves
In their own fashion, like a merriment.
 Dum. Our letters, madam, showed much more than jest.
 Long. So did our looks.
 Ros.   We did not quote them so.
 King. Now, at the latest minute of the hour,
Grant us your loves.
 Prin.   A time, methinks, too short
To make a world-without-end bargain in.
No, no, my lord, your grace is perjured much,
Full of dear guiltiness; and therefore this:—
If for my love—as there is no such cause—
You will do aught, this shall you do for me:
Your oath I will not trust; but go with speed
To some forlorn and naked hermitage,
Remote from all the pleasures of the world;
There stay, until the twelve celestial signs
Have brought about their annual reckoning.
If this austere insociable life
Change not your offer made in heat of blood;
If frosts, and fasts, hard lodging, and thin weeds,
Nip not the gaudy blossoms of your love,
But that it bear this trial, and last love;
Then, at the expiration of the year,
Come challenge, challenge me by these deserts,
And by this virgin palm, now kissing thine,
I will be thine; and, till that instant, shut
My woful self up in a mourning house,
Raining the tears of lamentation
For the remembrance of my father's death.
If this thou do deny, let our hands part:
Neither intitled in the other's heart.
 King. If this, or more than this, I would deny,
 To flatter up these powers of mine with rest,
The sudden hand of death close up mine eye.
 Hence ever then my heart is in thy breast.
 Dum. But what to me, my love? but what tó me?
 Kath. A wife?—A beard, fair health, and honesty;
With three-fold love I wish you all these three.
 Dum. O, shall I say, I thank you, gentle wife?
 Kath. Not so, my lord. A twelvemonth and a day
I'll mark no words that smooth-faced wooers say:

Come when the king doth to my lady come;
Then, if I have much love, I 'll give you some.
    Dum. I 'll serve thee true and faithfully till then.
    Kath. Yet swear not, lest you be forsworn again.
    Long.   What says Maria?
    Mar.   At the twelvemonth's end,
I'll change my black gown for a faithful friend.
    Long. I'll stay with patience; but the time is
    long.
    Mar. The liker you; few taller are so young.
    Biron. Studies my lady? mistress, look on me.
Behold the window of my heart, mine eye,
What humble suit attends thy answer there;
Impose some service on me for thy love.
    Ros. Oft have I heard of you, my Lord Biron,
Before I saw you, and the world's large tongue
Proclaims you for a man replete with mocks;
Full of comparisons and wounding flouts,
Which you on all estates will execute,
That lie within the mercy of your wit:
To weed this wormwood from your fruitful brain,
And, therewithal, to win me, if you please,
Without the which I am not to be won,
You shall this twelvemonth term, from day to day,
Visit the speechless sick, and still converse
With groaning wretches; and your task shall be,
With all the fierce endeavour of your wit,
To enforce the painéd impotent to smile.
    Biron. To move wild laughter in the throat of
    death?
It cannot be; it is impossible:
Mirth cannot move a soul in agony.
    Ros. Why, that's the way to choke a gibing spirit,
Whose influence is begot of that loose grace
Which shallow laughing hearers give to fools.
A jest's prosperity lies in the ear
Of him that hears it, never in the tongue
Of him that makes it: then, if sickly ears,
Deafed with the clamours of their own dear groans,
Will hear your idle scorns, continue them,
And I will have you and that fault withal;
But, if they will not, throw away that spirit,
And I shall find you empty of that fault,
Right joyful of your reformation.
    Biron. A twelvemonth! well, befall what will befall,
I'll jest a twelvemonth in an hospital.
    Prin. [*To the King*] Ay, sweet my lord; and so I
    take my leave.
    King. No, madam; we will bring you on your way.
    Biron. Our wooing doth not end like an old play;

Jack hath not Jill: these ladies' courtesy
Might well have made our sport a comedy.
 King. Come, sir, it wants a twelvemonth and a day,
And then 't will end.
 Biron.   That's too long for a play.

Enter ARMADO

 Arm. Sweet majesty, vouchsafe me,—
 Prin. Was not that Hector?
 Dum. The worthy knight of Troy.
 Arm. I will kiss thy royal finger, and take leave. I am
a votary: I have vowed to Jaquenetta to hold the plough
for her sweet love three years. But, most esteemed greatness, will you hear the dialogue that the two learned men
have compiled in praise of the owl and the cuckoo? it should
have followed in the end of our show.
 King. Call them forth quickly; we will do so.
 Arm. Holla! approach.

Enter HOLOFERNES, NATHANIEL, MOTH, COSTARD,
and others

This side is Hiems, Winter, this Ver, the Spring; the one
maintained by the owl, the other by the cuckoo. Ver,
begin.

SONG

SPRING

I

When daisies pied, and violets blue,
 And lady-smocks all silver-white,
And cuckoo-buds of yellow hue,
 Do paint the meadows with delight,
The cuckoo then, on every tree,
Mocks married men ; for thus sings he,
   Cuckoo ;
Cuckoo, cuckoo,—O word of fear,
Unpleasing to a married ear !

II

When shepherds pipe on oaten straws,
 And merry larks are ploughmen's clocks,
When turtles tread, and rooks, and daws,
 And maidens bleach their summer smocks,
The cuckoo then, on every tree,
Mocks married men; for thus sings he,
   Cuckoo ;
Cuckoo, cuckoo,—O word of fear,
Unpleasing to a married ear !

220

Winter

III

When icicles hang by the wall,
*   And Dick the shepherd blows his nail,*
And Tom bears logs into the hall,
*   And milk comes frozen home in pail,*
When blood is nipped, and ways be foul,
Then nightly sings the staring owl,
*   To-who ;*
Tu-whit, to-who,—a merry note,
While greasy Joan doth keel the pot.

When all aloud the wind doth blow,
*   And coughing drowns the parson's saw,*
And birds sit brooding in the snow,
*   And Marian's nose looks red and raw,*
When roasted crabs hiss in the bowl,
Then nightly sings the staring owl,
*   To-who ;*
Tu-whit, to-who,—a merry note,
While greasy Joan doth keel the pot.

Arm.   The words of Mercury are harsh after the songs of Apollo.   You, that way,—we, this way.   [*Exeunt*

MACBETH

DRAMATIS PERSONÆ

DUNCAN, *King of Scotland*
MALCOLM
DONALBAIN } *his sons*
MACBETH
BANQUO } *generals of the King's army*
MACDUFF
LENNOX
ROSS
MENTEITH - *noblemen of Scotland*
ANGUS
CAITHNESS
FLEANCE, *son to Banquo*
SIWARD, *Earl of Northumberland, general of the English forces*
Young SIWARD, *his son*
SEYTON, *an officer attending on Macbeth*
Boy, son to Macduff
An English doctor
A Scotch doctor
A Soldier
A Porter
An Old Man

LADY MACBETH
LADY MACDUFF
Gentlewoman attending on Lady Macbeth
HECATE, *and three witches*

Lords, Gentlemen, Officers, Soldiers, Murderers, Attendants,
and Messengers
The Ghost of Banquo, and other apparitions

SCENE.—*In the end of the Fourth Act, in England: through
the rest of the Play, in Scotland*

MACBETH

ACT ONE

SCENE I.—A Desert Place

Thunder and lightning.   Enter three Witches

First Witch.   When shall we three meet again,
In thunder, lightning, or in rain?
Sec. Witch.   When the hurley-burley's done,
When the battle's lost and won.
Third Witch.   That will be ere the set of sun.
First Witch.   Where the place?
Sec. Witch.   Upon the heath.
Third Witch.   There to meet with Macbeth.
First Witch.   I come, Graymalkin.
Sec. Witch.   Paddock calls.
Third Witch.   Anon!
All.   Fair is foul, and foul is fair:
Hover through the fog and filthy air.   [*Exeunt*

SCENE II.—A Camp near Forres

Alarum within.   Enter KING DUNCAN, MALCOLM, DONAL-
BAIN, LENNOX, *with attendants, meeting a bleeding
Sergeant*

Dun.   What bloody man is that?   He can report,
As seemeth by his plight, of the revolt
The newest state.
Mal.   This is the sergeant
Who like a good and hardy soldier fought
'Gainst my captivity: Hail, brave friend!
Say to the king the knowledge of the broil
As thou didst leave it.
Ser.   Doubtful it stood,
As two spent swimmers that do cling together
And choke their art.   The merciless Macdonwald—
Worthy to be a rebel, for to that
The multiplying villainies of nature
Do swarm upon him—from the Western Isles
Of kerns and gallowglasses is supplied,
And Fortune, on his damned quarrel smiling,
Showed like a rebel's whore: but all's too weak,
For brave Macbeth—well he deserved that name—

Disdaining Fortune, with his brandished steel,
Which smoked with bloody execution,
Like valour's minion
Carved out his passage till he faced the slave,
Which ne'er shook hands nor bade farewell to him
Till he unseamed him from the nave to the chaps,
And fixed his head upon our battlements.
   Dun. O valiant cousin! worthy gentleman.
   Ser. As whence the sun gins his reflection
Shipwrecking storms and direful thunders break,
So from that spring whence comfort seemed to come
Discomfort swells. Mark, King of Scotland, mark :
No sooner justice had, with valour armed,
Compelled these skipping kerns to trust their heels,
But the Norweyan lord, surveying vantage,
With furbished arms and new supplies of men,
Began a fresh assault.
   Dun.   Dismayed not this
Our captains, Macbeth and Banquo?
   Ser.   Yes,
As sparrows eagles, or the hare the lion.
If I say sooth, I must report they were
As cannons overcharged with double cracks;
So they
Doubly redoubled strokes upon the foe:
Except they meant to bathe in reeking wounds,
Or memorise another Golgotha,
I cannot tell—
But I am faint, my gashes cry for help.
   Dun. So well thy words become thee as thy wounds;
They smack of honour both.—Go, get him surgeons.
                   [Exit Sergeant, attended

Enter Ross

Who comes here?
   Mal.   The worthy thane of Ross.
   Len. What haste looks through his eyes! So should he look
That seems to speak things strange.
   Ross.   God save the king!
   Dun. Whence cam'st thou, worthy thane?
   Ross.   From Fife, great king,
Where the Norweyan banners flout the sky
And fan our people cold. Norway himself,
With terrible numbers,
Assisted by that most disloyal traitor
The thane of Cawdor, began a dismal conflict;
Till that Bellona's bridegroom, lapped in proof,
Confronted him with self-comparisons,
Point against point rebellious, arm 'gainst arm,

Curbing his lavish spirit; and, to conclude,
The victory fell on us.
    Dun.   Great happiness!
    Ross.   That now
Sweno, the Norway's king, craves composition;
Nor would we deign him burial of his men
Till he disburséd at Saint Colme's Inch
Ten thousand dollars to our general use.
    Dun.   No more that thane of Cawdor shall deceive
Our bosom interest:—Go, pronounce his present death,
And with his former title greet Macbeth.
    Ross.   I 'll see it done.
    Dun.   What he hath lost, noble Macbeth hath won.
                                         [Exeunt

Scene III.—A Heath

Thunder. Enter the three Witches

    First Witch.   Where hast thou been, sister?
    Sec. Witch.   Killing swine.
    Third Witch.   Sister, where thou?
    First Witch.   A sailor's wife had chestnuts in her lap,
And mounched, and mounched, and mounched:—"Give
    me," quoth I:—
"Aroint thee, witch!" the rump-fed ronyon cries.—
Her husband's to Aleppo gone, master o' the *Tiger;*
But in a sieve I 'll thither sail,
And, like a rat without a tail,
I 'll do, I 'll do, and I 'll do.
    Sec. Witch.   I 'll give thee a wind.
    First Witch.   Thou art kind.
    Third Witch.   And I another.
    First Witch.   I myself have all the other;
And to every point they blow,
All the quarters that they know
I' the shipman's card.
I will drain him dry as hay:
Sleep shall neither night nor day
Hang upon his penthouse lid;
He shall live a man forbid.
Weary seven-nights, nine times nine,
Shall he dwindle, peak, and pine.
Though his bark cannot be lost,
Yet it shall be tempest-tost.—
Look what I have.
    Sec. Witch.   Show me, show me.
    First Witch.   Here I have a pilot's thumb,
Wrecked as homeward he did come.   *[Drum within*

Third Witch.   A drum, a drum!
Macbeth doth come.
   All.   The weird sisters, hand in hand,
Posters of the sea and land,
Thus do go about, about:
Thrice to thine, and thrice to mine,
And thrice again, to make up nine.
Peace!—the charm's wound up.

Enter MACBETH *and* BANQUO

   Macb.   So foul and fair a day I have not seen.
   Ban.   How far is 't called to Forres?—What are these,
So withered, and so wild in their attire,
That look not like th' inhabitants o' th' earth,
And yet are on 't?   Live you, or are you aught
That man may question?   You seem to understand me,
By each at once her choppy finger laying
Upon her skinny lips: you should be women,
And yet your beards forbid me to interpret
That you are so.
   Macb.   Speak, if you can: what are you?
   First Witch.   All hail, Macbeth! hail to thee, thane of
      Glamis!
   Sec. Witch.   All hail, Macbeth! hail to thee, thane of
      Cawdor!
   Third Witch.   All hail, Macbeth! that shalt be King
      hereafter!
   Ban.   Good sir, why do you start, and seem to fear
Things that do sound so fair?—I' the name of truth,
Are ye fantastical, or that indeed
Which outwardly ye show?   My noble partner
You greet with present grace, and great prediction
Of noble having, and of royal hope
That he seems rapt withal: to me you speak not.
If you can look into the seeds of time
And say which grain will grow and which will not,
Speak then to me, who neither beg nor fear
Your favours nor your hate.
   First Witch.   Hail!
   Sec. Witch.   Hail!
   Third Witch.   Hail!
   First Witch.   Lesser than Macbeth, and greater.
   Sec. Witch.   Not so happy, yet much happier.
   Third Witch.   Thou shalt get kings, though thou be none.
So, all hail, Macbeth and Banquo!
   First Witch.   Banquo and Macbeth, all hail!
   Macb.   Stay, you imperfect speakers, tell me more.
By Sinel's death I know I am thane of Glamis;
But how of Cawdor? the thane of Cawdor lives,

A prosperous gentleman; and to be King
Stands not within the prospect of belief,
No more than to be Cawdor. Say, from whence
You owe this strange intelligence? or why
Upon this blasted heath you stop our way
With such prophetic greeting? Speak, I charge you.
                                        [*Witches vanish*
   Ban.   The earth hath bubbles, as the water has,
And these are of them. Whither are they vanished?
   Macb.   Into the air; and what seemed corporal melted
As breath into the wind.—Would they had stayed!
   Ban.   Were such things here as we do speak about,
Or have we eaten of the insane root
That takes the reason prisoner?
   Macb.   Your children shall be kings.
   Ban.   You shall be king.
   Macb.   And thane of Cawdor too; went it not so?
   Ban.   To the selfsame tune and words. Who 's here?

Enter Ross *and* Angus

   Ross.   The king hath happily received, Macbeth,
The news of thy success; and when he reads
Thy personal venture in the rebels' fight,
His wonders and his praises do contend
Which should be thine or his: silenced with that,
In viewing o'er the rest of the selfsame day,
He finds thee in the stout Norweyan ranks
Nothing afeared of, what thyself didst make,
Strange images of death. As thick as hail
Came post with post, and every one did bear
Thy praises in his kingdom's great defence,
And poured them down before him.
   Ang.   We are sent
To give thee from our royal master thanks;
Only to herald thee into his sight,
Not pay thee.
   Ross.   And, for an earnest of greater honour,
He bade me, from him, call thee thane of Cawdor:
In which addition, Hail, most worthy thane!
For it is thine.
   Ban.   What, can the devil speak true?
   Macb.   The thane of Cawdor lives: why do you dress me
In borrowed robes?
   Ang.   Who was the thane, lives yet:
But under heavy judgment bears that life
Which he deserves to lose. Whether he was combined
With those of Norway, or did line the rebel
With hidden help and vantage, or that with both
He laboured in his country's wreck, I know not:

But treasons capital, confessed and proved,
Have overthrown him.—
    Macb.   Glamis, and thane of Cawdor:
The greatest is behind.—Thanks for your pains.—
Do you not hope your children shall be kings,
When those that gave the thane of Cawdor to me
Promised no less to them?
    Ban.   That, trusted home,
Might yet enkindle you unto the crown,
Besides the thane of Cawdor. But 't is strange:
And oftentimes, to win us to our harm,
The instruments of darkness tell us truths;
Win us with honest trifles, to betray us
In deepest consequence.—
Cousins, a word, I pray you.—
    Macb.   Two truths are told,
As happy prologues to the swelling act
Of the imperial theme.—I thank you gentlemen.—
This supernatural soliciting
Cannot be ill; cannot be good: if ill,
Why hath it given me earnest of success,
Commencing in a truth? I am thane of Cawdor:
If good, why do I yield to that suggestion
Whose horried image doth unfix my hair,
And make my seated heart knock at my ribs,
Against the use of nature? Present fears
Are less than horrible imaginings.
My thought, whose murder yet is but fantastical,
Shakes so my single state of man, that function
Is smothered in surmise, and nothing is
But what is not.—
    Ban.   Look how our partner's rapt.—
    Macb. If chance will have me King, why, chance may
          crown me,
Without my stir.—
    Ban.   New honours come upon him
Like our strange garments, cleave not to their mould
But with the aid of use.—
    Macb.   Come what come may,
Time and the hour runs through the roughest day.
    Ban. Worthy Macbeth, we stay upon your leisure.
    Macb. Give me your favour: my dull brain was wrought
With things forgotten. Kind gentlemen, your pains
Are registered where every day I turn
The leaf to read them. Let us toward the king.—
Think upon what hath chanced, and at more time,
The interim having weighed it, let us speak
Our free hearts each to other.
    Ban.   Very gladly.
    Macb. Till then, enough.—Come, friends.   *[Exeunt*

SCENE IV.—Forres. A Room in the Palace

Flourish. Enter DUNCAN, MALCOLM, DONALBAIN, LENNOX,
and Attendants

    Dun. Is execution done on Cawdor? Are not
Those in commission yet returned?
    Mal.   My liege,
They are not yet come back. But I have spoke
With one that saw him die: who did report,
That very frankly he confessed his treasons,
Implored your highness' pardon, and set forth
A deep repentance. Nothing in his life
Became him like the leaving it: he died
As one that had been studied in his death
To throw away the dearest thing he owed
As 't were a careless trifle.
    Dun.   There 's no art
To find the mind's construction in the face:
He was a gentleman on whom I built
An absolute trust.—

    Enter MACBETH, BANQUO, ROSS, *and* ANGUS

                     O worthiest cousin!
The sin of my ingratitude even now
Was heavy on me. Thou art so far before,
That swiftest wing of recompense is slow
To overtake thee: would thou hadst less deserved,
That the proportion both of thanks and payment
Might have been mine: only I have left to say,
More is thy due than more than all can pay.
    Macb. The service and the loyalty I owe,
In doing it, pays itself. Your highness' part
Is to receive our duties: and our duties
Are to your throne and state, children and servants;
Which do but what they should by doing everything
Safe toward your love and honour.
    Dun.   Welcome hither:
I have begun to plant thee, and will labour
To make thee full of growing.—Noble Banquo,
That hast no less deserved, nor must be known
No less to have done so; let me infold thee
And hold thee to my heart.
    Ban.   There if I grow,
The harvest is your own.
    Dun.   My plenteous joys,
Wanton in fulness, seek to hide themselves
In drops of sorrow.—Sons, kinsmen, thanes,
And you whose places are the nearest, know,
We will establish our estate upon

Our eldest Malcolm; whom we name hereafter
The Prince of Cumberland: which honour must
Not, unaccompanied, invest him only,
But signs of nobleness, like stars, shall shine
On all deservers.—Hence to Inverness,
And bind us further to you.
    Macb.   The rest is labour, which is not used for you:
I'll be myself the harbinger, and make joyful
The hearing of my wife with your approach:
So humbly take my leave.
    Dun.   My worthy Cawdor!
    Macb. [*aside*] The Prince of Cumberland! That is a
         step
On which I must fall down, or else o'erleap,
For in my way it lies. Stars, hide your fires.
Let not light see my black and deep desires:
The eye wink at the hand; yet let that be,
Which the eye fears, when it is done, to see.—   [*Exit*
    Dun.   True, worthy Banquo: he is full so valiant,
And in his commendations I am fed;
It is a banquet to me. Let us after him,
Whose care is gone before to bid us welcome:
It is a peerless kinsman.   [*Flourish.*   *Exeunt*

Scene V.—Inverness. A Room in Macbeth's Castle

Enter Lady Macbeth, *reading a letter*

    Lady M.   *They met me in the day of success ; and I have
learned by the perfectest report, they have more in them than
mortal knowledge. When I burned in desire to question them
further, they made themselves air, into which they vanished.
Whiles I stood rapt in the wonder of it, came missives from
the king, who all-hailed me " Thane of Cawdor" ; by which
title, before, these weird sisters saluted me, and referred me
to the coming on of time, with "Hail, king that shalt be !"
This have I thought good to deliver thee, my dearest partner of
greatness, that thou mightest not lose the dues of rejoicing by
being ignorant of what greatness is promised thee. Lay it to
thy heart, and farewell.*

Glamis thou art, and Cawdor; and shalt be
What thou art promised. Yet do I fear thy nature;
It is too full o' the milk of human kindness
To catch the nearest way. Thou wouldst be great;
Art not without ambition: but without
The illness should attend it: what thou wouldst highly,
That wouldst thou holily; wouldst not play false,
And yet wouldst wrongly win: thou 'dst have, great Glamis,
That which cries "Thus thou must do, if thou have it;"

And that which rather thou dost fear to do
Than wishest should be undone.   Hie thee hither,
That I may pour my spirits in thine ear,
And chastise with the valour of my tongue
All that impedes thee from the golden round,
Which Fate and metaphysical aid doth seem
To have thee crowned withal.—

Enter an Attendant

                            What is your tidings?
    Att.   The king comes here to-night.
    Lady M.   Thou 'rt mad to say it.—
Is not thy master with him? who, were 't so,
Would have informed for preparation.
    Att.   So please you, it is true: our thane is coming:
One of my fellows had the speed of him,
Who, almost dead for breath, had scarcely more
Than would make up his message.
    Lady M.   Give him tending;
He brings great news. [*Exit Attendant*]   The raven himself
       is hoarse
That croaks the fatal entrance of Duncan
Under my battlements.   Come you spirits
That tend on mortal thoughts, unsex me here,
And fill me, from the crown to the toe, top-full
Of direst cruelty! make thick my blood,
Stop up the access and passage to remorse,
That no compunctious visitings of nature
Shake my fell purpose, nor keep peace between
The effect and it!   Come to my woman's breasts,
And take my milk for gall, you murdering ministers,
Wherever in your sightless substances
You wait on nature's mischief!   Come thick night,
And pall thee in the dunnest smoke of hell,
That my keen knife see not the wound it makes,
Nor heaven peep through the blanket of the dark,
To cry, "Hold, hold!"

Enter MACBETH

                     Great Glamis! worthy Cawdor!
Greater than both, by the all-hail hereafter!
Thy letters have transported me beyond
This ignorant present, and I feel now
The future in the instant.
    Macb.   My dearest love,
Duncan comes here to-night.
    Lady M.   And when goes hence?
    Macb.   To-morrow, as he purposes.
    Lady M.   O, never
Shall sun that morrow see.

Your face, my thane, is as a book where men
May read strange matters; to beguile the time,
Look like the time; bear welcome in your eye,
Your hand, your tongue: look like the innocent flower,
But be the serpent under 't. He that 's coming
Must be provided for: and you shall put
This night's great business into my despatch;
Which shall to all our nights and days to come
Give solely sovereign sway and masterdom.—
    Macb. We will speak further.
    Lady M.   Only look up clear:
To alter favour ever is to fear:—
Leave all the rest to me.   [*Exeunt*

SCENE VI.—The Same. Before the Castle

Hautboys and torches. Enter DUNCAN, MALCOLM, DONAL-
    BAIN, BANQUO, LENNOX, MACDUFF, ROSS, ANGUS, *and*
    Attendants

    Dun. This castle hath a pleasant seat; the air
Nimbly and sweetly recommends itself
Unto our gentle senses.
    Ban.   This guest of summer,
The temple-haunting martlet, does approve
By his loved mansionry that the heaven's breath
Smells wooingly here; no jutty, frieze,
Buttress, nor coign of vantage, but this bird
Hath made his pendent bed and procreant cradle:
Where they most breed and haunt, I have observed,
The air is delicate.

Enter LADY MACBETH

    Dun. See, see, our honoured hostess.—
The love that follows us sometime is our trouble,
Which still we thank as love. Herein I teach you
How you shall bid God yield us for your pains
And thank us for your trouble.
    Lady M.   All our service
In every point twice done, and then done double,
Were poor and single business to contend
Against those honours deep and broad wherewith
Your majesty loads our house: for those of old,
And the late dignities heaped up to them,
We rest your hermits.
    Dun.   Where 's the thane of Cawdor?
We coursed him at the heels, and had a purpose
To be his purveyor: but he rides well;
And his great love, sharp as his spur, hath holp him
To his home before us. Fair and noble hostess,
We are your guest to-night.

Lady M.   Your servants ever
Have theirs, themselves, and what is theirs, in compt,
To make their audit at your highness' pleasure,
Still to return your own.
　　Dun.   Give me your hand;
Conduct me to mine host: we love him highly,
And shall continue our graces towards him.
By your leave, hostess.   [*Exeunt*

SCENE VII.—The Same.   A Room in the Castle

Hautboys and torches. Enter, and pass over the stage, a
Sewer, and divers Servants with dishes and service.
Then enter MACBETH

　　Macb.   If it were done when 't is done, then 't were well
It were done quickly: if the assassination
Could trammel up the consequence, and catch
With his surcease success: that but this blow
Might be the be-all and the end-all here,
But here, upon this bank and shoal of time,
We 'd jump the life to come.   But in these cases
We still have judgment here; that we but teach
Bloody instructions, which, being taught, return
To plague th' inventor.   This even-handed justice
Commends the ingredients of our poisoned chalice
To our own lips.   He 's here in double trust:
First, as I am his kinsman and his subject,
Strong both against the deed; then, as his host,
Who should against his murderer shut the door,
Not bear the knife myself.   Beside, this Duncan
Hath borne his faculties so meek, hath been
So clear in his great office, that his virtues
Will plead like angels, trumpet-tongued, against
The deep damnation of his taking off;
And pity, like a naked new-born babe,
Striding the blast, or heaven's cherubin, horsed
Upon the sightless couriers of the air,
Shall blow the horrid deed in every eye,
That tears shall drown the wind.—I have no spur
To prick the sides of my intent, but only
Vaulting ambition, which o'erleaps itself,
And falls on the other—

Enter LADY MACBETH

　　　　　　　　　　　　　　　How now? what news?
　　Lady M.   He has almost supped.   Why have you left
　　　the chamber?
　　Macb.   Hath he asked for me?
　　Lady M.   Know you not, he has?

Macb.   We will proceed no further in this business:
He hath honoured me of late; and I have bought
Golden opinions from all sorts of people,
Which would be worn now in their newest gloss,
Not cast aside so soon.
    Lady M.   Was the hope drunk
Wherein you dressed yourself? hath it slept since,
And wakes it now, to look so green and pale
At what it did so freely?   From this time,
Such I account thy love.   Art thou afeard
To be the same in thine own act and valour
As thou art in desire?   Wouldst thou have that
Which thou esteem'st the ornament of life,
And live a coward in thine own esteem,
Letting "I dare not" wait upon "I would,"
Like the poor cat i' the adage?
    Macb.   Pr'ythee, peace.
I dare do all that may become a man;
Who dares do more, is none.
    Lady M.   What beast was 't then,
That made you break this enterprise to me?
When you durst do it, then you were a man;
And, to be more than what you were, you would
Be so much more the man.   Nor time nor place
Did then adhere, and yet you would make both:
They have made themselves, and that their fitness now
Does unmake you.   I have given suck, and know
How tender 't is to love the babe that milks me:
I would, while it was smiling in my face,
Have plucked my nipple from his boneless gums,
And dashed the brains out, had I so sworn as you
Have done to this.
    Macb.   If we should fail?
    Lady M.   We fail.
But screw your courage to the sticking place,
And we 'll not fail.   When Duncan is asleep—
Whereto the rather shall his day's hard journey
Soundly invite him—his two chamberlains
Will I with wine and wassail so convince,
That memory, the warder of the brain,
Shall be a fume, and the receipt of reason
A limbeck only: when in swinish sleep
Their drenchéd natures lie, as in a death,
What cannot you and I perform upon
Th' unguarded Duncan? what not put upon
His spongy officers, who shall bear the guilt
Of our great quell?
    Macb.   Bring forth men-children only;
For thy undaunted mettle should compose
Nothing but males.   Will it not be received,

When we have marked with blood those sleepy two
Of his own chamber, and used their very daggers,
That they have done 't?
 Lady M. Who dares receive it other,
As we shall make our griefs and clamour roar
Upon his death?
 Macb.   I am settled, and bend up
Each corporal agent to this terrible feat.
Away, and mock the time with fairest show:
False face must hide what the false heart doth know.
             [*Exeunt*

ACT TWO

SCENE I.—Inverness. Court within Macbeth's Castle

Enter BANQUO, *and* FLEANCE *with a torch before him*

Ban. How goes the night, boy?
Fle. The moon is down; I have not heard the clock.
Ban. And she goes down at twelve.
Fle.   I take 't, 't is later, sir.
Ban. Hold, take my sword.—There's husbandry in
  heaven;
Their candles are all out.—Take thee that too.—
A heavy summons lies like lead upon me,
And yet I would not sleep: merciful powers,
Restrain in me the cursèd thoughts that nature
Gives way to in repose!—Give me my sword.
Who 's there?

Enter MACBETH, *and a Servant with a torch*

 Macb. A friend.
 Ban. What, sir, not yet at rest? The king a-bed:
He hath been in unusual pleasure, and
Sent forth great largess to your offices.
This diamond he greets your wife withal,
By the name of most kind hostess; and shut up
In measureless content.
 Macb.   Being unprepared,
Our will became the servant to defect,
Which else should free have wrought.
 Ban.   All 's well.—
I dreamt last night of the three weird sisters:
To you they have showed some truth.
 Macb.   I think not of them.
Yet, when we can entreat an hour to serve,

We would spend it in some words upon that business,
If you would grant the time.
    Ban.   At your kind'st leisure.
    Macb.   If you shall cleave to my consent, when 't is,
It shall make honour for you.
    Ban.   So I lose none
In seeking to augment it, but still keep
My bosom franchised and allegiance clear,
I shall be counselled.
    Macb.   Good repose, the while!
    Ban. Thanks, sir: the like to you.
                     [Exeunt Banquo and Fleance
    Macb.   Go, bid my mistress, when my drink is ready,
She strike upon the bell.   Get thee to bed.—
                           [Exit Servant
Is this a dagger which I see before me,
The handle toward my hand? Come, let me clutch
      thee:—
I have thee not, and yet I see thee still.
Art thou not, fatal vision, sensible
To feeling as to sight? or art thou but
A dagger of the mind, a false creation
Proceeding from the heat-oppresséd brain?
I see thee yet, in form as palpable
As this which now I draw.
Thou marshall'st me the way that I was going;
And such an instrument I was to use.
Mine eyes are made the fools o' the other senses,
Or else worth all the rest: I see thee still;
And on thy blade and dudgeon gouts of blood,
Which was not so before. There 's no such thing.
It is the bloody business which informs
Thus to mine eyes.—Now o'er the one half-world
Nature seems dead, and wicked dreams abuse
The curtained sleep: witchcraft celebrates
Pale Hecate's offerings; and withered murder,
Alarumed by his sentinel, the wolf,
Whose howl 's his watch, thus with his stealthy pace,
With Tarquin's ravishing strides, towards his design
Moves like a ghost.—Thou sure and firm-set earth,
Hear not my steps, which way they walk, for fear
The very stones prate of my whereabout,
And take the present horror from the time,
Which now suits with it.—Whiles I threat, he lives:
Words to the heat of deeds too cold breath gives.—
                          [A bell rings
I go, and it is done: the bell invites me.
Hear it not, Duncan; for it is a knell
That summons thee to heaven or to hell.   *[Exit*

SCENE II.—The Same

Enter LADY MACBETH

Lady M.   That which hath made them drunk hath made
        me bold;
What hath quenched them hath given me fire.—Hark!—
        Peace!—
It was the owl that shrieked, the fatal bellman,
Which gives the stern'st good-night.—He is about it.—
The doors are open, and the surfeited grooms
Do mock their charge with snores: I have drugged their
        possets,
That death and nature do contend about them
Whether they live or die.
    Macb.   [*Within*]   Who's there?—what, ho!
    Lady M.   Alack!   I am afraid they have awaked
And 't is not done:—the attempt and not the deed
Confounds us.—Hark!—I laid their daggers ready;
He could not miss 'em.   Had he not resembled
My father as he slept, I had done 't.—My husband!

Enter MACBETH

    Macb.   I have done the deed.   Didst thou not hear a
        noise?
    Lady M.   I heard the owl scream and the crickets cry.
Did not you speak?
    Macb.   When?
    Lady M.   Now.
    Macb.   As I descended?
    Lady M.   Ay.
    Macb.   Hark!
Who lies i' the second chamber?
    Lady M.   Donalbain.
    Macb.   This is a sorry sight.
    Lady M.   A foolish thought to say a sorry sight.
    Macb.   There's one did laugh in 's sleep, and one cried
        "Murder!"
That they did wake each other: I stood and heard them;
But they did say their prayers, and addressed them
Again to sleep.
    Lady M.   There are two lodged together.
    Macb.   One cried, "God bless us!" and, "Amen," the
        other,
As they had seen me with these hangman's hands.
Listening their fear, I could not say "Amen,"
When they did say "God bless us."
    Lady M.   Consider it not so deeply.
    Macb.   But wherefore could not I pronounce "Amen"?

I had most need of blessing, and "Amen"
Stuck in my throat.
   Lady M.   These deeds must not be thought
After these ways: so, it will make us mad.
   Macb.   Methought I heard a voice cry, "Sleep no more!
Macbeth does murder sleep,"—the innocent sleep:
Sleep, that knits up the ravelled sleave of care,
The death of each day's life, sore labour's bath,
Balm of hurt minds, great nature's second course,
Chief nourisher in life's feast;—
   Lady M.   What do you mean?
   Macb.   Still it cried, "Sleep no more!" to all the house:
"Glamis hath murdered sleep, and therefore Cawdor
Shall sleep no more, Macbeth shall sleep no more!"
   Lady M.   Who was it that thus cried? Why, worthy
     thane,
You do unbend your noble strength, to think
So brainsickly of things. Go, get some water,
And wash this filthy witness from your hand.—
Why did you bring these daggers from the place?
They must lie there: go, carry them, and smear
The sleepy grooms with blood.
   Macb.   I 'll go no more:
I am afraid to think what I have done;
Look on 't again I dare not.
   Lady M.   Infirm of purpose!
Give me the daggers. The sleeping and the dead
Are but as pictures; 't is the eye of childhood
That fears a painted devil. If he do bleed
I'll gild the faces of the grooms withal,
For it must seem their guilt.—
            [Exit.—Knocking within
   Macb.   Whence is that knocking?—
How is 't with me, when every noise appals me?
What hands are here? ha! they pluck out mine eyes.
Will all great Neptune's ocean wash this blood
Clean from my hand? No, this my hand will rather
The multitudinous seas incarnadine,
Making the green one red.

Re-enter LADY MACBETH

   Lady.   My hands are of your colour: but I shame
To wear a heart so white. *[Knock]* I hear a knocking
At the south entry;—retire we to our chamber.
A little water clears us of this deed:
How easy is it then!—Your constancy
Hath left you unattended.—*[Knock]* Hark, more knocking.
Get on your night-gown, lest occasion call us,
And show us to be watchers.—Be not lost
So poorly in your thoughts.

Macb. To know my deed, 't were best not know myself.
                                              [*Knock*
Wake Duncan with thy knocking:—I would thou couldst!
                                              [*Exeunt*

SCENE III.—The Same

Enter a Porter

                                      [*Knocking within*
     Porter. Here's a knocking, indeed! If a man were
porter of hell-gate, he should have old turning the key:—
[*Knocking*] Knock, knock, knock. "Who's there, i' the
name of Beelzebub?"—"Here's a farmer, that hanged himself on the expectation of plenty:" "Come in, farmer: have
napkins enough about you, here you'll sweat for't." [*Knocking*] Knock, knock. "Who's there, i' the other devil's
name?"—"Faith, here is an equivocator, that could swear
in both the scales against either scale; who committed
treason enough for God's sake, yet could not equivocate to
heaven:" "O! come in, equivocator." [*Knocking*]
Knock, knock, knock. "Who 's there?"—"Faith, here 's
an English tailor come hither for stealing out of a French
hose:" "Come in, tailor; here you may roast your goose."
[*Knocking*] Knock, knock. Never at quiet! "What are
you?"—But this place is too cold for hell. I'll devil-porter
it no further. I had thought to have let in some of all
professions, that go the primrose way to the everlasting
bonfire. [*Knocking*] Anon, anon! I pray you remember
the porter.   [*Opens the gate*

Enter MACDUFF *and* LENNOX

     Macd. Was it so late, friend, ere you went to bed,
That you do lie so late?
     Port. Faith, sir, we were carousing till the second cock;
And drink, sir, is a great provoker of three things.
     Macd. What three things does drink especially provoke?
     Port. Marry, sir, nose-painting, sleep, and urine.
Lechery, sir, it provokes, and unprovokes; it provokes
the desire, but it takes away the performance. Therefore,
much drink may be said to be an equivocator with lechery:
it makes him, and it mars him; it sets him on, and it takes
him off; it persuades him, and disheartens him; makes
him stand to, and not stand to: in conclusion, equivocates
him in a sleep, and, giving him the lie, leaves him.
     Macd. I believe, drink gave thee the lie last night.
     Port. That it did, sir, i' the very throat o' me: but I
requited him for his lie: and, I think, being too strong for
him, though he took up my legs sometime, yet I made a
shift to cast him.

Macd.   Is thy master stirring?

Enter MACBETH

Our knocking has awaked him; here he comes.
  Len.   Good-morrow, noble sir.
  Macb.   Good-morrow, both.
  Macd.   Is the King stirring, worthy thane?
  Macb.   Not yet.
  Macd.   He did command me to call timely on him:
I have almost slipped the hour.
  Macb.   I 'll bring you to him.
  Macd.   I know this is a joyful trouble to you;
But yet 't is one.
  Macb.   The labour we delight in physics pain.
This is the door.
  Macd.   I 'll make so bold to call,
For 't is my limited service.   [*Exit*
  Len.   Goes the King hence to-day?
  Macb.   He does:—he did appoint so.
  Len.   The night has been unruly.   Where we lay,
Our chimneys were blown down, and, as they say,
Lamentings heard i' the air, strange screams of death,
And prophesying with accents terrible
Of dire combustion and confused events
New hatched to the woful time.   The obscure bird
Clamoured the livelong night: some say, the earth
Was feverous, and did shake.
  Macb.   'T was a rough night.
  Len.   My young remembrance cannot parallel
A fellow to it.

Re-enter MACDUFF

  Macd.   O horror, horror, horror!   Tongue, nor heart
Cannot conceive nor name thee!
  Macb., Len.   What's the matter?
  Macd.   Confusion now hath made his masterpiece!
Most sacrilegious murder hath broke ope
The Lord's anointed temple, and stole thence
The life o' the building.
  Macb.   What is 't you say? the life?
  Len.   Mean you his majesty?
  Macd.   Approach the chamber, and destroy your sight
With a new Gorgon.   Do not bid me speak:
See, and then speak yourselves.
                              [*Exeunt Macbeth and Lennox*
                              Awake! awake!—
Ring the alarum-bell.—Murder, and treason!
Banquo and Donalbain!   Malcolm! awake!
Shake off this downy sleep, death's counterfeit,
And look on death itself! up, up, and see

The great doom's image!—Malcolm! Banquo!
As from your graves rise up, and walk like sprites,
To countenance this horror!   [*Bell rings*

Enter LADY MACBETH

Lady M.   What 's the business,
That such a hideous trumpet calls to parley
The sleepers of the house? speak, speak!
  Macd.   O gentle lady,
'T is not for you to hear what I can speak:
The repetition, in a woman's ear,
Would murder as it fell.

Enter BANQUO

      O Banquo, Banquo,
Our royal master 's murdered!
  Lady M.   Woe, alas!
What! in our house?
  Ban.   Too cruel, anywhere.
Dear Duff, I pr'ythee contradict thyself
And say, it is not so.

Re-enter MACBETH *and* LENNOX

Macb.   Had I but died an hour before this chance,
I have lived a blessèd time: for, from this instant
There 's nothing serious in mortality,
All is but toys; renown and grace is dead;
The wine of life is drawn, and the mere lees
Is left this vault to brag of.

Enter MALCOLM *and* DONALBAIN

Don.   What is amiss?
  Macb.   You are, and do not know 't:
The spring, the head, the fountain of your blood
Is stopped; the very source of it is stopped.
  Macd.   Your royal father 's murdered.
  Mal.   O, by whom?
  Len.   Those of his chamber, as it seemed, had done 't:
Their hands and faces were all badged with blood;
So were their daggers, which, unwiped, we found
Upon their pillows:
They stared, and were distracted; no man's life
Was to be trusted with them.
  Macb.   O, yet I do repent me of my fury,
That I did kill them.
  Macd.   Wherefore did you so?
  Macb.   Who can be wise, amazed; temperate and
   furious;

Loyal and neutral, in a moment? No man.
The expedition of my violent love
Outrun the pauser reason.—Here lay Duncan,
His silver skin laced with his golden blood,
And his gashed stabs looked like a breach in nature
For ruin's wasteful entrance: there, the murderers,
Steeped in the colours of their trade, their daggers
Unmannerly breeched with gore. Who could refrain,
That had a heart to love, and in that heart
Courage to make 's love known?
   Lady M.   Help me hence, ho!
   Macd. Look to the lady.
   Mal.   Why do we hold our tongues
That most may claim this argument for ours?
   Don. What should be spoken
Here, where our fate, hid in an auger-hole,
May rush, and seize us? Let 's away; our tears
Are not yet brewed.
   Mal.   Nor our strong sorrow yet
Upon the foot of motion.
   Ban.   Look to the lady:—
                    [*Lady Macbeth is carried out*
And when we have our naked frailties hid,
That suffer in exposure, let us meet,
And question this most bloody piece of work,
To know it further. Fears and scruples shake us:
In the great hand of God I stand; and, thence,
Against the undivulged pretence I fight
Of treasonous malice.
   Macd.   And so do I.
   All.   So all.
   Macb. Let's briefly put on manly readiness,
And meet i' the hall together.
   All.   Well contended.
        [*Exeunt all but Malcolm and Donalbain*
   Mal. What will you do? Let's not consort with
      them:
To show an unfelt sorrow is an office
Which the false man does easy. I 'll to England.
   Don. To Ireland, I: our separated fortune
Shall keep us both the safer; where we are,
There's daggers in men's smiles: the near in blood
The nearer bloody.
   Mal.   This murderous shaft that's shot
Hath not yet lighted; and our safest way
Is to avoid the aim: therefore, to horse:
And let us not be dainty of leave-taking,
But shift away. There 's warrant in that theft
Which steals itself, when there 's no mercy left.
                         [*Exeunt*

SCENE IV.—Without the Castle

Enter Ross *and an Old Man*

Old M.   Threescore and ten I can remember well;
Within the volume of which time I have seen
Hours dreadful and things strange, but this sore night
Hath trifled former knowings.
Ross.   Ah, good father,
Thou seest, the heavens, as troubled with man's act,
Threaten his bloody stage: by the clock 't is day,
And yet dark night strangles the travelling lamp:
Is 't night's predominance, or the day's shame,
That darkness does the face of the earth entomb
When living light should kiss it?
Old M.   'T is unnatural,
Even like the deed that 's done.   On Tuesday last,
A falcon, towering in her pride of place,
Was by a mousing owl hawked at and killed.
Ross.   And Duncan's horses—a thing most strange and
          certain—
Beauteous and swift, the minions of their race,
Turned wild in nature, broke their stalls, flung out,
Contending 'gainst obedience, as they would make
War with mankind.
Old M.   'T is said, they ate each other.
Ross.   They did so; to the amazement of mine eyes,
That looked upon 't.—Here comes the good Macduff.

Enter MACDUFF

How goes the world, sir, now?
Macd.   Why, see you not?
Ross.   Is 't known who did this more than bloody deed?
Macd.   Those that Macbeth hath slain.
Ross.   Alas, the day
What good could they pretend?
Macd.   They were suborned.
Malcolm, and Donalbain, the king's two sons,
Are stolen away and fled; which puts upon them
Suspicion of the deed.
Ross.   'Gainst nature still:
Thriftless ambition, that wilt ravin up
Thine own life's means!—Then 't is most like
The sovereignty will fall upon Macbeth.
Macd.   He is already named, and gone to Scone
To be invested.
Ross.   Where 's Duncan's body?
Macd.   Carried to Colme-kill,
The sacred storehouse of his predecessors,
And guardian of their bones.
Ross.   Will you to Scone?

Macd.   No cousin: I 'll to Fife.
Ross.   Well, I will thither.
Macd.   Well,—may you see things well done there —
    adieu!—
Lest our old robes sit easier than our new!
Ross.   Farewell, father.
Old M.   God's benison go with you; and with those
That would make good of bad, and friends of foes!
                                              [*Exeunt*

ACT THREE

SCENE I.—Forres.   A Room in the Palace
Enter BANQUO

Ban.   Thou hast it now, King, Cawdor, Glamis, all,
As the weird women promised; and I fear,
Thou play'dst most foully for 't; yet it was said
It should not stand in thy posterity,
But that myself should be the root and father
Of many kings.   If there come truth from them,—
As upon thee, Macbeth, their speeches shine,—
Why, by the verities on thee made good,
May they not be my oracles as well,
And set me up in hope?   But, hush; no more.

Sennet sounded.   Enter MACBETH, *as King;* LADY MAC-
    BETH, *as Queen;* LENNOX, ROSS, *Lords, and Attendants*

Macb.   Here 's our chief guest.
Lady M.   If he had been forgotten,
It had been as a gap in our great feast,
And all-thing unbecoming.
Macb.   To-night we hold a solemn supper, sir,
And I' ll request your presence.
Ban.   Let your highness
Command upon me, to the which my duties
Are with a most indissoluble tie
For ever knit.
Macb.   Ride you this afternoon?
Ban.   Ay, my good lord.
Macb.   We should have else desired your good advice—
Which still hath been both grave and prosperous—
In this day's council; but we 'll take to-morrow.
Is 't far you ride?
Ban.   As far, my lord, as will fill up the time
'Twixt this and supper; go not my horse the better,
I must become a borrower of the night
For a dark hour or twain.
Macb.   Fail not our feast.
Ban.   My lord, I will not.

    Macb. We hear our bloody cousins are bestowed
In England and in Ireland; not confessing
Their cruel parricide, filling their hearers
With strange invention. But of that to-morrow,
When, therewithal, we shall have cause of state
Craving us jointly. Hie you to horse: adieu,
Till you return at night. Goes Fleance with you?
    Ban. Ay, my good lord: our time does call upon 's.
    Macb. I wish your horses swift, and sure of foot,
And so I do commend you to their backs.
Farewell.—   [*Exit Banquo*
Let every man be master of his time
Till seven at night; to make society
The sweet welcome, we will keep ourself
Till supper time alone; while then, God be with you.
            [*Exeunt Lady Macbeth, Lords, etc.*
Sirrah, a word with you. Attend those men
Our pleasure?
    Atten. They are, my lord, without the palace gate.
    Macb. Bring them before us.   [*Exit Attendant*
                  To be thus is nothing;
But to be safely thus. Our fears in Banquo
Stick deep, and in his royalty of nature
Reigns that which would be feared: 't is much he dares;
And, to that dauntless temper of his mind,
He hath a wisdom that doth guide his valour
To act in safety. There is none but he
Whose being I do fear: and under him
My genius is rebuked; as it is said,
Mark Antony's was by Cæsar. He chid the sisters
When first they put the name of King upon me,
And bade them speak to him: then, prophet-like,
They hailed him father to a line of kings.
Upon my head they placed a fruitless crown,
And put a barren sceptre in my gripe,
Then to be wrenched with an unlineal hand,
No son of mine succeeding. If 't be so,
For Banquo's issue have I filed my mind;
For them the gracious Duncan have I murdered;
Put rancours in the vessel of my peace,
Only for them; and mine eternal jewel
Given to the common enemy of man,
To make them kings, the seed of Banquo kings!
Rather than so, come, Fate, into the list,
And champion me to the utterance!—Who 's there?

       Re-enter Attendant with two Murderers

Now, go to the door, and stay there till we call.
                  [*Exit Attendant*
Was it not yesterday we spoke together?

First Mur.   It was, so please your highness.
   Macb.   Well then, now
Have you considered of my speeches?   Know,
That is was he, in the times past, which held you
So under fortune, which you thought had been
Our innocent self.   This I made good to you
In our last conference; passed in probation with you
How you were borne in hand; how crossed; the instru-
      ments;
Who wrought with them; and all things else, that might
To half a soul and to a notion crazed
Say "Thus did Banquo."
   First Mur.   You made it known to us.
   Macb.   I did so; and went further, which is now
Our point of second meeting.   Do you find
Your patience so predominant in your nature,
That you can let this go?   Are you so gospelled
To pray for this good man, and for his issue,
Whose heavy hand hath bowed you to the grave
And beggared yours for ever?
   First Mur.   We are men, my liege.
   Macb.   Ay, in the catalogue ye go for men;
As hounds, and greyhounds, mongrels, spaniels, curs,
Shoughs, water-rugs, and demi-wolves, are clept
All by the name of dogs: the valued file
Distinguishes the swift, the slow, the subtle,
'The housekeeper, the hunter, every one
According to the gift which bounteous nature
Hath in him closed; whereby he does receive
Particular addition, from the bill
That writes them all alike: and so of men.
Now, if you have a station in the file
Not i' the worst rank of manhood, say it,
And I will put that business in your bosoms
Whose execution takes your enemy off,
Grapples you to the heart and love of us,
Who wear our health but sickly in his life,
Which in his death were perfect.
   Sec. Mur.   I am one, my liege,
Whom the vile blows and buffets of the world
Have so incensed, that I am reckless what
I do to spite the world.
   First Mur.   And I another,
So weary with disasters, tugged with fortune,
That I would set my life on any chance,
To mend it or be rid on 't.
   Macb.   Both of you
Know, Banquo was your enemy.
   Sec. Mur.   True, my lord.
   Macb.   So is he mine; and in such bloody distance,

That every minute of his being thrusts
Against my near'st of life: and though I could
With barefaced power sweep him from my sight,
And bid my will avouch it, yet I must not—
For certain friends that are both his and mine,
Whose loves I may not drop—but wail his fall
Who I myself struck down: and thence it is
That I to your assistance do make love,
Masking the business from the common eye
For sundry weighty reasons.
 Sec. Mur.   We shall, my lord,
Perform what you command us.
 First Mur.   Though our lives—
 Macb. Your spirits shine through you. Within this hour, at most,
I will advise you where to plant yourselves,
Acquaint you with the perfect spy o' the time,
The moment on 't; for 't must be done to-night,
And something from the palace; always thought,
That I require a clearness: and with him,—
To leave no rubs nor botches in the work—
Fleance his son, that keeps him company,
Whose absence is no less material to me
Than is his father's, must embrace the fate
Of that dark hour. Resolve yourselves apart;
I 'll come to you anon.
 Sec. Mur.   We are resolved, my lord.
 Macb. I 'll come upon you straight: abide within.—
           [Exeunt Murderers
It is concluded: Banquo, thy soul's flight,
If it find heaven, must find it out to-night. *[Exit*

SCENE II.—The Same. Another Room

Enter LADY MACBETH *and a Servant*

 Lady M. Is Banquo gone from court?
 Serv. Ay, madam, but returns again to-night.
 Lady M. Say to the king, I would attend his leisure
For a few words.
 Serv.   Madam, I will.   *[Exit*
 Lady M.   Naught's had, all's spent,
Where our desire is got without content:
'T is safer to be that which we destroy
Than by destruction dwell in doubtful joy.

Enter MACBETH

How now, my lord? why do you keep alone,
Of sorriest fancies your companions making,

Using those thoughts which should indeed have died
With them they think on?   Things without remedy
Should be without regard: what 's done, is done.
  Macb.   We have scotched the snake, not killed it:
She 'll close, and be herself, whilst our poor malice
Remains in danger of her former tooth.
But let the frame of things disjoint, both the worlds suffer
Ere we will eat our meal in fear, and sleep
In the affliction of these terrible dreams
That shake us nightly.   Better be with the dead
Whom we, to gain our place, have sent to peace,
Than on the torture of the mind to lie
In restless ecstasy.   Duncan is in his grave:
After life's fitful fever he sleeps well.
Treason has done his worst: nor steel, nor poison,
Malice domestic, foreign levy, nothing
Can touch him further.
  Lady M.   Come on; gentle my lord,
Sleek o'er your rugged looks; be bright and jovial
Among your guests to-night.
  Macb.   So shall I, love,
And so, I pray, be you.   Let your remembrance
Apply to Banquo; present him eminence, both
With eye and tongue: unsafe the while that we
Must lave our honours in these flattering streams,
And make our faces visards to our hearts,
Disguising what they are.
  Lady M.   You must leave this.
  Macb.   O, full of scorpions is my mind, dear wife!
Thou know'st that Banquo, and his Fleance, lives.
  Lady M.   But in them nature's copy 's not eterne.
  Macb.   There 's comfort yet: they are assailable:
Then be thou jocund.   Ere the bat hath flown
His cloistered flight; ere to black Hecate's summons
The shard-borne beetle with his drowsy hums
Hath rung night's yawning peal,
There shall be done a deed of dreadful note.—
  Lady M.   What 's to be done?
  Macb.   Be innocent of the knowledge, dearest chuck,
Till thou applaud the deed.—Come, seeling night,
Scarf up the tender eye of pitiful day,
And with thy bloody and invisible hand
Cancel and tear to pieces that great bond
Which keeps me pale!—Light thickens; and the crow
Makes wing to the rooky wood;
Good things of day begin to droop and drowse,
Whiles night's black agents to their preys do rouse.—
Thou marvell'st at my words; but hold thee still:
Things bad begun make strong themselves by ill.
So, pr'ythee, go with me.   *[Exeunt*

SCENE III.—The Same. A Park with a Gate leading to
the Palace

Enter three Murderers

First Mur.   But who did bid thee join with us?
Third Mur.   Macbeth.
Sec. Mur.   He needs not our mistrust since he delivers
Our offices, and what we have to do
To the direction just.
First Mur.   Then stand with us.
The west yet glimmers with some streaks of day;
Now spurs the lated traveller apace
To gain the timely inn; and near approaches
The subject of our watch.
Third Mur.   Hark, I hear horses.
Ban. [*Within*]   Give us a light there, ho!
Sec. Mur.   Then it is he: the rest
That are within the note of expectation,
Already are i' th' court.
First Mur.   His horses go about.
Third Mur.   Almost a mile; but he does usually,
So all men do, from hence to the palace gate
Make it their walk.

Enter BANQUO, *and* FLEANCE *with a torch*

Sec. Mur.   A light, a light!
Third Mur.   'T is he.
First Mur.   Stand to 't.
Ban.   It will be rain to-night.
First Mur.   Let it come down.
                              [*Assaults Banquo*
Ban.   O, treachery! Fly, good Fleance, fly, fly, fly!
Thou may'st avenge—O slave!
                              [*Dies. Fleance escapes*
Third Mur.   Who did strike out the light?
First Mur.   Was 't not the way?
Third Mur.   There's but one down: the son is fled.
Sec. Mur.   We have lost
Best half of our affair.
First Mur.   Well, let's away, and say how much is done.
                              [*Exeunt*

SCENE IV.—A Room of State in the Palace

A Banquet prepared. Enter MACBETH, LADY MACBETH,
ROSS, LENNOX, *Lords, and Attendants*

Macb.   You know your own degrees, sit down: at first
and last,
The hearty welcome.

251

Lords.   Thanks to your majesty.
Macb.   Ourself will mingle with society
And play the humble host.
Our hostess keeps her state; but, in best time,
We will require her welcome.
Lady M.   Pronounce it for me, sir, to all our friends;
For my heart speaks, they are welcome.

Enter first Murderer to the door

Macb.   See, they encounter thee with their hearts'
            thanks.
Both sides are even: here I 'll sit i' the midst.
Be large in mirth; anon, we 'll drink a measure
The table round.—There's blood upon thy face.
Mur.   'T is Banquo's, then.
Macb.   'T is better thee without than him within.
Is he despatched?
Mur.   My lord, his throat is cut; that I did for him.
Macb.   Thou art the best o' the cut-throats; yet he 's good,
That did the like for Fleance: if thou didst it,
Thou art the nonpareil.
Mur.   Most royal sir,
Fleance is 'scaped.
Macb.   Then comes my fit again: I had else been perfect;
Whole as the marble, founded as the rock,
As broad and general as the casing air:
But now, I am cabined, cribbed, confined, bound in
To saucy doubts and fears.   But Banquo's safe?
Mur.   Ay, my good lord, safe in a ditch he bides,
With twenty trenchéd gashes on his head,
The least a death to nature.
Macb.   Thanks for that.
There the grown serpent lies: the worm that 's fled
Hath nature that in time will venom breed,
No teeth for the present.—Get thee gone; to-morrow
We 'll hear ourselves again.—   [*Exit Murderer*
Lady M.   My royal lord,
You do not give the cheer.   The feast is sold,
That is not often vouched, while 't is a-making,
'T is given with welcome; to feed were best at home;
From thence, the sauce to meat is ceremony,
Meeting were bare without it.
Macb.   Sweet remembrancer!—
Now, good digestion wait on appetite,
And health on both!
Len.   May 't please your highness sit?

The Ghost of Banquo enters, and sits in Macbeth's place

Macb.   Here had we now our country's honour roofed,
Were the graced person of our Banquo present;

Who I may rather challenge for unkindness
Than pity for mischance!
   Ross. His absence, sir,
Lays blame upon his promise. Please it your highness
To grace us with your royal company?
   Macb. The table's full.
   Len. Here is a place reserved, sir.
   Macb. Where?
   Len. Here, my good lord. What is 't that moves your
      highness?
   Macb. Which of you have done this?
   Lords. What, my good lord?
   Macb. Thou canst not say, I did it: never shake
Thy gory locks at me.
   Ross. Gentlemen, rise; his highness is not well.
   Lady M. Sit, worthy friends. My lord is often thus,
And hath been from his youth: pray you, keep seat;
The fit is momentary; upon a thought
He will again be well. If much you note him,
You shall offend him, and extend his passion;
Feed, and regard him not.—Are you a man?
   Macb. Ay, and a bold one, that dare look on that
Which might appal the devil.
   Lady M. O proper stuff!
This is the very painting of your fear:
This is the air-drawn dagger, which, you said,
Led you to Duncan. O, these flaws, and starts,
Impostors to true fear, would well become
A woman's story at a winter's fire,
Authorised by her grandam. Shame itself!
Why do you make such faces? When all 's done,
You look but on a stool.
   Macb. Pr'ythee, see there! behold! look! lo! how
      say you?—
Why, what care I? If thou canst nod, speak too.—
If charnelhouses, and our graves, must send
Those that we bury, back, our monuments
Shall be the maws of kites.   *[Ghost vanishes*
   Lady M. What, quite unmanned in folly?
   Macb. If I stand here, I saw him.
   Lady M. Fie, for shame!
   Macb. Blood hath been shed ere now, i' th' olden time,
Ere human statute purged the gentle weal,
Ay, and since too, murders have been performed
Too terrible for the ear; the time has been
That when the brains were out the man would die
And there an end: but now, they rise again
With twenty mortal murders on their crowns,
And push us from our stools. This is more strange
Than such a murder is.

Lady M.   My worthy lord,
Your noble friends do lack you.
 Macb.   I do forget.—
Do not muse at me, my most worthy friends;
I have a strange infirmity, which is nothing
To those that know me.   Come, love and health to all;
Then I'll sit down.   Give me some wine: fill full:
I drink to the general joy of the whole table,
And to our dear friend Banquo, whom we miss;
Would he were here! to all, and him, we thirst,
And all to all.
 Lords.   Our duties, and the pledge.

Re-enter Ghost

 Macb.   Avaunt, and quit my sight!   Let the earth hide
  thee!
Thy bones are marrowless, thy blood is cold;
Thou hast no speculation in those eyes
Which thou dost glare with.
 Lady M.   Think of this, good peers
But as a thing of custom; 't is no other;
Only it spoils the pleasure of the time.
 Macb.   What man dare, I dare:
Approach thou like the rugged Russian bear,
The armed rhinoceros, or the Hyrcan tiger;
Take any shape but that, and my firm nerves
Shall never tremble: or, be alive again,
And dare me to the desert with thy sword;
If trembling I inhabit then, protest me
The baby of a girl.   Hence, horrible shadow!
Unreal mockery, hence!   [*Ghost vanishes*
    Why, so;—being gone,
I am a man again.—Pray you, sit still.
 Lady M.   You have displaced the mirth, broke the good
  meeting
With most admired disorder.
 Macb.   Can such things be,
And overcome us like a summer's cloud,
Without our special wonder?   You make me strange
Even to the disposition that I owe,
When now I think you can behold such sights,
And keep the natural ruby of your cheeks
When mine is blanched with fear.
 Ross.   What sights, my lord?
 Lady M.   I pray you, speak not; he grows worse and
  worse;
Question enrages him: At once, good night:—
Stand not upon the order of your going,
But go at once.

   Len.   Good night, and better health
Attend his majesty!
   Lady M.   A kind good night to all!
                     [Exeunt Lords and Attendants
   Macb.   It will have blood, they say; blood will have
     blood:
Stones have been known to move, and trees to speak:
Augurs and understood relations have
By magot-pies and choughs and rooks brought forth
The secret'st man of blood.—What is the night?
   Lady M. Almost at odds with morning, which is which.
   Macb. How say'st thou, that Macduff denies his person
At our great bidding?
   Lady M.   Did you send to him, sir?
   Macb. I hear it by the way; but I will send.
There 's not a one of them but in his house
I keep a servant fee'd. I will to-morrow,
And betimes I will, to the weird sisters:
More shall they speak; for now I am bent to know,
By the worst means, the worst. For mine own good
All causes shall give way: I am in blood
Stepped in so far, that, should I wade no more,
Returning were as tedious as go o'er.
Strange things I have in head that will to hand,
Which must be acted ere they may be scanned.
   Lady M. You lack the season of all natures, sleep.
   Macb. Come, we'll to sleep. My strange and self-abuse
Is the initiate fear, that wants hard use:
We are yet but young in deed.   *[Exeunt*

Scene V.—The Heath

Thunder. Enter the three Witches, meeting Hecate

   First Witch. Why, how now, Hecate? you look angerly.
   Hec. Have I not reason, beldams as you are,
Saucy, and overbold? How did you dare
To trade and traffic with Macbeth
In riddles and affairs of death;
And I, the mistress of your charms,
The close contriver of all harms,
Was never called to bear my part,
Or show the glory of our art?
And, which is worse, all you have done
Hath been but for a wayward son,
Spiteful and wrathful, who, as others do
Loves for his own ends, not for you.—
But makes amends now; get you gone,
And at the pit of Acheron

Meet me i' the morning: thither he
Will come to know his destiny.
Your vessels and your spells provide
Your charms and everything beside.
I am for the air; this night I'll spend
Unto a dismal and a fatal end:
Great business must be wrought ere noon.
Upon the corner of the moon
There hangs a vaporous drop profound;
I 'll catch it ere it come to ground:
And that, distilled by magic sleights,
Shall raise such artificial sprites
As, by the strength of their illusion,
Shall draw him on to his confusion.
He shall spurn fate, scorn death, and bear
His hopes 'bove wisdom, grace, and fear:
And you all know, security
Is mortals' chiefest enemy.

        [Song, within: " Come away, come away," etc.
Hark! I am called: my little spirit, see,
Sits in a foggy cloud, and stays for me.   *[Exit*
   First Witch. Come, let 's make haste: she 'll soon be
      back again.   *[Exeunt*

SCENE VI.—Forres. A Room in the Palace

Enter LENNOX *and another Lord*

   Len. My former speeches have but hit your thoughts,
Which can interpret further: only, I say,
Things have been strangely borne. The gracious Duncan
Was pitied of Macbeth: marry, he was dead.
And the right-valiant Banquo walked too late;
Whom, you may say, if 't please you, Fleance killed,
For Fleance fled. Men must not walk too late.
Who cannot want the thought, how monstrous
It was for Malcolm and for Donalbain
To kill their gracious father? damnéd fact,
How it did grieve Macbeth! did he not straight,
In pious rage, the two delinquents tear,
That were the slaves of drink and thralls of sleep?
Was not that nobly done? Ay, and wisely too;
For 't would have angered any heart alive
To hear the men deny it. So that, I say,
He has borne all things well: and I do think,
That, had he Duncan's sons under his key,—
As, an 't please Heaven, he shall not,—they should find
What 't were to kill a father; so should Fleance.
But, peace!—for from broad words, and 'cause he failed

His presence at the tyrant's feast, I hear
Macduff lives in disgrace.   Sir, can you tell
Where he bestows himself?
    Lord.   The son of Duncan
From whom this tyrant holds the due of birth
Lives in the English court; and is received
Of the most pious Edward with such grace,
That the malevolence of fortune nothing
Takes from his high respect.   Thither Macduff
Is gone to pray the holy king, upon his aid
To wake Northumberland and warlike Siward;
That, by the help of these,—with Him above
To ratify the work,—we may again
Give to our tables meat, sleep to our nights;
Free from our feasts and banquets bloody knives;
Do faithful homage, and receive free honours,
All which we pine for now: and this report
Hath so exasperate the king, that he
Prepares for some attempt of war.
    Len.   Sent he to Macduff?
    Lord. He did: and with an absolute, "Sir, not I,"
The cloudy messenger turns me his back,
And hums, as who should say, "You 'll rue the time
That clogs me with this answer."
    Len.   And that well might
Advise him to a caution, to hold what distance
His wisdom can provide.   Some holy angel
Fly to the court of England, and unfold
His message ere he come, that a swift blessing
May soon return to this our suffering country
Under a hand accursed!
    Lord.   I 'll send my prayers with him.
                             [*Exeunt*

ACT FOUR

Scene I.—A Cavern.   In the middle **a** Cauldron boiling

Thunder.   Enter the three Witches

    First Witch. Thrice the brinded cat hath mewed.
    Sec. Witch. Thrice and once the hedge-pig whined.
    Third Witch. Harpier cries:—'T is time, 't is time.
    First Witch. Round about the cauldron go;
In the poisoned entrails throw.—
Toad, that under a cold stone
Days and nights has thirty-one
Sweltered venom, sleeping got,
Boil thou first i' the charméd pot.

All.   Double, double toil and trouble:
Fire, burn; and, cauldron, bubble.
   Sec. Witch.   Fillet of a fenny snake,
In the cauldron boil and bake;
Eye of newt, and toe of frog,
Wool of bat, and tongue of dog,
Adder's fork, and blind-worm's sting,
Lizard's leg, and howlet's wing,
For a charm of powerful trouble,
Like a hell-broth boil and bubble.
   All.   Double, double toil and trouble:
Fire, burn; and, cauldron, bubble.
   Third Witch.   Scale of dragon, tooth of wolf:
Witches' mummy; maw, and gulf,
Of the ravined salt-sea shark;
Root of hemlock, digged i' the dark;
Liver of blaspheming Jew;
Gall of goat, and slips of yew
Slivered in the moon's eclipse;
Nose of Turk, and Tartar's lips;
Finger of birth-strangled babe
Ditch-delivered by a drab,
Make the gruel thick and slab:
Add thereto a tiger's chaudron,
For the ingredients of our cauldron.
   All.   Double, double toil and trouble:
Fire, burn; and, cauldron, bubble.
   Sec. Witch.   Cool it with a baboon's blood:
Then the charm is firm and good.

Enter HECATE

   Hec.   O, well done!   I commend your pains,
And every one shall share i' the gains.
   And now about the cauldron sing
   Like elves and fairies in a ring,
   Enchanting all that you put in.
                  [*Music and a Song, "Black spirits," etc.*
   Sec. Witch.   By the pricking of my thumbs,
Something wicked this way comes: [*Knocking*
Open, locks,
Whoever knocks.

Enter MACBETH

   Macb.   How now, you secret, black, and midnight hags!
What is 't you do?
   All.   A deed without a name.
   Macb.   I cónjure you, by that which you profess,—
Howe'er you come to know it, answer me:
Though you untie the winds, and let them fight

Against the churches; though the yesty waves
Confound and swallow navigation up;
Though bladed corn be lodged, and trees blown down;
Though castles topple on their warders' heads;
Though palaces, and pyramids do slope
Their head to their foundations; though the treasure
Of nature's germen tumble all together,
Even till destruction sicken: answer me
To what I ask you.
    First Witch.   Speak.
    Sec. Witch.   Demand.
    Third Witch.   We'll answer.
    First Witch. Say, if thou 'dst rather hear it from our
      mouths,
Or from our masters?
    Macb.   Call 'em: let me see 'em.
    First Witch. Pour in sow's blood, that hath eaten
Her nine farrow: grease, that 's sweaten
From the murderer's gibbet throw
Into the flame.
    All.   Come, high or low;
Thyself and office deftly show.

     Thunder.   First Apparition; an armed Head

    Macb. Tell me, thou unknown power,—
    First Witch.   He knows thy thought.
Hear his speech, but say thou nought.
    First App. Macbeth! Macbeth! Macbeth! beware
      Macduff;
Beware the thane of Fife.—Dismiss me.—Enough.
                          [Descends
    Macb. Whate'er thou art, for thy good caution, thanks:
Thou hast harped my fear aright. But one word more:—
    First Witch. He will not be commanded. Here's
      another,
More potent than the first.

     Thunder.   Second Apparition: a bloody Child

    Sec. App. Macbeth! Macbeth! Macbeth!—
    Macb. Had I three ears, I'd hear thee.
    Sec. App. Be bloody, bold, and resolute: laugh to
      scorn
The power of man, for none of woman born
Shall harm Macbeth.   *[Descends*
    Macb. Then live, Macduff: what need I fear of thee?
But yet I'll make assurance double sure,
And take a bond of fate: thou shalt not live;
That I may tell pale-hearted fear it lies,
And sleep in spite of thunder.

*Thunder.   Third Apparition: a Child crowned,
with a tree in his hand*

                                What is this,
That rises like the issue of a king;
And wears upon his baby-brow the round
And top of sovereignty?
        All.   Listen, but speak not to 't.
    Third App.   Be lion-mettled, proud, and take no care
Who chafes, who frets, or where conspirers are:
Macbeth shall never vanquished be, until
Great Birnam Wood to high Dunsinane hill
Shall come against him.   [*Descends*
        Macb.   That will never be:
Who can impress the forest; bid the tree
Unfix his earth-bound root?   Sweet bodements! good!
Rebellion's head rise never, till the wood
Of Birnam rise; and our high-placed Macbeth
Shall live the lease of nature, pay his breath
To time and mortal custom.—Yet my heart
Throbs to know one thing: tell me—if your art
Can tell so much—shall Banquo's issue ever
Reign in this kingdom?
        All.   Seek to know no more.
    Macb.   I will be satisfied: deny me this,
And an eternal curse fall on you!   Let me know.—
Why sinks that cauldron? and what noise is this?
                                                    [*Hautboys*

    First Witch.   Show!
    Sec. Witch.   Show!
    Third Witch.   Show!
    All.   Show his eyes, and grieve his heart;
Come like shadows, so depart.

*A show of eight Kings, the last with a glass in his
hand; Banquo's Ghost following*

    Macb.   Thou art too like the spirit of Banquo: down!
Thy crown does sear mine eye-balls:—and thy hair,
Thou other gold-bound brow, is like the first:—
A third is like the former:—filthy hags!
Why do you show me this?—A fourth?—Start, eyes!
What! will the line stretch out to the crack of doom?
Another yet?—A seventh?—I'll see no more:—
And yet the eighth appears, who bears a glass,
Which shows me many more; and some I see,
That two-fold balls and treble-sceptres carry.
Horrible sight!—Now, I see, 't is true;
For the blood-boltered Banquo smiles upon me,
And points at them for his.—What! is this so?
    First Witch.   Ay, sir, all this is so: but why

Stands Macbeth thus amazedly?
Come, sisters, cheer we up his sprites,
And show the best of our delights.
I'll charm the air to give a sound,
While you perform your antick round;
That this great king may kindly say,
Our duties did his welcome pay.
            [*Music. The Witches dance, and vanish*
   Macb. Where are they? Gone?—Let this pernicious hour
Stand aye accursèd in the calendar!—
Come in, without there!

Enter LENNOX

Len.   What 's your grace's will?
Macb. Saw you the weird sisters?
Len.   No, my lord.
Macb. Came they not by you?
Len.   No, indeed, my lord.
   Macb. Infected be the air whereon they ride,
And damned all those that trust them!—I did hear
The galloping of horse: who was 't came by?
   Len. 'T is two or three, my lord, that bring you word,
Macduff is fled to England.
   Macb.   Fled to England?
Len. Ay, my good lord.
   Macb. Time, thou anticipat'st my dread exploits:
The flighty purpose never is o'ertook,
Unless the deed go with it. From this moment,
The very firstlings of my heart shall be
The firstlings of my hand. And even now,
To crown my thoughts with acts, be it thought and done:
The castle of Macduff I will surprise;
Seize upon Fife; give to the edge o' the sword
His wife, his babes, and all unfortunate souls
That trace him in his line. No boasting like a fool;
This deed I'll do, before this purpose cool:
But no more sights!—Where are these gentlemen?
Come, bring me where they are.   [*Exeunt*

SCENE II.—Fife. A Room in MACDUFF's Castle

Enter LADY MACDUFF, *her Son, and* ROSS

Wife. What had he done, to make him fly the land?
Ross. You must have patience, madam.
Wife.   He had none:
His flight was madness: when our actions do not,
Our fears do make us traitors.
   Ross.   You know not
Whether it was his wisdom or his fear.

261

Wife. Wisdom! to leave his wife, to leave his babes
His mansion, and his titles, in a place
From whence himself does fly?   He loves us not;
He wants the natural touch: for the poor wren
The most diminutive of birds, will fight,
Her young ones in her nest, against the owl.
All is the fear, and nothing is the love;
As little is the wisdom, where the flight
So runs against all reason.
    Ross.   My dear'st coz,
I pray you, school yourself: but, for your husband,
He is noble, wise, judicious, and best knows
The fits o' the season.   I dare not speak much further:
But cruel are the times, when we are traitors
And do not know ourselves; when we hold rumour
From what we fear, yet know not what we fear,
But float upon a wild and violent sea
And each way move.—I take my leave of you:
Shall not be long but I'll be here again;
Things at the worst will cease, or else climb upward
To what they were before.—My pretty cousin,
Blessing upon you!
    Wife. Fathered he is, and yet he 's fatherless.
    Ross. I am so much a fool, should I stay longer,
It would be my disgrace, and your discomfort:
I take my leave at once.   [*Exit*
    Wife.   Sirrah, your father 's dead:
And what will you do now?   How will you live?
    Son. As birds do, mother.
    Wife.   What, with worms and flies?
    Son. With what I get, I mean; and so do they.
    Wife. Poor bird! thou 'dst never fear the net, nor lime,
The pit-fall, nor the gin.
    Son. Why should I, mother?   Poor birds they are
        not set for.
My father is not dead, for all your saying.
    Wife. Yes, he is dead: how wilt thou do for a father?
    Son. Nay, how will you do for a husband?
    Wife. Why, I can buy me twenty at any market.
    Son. Then you 'll buy 'em to sell again.
    Wife. Thou speak'st with all thy wit;
And yet, i' faith, with wit enough for thee.
    Son. Was my father a traitor, mother?
    Wife. Ay, that he was.
    Son. What is a traitor?
    Wife. Why, one that swears and lies.
    Son. And be all traitors that do so?
    Wife. Every one that does so is a traitor, and must
be hanged.
    Son. And must they all be hanged that swear and lie?

Wife. Every one.
Son. Who must hang them?
Wife. Why, the honest men.
Son. Then the liars and swearers are fools; for there are liars and swearers enough to beat the honest men, and hang up them.
Wife. Now God help thee, poor monkey!
But how wilt thou do for a father?
Son. If he were dead, you'd weep for him: if you would not, it were a good sign that I should quickly have a new father.
Wife. Poor prattler, how thou talk'st!

Enter a Messenger

Mess. Bless you, fair dame! I am not to you known,
Though in your state of honour I am perfect.
I doubt, some danger does approach you nearly:
If you will take a homely man's advice,
Be not found here; hence, with your little ones.
To fright you thus, methinks, I am too savage;
To do worse to you were fell cruelty,
Which is too nigh your person.   Heaven preserve you!
I dare abide no longer.   [*Exit*
Wife.   Whither should I fly?
I have done no harm.   But I remember now
I am in this earthly world where to do harm
Is often laudable; to do good, sometime
Accounted dangerous folly: why then, alas!
Do I put up that womanly defence,
To say, I have done no harm?   What are these faces?

Enter Murderers

Mur. Where is your husband?
Wife. I hope, in no place so unsanctified
Where such as thou may'st find him.
Mur.   He's a traitor.
Son. Thou liest, thou shag-haired villain!
Mur.   What, you egg! [*Stabbing him*
Young fry of treachery!
Son. He has killed me, mother; run away, I pray you.
                                                   [*Dies*
          [*Exit Lady Macduff, crying " Murder!"
                    and pursued by the Murderers*

SCENE III.—England. Before the KING's Palace

Enter MALCOLM and MACDUFF

Mal. Let us seek out some desolate shade, and there
Weep our sad bosoms empty.
Macd.   Let us rather

263

Hold fast the mortal sword, and like good men
Bestride our down-fall'n birthdom.   Each new morn
New widows howl, new orphans cry, new sorrows
Strike heaven on the face, that it resounds
As if it felt with Scotland and yelled out
Like syllable of dolour.
    Mal.   What I believe, I'll wail;
What know, believe; and what I can redress,
As I shall find the time to friend, I will.
What you have spoke, it may be so, perchance.
This tyrant, whose sole name blisters our tongues,
Was once thought honest; you have loved him well;
He hath not touched you yet.   I am young; but some-
       thing
You may deserve of him through me; and wisdom
To offer up a weak, poor, innocent lamb
To appease an angry God.
    Macd.   I am not treacherous.
    Mal.   But Macbeth is.
A good virtuous nature may recoil
In an imperial charge.   But I shall crave your pardon:
That which you are, my thoughts cannot transpose,
Angels are bright still, though the brightest fell;
Though all things foul would wear the brows of grace,
Yet grace must still look so.
    Macd.   I have lost my hopes.
    Mal.   Perchance even there where I did find my doubts.
Why in that rawness left you wife and child—
Those precious motives, those strong knots of love—
Without leave-taking?—I pray you
Let not my jealousies be your dishonours,
But mine own safeties: you may be rightly just
Whatever I shall think.
    Macd.   Bleed, bleed, poor country!
Great tyranny, lay thou thy basis sure,
For goodness dare not check thee! wear thou thy wrongs;
The title is affeered!—Fare thee well, lord:
I would not be the villain that thou think'st
For the whole space that 's in the tyrant's grasp
And the rich East to boot.
    Mal.   Be not offended:
I speak not as in absolute fear of you.
I think our country sinks beneath the yoke;
It weeps, it bleeds; and each new day a gash
Is added to her wounds: I think, withal,
There would be hands uplifted in my right;
And here, from gracious England, had I offer
Of goodly thousands: but, for all this,
When I shall tread upon the tyrant's head
Or wear it on my sword, yet my poor country

Shall have more vices than it had before,
More suffer, and more sundry ways than ever,
By him that shall succeed.
   Macd.   What should he be?
   Mal.   It is myself I mean; in whom I know
All the particulars of vice so grafted,
That, when they shall be opened, black Macbeth
Will seem as pure as snow, and the poor state
Esteem him as a lamb, being compared
With my confineless harms.
   Macd.   Not in the legions
Of horrid hell can come a devil more damned
In evils, to top Macbeth.
   Mal.   I grant him bloody,
Luxurious, avaricious, false, deceitful,
Sudden, malicious, smacking of every sin
That has a name; but there's no bottom, none,
In my voluptuousness; your wives, your daughters,
Your matrons, and your maids, could not fill up
The cistern of my lust; and my desire
All continent impediments would o'erbear,
That did oppose my will: better Macbeth,
Than such a one to reign.
   Macd.   Boundless intemperance
In nature is a tyranny; it hath been
The untimely emptying of the happy throne,
And fall of many kings: but fear not yet
To take upon you what is yours: you may
Convey your pleasures in a spacious plenty
And yet seem cold, the time you may so hoodwink.
We have willing dames enough; there cannot be
That vulture in you, to devour so many
As will to greatness dedicate themselves,
Finding it so inclined.
   Mal.   With this, there grows
In my most ill-composed affection such
A stanchless avarice, that, were I king,
I should cut off the nobles for their lands;
Desire his jewels, and this other's house;
And my more-having would be as a sauce
To make me hunger more, that I should forge
Quarrels unjust against the good and loyal,
Destroying them for wealth.
   Macd.   This avarice
Sticks deeper, grows with more pernicious root
Than summer-seeking lust; and it hath been
The sword of our slain kings.   Yet do not fear;
Scotland hath foisons to fill up your will,
Of your mere own.   All these are portable,
With other graces weighed.

Mal.   But I have none: the king-becoming graces,
As justice, verity, temperance, stableness,
Bounty, persévérance, mercy, lowliness,
Devotion, patience, courage, fortitude,
I have no relish of them; but abound
In the division of each several crime,
Acting it many ways.   Nay, had I power, should
Pour the sweet milk of concord into hell,
Uproar the universal peace, confound
All unity on earth.
      Macd.   O Scotland, Scotland!
      Mal.   If such a one be fit to govern, speak:
I am as I have spoken.
      Macd.   Fit to govern?
No, not to live.—O nation miserable,
With an untitled tyrant bloody-sceptered,
When shalt thou see thy wholesome days again,
Since that the truest issue of thy throne
By his own interdiction stands accursed,
And does blaspheme his breed?   Thy royal father
Was a most sainted king; the queen, that bore thee,
Oft'ner upon her knees than on her feet,
Died every day she livéd.   Fare thee well!
These evils thou repeat'st upon thyself
Have banished me from Scotland.—O my breast,.
Thy hope ends here!
      Mal.   Macduff, this noble passion,
Child of integrity, hath from my soul
Wiped the black scruples, reconciled my thoughts
To thy good truth and honour.   Devilish Macbeth
By many of these trains hath sought to win me
Into his power, and modest wisdom plucks me
From over-credulous haste: but God above
Deal between thee and me! for even now
I put myself to thy direction, and
Unspeak mine own detraction; here abjure
The taints and blames I laid upon myself,
For strangers to my nature.   I am yet
Unknown to woman; never was forsworn;
Scarcely have coveted what was mine own;
At no time broke my faith, would not betray
The devil to his fellow; and delight
No less in truth, than life: my first false speaking
Was this upon myself.   What I am truly,
Is thine, and my poor country's, to command:
Whither, indeed, before thy here-approach,
Old Siward, with ten thousand warlike men
Already at a point, was setting forth.
Now, we'll together, and the chance of goodness
Be like our warranted quarrel.   Why are you silent?

Macd. Such welcome and unwelcome things at once
'T is hard to reconcile.
Enter a Doctor

Mal. Well; more anon.—Comes the king forth, I
          pray you?
Doct. Ay, sir; there are a crew of wretched souls
That stay his cure; their malady convinces
The great assay of art; but at his touch,
Such sanctity hath Heaven given his hand,
They presently amend.
Mal.   I thank you, doctor. [*Exit Doctor*
Macd. What's the disease he means?
Mal.   'T is called the evil;
A most miraculous work in this good king,
Which often, since my here-remain in England,
I have seen him do.   How he solicits Heaven,
Himself best knows; but strangely-visited people,
All swoln and ulcerous, pitiful to the eye,
The mere despair of surgery, he cures;
Hanging a golden stamp about their necks,
Put on with holy prayers; and 't is spoken,
To the succeeding royalty he leaves
The healing benediction.   With this strange virtue,
He hath a heavenly gift of prophecy;
And sundry blessings hang about his throne,
That speak him full of grace.

Enter Ross

Macd.   See, who comes here?
Mal. My countryman; but yet I know him not.
Macd. My ever-gentle cousin, welcome hither.
Mal. I know him now.   Good God, betimes remove
The means that makes us strangers!
Ross.   Sir, Amen.
Macd. Stand Scotland where it did?
Ross.   Alas, poor country!
Almost afraid to know itself.   It cannot
Be called our mother, but our grave; where nothing,
But who knows nothing, is once seen to smile;
Where sighs, and groans, and shrieks that rend the air,
Are made, not marked; where violent sorrow seems
A modern ecstasy; the dead man's knell
Is there scarce asked for who; and good men's lives
Expire before the flowers in their caps,
Dying or ere they sicken.
Macd.   O relation
Too nice, and yet too true!
Mal.   What is the newest grief?
Ross. That of an hour's age doth hiss the speaker;
Each minute teems a new one.

267

Macd.   How does my wife?
Ross.   Why, well.
Macd.   And all my children?
Ross.   Well too.
Macd.   The tyrant has not battered at their peace?
Ross.   No; they were well at peace, when I did leave
   them.
Macd.   Be not a niggard of your speech: how goes it?
Ross.   When I came hither to transport the tidings
Which I have heavily borne, there ran a rumour
Of many worthy fellows that were out;
Which was to my belief witnessed the rather,
For that I saw the tyrant's power afoot.
Now is the time of help.   Your eye in Scotland
Would create soldiers, make our women fight
To doff their dire distresses.
Mal.   Be 't their comfort
We are coming thither.   Gracious England hath
Lent us good Siward and ten thousand men;
An older and a better soldier none
That Christendom gives out.
Ross.   Would I could answer
This comfort with the like!   But I have words
That would be howled out in the desert air
Where hearing should not latch them.
Macd.   What concern they?
The general cause? or is it a fee-grief,
Due to some single breast?
Ross.   No mind that 's honest
But in it shares some woe, though the main part
Pertains to you alone.
Macd.   If it be mine
Keep it not from me; quickly let me have it.
Ross.   Let not your ears despise my tongue for ever,
Which shall possess them with the heaviest sound
That ever yet they heard.
Macd.   Humph! I guess at it.
Ross.   Your castle is surprised; your wife and babes
Savagely slaughtered: to relate the manner,
Were on the quarry of these murdered deer
To add the death of you.
Mal.   Merciful Heaven!—
What, man! ne'er pull your hat upon your brows:
Give sorrow words; the grief that does not speak
Whispers the o'er-fraught heart and bids it break.
Macd.   My children too?
Ross.   Wife, children, servants, all
That could be found.
Macd.   And I must be from thence!
My wife killed too?

Ross.   I have said.
Mal.   Be comforted:
Let 's make our medicines of our great revenge
To cure this deadly grief.
Macd. He has no children.—All my pretty ones?
Did you say, all?—O hell-kite!—All?
What, all my pretty chickens and their dam
At one fell swoop?
Mal. Dispute it like a man.
Macd.   I shall do so.
But I must also feel it as a man:
I cannot but remember such things were,
That were most precious to me.—Did Heaven look on,
And would not take their part? Sinful Macduff!
They were all struck for thee. Naught that I am,
Not for their own demerits but for mine
Fell slaughter on their souls. Heaven rest them now!
Mal. Be this the whetstone of your sword: let grief
Convert to anger; blunt not the heart, enrage it.
Macd. O, I could play the woman with mine eyes
And braggart with my tongue.—But, gentle heavens,
Cut short all intermission. Front to front
Bring thou this fiend of Scotland and myself;
Within my sword's length set him. If he 'scape,
Heaven forgive him too!
Mal.   This tune goes manly.
Come, go we to the king: our power is ready;
Our lack is nothing but our leave. Macbeth
Is ripe for shaking, and the powers above
Put on their instruments. Receive what cheer you may:
The night is long that never finds a day.   [*Exeunt*

ACT FIVE

Scene I.—Dunsinane. A Room in the Castle

Enter a Doctor of Physic and a waiting Gentlewoman

Doct. I have two nights watched with you, but can perceive no truth in your report. When was it she last walked?
Gent. Since his majesty went into the field, I have seen her rise from her bed, throw her nightgown upon her, unlock her closet, take forth paper, fold it, write upon it, read it, afterwards seal it, and again return to bed; yet all this while in a most fast sleep.
Doct. A great perturbation in nature, to receive at once the benefit of sleep, and do the effects of watching. In this slumbery agitation, besides her walking and other actual performances, what, at any time, have you heard her say?
Gent. That, sir, which I will not report after her.

Doct. You may, to me: and 't is most meet you should.

Gent. Neither to you nor any one; having no witness to confirm my speech. Lo you! here she comes.

Enter LADY MACBETH *with a taper*

This is her very guise; and, upon my life, fast asleep. Observe her: stand close.

Doct. How came she by that light?

Gent. Why, it stood by her: she has light by her continually; 't is her command.

Doct. You see, her eyes are open.

Gent. Ay, but their sense' are shut.

Doct. What is it she does now? Look, how she rubs her hands.

Gent. It is an accustomed action with her, to seem thus washing her hands. I have known her continue in this a quarter of an hour.

Lady M. Yet here's a spot.

Doct. Hark! she speaks: I will set down what comes from her, to satisfy my remembrance the more strongly.

Lady M. Out, damned spot! out, I say!—One; two: why, then 't is time to do 't.—Hell is murky!—Fie, my lord, fie! a soldier, and afeard? What need we fear who knows it, when none can call our power to account?—Yet who would have thought the old man to have had so much blood in him?

Doct. Do you mark that?

Lady M. The thane of Fife had a wife: where is she now?—What, will these hands ne'er be clean?—No more o' that, my lord, no more o' that: you mar all with this starting.

Doct. Go to, go to; you have known what you should not.

Gent. She has spoke what she should not, I am sure of that: Heaven knows what she has known.

Lady M. Here's the smell of the blood still: all the perfumes of Arabia will not sweeten this little hand. Oh . . . . oh . . . oh!

Doct. What a sigh is there! Thy heart is sorely charged.

Gent. I would not have such a heart in my bosom, for the dignity of the whole body.

Doct. Well, well, well.—

Gent. Pray God, it be, sir.

Doct. This disease is beyond my practice: yet I have known those which have walked in their sleep, who have died holily in their beds.

Lady M. Wash your hands, put on your nightgown; look not so pale.—I tell you yet again, Banquo's buried; he cannot come out on 's grave.

Doct. Even so?—

Lady M. To bed, to bed: there 's knocking at the

gate. Come, come, come, come, give me your hand:—
What 's done cannot be undone:—To bed, to bed, to bed.

                                                      [*Exit*

   Doct. Will she go now to bed?
   Gent. Directly.
   Doct. Foul whisperings are abroad. Unnatural deeds
Do breed unnatural troubles: infected minds
To their deaf pillows will discharge their secrets.
More needs she the divine than the physician.—
God, God, forgive us all!—Look after her;
Remove from her the means of all annoyance,
And still keep eyes upon her:—so, good night:
My mind she has mated, and amazed my sight:
I think, but dare not speak.
   Gent.   Good night, good doctor.

                                                    [*Exeunt*

Scene II.—The Country near Dunsinane

Enter, with drum and colours, MENTEITH, CAITHNESS, ANGUS,
LENNOX, *and Soldiers*

   Ment. The English power is near, led on by Malcolm,
His uncle Siward, and the good Macduff.
Revenges burn in them; for their dear causes
Would to the bleeding and the grim alarm
Excite the mortified man.
   Ang.   Near Birnam wood
Shall we well meet them; that way are they coming.
   Caith. Who knows if Donalbain be with his brother?
   Len. For certain, sir, he is not. I have a file
Of all the gentry: there is Siward's son,
And many unrough youths that even now
Protest their first of manhood.
   Ment.   What does the tyrant?
   Caith. Great Dunsinane he strongly fortifies.
Some say he 's mad; others, that lesser hate him,
Do call it valiant fury: but, for certain,
He cannot buckle his distempered cause
Within the belt of rule.
   Ang.   Now does he feel
His secret murders sticking on his hands;
Now minutely revolts upbraid his faith-breach;
Those he commands move only in command,
Nothing in love; now does he feel his title
Hang loose about him, like a giant's robe
Upon a dwarfish thief.
   Ment.   Who then shall blame
His pestered senses to recoil and start,
When all that is within him does condemn
Itself for being there?

Caith.   Well, march we on,
To give obedience where 't is truly owed:
Meet we the medicine of the sickly weal,
And with him pour we in our country's purge
Each drop of us.
Len.   Or so much as it needs
To dew the sovereign flower and drown the weeds.
Make we our march towards Birnam.   [*Exeunt, marching*

SCENE III.—Dunsinane.   A Room in the Castle

Enter MACBETH, *Doctor, and Attendants*

Macb.   Bring me no more reports; let them fly all:
Till Birnam wood remove to Dunsinane,
I cannot taint with fear.   What 's the boy Malcolm?
Was he not born of woman?   The spirits that know
All mortal consequences have pronounced me thus:
"Fear not, Macbeth; no man that 's born of woman
Shall e'er have power upon thee."—Then fly, false thanes,
And mingle with the English epicures:
The mind I sway by, and the heart I bear,
Shall never sag with doubt nor shake with fear.

Enter a Servant

The devil damn thee black, thou cream-faced loon!
Where gott'st thou that goose look?
Serv.   There is ten thousand—
Macb.   Geese, villain?
Serv.   Soldiers, sir.
Macb.   Go, prick thy face, and over-red thy fear,
Thou lily-livered boy.   What soldiers, patch?
Death of thy soul! those linen cheeks of thine
Are counsellors to fear.   What soldiers, whey-face?
Serv.   The English force, so please you.
Macb.   Take thy face hence.   [*Exit Servant*
          —Seyton!—I am sick at heart,
When I behold—Seyton, I say!—This push
Will chair me ever, or disseat me now.
I have lived long enough: my way of life
Is fall'n into the sere, the yellow leaf;
And that which should accompany old age,
As honour, love, obedience, troops of friends,
I must not look to have; but, in their stead,
Curses, not loud, but deep, mouth-honour, breath
Which the poor heart would fain deny, and dare not.—
Seyton!—

Enter SEYTON

Sey.   What is your gracious pleasure?
Macb.   What news more?

272

Sey. All is confirmed, my lord, which was reported.
Macb. I 'll fight till from my bones my flesh be hacked.
Give me my armour.
Sey.   'T is not needed yet.
Macb. I 'll put it on.—
Send out more horses, skirr the country round;
Hang those that talk of fear.—Give me mine armour.—
How does your patient, doctor?
Doct.   Not so sick, my lord,
As she is troubled with thick-coming fancies
That keep her from her rest.
Macb.   Cure her of that:
Canst thou not minister to a mind diseased,
Pluck from the memory a rooted sorrow,
Raze out the written troubles of the brain,
And with some sweet oblivious antidote
Cleanse the stuffed bosom of that perilous stuff
Which weighs upon the heart?
Doct.   Therein the patient
Must minister to himself.
Macb. Throw physic to the dogs, I'll none of it.—
Come, put mine armour on; give me my staff—
Seyton, send out—Doctor, the thanes fly from me—
Come, sir, despatch—if thou couldst, doctor, cast
The water of my land, and her disease,
And purge it to a sound and pristine health,
I would applaud thee to the very echo
That should applaud again—Pull 't off, I say—
What rhubarb, senna, or what purgative drug,
Would scour these English hence? Hear'st thou of them?
Doct. Ay, my good lord; your royal preparation
Makes us hear something.
Macb.   Bring it after me.—
I will not be afraid of death and bane,
Till Birnam forest come to Dunsinane.   [*Exit*
Doct. [*Aside*] Were I from Dunsinane away and clear,
Profit again should hardly draw me here.   [*Exeunt*

SCENE IV.—Country near Dunsinane
A Wood in view

Enter, with drum and colours, MALCOLM, *Old* SIWARD *and
his Son,* MACDUFF, MENTEITH, CAITHNESS, ANGUS,
LENNOX, ROSS, *and Soldiers, marching*

Mal. Cousins, I hope the days are near at hand
That chambers will be safe.
Ment.   We doubt it nothing.
Siw. What wood is this before us?
Ment.   The wood of Birnam.

Mal. Let every soldier hew him down a bough,
And bear 't before him: thereby shall we shadow
The numbers of our host and make discovery
Err in report of us.
　　Sold.　　　　　It shall be done.
　　Siw. We learn no other, but the confident tyrant
Keeps still in Dunsinane, and will endure
Our setting down before 't.
　　Mal.　　　　　'T is his main hope;
For where there is advantage to be given
Both more and less hath given him the revolt,
And none serve with him but constrainéd things
Whose hearts are absent too.
　　Macd.　　　　　Let our just censures
Attend the true event, and put we on
Industrious soldiership.
　　Siw.　　　　　The time approaches
That will with due decision make us know
What we shall say we have and what we owe.
Thoughts speculative their unsure hopes relate,
But certain issue strokes must arbitrate:
Towards which advance the war.　　*[Exeunt, marching*

SCENE V.—Dunsinane. Within the Castle

Enter, with drum and colours, MACBETH, SEYTON, *and Soldiers*

　　Macb. Hang out our banners on the outward walls;
The cry is still, "They come!" Our castle's strength
Will laugh a siege to scorn: here let them lie
Till famine and the ague eat them up.
Were they not forced with those that should be ours,
We might have met them dareful, beard to beard,
And beat them backward home. What is that noise?
　　　　　　　　[A cry of Women within
　　Sey. It is the cry of women, my good lord.　　*[Exit*
　　Macb. I have almost forgot the taste of fears.
The time has been, my senses would have cooled
To hear a night-shriek; and my fell of hair
Would at a dismal treatise rouse and stir
As life were in 't. I have supped full with horrors:
Direness, familiar to my slaughterous thoughts,
Cannot once start me.

Re-enter SEYTON

　　　　　　　　Wherefore was that cry?
　　Sey. The queen, my lord, is dead.
　　Macb. She should have died hereafter:
There would have been a time for such a word.—
To-morrow, and to-morrow, and to-morrow,

Creeps in this pretty pace from day to day,
To the last syllable of recorded time;
And all our yesterdays have lighted fools
The way to dusty death.   Out, out, brief candle!
Life's but a walking shadow; a poor player,
That struts and frets his hour upon the stage,
And then is heard no more: it is a tale
Told by an idiot, full of sound and fury,
Signifying nothing.

Enter a Messenger

Thou com'st to use thy tongue; thy story quickly.
   Mess.   Gracious my lord,
I should report which I say I saw,
But know not how to do it.
   Macb.   Well, say, sir.
   Mess.   As I did stand my watch upon the hill,
I looked toward Birnam, and anon, methought,
The wood began to move.
   Macb.   Liar and slave!
   Mess.   Let me endure your wrath if 't be not so.
Within three mile may you see it coming;
I say, a moving grove.
   Macb.   If thou speak'st false,
Upon the next tree shalt thou hang alive
Till famine cling thee: if thy speech be sooth,
I care not if thou dost for me as much.—
I pull in resolution; and begin
To doubt the equivocation of the fiend,
That lies like truth: "Fear not, till Birnam wood
Do come to Dunsinane;"—and now a wood
Comes towards Dunsinane.—Arm, arm, and out!
If this which avouches doth appear,
There is nor flying hence, nor tarrying here.—
I gin to be aweary of the sun,
And wish the estate o' the world were now undone.—
Ring the alarum-bell!—Blow, wind! come, wrack!
At least we'll die with harness on our back.   [*Exeunt*

SCENE VI.—The Same.   A Plain before the Castle

Enter, with drum and colours, MALCOLM, *Old* SIWARD,
MACDUFF, *etc., and their Army, with boughs*

   Mal. Now, near enough: your leafy screens throw down,
And show like those you are.—You, worthy uncle,
Shall, with my cousin, your right-noble son,
Lead our first battle: worthy Macduff, and we,
Shall take upon 's what else remains to do,
According to our order.
   Siw.   Fare you well.

Do we but find the tyrant's power to-night,
Let us be beaten if we cannot fight.
    Macd. Make all our trumpets speak; give them all breath,
Those clamorous harbingers of blood and death.
                         [*Exeunt. Alarums continued*

SCENE VII.—The Same. Another Part of the Plain
Enter MACBETH

    Macb. They have tied me to a stake; I cannot fly,
But, bear-like, I must fight the course.—What 's he
That was not born of woman?   Such a one
Am I to fear, or none.

Enter Young SIWARD

    Yo. Siw. What is thy name?
    Macb.   Thou 'lt be afraid to hear it.
    Yo. Siw. No; though thou call'st thyself a hotter name
Than any is in hell.
    Macb.   My name's Macbeth.
    Yo. Siw. The devil himself could not pronounce a title
More hateful to mine ear.
    Macb.   No, nor more fearful.
    Yo. Siw. Thou liest, abhorréd tyrant: with my sword
I'll prove the lie thou speak'st.
                [*They fight, and Young Siward is slain*
    Macb.   Thou wast born of woman.—
But swords I smile at, weapons laugh to scorn,
Brandished by man that 's of a woman born.   [*Exit*

Alarums. Enter MACDUFF

    Macd. That way the noise is.—Tyrant, show thy face!
If thou be'st slain, and with no stroke of mine,
My wife and children's ghosts will haunt me still.
I cannot strike at wretched kerns, whose arms
Are hired to bear their staves: either thou, Macbeth,
Or else my sword, with an unbattered edge,
I sheathe again undeeded.—There thou shouldst be,—
By this great clatter one of greatest note
Seems bruited.   Let me find him, fortune!
And more I beg not.   [*Exit. Alarums*

Enter MALCOLM *and Old* SIWARD

    Siw. This way, my lord;—the castle's gently rendered:
The tyrant's people on both sides do fight;
The noble thanes do bravely in the war.
The day almost itself professes yours,
And little is to do.
    Mal.   We have met with foes
That strike beside us.

Siw.					Enter, sir, the castle.
					[*Exeunt.	Alarums*

SCENE VIII.—Another Part of the Plain

Enter MACBETH

Macb.	Why should I play the Roman fool, and die
On mine own sword?	Whiles I see lives, the gashes
Do better upon them.

Enter MACDUFF

Macd.				Turn, hell-hound, turn!
Macb.	Of all men else I have avoided thee:
But get thee back, my soul is too much charged
With blood of thine already.
Macd.				I have no words;
My voice is in my sword; thou bloodier villain
Than terms can give thee out!		[*They fight*
Macb.			Thou losest labour:
As easy mayst thou the intrenchant air
With thy keen sword impress, as make me bleed:
Let fall thy blade on vulnerable crests;
I bear a charméd life, which must not yield
To one of woman born.
Macd.			Despair thy charm;
And let the angel whom thou still hast served
Tell thee, Macduff was from his mother's womb
Untimely ripped.
Macb.	Acccurséd be that tongue that tells me so,
For it hath cowed my better part of man!
And be these juggling fiends no more believed,
That palter with us in a double sense;
That keep the word of promise to our ear,
And break it to our hope.—I'll not fight with thee.
Macd.	Then yield thee, coward,
And live to be the show and gaze o' the time:
We'll have thee, as our rarer monsters are,
Painted upon a pole, and underwrit,
"Here may you see the Tyrant."
Macb.				I will not yield,
To kiss the ground before young Malcolm's feet
And to be baited with the rabble's curse.
Though Birnam wood be come to Dunsinane,
And thou opposed, being of no woman born,
Yet I will try the last: before my body
I throw my warlike shield: lay on, Macduff;
And damned be he that first cries, "Hold, enough!"
				[*Exeunt, fighting*

*Retreat.	Flourish.	Re-enter, with drum and colours,*
MALCOLM, *Old* SIWARD, ROSS, *Thanes, and Soldiers*

277

Mal.   I would the friends we miss were safe arrived.
Siw.   Some must go off; and yet, by these I see,
So great a day as this is cheaply bought.
Mal.   Macduff is missing, and your noble son.
Ross.   Your son, my lord, has paid a soldier's debt:
He only lived but till he was a man;
The which no sooner had his prowess confirmed
In the unshrinking station where he fought,
But like a man he died.
Siw.   Then he is dead?
Ross.   Ay, and brought off the field.   Your cause of
    sorrow
Must not be measured by his worth, for then
It hath no end.
Siw.   Had he his hurts before?
Ross.   Ay, on the front.
Siw.   Why then, God's soldier be he!
Had I as many sons as I have hairs,
I would not wish them to a fairer death:
And so, his knell is knolled.
Mal.   He 's worth more sorrow,
And that I 'll spend for him.
Siw.   He 's worth no more;
They say, he parted well, and paid his score:
And so, God be with him!—Here comes newer comfort.

Re-enter MACDUFF, *with* MACBETH'S *head*

Macd.   Hail, King! for so thou art.   Behold, where stands
The usurper's cursèd head: the time is free.
I see thee compassed with thy kingdom's pearl,
That speak my salutation in their minds;
Whose voices I desire aloud with mine,—
Hail, King of Scotland!
All.   Hail, King of Scotland!   [*Flourish*
Mal.   We shall not spend a large expense of time,
Before we reckon with your several loves,
And make us even with you.   My thanes and kinsmen,
Henceforth be earls, the first that ever Scotland
In such an honour named.   What 's more to do,
Which would be planted newly with the time,—
As calling home our exiled friends abroad,
That fled the snares of watchful tyranny;
Producing forth the cruel ministers
Of this dead butcher, and this fiend-like queen,
Who, as 't is thought, by self and violent hands
Took off her life,—this, and what needful else
That calls upon us, by the grace of Grace,
We will perform in measure, time, and place.
So thanks to all at once and to each one,
Whom we invite to see us crowned at Scone.   [*Exeunt*

MEASURE FOR MEASURE

DRAMATIS PERSONÆ

VINCENTIO, *the Duke*
ANGELO, *the deputy in the Duke's absence*
ESCALUS, *joined with Angelo in the government*
CLAUDIO, *a young gentleman*
LUCIO, *a fantastic*
Two other gentlemen
Provost
THOMAS } *Friars*
PETER }
A Justice
VARRIUS
ELBOW, *a constable*
FROTH, *a foolish gentleman*
POMPEY, *servant to Mistress Overdone*
ABHORSON, *an executioner*
BARNARDINE, *a prisoner*

ISABELLA, *sister to Claudio*
MARIANA, *betrothed to Angelo*
JULIET, *beloved of Claudio*
FRANCISCA, *a nun*
MISTRESS OVERDONE, *a bawd*

Lords, Officers, Citizens, Boy, and Attendants

SCENE.—*Vienna*

MEASURE FOR MEASURE

ACT ONE

Scene I.—A Room in the Duke's Palace

Enter Duke, Escalus, *and Attendants*

Duke. Escalus,—
Escal. My lord?
Duke. Of government the properties to unfold
Would seem in me to affect speech and discourse;
Since I am put to know that your own science
Exceeds, in that, the lists of all advice
My strength can give you: then no more remains
But that to your sufficiency, as your worth is able,
And let them work. The nature of our people,
Our city's institutions, and the terms
For common justice, you 're as pregnant in
As art and practice hath enrichéd any
That we remember. There is our commission, *[Giving it*
From which we would not have you warp.—Call hither,
I say, bid come before us, Angelo.— *[Exit an Attendant*
What figure of us think you he will bear?
For you must know, we have with special soul
Elected him our absence to supply,
Lent him our terror, dressed him with our love,
And given his deputation all the organs
Of our own power: what think you of it?
    Escal. If any in Vienna be of worth
To undergo such ample grace and honour,
It is Lord Angelo.
    Duke.   Look where he comes.

Enter Angelo

    Ang. Always obedient to your grace's will,
I come to know your pleasure.
    Duke.   Angelo,
There is a kind of character in thy life,
That to the observer doth thy history
Fully unfold. Thyself and thy belongings
Are not thine own so proper, as to waste
Thyself upon thy virtues, they on thee.
Heaven doth with us, as we with torches do,
Not light them for themselves; for if our virtues
Did not go forth of us, 't were all alike

281

As if we had them not.   Spirits are not finely touched,
But to fine issues; nor Nature never lends
The smallest scruple of her excellence
But, like a thrifty goddess, she determines
Herself the glory of a creditor,
Both thanks and use.   But I do bend my speech
To one that can my part in him advértise;
Hold, therefore, Angelo:—
                              [*Tendering his commission*
In our remove, be thou at full ourself;
Mortality and mercy in Vienna
Live in thy tongue and heart: old Escalus,
Though first in question, is thy secondary:—
Take thy commission.   [*Giving it*
     Ang.   Now, good my lord,
Let there be some more test made of my metal,
Before so noble and so great a figure
Be stamped upon 't.
     Duke.   No more evasion: we
Have with a leavened and preparéd choice
Proceeded to you; therefore take your honours.
Our haste from hence is of so quick condition,
That it prefers itself, and leaves unquestioned
Matters of needful value.   We shall write to you,
As time and our concernings shall impórtune,
How it goes with us; and do look to know
What doth befall you here.   So, fare you well.
To the hopeful execution do I leave you
Of your commissions.
     Ang.   Yet, give leave, my lord,
That we may bring you something on the way.
     Duke.   My haste may not admit it;
Nor need you, on mine honour, have to do
With any scruple: your scope is as mine own,
So to enforce or qualify the laws
As to your soul seems good.   Give me your hand:
I'll privily away: I love the people,
But do not like to stage me to their eyes.
Though it do well, I do not relish well
Their loud applause, and Aves vehement;
Nor do I think the man of safe discretion
That does affect it.   Once more, fare you well.
     Ang.   The heavens give safety to your purposes!
     Escal.   Lead forth and bring you back in happiness!
     Duke.   I thank you.   Fare you well.   [*Exit*
     Escal.   I shall desire you, sir, to give me leave
To have free speech with you; and it concerns me
To look into the bottom of my place;
A power I have, but of what strength and nature
I am not yet instructed.

Ang. 'T is so with me. Let us withdraw together,
And we may soon our satisfaction have
Touching the point.
    Escal.   I 'll wait upon your honour.

                                    [*Exeunt*

SCENE II.—A Street

Enter LUCIO *and two Gentlemen*

Lucio. If the duke, with the other dukes, come not to
composition with the King of Hungary, why then, all the
dukes fall upon the king.
    First Gent. Heaven grant us its peace, but not the King
of Hungary's !
    Sec. Gent. Amen.
    Lucio. Thou concludest like the sanctimonious pirate,
that went to sea with the Ten Commandments, but scraped
one out of the table.
    Sec. Gent. "Thou shalt not steal?"
    Lucio. Ay, that he razed.
    First Gent. Why, 't was a commandment to command
the captain and all the rest from their functions: they
put forth to steal. There 's not a soldier of us all, that,
in the thanksgiving before meat, doth relish the petition
well that prays for peace.
    Sec. Gent. I never heard any soldier dislike it.
    Lucio. I believe thee; for, I think, thou never wast
where grace was said.
    Sec. Gent. No? a dozen times at least.
    First Gent. What, in metre?
    Lucio. In any proportion or in any language.
    First Gent. I think, or in any religion.
    Lucio. Ay, why not? Grace is grace, despite of all
controversy: as for example,—thou thyself art a wicked
villain, despite of all grace.
    First Gent. Well, there went but a pair of shears
between us.
    Lucio. I grant; as there may between the list and the
velvet: thou art the list.
    First Gent. And thou the velvet: thou art good vel-
vet; thou art a three-piled piece, I warrant thee. I had
as lief be a list of an English kersey, as be piled, as thou art
piled, for a French velvet. Do I speak feelingly now?
    Lucio. I think thou dost; and, indeed, with most pain-
ful feeling of thy speech: I will, out of thine own confession,
learn to begin thy health; but, whilst I live, forget to
drink after thee.
    First Gent. I think I have done myself wrong, have I
not?

Sec. Gent.   Yes, that thou hast, whether thou art tainted or free.

Lucio.   Behold, behold, where Madam Mitigation comes!

First Gent.   I have purchased as many diseases under her roof as come to—

Sec. Gent.   To what, I pray?

Lucio.   Judge.

Sec. Gent.   To three thousand dolours a year.

First Gent.   Ay, and more.

Lucio.   A French crown more.

First Gent.   Thou art always figuring diseases in me; but thou art full of error,—I am sound.

Lucio.   Nay, not as one would say, healthy; but so sound as things that are hollow: thy bones are hollow; impiety has made a feast of thee.

Enter MISTRESS OVERDONE

First Gent.   How now? Which of your hips has the most profound sciatica?

Mrs. Ov.   Well, well; there 's one yonder arrested and carried to prison was worth five thousand of you all.

Sec. Gent.   Who 's that, I pray thee?

Mrs. Ov.   Marry, sir, that 's Claudio, Signior Claudio.

First Gent.   Claudio to prison! 't is not so.

Mrs. Ov.   Nay, but I know, 't is so: I saw him arrested; saw him carried away; and, which is more, within these three days his head 's to be chopped off.

Lucio.   But, after all this fooling, I would not have it so. Art thou sure of this?

Mrs. Ov.   I am too sure of it; and it is for getting Madam Julietta with child.

Lucio.   Believe me, this may be: he promised to meet me two hours since, and he was ever precise in promise-keeping.

Sec. Gent.   Besides, you know, it draws something near to the speech we had to such a purpose.

First Gent.   But most of all, agreeing with the proclamation.

Lucio.   Away: let 's go learn the truth of it.

[*Exeunt Lucio and Gentlemen*

Mrs. Ov.   Thus: what with the war, what with the sweat, what with the gallows, and what with poverty, I am custom-shrunk.

Enter POMPEY

How now? what 's the news with you?

Pom.   Yonder man is carried to prison.

Mrs. Ov.   Well: what has he done?

Pom.   A woman.

Mrs. Ov.   But what 's his offence?

Pom.   Groping for trouts in a peculiar river.

Mrs. Ov.   What, is there a maid with child by him?

Pom.   No; but there 's a woman with maid by him. You have not heard of the proclamation, have you?

Mrs. Ov.   What proclamation, man?

Pom.   All houses in the suburbs of Vienna must be plucked down.

Mrs. Ov.   And what shall become of those in the city?

Pom.   They shall stand for seed: they had gone down too, but that a wise burgher put in for them.

Mrs. Ov.   But shall all our houses of resort in the suburbs be pulled down?

Pom.   To the ground, mistress.

Mrs. Ov.   Why, here 's a change, indeed, in the commonwealth! what shall become of me?

Pom.   Come; fear not for you: good counsellors lack no clients: though you change your place, you need not change your trade; I'll be your tapster still.   Courage! there will be pity taken on you; you that have worn your eyes almost out in the service, you will be considered.

Mrs. Ov.   What 's to do here, Thomas Tapster?   Let 's withdraw.

Pom.   Here comes Signior Claudio, led by the provost to prison; and there 's Madam Juliet.

[*Exeunt*

Scene III.—The Same

Enter Provost, Claudio, Juliet, *and Officers*

Claud.   Fellow, why dost thou show me thus to the world?
Bear me to prison, where I am committed.

Prov.   I do it not in evil disposition,
But from Lord Angelo by special charge.

Claud.   Thus can the demi-god Authority
Make us pay down for our offence by weight.—
The sword of Heaven;—on whom it will, it will;
On whom it will not, so: yet still 't is just.

Enter Lucio *and two Gentlemen*

Lucio.   Why, how now, Claudio? whence comes this restraint?

Claud.   From too much liberty, my Lucio, liberty:
As surfeit is the father of much fast,
So every scope by the immoderate use
Turns to restraint.   Our natures do pursue,
Like rats that ravin down their proper bane,
A thirsty evil; and when we drink we die.

Lucio.   If I could speak so wisely under an arrest, I would send for certain of my creditors: and yet, to say the

truth, I had as lief have the foppery of freedom, as the
morality of imprisonment.—What's thy offence, Claudio?

Claud. What but to speak of would offend again.

Lucio. What, is it murder?

Claud. No.

Lucio. Lechery?

Claud. Call it so.

Prov. Away, sir; you must go.

Claud. One word, good friend.—Lucio, a word with you.
                                        [*Takes him aside*

Lucio. A hundred, if they 'll do you any good.
Is lechery so looked after?

Claud. Thus stands it with me: upon a true contráct,
I got possession of Julietta's bed:
You know the lady; she is fast my wife,
Save that we do the denunciation lack
Of outward order: this we came not to,
Only for propagation of a dower
Remaining in the coffer of her friends,
From whom we thought it meet to hid our love,
Till time had made them for us. But it chances
The stealth of our most mutual entertainment
With character too gross is writ on Juliet.

Lucio. With child, perhaps?

Claud.   Unhappily, even so.
And the new deputy now for the duke,—
Whether it be the fault and glimpse of newness,
Or whether that the body public be
A horse whereon the governor doth ride,
Who, newly in the seat, that it may know
He can command, lets it straight feel the spur;
Whether the tyranny be in his place,
Or in his eminence that fills it up,
I stagger in;—but this new governor
Awakes me all the enrollèd penalties,
Which have, like unscoured armour, hung by the wall
So long, that nineteen zodiacs have gone round,
And none of them been worn; and, for a name,
Now puts the drowsy and neglected act
Freshly on me:—'t is surely for a name.

Lucio. I warrant, it is: and thy head stands so tickle
on thy shoulders, that a milk-maid, if she be in love, may
sigh it off. Send after the duke, and appeal to him.

Claud. I have done so, but he 's not to be found.
I prithee, Lucio, do me this kind service:—
This day my sister should the cloister enter,
And there receive her approbation:
Acquaint her with the danger of my state;
Implore her, in my voice, that she make friends
To the strict deputy; bid herself assay him:

I have great hope in that; for in her youth
There is a prone and speechless dialect,
Such as moves men: besides, she hath prosperous art,
When she will play with reason and discourse,
And well she can persuade.

　　Lucio. I pray, she may: as well for the encouragement
of the like, which else would stand under grievous imposition, as for the enjoying of thy life, who I would be sorry
should be thus foolishly lost at a game of tick-tack.　　I'll
to her.

　　Claud. I thank you, good friend Lucio.

　　Lucio. Within two hours—

　　Claud.　　　　　　　　　　Come, officer, away! [*Exeunt*

SCENE IV.—A Monastery

Enter DUKE *and* FRIAR THOMAS

　　Duke. No, holy father; throw away that thought:
Believe not that the dribbling dart of love
Can pierce a complete bosom.　　Why I desire thee
To give me secret harbour, hath a purpose
More grave and wrinkled than the aims and ends
Of burning youth.

　　Fri.　　　　　　May your grace speak of it?

　　Duke. My holy sir, none better knows than you
How I have ever loved the life removed,
And held in idle price to haunt assemblies,
Where youth, and cost, and witless bravery keep.
I have delivered to Lord Angelo—
A man of stricture and firm abstinence—
My absolute power and place here in Vienna,
And he supposes me travelled to Poland;
For so I've strewed it in the common ear,
And so it is received.　　Now, pious sir,
You will demand of me, why I do this?

　　Fri. Gladly, my lord.

　　Duke. We have strict statutes and most biting laws,—
The needful bits and curbs to headstrong steeds,—
Which for this fourteen years we have let sleep;
Even like an o'ergrown lion in a cave,
That goes not out to prey.　　Now, as fond fathers,
Having bound up the threatening twigs of birch,
Only to stick it in their children's sight
For terror, not to use, in time the rod
Becomes more mocked than feared; so our decrees,
Dead to infliction, to themselves are dead;
And liberty plucks justice by the nose,
The baby beats the nurse, and quite athwart
Goes all decorum.

287

Fri.   It rested in your grace
To unloose this tied-up justice when you pleased;
And it in you more dreadful would have seemed,
Than in Lord Angelo.
   Duke.   I do fear, too dreadful:
Sith 't was my fault to give the people scope,
'T would be my tyranny to strike and gall them
For what I bid them do: for we bid this be done,
When evil deeds have their permissive pass
And not the punishment. Therefore, indeed, my father,
I have on Angelo imposed the office;
Who may, in the ambush of my name, strike home,
And yet my nature never in the sight,
To do it slander. And to behold his sway.
I will, as 't were a brother of your order,
Visit both prince and people: therefore, I prithee,
Supply me with the habit, and instruct me
How I may formally in person bear me
Like a true friar. More reasons for this action
At our more leisure shall I render you;
Only, this one:—Lord Angelo is precise;
Stands at a guard with envy; scarce confesses
That his blood flows, or that his appetite
Is more to bread than stone: hence shall we see,
If power change purpose, what our seemers be.   [*Exeunt*

Scene V.—A Nunnery

Enter Isabella *and* Francisca

   Isab.   And have you nuns no further privileges?
   Fran.   Are not these large enough?
   Isab.   Yes, truly: I speak not as desiring more;
But rather wishing a more strict restraint
Upon the sisterhood, votarists of Saint Clare.
   Lucio.   [*Within*] Ho! Peace be in this place!
   Isab.   Who 's that which calls?
   Fran.   It is a man's voice. Gentle Isabella,
Turn you the key, and know his business of him;
You may, I may not; you are yet unsworn.
When you have vowed, you must not speak with men
But in the presence of the prioress:
Then, if you speak, you must not show your face;
Or, if you show your face, you must not speak.
He calls again; I pray you, answer him.   [*Exit*
   Isab.   Peace and prosperity! Who is 't that calls?

Enter Lucio

   Lucio.   Hail, virgin, if you be,—as those cheek-roses
Proclaim you are no less! Can you so stead me,

As bring me to the sight of Isabella,
A novice of this place, and the fair sister
To her unhappy brother Claudio!
   Isab. Why her unhappy brother? let me ask:
The rather, for I now must make you know
I am that Isabella and his sister.
   Lucio. Gentle and fair, your brother kindly greets you:
Not to be weary with you, he's in prison.
   Isab. Woe me! for what?
   Lucio. For that which, if myself might be his judge,
He should receive his punishment in thanks:
He hath got his friend with child.
   Isab. Sir, make me not your story.
   Lucio.   'T is true.
I would not, though 't is my familiar sin
With maids to seem the lapwing and to jest
Tongue far from heart, play with all virgins so:
I hold you as a thing enskied and sainted;
By your renouncement, an immortal spirit;
And to be talked with in sincerity,
As with a saint.
   Isab. You do blaspheme the good in mocking me.
   Lucio. Do not believe it. Fewness and truth 't is
        thus:—
Your brother and his lover have embraced:
As those that feed grow full: as blossoming time,
That from the seedness the bare fallow brings
To teeming foison, e'en so her plenteous womb
Expresseth his full tilth and husbandry.
   Isab. Some one with child by him?—My cousin Juliet?
   Lucio. Is she your cousin?
   Isab. Adoptedly; as school-maids change their names
By vain, though apt, affection.
   Lucio.   She it is.
   Isab. O, let him marry her.
   Lucio.   This is the point.
The duke is very strangely gone from hence;
Bore many gentlemen, myself being one,
In hand, and hope of action; but we do learn
By those that know the very nerves of state,
His givings-out were of an infinite distance
From his true-meant design. Upon his place,
And with full line of his authority,
Governs Lord Angelo; a man whose blood
Is very snow-broth; one who never feels
The wanton stings and motions of the sense,
But doth rebate and blunt his natural edge
With profits of the mind, study and fast.
He—to give fear to use and liberty,
Which have for long run by the hideous law,

As mice by lions—hath picked out an act,
Under whose heavy sense your brother's life
Falls into forfeit: he arrests him on it,
And follows close the rigour of the statute,
To make him an example. All hope 's gone,
Unless you have the grace by your fair prayer
To soften Angelo; and that 's my pith
Of business 'twixt you and your poor brother.
    Isab. Doth he so seek his life?
    Lucio.   Has censured him
Already; and, as I hear, the provost hath
A warrant for his execution.
    Isab. Alas, what poor ability 's in me
To do him good?
    Lucio.   Assay the power you have.
    Isab. My power! Alas, I doubt,—
    Lucio.   Our doubts are traitors,
And make us lose the good we oft might win,
By fearing to attempt. Go to Lord Angelo,
And let him learn to know, when maidens sue,
Men give like gods; but when they weep and kneel,
All their petitions are as freely theirs
As they themselves would owe them.
    Isab. I'll see what I can do.
    Lucio.   But speedily.
    Isab. I will about it straight,
No longer staying but to give the mother
Notice of my affair. I humbly thank you:
Commend me to my brother; soon at night
I'll send him certain word of my success.
    Lucio. I take my leave of you.
    Isab.   Good, sir, adieu.
                                   [Exeunt

ACT TWO

Scene I.—A Hall in Angelo's House

Enter Angelo, Escalus, *and a Justice; Provost, Officers,*
and other Attendants

    Ang. We must not make a scarecrow of the law,
Setting it up to fear the birds of prey,
And let it keep one shape till custom make it
Their perch and not their terror.
    Escal.   Ay, but yet
Let us be keen, and rather cut a little,
Than fall, and bruise to death. Alas, this gentleman,
Whom I would save, had a most noble father.
Let but your honour know,—

Whom I believe to be most strait in virtue,—
That, in the working of your own affections,
Had time cohered with place, or place with wishing,
Or that the resolute acting of your blood
Could have attained the effect of your own purpose,
Whether you had not, sometime in your life,
Erred in this point which now you censure him,
And pulled the law upon you.

    Ang. 'T is one thing to be tempted, Escalus,
Another thing to fall. I not deny,
The jury, passing on the prisoner's life,
May in the sworn twelve have a thief or two
Guiltier than him they try; what's open made to justice,
That justice seizes: what knows the laws
That thieves do pass on thieves? 'T is very pregnant,
The jewel that we find, we stoop and take 't,
Because we see 't; but what we do not see
We tread upon, and never think of it.
You may not so extenuate his offence,
For I have had such faults; but rather tell me,
When I, that censure him, do so offend,
Let mine own judgment pattern out my death,
And nothing come in partial. Sir, he must die.

    Escal. Be 't as your wisdom will.
    Ang.   Where is the provost?
    Prov. Here, if it like your honour.
    Ang.   See that Claudio
Be executed by nine to-morrow morning.
Bring him his confessor, let him be prepared;
For that's the utmost of his pilgrimage.   [*Exit Provost*

    Escal. Well, Heaven forgive him, and forgive us all!
Some rise by sin, and some by virtue fall;
Some run from brakes of vice and answer none,
And some condemnéd for a fault alone.

Enter ELBOW *and Officers, with* FROTH *and* POMPEY

    Elb. Come, bring them away. If these be good people
in a commonweal that do nothing but use their abuses in
common houses, I know no law: bring them away.

    Ang. How now, sir! What's your name, and what's
the matter?

    Elb. If it please your honour, I am the poor duke's
constable, and my name is Elbow: I do lean upon justice,
sir; and do bring in here before your good honour two
notorious benefactors.

    Ang. Benefactors! Well, what benefactors are they?
are they not malefactors?

    Elb. If it please your honour, I know not well what they
are; but precise villains they are, that I am sure of, and

void of all profanation in the world that good Christians ought to have.

Escal. This comes off well: here's a wise officer.

Ang. Go to: what quality are they of? Elbow is your name: why dost thou not speak, Elbow?

Pom. He cannot, sir: he's out at elbow.

Ang. What are you, sir?

Elb. He, sir? a tapster, sir; parcel-bawd; one that serves a bad woman, whose house, sir, was, as they say, plucked down in the suburbs; and now she professes a hot-house, which, I think, is a very ill house too.

Escal. How know you that?

Elb. My wife, sir, whom I detest before Heaven and your honour,—

Escal. How! thy wife?

Elb. Ay, sir;—whom, I thank Heaven, is an honest woman,—

Escal. Dost thou detest her therefore?

Elb. I say, sir, I will detest myself also, as well as she, that this house, if it be not a bawd's house, it is pity of her life, for it is a naughty house.

Escal. How dost thou know that, constable?

Elb. Marry, sir, by my wife; who, if she had been a woman cardinally given, might have been accused in fornication, adultery, and all uncleanliness there.

Escal. By the woman's means?

Elb. Ay, sir, by Mistress Overdone's means; but as she spit in his face, so she defied him.

Pom. Sir, if it please your honour, this is not so.

Elb. Prove it before these varlets here, thou honourable man; prove it.

Escal. [*To Angelo*] Do you hear how he misplaces?

Pom. Sir, she came in great with child, and longing—saving your honour's reverence—for stewed prunes. Sir, we had but two in the house, which at that very distant time stood, as it were, in a fruit-dish, a dish of some three-pence; your honours have seen such dishes; they are not China dishes, but very good dishes,—

Escal. Go to, go to: no matter for the dish, sir.

Pom. No, indeed, sir, not of a pin; you are therein in the right:—but to the point. As I say, this Mistress Elbow, being, as I say, with child, and being great-bellied, and longing, as I said, for prunes, and having but two in the dish, as I said, Master Froth here, this very man, having eaten the rest, as I said, and, as I say, paying for them very honestly;—for, as you know, Master Froth, I could not give you three-pence again,—

Froth. No, indeed.

Pom. Very well;—you being then, if you be remembered, cracking the stones of the foresaid prunes,—

Froth. Ay, so I did, indeed.

Pom. Why, very well;—I telling you then, if you be remembered, that such a one, and such a one, were past cure of the thing you wot of, unless they kept very good diet, as I told you,—

Froth. All this is true.

Pom. Why, very well then,—

Escal. Come; you are a tedious fool: to the purpose.— What was done to Elbow's wife, that he hath cause to complain of? Come me to what was done to her.

Pom. Sir, your honour cannot come to that yet.

Escal. No, sir, nor I mean it not.

Pom. Sir, but you shall come to it, by your honour's leave. And, I beseech you, look into Master Froth here, sir; a man of fourscore pound a year, whose father died at Hallowmas:—Was't not at Hallowmas, Master Froth?—

Froth. All-Hallownd eve.

Pom. Why, very well; I hope here be truths. He, sir, sitting, as I say, in a lower chair, sir;—'t was in the Bunch of Grapes, where, indeed, you have a delight to sit, have you not?

Froth. I have so; because it is an open room, and good for winter.

Pom. Why, very well then; I hope here be truths.

Ang. This will last out a night in Russia,
When nights are longest there: I'll take my leave,
And leave you to the hearing of the cause;
Hoping you'll find good cause to whip them all.

Escal. I think no less. Good morrow to your lordship. [*Exit Angelo*] Now, sir, come on: what was done to Elbow's wife, once more?

Pom. Once, sir! there was nothing done to her once.

Elb. I beseech you, sir, ask him what this man did to my wife.

Pom. I beseech your honour, ask me.

Escal. Well, sir, what did this gentleman to her?

Pom. I beseech you, sir, look in this gentleman's face.— Good Master Froth, look upon his honour; 't is for a good purpose.—Doth your honour mark his face?

Escal. Ay, sir, very well.

Pom. Nay, I beseech you, mark it well.

Escal. Well, I do so.

Pom. Doth your honour see any harm in his face?

Escal. Why, no.

Pom. I'll be supposed upon a book, his face is the worst thing about him. Good then; if his face be the worst thing about him, how could Master Froth do the constable's wife any harm? I would know that of your honour.

Escal. He's in the right.—Constable, what say you to it?

Elb. First, an it like you, the house is a respected house; next, this is a respected fellow; and his mistress is a respected woman.

Pom. By this hand, sir, his wife is a more respected person than any of us all.

Elb. Varlet, thou liest: thou liest, wicked varlet! The time is yet to come that she was ever respected with man, woman, or child.

Pom. Sir, she was respected with him before he married with her.

Escal. Which is the wiser here? Justice, or Iniquity? —Is this true?

Elb. O thou caitiff! O thou varlet! O thou wicked Hannibal! I respected with her, before I was married to her?—If ever I was respected with her, or she with me, let not your worship think me the poor duke's officer. Prove this, thou wicked Hannibal, or I'll have mine action of battery on thee.

Escal. If he took you a box o' th' ear, you might have your action of slander too.

Elb. Marry, I thank your good worship for it. What is 't your worship's pleasure I shall do with this wicked caitiff?

Escal. Truly, officer, because he hath some offences in him, that thou wouldst discover if thou couldst, let him continue in his courses, till thou knowest what they are.

Elb. Marry, I thank your worship for it. Thou seest, thou wicked varlet, now, what's come upon thee: thou art to continue; now, thou varlet; thou art to continue.

Escal. Where were you born, friend?

Froth. Here in Vienna, sir.

Escal. Are you of fourscore pounds a year?

Froth. Yes, an 't please you, sir.

Escal. So.—What trade are you of, sir?

Pom. A tapster; a poor widow's tapster.

Escal. Your mistress' name?

Pom. Mistress Overdone.

Escal. Hath she had any more than one husband?

Pom. Nine, sir; Overdone by the last.

Escal. Nine! Come hither to me, Master Froth. Master Froth, I would not have you acquainted with tapsters; they will draw you, Master Froth, and you will hang them. Get you gone, and let me hear no more of you.

Froth. I thank your worship. For mine own part, I never came into any room in a taphouse, but I am drawn in.

Escal. Well, no more of it, Master Froth: farewell. [*Exit Froth*]—Come you hither to me, master tapster. What's your name, master tapster?

Pom. Pompey.

Escal.   What else?

Pom.   Bum, sir.

Escal.   Troth, and your bum is the greatest thing about you, so that, in the beastliest sense, you are Pompey the Great.   Pompey, you are partly a bawd, Pompey, howsoever you colour it in being a tapster.   Are you not? come, tell me true: it shall be the better for you.

Pom.   Truly, sir, I am a poor fellow that would live.

Escal.   How would you live, Pompey? by being a bawd?   What do you think of the trade, Pompey? is it a lawful trade?

Pom.   If the law would allow it, sir.

Escal.   But the law will not allow it, Pompey; nor it shall not be allowed in Vienna.

Pom.   Does your worship mean to geld and splay all the youth of the city?

Escal.   No, Pompey.

Pom.   Truly, sir, in my poor opinion, they will to't then.   If your worship will take order for the drabs and the knaves, you need not to fear the bawds.

Escal.   There are pretty orders beginning, I can tell you: it is but heading and hanging.

Pom.   If you head and hang all that offend that way but for ten year together, you'll be glad to give out a commission for more heads.   If this law hold in Vienna ten year, I'll rent the fairest house in it after three-pence a bay.   If you live to see this come to pass, say, Pompey told you so.

Escal.   Thank you, good Pompey; and, in requital of your prophecy, hark you:—I advise you, let me not find you before me again upon any complaint whatsoever; no, not for dwelling where you do: if I do, Pompey, I shall beat you to your tent, and prove a shrewd Cæsar to you; in plain dealing, Pompey, I shall have you whipt.   So, for this time, Pompey, fare you well.

Pom.   I thank your worship for your good counsel. —[*Aside*] But I shall follow it as the flesh and fortune shall better determine.

Whip me?   No, no, let carman whip his jade;
The valiant heart's not whipt out of his trade.   [*Exit*

Escal.   Come hither to me, Master Elbow; come hither, master constable.   How long have you been in this place of constable?

Elb.   Seven year and a half, sir.

Escal.   I thought, by the readiness in the office, you had continued in it some time.   You say, seven years together?

Elb.   And a half, sir.

Escal.   Alas, it hath been great pains to you.   They do you wrong to put you so oft upon 't.   Are there not men in your ward sufficient to serve it?

Elb. Faith, sir, few of any wit in such matters. As
they are chosen, they are glad to choose me for them; I
do it for some piece of money, and go through with all.

Escal. Look you bring me in the names of some six or
seven, the most sufficient of your parish.

Elb. To your worship's house, sir?

Escal. To my house. Fare you well.   [*Exit Elbow*
What's o'clock, think you?

Just. Eleven, sir.

Escal. I pray you home to dinner with me.

Just. I humbly thank you.

Escal. It grieves me for the death of Claudio;
But there's no remedy.

Just. Lord Angelo is severe.

Escal.   It is but needful:
Mercy is not itself, that oft looks so;
Pardon is still the nurse of second woe,
But yet,—poor Claudio!—There's no remedy.—
Come, sir.   [*Exeunt*

SCENE II.—Another Room in ANGELO'S House

Enter Provost, and a Servant

Serv. He's hearing of a cause; he will come straight:
I'll tell him of you.

Prov. Pray you, do. [*Exit Serv.*] I'll know
His pleasure; may be, he'll relent. Alas,
He hath but as offended in a dream:
All sects, all ages smack of this vice, and he
To die for it!—

Enter ANGELO

Ang.   Now, what's the matter, provost?

Prov. Is it your will Claudio shall die to-morrow?

Ang. Did I not tell thee, yea? hadst thou not order?
Why dost thou ask again?

Prov.   Lest I might be too rash.
Under your good correction, I have seen,
When, after execution, judgment hath
Repented o'er his doom.

Ang.   Go to; let that be mine:
Do you your office, or give up your place
And you shall well be spared.

Prov.   I crave your honour's pardon.
What shall be done, sir, with the groaning Juliet?
She's very near her hour.

Ang.   Dispose of her
To some more fitter place, and that with speed.

Re-enter Servant

Serv.   Here is the sister of the man condemned
Desires access to you.
Ang.   Hath he a sister?
Prov.   Ay, my good lord; a very virtuous maid,
And to be shortly of a sisterhood,
If not already.
Ang.   Well, let her be admitted.   *[Exit Servant*
See you the fornicatress be removed:
Let her have needful, but not lavish, means;
There shall be order for 't.

Enter Lucio *and* Isabella

Prov.   God save your honour!
Ang.   Stay a little while.—[*To Isab.*] You're welcome:
        what's your will?
Isab.   I am a woful suitor to your honour,
Please but your honour hear me.
Ang.   Well; what's your suit?
Isab.   There is a vice that most I do abhor,
And most desire should meet the blow of justice,
For which I would not plead, but that I must;
For which I must not plead, but that I am
At war 'twixt will and will not.
Ang.   Well; the matter?
Isab.   I have a brother is condemned to die:
I do beseech you, let it be his fault
And not my brother.
Prov.   [*Aside*] Heaven give thee moving graces!
Ang.   Condemn the fault, and not the actor of it!
Why, every fault's condemned ere it be done.
Mine were the very cipher of a function,
To find the fault, whose fine stands in record,
And let go by the actor.
Isab.   O just, but severe law!
I had a brother then.—Heaven keep your honour!
Lucio.   [*To Isab.*] Give 't not o'er so: to him again,
        entreat him;
Kneel down before him, hang upon his gown;
You are too cold; if you should need a pin,
You could not with more tame a tongue desire it.
To him, I say.
Isab.   Must he needs die?
Ang.   Maiden, no remedy.
Isab.   Yes; I do think that you might pardon him,
And neither Heaven, nor man, grieve at the mercy.
Ang.   I will not do 't.
Isab.   But can you, if you would?
Ang.   Look; what I will not, that I cannot do.

297

Isab. But might you do 't and do the world no wrong,
If so your heart were touched with that remorse
As mine is to him?
    Ang.   He's sentenced: 't is too late.
    Lucio. [*To Isab.*] You are too cold.
    Isab. Too late! why, no; I, that do speak a word,
May call it back again.   Well, believe this,
No ceremony that to great ones 'longs,
Not the king's crown, nor the deputed sword,
The marshal's truncheon, nor the judge's robe,
Become them with one half so good a grace
As mercy does.
If he had been as you, and you as he,
You would have slipped like him; but he, like you,
Would not have been so stern.
    Ang.   Pray you, be gone.
    Isab. I would to Heaven I had your potency,
And you were Isabel! should it then be thus?
No; I would tell what 't were to be a judge,
And what a prisoner.
    Lucio. [*To Isab.*] Ay, touch him; there's the vein.
    Ang. Your brother is a forfeit of the law,
And you but waste your words.
    Isab.   Alas! alas!
Why, all the souls that were were forfeit once;
And He that might the vantage best have took,
Found out the remedy.   How would you be,
If He, which is the top of judgment, should
But judge you as you are?   O, think on that,
And mercy then will breathe within your lips
Like man new-made!
    Ang.   Be you content, fair maid,
It is the law, not I, condemns your brother:
Were he my kinsman, brother, or my son,
It should be thus with him:—he must die to-morrow.
    Isab. To-morrow? O, that's sudden! Spare him,
        spare him!—
He's not prepared for death.   Even for our kitchens
We kill the fowl of season: shall we serve Heaven
With less respect than we do minister
To our gross selves?   Good, good my lord, bethink you:
Who is it that hath died for this offence?
There's many have committed it.
    Lucio. [*To Isab.*]   Ay, well said.
    Ang. The law hath not been dead, though it hath
    slept:
Those many had not dared to do that evil,
If the first that did the edict infringe
Had answered for his deed: now, 't is awake,
Takes note of what is done, and, like a prophet,

Looks in a glass that shows what future evils,—
Either new, or by remissness new-conceived,
And so in progress to be hatched and born,—
Are now to have no súccessive degrees,
But, ere they live, to end.
    Isab.   Yet show some pity.
    Ang. I show it most of all when I show justice;
For then I pity those I do not know,
Which a dismissed offence would after gall,
And do him right that, answering one foul wrong,
Lives not to act another. Be satisfied;
Your brother dies to-morrow; be content.
    Isab. So you must be the first that gives this sentence,
And he that suffers. O! 't is excellent
To have a giant's strength, but tyrannous
To use it like a giant.
    Lucio. [*To Isab.*] That's well said.
    Isab. Could great men thunder
As Jove himself does, Jove would ne'er be quiet,
For every pelting, petty officer
Would use his heaven for thunder; nothing but thunder.—
Merciful Heaven!
Thou rather with thy sharp and sulphurous bolt
Splitt'st the unwedgeable and gnarléd oak,
Than the soft myrtle; but man, proud man,
Drest in a little brief authority,
Most ignorant of what he's most assured,
His glassy essence,—like an angry ape,
Plays such fantastic tricks before high heaven
As make the angels weep; who, with our spleens,
Would all themselves laugh mortal.
    Lucio. [*To Isab.*] O, to him, to him, wench! He will
      relent:
He's coming; I perceive 't.
    Prov. [*Aside*] Pray Heaven, she win him!
    Isab. We cannot weigh our brother with ourself:
Great men may jest with saints; 't is wit in them,
But in the less foul profanation.
    Lucio. [*To Isab.*] Thou 'rt in the right, girl; more
      o' that.
    Isab. That in the captain's but a choleric word,
Which in the soldier is flat blasphemy.
    Lucio. [*To Isab.*] Art advised o' that? more on 't.
    Ang. Why do you put these sayings upon me?
    Isab. Because authority, though it err like others,
Hath yet a kind of medicine in itself,
That skins the vice o' the top. Go to your bosom;
Knock there, and ask your heart, what it doth know
That's like my brother's fault: if it confess
A natural guiltiness, such as is his,

Let it not sound a thought upon your tongue
Against my brother's life.
    Ang.   *[Aside]*   She speaks, and 't is
Such sense, that my sense breeds with 't.   Fare you well.
    Isab.   Gentle my lord, turn back.
    Ang.   I will bethink me.—Come again to-morrow.
    Isab.   Hark, how I'll bribe you.   Good my lord turn back.
    Ang.   How, bribe me?
    Isab.   Ay, with such gifts that Heaven shall share with
      you.
    Lucio.   *[To Isab.]*   You had marred all else.
    Isab.   Not with fond shekels of the tested gold,
Or stones, whose rates are either rich or poor
As fancy values them; but with true prayers,
That shall be up at heaven, and enter there
Ere sunrise,—prayers from preservéd souls,
From fasting maids, whose minds are dedicate
To nothing temporal.
    Ang.   Well; come to me to-morrow.
    Lucio.   *[To Isab.]*   Go to; 't is well; away!
    Isab.   Heaven keep your honour safe!
    Ang.   *[Aside]*   Amen:
For I am that way going to temptation,
Where prayers cross.
    Isab.   At what hour to-morrow
Shall I attend your lordship?
    Ang.   At any time 'fore noon.
    Isab.   Save your honour!
                [Exeunt Lucio, Isabella, and Provost
    Ang.   From thee,—even from thy virtue!—
What 's this? what 's this?   Is this her fault or mine?
The tempter or the tempted, who sins most, ha?
Not she; nor doth she tempt; but it is I,
That, lying by the violet in the sun,
Do, as the carrion does, not as the flower,
Corrupt with virtuous season.   Can it be,
That modesty may more betray our sense
Than woman's lightness?   Having waste ground enough,
Shall we desire to raze the sanctuary,
And pitch our evils there?   O, fie, fie, fie!
What dost thou, or what art thou, Angelo?
Dost thou desire her foully for those things
That make her good?   O, let her brother live:
Thieves for their robbery have authority
When judges steal themselves.   What, do I love her,
That I desire to hear her speak again,
And feast upon her eyes?   What is 't I dream on?
O cunning enemy, that, to catch a saint,
With saints dost bait thy hook!   Most dangerous
Is that temptation that doth goad us on

To sin in loving virtue. Ne'er could the strumpet,
With all her double vigour, art and nature,
Once stir my temper, but this virtuous maid
Subdues me quite.—Ever, till now,
When men were fond, I smiled, and wondered how. [*Exit*

SCENE III.—A Room in a Prison

Enter DUKE, *disguised as a friar, and Provost*

Duke. Hail to you, provost!—so I think you are.
Prov. I am the provost. What's your will, good friar?
Duke. Bound by my charity and my blessed order,
I come to visit the afflicted spirits
Here in the prison. Do me the common right
To let me see them, and to make me know
The nature of their crimes, that I may minister
To them accordingly.
Prov. I would do more than that, if more were needful.
Look, here comes one,—a gentlewoman of mine,
Who, falling in the flames of her own youth,
Hath blistered her report. She is with child,
And he that got it, sentenced,—a young man
More fit to do another such offence
Than die for this.

Enter JULIET

Duke. When must he die?
Prov.   As I do think, to-morrow.—
[*To Juliet*] I have provided for you: stay awhile,
And you shall be conducted.
Duke. Repent you, fair one, of the sin you carry?
Juliet. I do, and bear the shame most patiently.
Duke. I'll teach you how you shall arraign your con-
        science,
And try your penitence, if it be sound,
Or hollowly put on.
Juliet.   I'll gladly learn.
Duke. Love you the man that wronged you?
Juliet. Yes, as I love the woman that wronged him.
Duke. So then, it seems, your most offenceful act
Was mutually committed?
Juliet.   Mutually.
Duke. Then was your sin of heavier kind than his.
Juliet. I do confess it, and repent it, father.
Duke. 'T is meet so, daughter: but lest you do repent,
As that the sin hath brought you to this shame,—
Which sorrow is always toward ourselves, not Heaven,
Showing, we would not spare Heaven as we love it,
But as we stand in fear,—

301

Juliet. I do repent me, as it is an evil,
And take the shame with joy.
   Duke.   There rest.
Your partner, as I hear, must die to-morrow,
And I am going with instruction to him.
   Juliet. Grace go with you!
   Duke. *Benedicite!*   *[Exit*
   Juliet. Must die to-morrow! O, injurious love,
That respites me a life, whose very comfort
Is still a dying horror!
   Prov.   'T is pity of him.   *[Exeunt*

SCENE IV.—A Room in ANGELO's House

Enter ANGELO

   Ang. When I would pray and think, I think and pray
To several subjects: Heaven hath my empty words,
Whilst my invention, hearing not my tongue,
Anchors on Isabel: Heaven in my mouth,
As if I did but only chew his name,
And in my heart the strong and swelling evil
Of my conception. The state, whereon I studied,
Is like a good thing, being often read,
Grown seared and tedious; yea, my gravity,
Wherein—let no man hear me—I take pride,
Could I, with boot, change for an idle plume
Which the air beats for vain. O place! O form!
How often dost thou with thy case, thy habit,
Wrench awe from fools, and tie the wiser souls
To thy false seeming!—Blood, thou still art blood:
Let's write good angel on the devil's horn,
'T is not the devil's crest.

Enter a Servant

How now! who's there?
   Serv.   One Isabel, a sister,
Desires access to you.
   Ang. .   Teach her the way. *[Exit Servant*
O heavens!
Why does my blood thus muster to my heart,
Making both it unable for itself,
And dispossessing all my other parts
Of necessary fitness?
So play the foolish throngs with one that swoons;
Come all to help him, and so stop the air
By which he should revive: and even so
The general, subject to a well-wished king,
Quit their own part, and in obsequious fondness
Crowd to his presence, where their untaught love
Must needs appear offence.

Enter ISABELLA

                         How now, fair maid?
Isab.   I am come to know your pleasure.
Ang.   That you might know it, would much better
    please me
Than to demand what 't is.   Your brother cannot live.
Isab.   Even so.—Heaven keep your honour!   [*Retiring*
Ang.   Yet may he live awhile; and, it may be,
As long as you, or I: yet he must die.
Isab.   Under your sentence.
Ang.   Yea.
Isab.   When, I beseech you? that in his reprieve,
Longer or shorter, he may be so fitted
That his soul sicken not.
    Ang.   Ha! fie, these filthy vices!   'T were as good
To pardon him that hath from nature stolen
A man already made, as to remit
Their saucy sweetness that do coin Heaven's image
In stamps that are forbid: 't is all as easy
Falsely to take away a life true made,
As to put metal in restrainéd means,
To make a false one.
    Isab.   'T is set down so in heaven, but not in earth.
Ang.   Say you so? then I shall pose you quickly.
Which had you rather, that the most just law
Now took your brother's life; or, to redeem him,
Give up your body to such sweet uncleanness
As she that he hath stained?
    Isab.   Sir, believe this,
I had rather give my body than my soul.
    Ang.   I talk not of your soul.   Our compelled sins
Stand more for number than accompt.
    Isab.   How say you?
    Ang.   Nay, I'll not warrant that; for I can speak
Against the thing I say.   Answer to this:—
I, now the voice of the recorded law,
Pronounce a sentence on your brother's life:
Might there not be a charity in sin
To save this brother's life?
    Isab.   Please you to do 't,
I'll take it as a peril to my soul:
It is no sin at all, but charity.
    Ang.   Pleased you to do 't, at peril of your soul,
Were equal poise of sin and charity.
    Isab.   That I do beg his life, if it be sin,
Heaven, let me bear 't! you granting of my suit,
If that be sin, I'll make it my morn-prayer
To have it added to the faults of mine,
And nothing of your answer.

Ang.   Nay, but hear me.
Your sense pursues not mine: either you are ignorant,
Or seem so, craftily; and that's not good.
   Isab. Let me be ignorant, and in nothing good
But graciously to know I am no better.
   Ang. Thus wisdom wishes to appear most bright
When it doth tax itself: as these black masks
Proclaim an enshield beauty ten times louder
Than beauty could, displayed.—But mark me;
To be receivéd plain, I'll speak more gross:
Your brother is to die.
   Isab. So.
   Ang. And his offence is so, as it appears
Accountant to the law upon that pain.
   Isab. True.
   Ang. Admit no other way to save his life,—
As I subscribe not that, nor any other,
But in the loss of question,—that you, his sister,
Finding yourself desired of such a person,
Whose credit with the judge, or own great place,
Could fetch your brother from the manacles
Of the all-building law; and that there were
No earthly mean to save him, but that either
You must lay down the treasures of your body
To this supposed, or else to let him suffer;
What would you do?
   Isab. As much for my poor brother as myself:
That is, were I under the terms of death,
The impression of keen whips I'd wear as rubies,
And strip myself to death, as to a bed
That longing I've been sick for, ere I'd yield
My body up to shame.
   Ang.   Thus must your brother die.
   Isab. And 't were the cheaper way.
Better it were, a brother died at once
Than that a sister, by redeeming him,
Should die for ever.
   Ang. Were not you then as cruel as the sentence
That you have slandered so?
   Isab. Ignomy in ransom, and free pardon,
Are of two houses: lawful mercy
Is nothing akin to foul redemption.
   Ang. You seemed of late to make the law a tyrant;
And rather proved the sliding of your brother
A merriment than a vice.
   Isab. O, pardon me, my lord! it oft falls out,
To have what we would have, we speak not what we mean.
I something do excuse the thing I hate,
For his advantage that I dearly love.
   Ang. We are all frail.

Isab.   Else let my brother die,
If not a fedary, but only he,
Owe and succeed thy weakness.
    Ang. Nay, women are frail too.
    Isab. Ay, as the glasses where they view themselves;
Which are as easy broke as they make forms.
Women!—Help Heaven! men their creation mar
In profiting by them. Nay, call us ten times frail,
For we are soft as our complexions are,
And credulous to false prints.
    Ang.   I think it well:
And from this testimony of your own sex,—
Since, I suppose, we're made to be no stronger
Than faults may shake our frames,—let me be bold:—
I do arrest your words. Be that you are,
That is, a woman; if you be more, you're none;
If you be one,—as you are well expressed
By all external warrants,—show it now
By putting on the destined livery.
    Isab. I have no tongue but one: gentle my lord,
Let me entreat you speak the former language.
    Ang. Plainly conceive, I love you.
    Isab. My brother did love Juliet; and you tell me,
That he shall die for 't.
    Ang. He shall not, Isabel, if you give me love.
    Isab. I know, your virtue hath a license in 't,
Which seems a little fouler that it is,
To pluck on others.
    Ang.   Believe me, on mine honour,
My words express my purpose.
    Isab. Ha! little honour to be much believed,
And most pernicious purpose!—Seeming, seeming!—
I will proclaim thee, Angelo; look for 't:
Sign me a present pardon for my brother,
Or with an outstretched throat I'll tell the world
Aloud what man thou art.
    Ang.   Who will believe thee, Isabel?
My unsoiled name, the austereness of my life,
My vouch against you, and my place i' the state,
Will so your accusation overweigh,
That you shall stifle in your own report,
And smell of calumny. I have begun,
And now I give my sensual race the rein;
Fit thy consent to my sharp appetite,
Lay by all nicety and prolixious blushes
That banish what they sue for, redeem thy brother
By yielding up thy body to my will;
Or else he must not only die the death,
But thy unkindness shall his death draw out
To lingering sufferance. Answer me to-morrow,

Or, by the affection that now guides me most,
I'll prove a tyrant to him.   As for you,
Say what you can, my false o'erweighs your true.   [*Exit*
  Isab. To whom should I complain?   Did I tell this,
Who would believe me?   O perilous mouths!
That bear in them one and the selfsame tongue,
Either of condemnation or approof,
Bidding the law make court'sy to their will,
Hooking both right and wrong to the appetite,
To follow as it draws!   I'll to my brother:
Though he hath fallen by prompture of the blood,
Yet hath he in him such a mind of honour,
That, had he twenty heads to tender down
On twenty bloody blocks, he'd yield them up,
Before his sister should her body stoop
To such abhorred pollution.
Then, Isabel, live chaste, and, brother, die:
More than our brother is our chastity.
I'll tell him yet of Angelo's request,
And fit his mind to death, for his soul's rest.   [*Exit*

ACT THREE

Scene I.—A Room in the Prison

Enter Duke, *as a friar,* Claudio, *and Provost*

  Duke. So, then you hope of pardon from Lord Angelo?
  Claud. The miserable have no other medicine,
But only hope:
I have hope to live, and am prepared to die.
  Duke. Be absolute for death; either death or life
Shall thereby be the sweeter.   Reason thus with life:—
If I do lose thee, I do lose a thing
That none but fools would keep; a breath thou art,
Servile to all the skyey influences
That dost this habitation, where thou keep'st,
Hourly inflict: merely, thou art death's fool; ·
For him thou labour'st by thy flight to shun,
And yet runn'st toward him still.   Thou art not noble;
For all the accommodations that thou bear'st
Are nursed by baseness.   Thou art by no means valiant;
For thou dost fear the soft and tender fork
Of a poor worm.   Thy best of rest is sleep,
And that thou oft provok'st, yet grossly fear'st
Thy death, which is no more.   Thou'rt not thyself;
For thou exist'st on many a thousand grains
That issue out of dust.   Happy thou art not;
For what thou hast not, still thou striv'st to get,

And what thou hast, forgett'st. Thou art not certain;
For thy complexion shifts to strange effects,
After the moon. If thou art rich, thou'rt poor;
For, like an ass whose back with ingots bows,
Thou bear'st thy heavy riches but a journey,
And death unloads thee. Friend hast thou none;
For thine own bowels, which do call thee sire,
The mere effusion of thy proper loins,
Do curse the gout, serpigo, and the rheum,
For ending thee no sooner. Thou hast nor youth nor age,
But, as it were, an after-dinner's sleep,
Dreaming on both; for all thy blessèd youth
Becomes as agéd and doth beg the alms
Of palsied eld; and when thou 'rt old and rich,
Thou 'st neither heat, affection, limb, nor beauty,
To make thy riches pleasant. What 's yet in this,
That bears the name of life? Yet in this life
Lie hid more thousand deaths: yet death we fear,
That makes these odds all even.
    Claud.   I humbly thank you.
To sue to live, I find I seek to die;
And, seeking death, find life: let it come on.
    Isab. [*Without*] What, ho! Peace here; grace and
        good company!
    Prov. Who's there? come in: the wish deserves a
        welcome.
    Duke. Dear sir, ere long I'll visit you again.
    Claud. Most holy sir, I thank you.

Enter ISABELLA

    Isab. My business is a word or two with Claudio.
    Prov. And very welcome.—Look, signior; here's your
        sister.
    Duke. Provost, a word with you.
    Prov.   As many as you please.
    Duke. Bring me to hear them speak, where I may be
Concealed.   [*Exeunt Duke and Provost*
    Claud. Now, sister, what 's the comfort?
    Isab.   Why, as
All comforts are; most good, most good, indeed.
Lord Angelo, having affairs to heaven,
Intends you for his swift ambassador,
Where you shall be an everlasting leiger:
Therefore, your best appointment make with speed;
To-morrow you set on.
    Claud.   Is there no remedy?
    Isab. None, but such remedy as, to save a head
To cleave a heart in twain.
    Claud.   But is there any?
    Isab. Yes, brother, you may live:

There is a devilish mercy in the judge,
If you'll implore it, that will free your life,
But fetter you till death.
 Claud.   Perpetual durance?
 Isab. Ay, just; perpetual durance,—a restraint,
Though all the world's vastidity you had,
To a determined scope.
 Claud.   But in what nature?
 Isab. In such a one as, you consenting to't,
Would bark your honour from that trunk you bear,
And leave you naked.
 Claud.   Let me know the point.
 Isab. O, I do fear thee, Claudio; and I quake,
Lest thou a feverous life shouldst entertain,
And six or seven winters more respect
Than a perpetual honour. Dar'st thou die?
The sense of death is most in apprehension,
And the poor beetle that we tread upon,
In corporal sufferance finds a pang as great
As when a giant dies.
 Claud.   Why give you me this shame?
Think you I can a resolution fetch
From flowery tenderness? If I must die,
I will encounter darkness as a bride
And hug it in mine arms.
 Isab. There spake my brother: there my father's grave
Did utter forth a voice. Yes, thou must die:
Thou art too noble to conserve a life
In base appliances. This outward-sainted deputy—
Whose settled visage and deliberate word
Nips youth i' the head, and follies doth emmew
As falcon doth the fowl—is yet a devil:
His filth within being cast, he would appear
A pond as deep as hell.
 Claud.   The princely Angelo?
 Isab. O, 't is the cunning livery of hell,
The damned'st body to invest and cover
In princely guards! Dost thou think, Claudio,—
If I would yield him my virginity,
Thou mightst be freed.
 Claud.   O heavens! it cannot be.
 Isab. Yes, he would give 't thee, from this rank offence,
So to offend him still. This night's the time
That I should do what I abhor to name,
Or else thou diest to-morrow.
 Claud.   Thou shalt not do't.
 Isab. O, were it but my life,
I'd throw it down for your deliverance
As frankly as a pin.
 Claud.   Thanks, dear Isabel.

Isab.   Be ready, Claudio, for your death to-morrow.
Claud.   Yes.—Has he affections in him,
That thus can make him bite the law by the nose,
When he would force it?   Sure, it is no sin;
Or of the deadly seven it is the least.
Isab.   Which is the least?
Claud.   If it were damnable, he, being so wise,
Why would he for the momentary trick
Be perdurably fined?—O Isabel!
Isab.   What says my brother?
Claud.   Death is a fearful thing.
Isab.   And shaméd life a hateful.
Claud.   Ay, but to die, and go we know not where;
To lie in cold obstruction, and to rot;
This sensible warm motion to become
A kneaded clod; and the delighted spirit
To bathe in fiery floods, or to reside
In thrilling regions of thick-ribbéd ice;
To be imprisoned in the viewless winds,
And blown with restless violence round about
The pendant world; or to be worse than worst
Of those that lawless and incertain thoughts
Imagine howling!—'t is too horrible.
The weariest and most loathéd worldly life,
That age, ache, penury, and imprisonment
Can lay on nature, is a paradise
To what we fear of death.
Isab.   Alas! alas!
Claud.   Sweet sister, let me live.
What sin you do to save a brother's life,
Nature dispenses with the deed so far
That it becomes a virtue.
Isab.   O you beast!
O faithless coward!   O dishonest wretch!
Wilt thou be made a man out of my vice?
Is't not a kind of incest, to take life
From thine own sister's shame?   What should I think?
Heaven shield, my mother played my father fair!
For such a warpéd slip of wilderness
Ne'er issued from his blood.   Take my defiance;
Die, perish!   Might but my bending down
Reprieve thee from thy fate, it should proceed.
I'll pray a thousand prayers for thy death,—
No word to save thee.
Claud.   Nay, hear me, Isabel.
Isab.   O, fie, fie, fie!
Thy sin's not accidental, but a trade.
Mercy to thee would prove itself a bawd:
'T is best that thou diest quickly.   [*Going*
Claud.   O hear me, Isabella!

Act III Sc i

Re-enter DUKE

Duke. Vouchsafe a word, young sister, but one word.
Isab. What is your will?
Duke. Might you dispense with your leisure, I would by-and-by have some speech with you: the satisfaction I would require is likewise your own benefit.
Isab. I have no superfluous leisure: my stay must be stolen out of other affairs; but I will attend you awhile.
Duke. [*Aside to Claudio*] Son, I have overheard what hath passed between you and your sister. Angelo had never the purpose to corrupt her; only he hath made an assay of her virtue, to practise his judgment with the disposition of natures: she, having the truth of honour in her, hath made him that gracious denial which he is most glad to receive. I am confessor to Angelo, and I know this to be true; therefore prepare yourself to death: do not satisfy your resolution with hopes that are fallible: to-morrow you must die. Go to your knees, and make ready.
Claud. Let me ask my sister pardon. I am so out of love with life, that I will sue to be rid of it.
Duke. Hold you there: farewell. [*Exit Claudio* Provost, a word with you.

Re-enter Provost

Prov. What's your will, father?
Duke. That now you are come, you will be gone. Leave me awhile with the maid: my mind promises with my habit no loss shall touch her by my company.
Prov. In good time. [*Exit*
Duke. The hand that hath made you fair hath made you good: the goodness that is cheap in beauty makes beauty brief in goodness; but grace, being the soul of your complexion, shall keep the body of it ever fair. The assault that Angelo hath made to you, fortune hath conveyed to my understanding; and but that frailty hath examples for his falling, I should wonder at Angelo. How will you do to content this substitute, and to save your brother?
Isab. I am now going to resolve him, I had rather my brother die by the law than my son should be unlawfully born. But O how much is the good duke deceived in Angelo! If ever he return, and I can speak to him, I will open my lips in vain, or discover his government.
Duke. That shall not be much amiss: yet, as the matter now stands, he will avoid your accusation,—he made trial of you only. Therefore fasten your ear on my advisings: to the love I have in doing good a remedy presents itself. I do make myself believe that you may most uprighteously do a poor wronged lady a merited benefit; redeem your brother from the angry law; do no stain to your own gracious

310

person; and much please the absent duke, if, peradventure, he shall ever return to have hearing of this business.

Isab. Let me hear you speak further. I have spirit to do anything that appears not foul in the truth of my spirit.

Duke. Virtue is bold, and goodness never fearful. Have you not heard speak of Mariana, the sister of Frederick, the great soldier who miscarried at sea?

Isab. I have heard of the lady, and good words went with her name.

Duke. She should this Angelo have married; was affianced to him by oath, and the nuptial appointed: between which time of the contract, and limit of the solemnity, her brother Frederick was wrecked at sea, having in that perished vessel the dowry of his sister. But mark how heavily this befell to the poor gentlewoman: there she lost a noble and renowned brother, in his love toward her ever most kind and natural; with him the portion and sinew of her fortune, her marriage-dowry; with both, her combinate husband, this well-seeming Angelo.

Isab. Can this be so? Did Angelo so leave her?

Duke. Left her in her tears, and dried not one of them with his comfort; swallowed his vows whole, pretending in her discoveries of dishonour; in few, bestowed her on her own lamentation, which she yet wears for his sake; and he, a marble to her tears, is washed with them, but relents not.

Isab. What a merit were it in death to take this poor maid from the world! What corruption in this life, that it will let this man live!—But how out of this can she avail?

Duke. It is a rupture that you may easily heal; and the cure of it not only saves your brother, but keeps you from dishonour in doing it.

Isab. Show me how, good father.

Duke. This fore-named maid hath yet in her the continuance of her first affection: his unjust unkindness, that in all reason should have quenched her love, hath, like an impediment in the current, made it more violent and unruly. Go you to Angelo; answer his requiring with a plausible obedience; agree with his demands to the point; only refer yourself to this advantage,—first, that your stay with him may not be long; that the time may have all shadow and silence in it; and the place answer to convenience. This being granted in course, now follows all:—we shall advise this wronged maid to stead up your appointment, go in your place; if the encounter acknowledge itself hereafter, it may compel him to her recompense: and here, by this, is your brother saved, your honour untainted, the poor Mariana advantaged, and the corrupt deputy scaled. The maid will I frame, and make fit for his attempt. If you think well to carry this as you may, the doubleness of the benefit defends the deceit from reproof. What think you of it?

Isab. The image of it gives me content already; and I trust it will grow to a most prosperous perfection.

Duke. It lies much in your holding up. Haste you speedily to Angelo: if for this night he entreat you to his bed, give him promise of satisfaction. I will presently to St. Luke's; there, at the moated grange, resides this dejected Mariana. At that place call upon me; and dispatch with Angelo, that it may be quickly.

Isab. I thank you for this comfort. Fare you well, good father.   [*Exeunt*

SCENE II.—The Street before the Prison

Enter, on one side, the DUKE, *as friar; on the other,* ELBOW *and Officers, with* POMPEY

Elb. Nay, if there be no remedy for it, but that you will needs buy and sell men and women like beasts, we shall have all the world drink brown and white bastard.

Duke. O heavens! what stuff is here?

Pom. 'T was never merry world, since, of two usuries, the merriest was put down, and the worser allowed by order of law a furred gown to keep him warm; and furred with fox and lamb-skins too, to signify that craft, being richer than innocency, stands for the facing.

Elb. Come your way, sir.—Bless you, good father friar.

Duke. And you, good brother father. What offence hath this man made you, sir?

Elb. Marry, sir, he hath offended the law: and, sir, we take him to be a thief too, sir; for we have found upon him, sir, a strange picklock, which we have sent to the deputy.

Duke. Fie, sirrah! a bawd, a wicked bawd!
The evil that thou causest to be done,
That is thy means to live. Do thou but think
What 't is to cram a maw or clothe a back
From such a filthy vice: say to thyself,—
From their abominable and beastly touches
I drink, I eat, array myself, and live:
Canst thou believe thy living is a life,
So stinkingly depending? Go mend, go mend.

Pom. Indeed, it does stink in some sort, sir; but yet, sir, I would prove—

Duke. Nay, if the devil have given thee proofs for sin, Thou wilt prove his. Take him to prison, officer;
Correction and instruction must both work
Ere this rude beast will profit.

Elb. He must before the deputy, sir; he has given him warning. The deputy cannot abide a whoremaster: if he be a whoremonger, and comes before him, he were as good go a mile on his errand.

Duke. That we were all, as some would seem to be,
Free from our faults as from faults seeming free!
Elb. His neck will come to your waist,—a cord, sir.
Pom. I spy comfort: I cry, bail. Here's a gentleman,
and a friend of mine.

Enter LUCIO

Lucio. How now, noble Pompey! What, at the wheels
of Cæsar? Art thou led in triumph? What, is there none
of Pygmalion's images, newly made woman, to be had now,
for putting the hand in the pocket and extracting it
clutched? What reply? Ha? What say'st thou to this
tune, matter, and method? Is't not drowned i' the last
rain, ha? What say'st thou, trot? Is the world as it
was, man? Which is the way? Is it sad and few words,
or how? The trick of it?
Duke. Still thus, and thus: still worse!
Lucio. How doth my dear morsel, thy mistress?
Procures she still, ha?
Pom. Troth, sir, she hath eaten up all her beef, and she
is herself in the tub.
Lucio. Why, 't is good; it is the right of it; it must
be so: ever your fresh whore, and your powdered bawd:
an unshunned consequence; it must be so. Art going to
prison, Pompey?
Pom. Yes, faith, sir.
Lucio. Why, 't is not amiss, Pompey. Farewell: go;
say, I sent thee thither. For debt, Pompey, or how?
Elb. For being a bawd, for being a bawd.
Lucio. Well, then imprison him. If imprisonment be
the due of a bawd, why, 't is his right: bawd is he, doubt-
less, and of antiquity too; bawd-born. Farewell, good
Pompey. Commend me to the prison, Pompey. You will
turn good husband now, Pompey; you will keep the
house.
Pom. I hope, sir, your good worship, will be my bail.
Lucio. No, indeed, will I not, Pompey; it is not the
wear. I will pray, Pompey, to increase your bondage: if
you take it not patiently, why, your mettle is the more.
Adieu, trusty Pompey.—Bless you, friar.
Duke. And you.
Lucio. Does Bridget paint still, Pompey, ha?
Elb. Come your ways, sir; come.
Pom. You will not bail me then, sir?
Lucio. Then, Pompey, nor now.—What news abroad,
friar? What news?
Elb. Come your ways, sir; come.
Lucio. Go to kennel, Pompey; go. [*Exeunt Elbow,
and Officers with Pompey*] What news, friar, of the duke
Duke. I know none. Can you tell me of any?

Lucio. Some say, he is with the emperor of Russia; other some, he is in Rome: but where is he, think you?

Duke. I know not where; but wheresoever, I wish him well.

Lucio. It was a mad fantastical trick of him, to steal from the state, and usurp the beggary he was never born to. Lord Angelo dukes it well in his absence: he puts transgression to 't.

Duke. He does well in 't.

Lucio. A little more lenity to lechery would do no harm in him: something too crabbed that way, friar.

Duke. It is too general a vice, and severity must cure it.

Lucio. Yes, in good sooth, the vice is of a great kindred; it is well allied; but it is impossible to extirp it quite, friar, till eating and drinking be put down. They say, this Angelo was not made by man and woman, after this downright way of creation: is it true, think you?

Duke. How should he be made, then?

Lucio. Some report, a sea-maid spawned him; some, that he was begot between two stock-fishes. But it is certain, that when he makes water, his urine is congealed ice: that I know to be true; and he is a motion generative, that's infallible.

Duke. You are pleasant, sir, and speak apace.

Lucio. Why, what a ruthless thing is this in him, for the rebellion of a codpiece to take away the life of a man? Would the duke that is absent have done this? Ere he would have hanged a man for the getting a hundred bastards, he would have paid for the nursing a thousand. He had some feeling of the sport: he knew the service, and that instructed him to mercy.

Duke. I never heard the absent duke much detected for women: he was not inclined that way.

Lucio. O, sir, you are deceived.

Duke. 'T is not possible.

Lucio. Who? not the duke? yes, your beggar of fifty, and his use was to put a ducat in her clack-dish. The duke had crotchets in him: he would be drunk too; that let me inform you.

Duke. You do him wrong, surely.

Lucio. Sir, I was an inward of his. A shy fellow was the duke; and I believe I know the cause of his withdrawing.

Duke. What, I prithee, might be the cause?

Lucio. No,—pardon; 't is a secret must be locked within the teeth and the lips; but this I can let you understand,— the greater file of the subject held the duke to be wise.

Duke. Wise? why, no question but he was.

Lucio. A very superficial, ignorant, unweighing fellow.

Duke. Either this is envy in you, folly, or mistaking: the very stream of his life, and the business he hath helmed.

must, upon a warranted need, give him a better proclamation. Let him be but testimonied in his own bringings-forth,
and he shall appear to the envious a scholar, a statesman,
and a soldier.   Therefore, you speak unskilfully; or, if your
knowledge be more, it is much darkened in your malice.

Lucio. Sir, I know him, and I love him.

Duke. Love talks with better knowledge, and knowledge with dearer love.

Lucio. Come, sir, I know what I know.

Duke. I can hardly believe that, since you know not
what you speak. But, if ever the duke returns—as our
prayers are he may—let me desire you to make your
answer before him: if it be honest you have spoke, you
have courage to maintain it: I am bound to call upon you;
and, I pray you, your name?

Lucio. Sir, my name is Lucio, well known to the duke.

Duke. He shall know you better, sir, if I may live to
report you.

Lucio. I fear you not.

Duke. O, you hope the duke will return no more, or
you imagine me too unhurtful an opposite. But, indeed,
I can do you little harm; you'll forswear this again.

Lucio. I'll be hanged first: thou art deceived in me,
friar. But no more of this. Canst thou tell if Claudio
die to-morrow or no?

Duke. Why should he die, sir?

Lucio. Why! for filling a bottle with a tun-dish. I
would the duke we talk of were returned again: this un-
genitured agent will unpeople the province with con-
tinency; sparrows must not build in his house-eaves, because they are lecherous. The duke yet would have dark
deeds darkly answered; he would never bring them to light:
would he were returned! Marry, this Claudio is condemned
for untrussing. Farewell, good friar; I prithee, pray for me.
The duke, I say to thee again, would eat mutton on Fridays.
He's now past it; yet, and I say to thee, he would mouth
with a beggar, though she smelt brown bread and garlic:
say, that I said so. Farewell.   [*Exit*

Duke. No might nor greatness in mortality
Can censure scape; back-wounding calumny
The whitest virtue strikes. What king so strong
Can tie the gall up in the slanderous tongue?
But who comes here?

Enter ESCALUS, *Provost, and Officers, with* MISTRESS
OVERDONE

Escal. Go; away with her to prison!

Mrs. Ov. Good my lord, be good to me; your honour
is accounted a merciful man; good my lord.

Escal. Double and treble admonition, and still forfeit

in the same kind? This would make mercy swear and play
the tyrant.

Prov. A bawd of eleven years' continuance, may it
please your honour.

Mrs. Ov. My lord, this is one Lucio's information against
me. Mistress Kate Keepdown was with child by him in
the duke's time; he promised her marriage; his child is a
year and a quarter old, come Philip and Jacob; I have
kept it myself; and see how he goes about to abuse me!

Escal. That fellow is a fellow of much license:—let
him be called before us.—Away with her to prison! Go
to; no more words. [*Exeunt Officers with Mistress Ov.*]
Provost, my brother Angelo will not be altered; Claudio
must die to-morrow. Let him be furnished with divines,
and have all charitable preparation: if my brother wrought
by my pity, it should not be so with him.

Prov. So please you, this friar hath been with him,
and advised him for the entertainment of death.

Escal. Good even, good father.

Duke. Bliss and goodness on you.

Escal. Of whence are you?

Duke. Not of this country, though my chance is now
To use it for my time: I am a brother
Of gracious order, late come from the See
In special business from his holiness.

Escal. What news abroad i' the world?

Duke. None, but that there is so great a fever on goodness, that the dissolution of it must cure it: novelty is
only in request; and it is as dangerous to be aged in any
kind of course, as it is virtuous to be constant in any under-
taking. There is scarce truth enough alive to make societies
secure, but security enough to make fellowships accursed.
Much upon this riddle runs the wisdom of the world. This
news is old enough, yet it is every day's news. I pray you,
sir, of what disposition was the duke?

Escal. One that, above all other strifes, contended
especially to know himself.

Duke. What pleasure was he given to?

Escal. Rather rejoicing to see another merry, than
merry at anything which professed to make him rejoice:
a gentleman of all temperance. But leave we him to his
events, with a prayer they may prove prosperous; and
let me desire to know how you find Claudio prepared. I
am made to understand that you have lent him visitation.

Duke. He professes to have received no sinister measure
from his judge, but most willingly humbles himself to the
determination of justice; yet had he framed to himself,
by the instruction of his frailty, many deceiving promises
of life; which I, by my good leisure, have discredited to
him, and now is he resolved to die.

Escal. You have paid the heavens your function, and the prisoner the very debt of your calling. I have laboured for the poor gentleman to the extremest shore of my modesty; but my brother justice have I found so severe, that he hath forced me to tell him he is indeed Justice.

Duke. If his own life answer the straitness of his proceeding, it shall become him well; wherein if he chance to fail, he hath sentenced himself.

Escal. I am going to visit the prisoner. Fare you well.

Duke. Peace be with you!

                               [Exeunt Escalus and Provost

He who the sword of heaven will bear
Should be as holy as severe;
Pattern in himself to know,
Grace to stand, and virtue go;
More nor less to others paying
Than by self-offences weighing.
Shame to him whose cruel striking
Kills for faults of his own liking!
Twice treble shame on Angelo,
To weed my vice and let his grow!
O, what may man within him hide,
Though angel on the outward side!
How may likeness made in crimes
Masking, practise on the times,
To draw with idle spiders' strings
Most ponderous and substantial things!
Craft against vice I must apply:
With Angelo to-night shall lie
His old betrothéd, but despised:
So disguise shall, by the disguised:
Pay with falsehood false exacting,
And perform an old contracting.   *[Exit*

ACT FOUR

Scene I.—The Moated Grange at St. Luke's

Mariana discovered sitting ; a Boy singing

Song

> Take, O, take those lips away,
>   That so sweetly were forsworn ;
> And those eyes, the break of day,
>   Lights that do mislead the morn :
> But my kisses bring again,
>   Bring again,
> Seals of love, but sealed in vain,
>   Sealed in vain.

Mari. Break off thy song, and haste thee quick away:
Here comes a man of comfort, whose advice
Hath often stilled my brawling discontent.—   [*Exit Boy*

Enter DUKE, *disguised as before*

I cry you mercy, sir; and well could wish
You had not found me here so musical:
Let me excuse me, and believe me so,
My mirth it much displeased, but pleased my woe.
    Duke. 'T is good: though music oft hath such a charm
To make bad good, and good provoke to harm.
I pray you, tell me, hath anybody inquired for me here
to-day? much upon this time have I promised here to
meet.
    Mari. You have not been inquired after: I have sat
here all day.
    Duke. I do constantly believe you.—The time is come,
even now. I shall crave your forbearance a little: may
be, I will call upon you anon, for some advantage to yourself.
    Mari. I am always bound to you.   [*Exit*

Enter ISABELLA

    Duke. Very well met, and welcome.
What is the news from this good deputy?
    Isab. He hath a garden circummured with brick,
Whose western side is with a vineyard backed;
And to that vineyard is a planchéd gate
That makes his opening with this bigger key;
This other doth command a little door
Which from the vineyard to the garden leads;
There have I made my promise
Upon the heavy middle of the night
To call upon him.
    Duke. But shall you on your knowledge find this way?
    Isab. I've ta'en a due and wary note upon't:
With whispering and most guilty diligence,
In action all of precept, he did show me
The way twice o'er.
    Duke.   Are there no other tokens
Between you 'greed, concerning her observance?
    Isab. No, none, but only a repair i' the dark;
And that I have possessed him my most stay
Can be but brief; for I have made him know
I have a servant comes with me along,
That stays upon me; whose persuasion is
I come about my brother.
    Duke.   'T is well borne up.
I have not yet made known to Mariana
A word of this.—What, ho! within! come forth!

318

Re-enter MARIANA

I pray you, be acquainted with this maid;
She comes to do you good.
   Isab.   I do desire the like.
   Duke. Do you persuade yourself that I respect you?
   Mari. Good friar, I know you do, and have found it.
   Duke. Take then this your companion by the hand,
Who hath a story ready for your ear.
I shall attend your leisure: but make haste;
The vaporous night approaches.
   Mari. Will 't please you walk aside?
                     [Exeunt Mariana and Isabella
   Duke. O place and greatness, millions of false eyes
Are struck upon thee! volumes of report
Run with these false and most contrarious quests
Upon thy doings! thousand escapes of wit
Make thee the father of their idle dreams,
And rack thee in their fancies!

Re-enter MARIANA *and* ISABELLA

                  Welcome! How agreed?
   Isab. She 'll take the enterprise upon her, father,
If you advise it.
   Duke.   'T is not my consent,
But my entreaty too.
   Isab.   Little have you to say
When you depart from him, but, soft and low,
"Remember now my brother."
   Mari.   Fear me not.
   Duke. Nor, gentle daughter, fear you not at all.
He is your husband on a pre-contract:
To bring you thus together, 't is no sin,
Sith that the justice of your title to him
Doth flourish the deceit. Come, let us go:
Our corn 's to reap, for yet our tilth 's to sow.   *[Exeunt*

SCENE II.—A Room in the Prison

Enter Provost and POMPEY

   Prov. Come hither, sirrah. Can you cut off a man's
head?
   Pom. If the man be a bachelor, sir, I can; but if he
be a married man, he is his wife's head, and I can never
cut off a woman's head.
   Prov. Come, sir: leave me your snatches, and yield
me a direct answer. To-morrow morning are to die
Claudio and Barnardine. Here is in our prison a common
executioner, who in his office lacks a helper: if you will

take it on you to assist him, it shall redeem you from your
gyves; if not, you shall have your full time of imprisonment, and your deliverance with an unpitied whipping, for
you have been a notorious bawd.

Pom. Sir, I have been an unlawful bawd, time out of
mind; but yet I will be content to be a lawful hangman.
I would be glad to receive some instruction from my fellow
partner.

Prov. What ho, Abhorson! Where's Abhorson there?

Enter ABHORSON

Abhor. Do you call, sir?

Prov. Sirrah, here's a fellow will help you to-morrow
in your execution. If you think it meet, compound with
him by the year, and let him abide here with you; if not,
use him for the present, and dismiss him. He cannot
plead his estimation with you: he hath been a bawd.

Abhor. A bawd, sir! fie upon him! he will discredit
our mystery.

Prov. Go to, sir; you weigh equally; a feather will
turn the scale.   [*Exit*

Pom. Pray, sir, by your good favour,— for surely, sir,
a good favour you have, but that you have a hanging
look,—do you call, sir, your occupation a mystery?

Abhor. Ay, sir; a mystery.

Pom. Painting, sir, I have heard say, is a mystery;
and your whores, sir, being members of my occupation,
using painting, do prove my occupation a mystery: but
what mystery there should be in hanging, if I should be
hanged, I cannot imagine.

Abhor. Sir, it is a mystery.

Pom. Proof?

Abhor. Every true man's apparel fits your thief. If
it be too little for your thief, your true man thinks it big
enough; if it be too big for your thief, your thief thinks it
little enough: so, every true man's apparel fits your thief.

Re-enter PROVOST

Prov. Are you agreed?

Pom. Sir, I will serve him; for I do find your hangman
is a more penitent trade than your bawd,—he doth oftener
asked forgiveness.

Prov. You, sirrah, provide your block and your axe
to-morrow four o'clock.

Abhor. Come on, bawd; I will instruct thee in my
trade; follow.

Pom. I do desire to learn, sir; and, I hope, if you have
occasion to use me for your own turn, you shall find me
yare; for, truly, sir, for your kindness I owe you a good
turn.

Prov. Call hither Barnardine and Claudio:

                       [Exeunt Pompey and Abhorson

The one has my pity; not a jot the other,

Being a murderer, though he were my brother.

Enter CLAUDIO

Look, here's the warrant, Claudio, for thy death:

'T is now dead midnight, and by eight to-morrow

Thou must be made immortal.   Where's Barnardine?

   Claud. As fast locked up in sleep as guiltless labour

When it lies starkly in the traveller's bones:

He will not wake.

      Prov.   Who can do good on him?

Well, go, prepare yourself.

But hark, what noise?   *[Knocking within*

Heaven give your spirits comfort!   *[Exit Claudio*

      By-and-by.—

I hope it is some pardon or reprieve

For the most gentle Claudio.—

Enter DUKE, *disguised as before*

                    Welcome, father.

   Duke. The best and wholesom'st spirits of the night

Envelop you, good provost!   Who called here of late?

   Prov. None, since the curfew rung.

   Duke. Not Isabel?

   Prov.   No.

   Duke.   They will, then, ere't be long.

   Prov. What comfort is for Claudio?

   Duke. There's some in hope.

   Prov.   It is a bitter deputy.

   Duke. Not so, not so: his life is paralleled

Even with the stroke and line of his great justice.

He doth with holy abstinence subdue

That in himself which he spurs on his power

To qualify in others: were he mealed with that

Which he corrects, then were he tyrannous;

But this being so, he's just.—*[Knocking within]* Now

      are they come.—   *[Exit Provost*

This is a gentle provost: seldom when

The steelèd gaoler is the friend of men.

                      [Knocking within

How now?   What noise?   That spirit 's possessed with

      haste

That wounds the unsisting postern with these strokes.

Re-enter Provost

   Prov. [*speaking to one at the door*] There he must stay,

      until the officer

Arise to let him in; he is called up.

Duke. Have you no countermand for Claudio yet,
But he must die to-morrow?
Prov.   None, sir, none.
Duke. As near the dawning, provost, as it is,
You shall hear more ere morning.
Prov.   Happily
You something know; yet I believe there comes
No countermand; no such example have we.
Besides, upon the very siege of justice
Lord Angelo hath to the public ear
Professed the contrary.

Enter a Messenger

                                   This is his lordship's man.
Duke. And here comes Claudio's pardon.
Mess. My lord hath sent you this note; and by me
this further charge,—that you swerve not from the smallest
article of it, neither in time, matter, or other circumstance.
—Good morrow; for, as I take it, it is almost day.
Prov. I shall obey him.   [*Exit Messenger*
Duke. [*Aside*] This is his pardon, purchased by such
          sin
For which the pardoner himself is in.
Hence hath offence his quick celerity,
When it is borne in high authority:
When vice makes mercy, mercy's so extended,
That for the fault's love is the offender friended.—
Now, sir, what news?
Prov. I told you, Lord Angelo, belike thinking me
remiss in mine office, awakens me with this unwonted
putting-on; methinks strangely, for he hath not used
it before.
Duke. Pray you, let's hear.
Prov. [*Reads*] *Whatsoever you may hear to the contrary,
let Claudio be executed by four of the clock; and, in the
afternoon, Barnardine. For my better satisfaction, let me
have Claudio's head sent me by five. Let this be duly performed; with a thought, that more depends on it than we
must yet deliver. Thus fail not to do your office, as you
will answer it at your peril.*—What say you to this, sir?
Duke. What is that Barnardine, who is to be executed
in the afternoon?
Prov. A Bohemian born, but here nursed up and bred;
one that is a prisoner nine years old.
Duke. How came it that the absent duke had not either
delivered him to his liberty or executed him? I have
heard it was ever his manner to do so.
Prov. His friends still wrought reprieves for him: and,
indeed, his fact, till now in the government of Lord Angelo,
came not to an undoubtful proof.

Duke. It is now apparent?

Prov. Most manifest, and not denied by himself.

Duke. Hath he borne himself penitently in prison? how seems he to be touched?

Prov. A man that apprehends death no more dreadfully but as a drunken sleep; careless, reckless, and fearless of what 's past, present, or to come; insensible of mortality, and desperately mortal.

Duke. He wants advice.

Prov. He will hear none. He hath evermore had the liberty of the prison; give him leave to escape hence, he would not: drunk many times a day, if not many days entirely drunk. We have very oft awaked him, as if to carry him to execution, and showed him a seeming warrant for it: it hath not moved him at all.   •

Duke. More of him anon. There is written in your brow, provost, honesty and constancy: if I read it not truly, my ancient skill beguiles me: but in the boldness of my cunning I will lay myself in hazard. Claudio, whom here you have warrant to execute, is no greater forfeit to the law than Angelo who hath sentenced him. To make you understand this in a manifested effect, I crave but four days' respite, for the which you are to do me both a present and a dangerous courtesy.

Prov. Pray, sir, in what?

Duke. In the delaying death.

Prov. Alack, how may I do it,—having the hour limited, and an express command, under penalty, to deliver his head in the view of Angelo? I may make my case as Claudio's, to cross this in the smallest.

Duke. By the vow of mine order, I warrant you, if my instructions may be your guide. Let this Barnardine be this morning executed, and his head borne to Angelo.

Prov. Angelo hath seen them both, and will discover the favour.

Duke. O, death's a great disguiser, and you may add to it. Shave the head, and tie the beard; and say, it was the desire of the penitent to be so bared before his death: you know, the course is common. If anything fall to you upon this, more than thanks and good fortune, by the saint whom I profess, I will plead against it with my life.

Prov. Pardon me, good father; it is against my oath.

Duke. Were you sworn to the duke, or to the deputy?

Prov. To him, and to his substitutes.

Duke. You will think you have made no offence, if the duke avouch the justice of your dealing.

Prov. But what likelihood is in that?

Duke. Not a resemblance, but a certainty. Yet since I see you fearful, that neither my coat, integrity, nor persuasion can with ease attempt you, I will go further than I meant, to pluck all fears out of you. Look you, sir, here is the hand and seal of the duke: you know the character, I doubt not; and the signet is not strange to you.

Prov. I know them both.

Duke. The contents of this is the return of the duke: you shall anon over-read it at your pleasure; where you shall find, within these two days he will be here. This is a thing that Angelo knows not, for he this very day receives letters of strange tenour; perchance, of the duke's death, perchance, entering into some monastery; but, by chance, nothing of what is writ. Look, the unfolding star calls up the shepherd. Put not yourself into amazement how these things should be: all difficulties are but easy when they are known. Call your executioner, and off with Barnardine's head: I will give him a present shrift, and advise him for a better place. Yet you are amazed; but this shall absolutely resolve you. Come away; it is almost clear dawn.   [*Exeunt*

SCENE III.—Another Room in the Same

Enter POMPEY

Pom. I am as well acquainted here, as I was in our house of profession: one would think, it were Mistress Overdone's own house, for here be many of her old customers. First, here's young Master Rash; he's in for a commodity of brown paper and old ginger, nine-score and seventeen pounds; of which he made five marks, ready money: marry, then, ginger was not much in request, for the old women were all dead. Then is there here one Master Caper, at the suit of Master Three-pile the mercer, for some four suits of peach-coloured satin, which now peaches him a beggar. Then have we here young Dizzy, and young Master Deep-vow, and Master Copper-spur, and Master Starve-lackey the rapier-and-dagger-man, and young Drop-heir that killed lusty Pudding, and Master Forthright the tilter, and brave Master Shoe-tie the great traveller, and wild Half-can that stabbed Pots, and, I think, forty more; all great doers in our trade, and are now "for the Lord's sake."

Enter ABHORSON

Abhor. Sirrah, bring Barnardine hither.

Pom. Master Barnardine! you must rise and be hanged, Master Barnardine.

Abhor. What, ho, Barnardine!

Bar. [*Within*] A pox o' your throats! Who makes that noise there? What are you?

Pom. Your friends, sir; the hangman. You must be so good, sir, to rise and be put to death.

Bar. [*Within*] Away, you rogue, away! I am sleepy.

Abhor. Tell him, he must awake, and that quickly too.

Pom. Pray, Master Barnardine, awake till you are executed, and sleep afterwards.

Abhor. Go in to him, and fetch him out.

Pom. He is coming, sir, he is coming: I hear his straw rustle.

Abhor. Is the axe upon the block, sirrah?

Pom. Very ready, sir.

Enter BARNARDINE

Bar. How now, Abhorson? what's the news with you?

Abhor. Truly, sir, I would desire you to clap into your prayers; for, look you, the warrant's come.

Bar. You rogue, I have been drinking all night: I am not fitted for 't.

Pom. O, the better, sir; for he that drinks all night, and is hanged betimes in the morning, may sleep the sounder all the next day.

Abhor. Look you, sir; here comes your ghostly father. Do we jest now, think you?

Enter DUKE, *disguised as before*

Duke. Sir, induced by my charity, and hearing how hastily you are to depart, I am come to advise you, comfort you, and pray with you.

Bar. Friar, not I: I have been drinking hard all night, and I will have more time to prepare me, or they shall beat out my brains with billets. I will not consent to die this day, that's certain.

Duke. O, sir, you must; and, therefore, I beseech you, Look forward on the journey you shall go.

Bar. I swear, I will not die to-day for any man's persuasion.

Duke. But hear you,—

Bar. Not a word: if you have anything to say to me, come to my ward; for thence will not I to-day.   [*Exit*

Duke. Unfit to live, or die. O gravel heart!— After him, fellows: bring him to the block.

[*Exeunt Abhorson and Pompey*

Enter Provost

Prov. Now, sir, how do you find the prisoner?

Duke. A creature unprepared, unmeet for death; And, to transport him in the mind he is, Were damnable.

Prov.   Here in the prison, father, There died this morning of a cruel fever

One Ragozine, a most notorious pirate,
A man of Claudio's years; his beard and head
Just of his colour.   What if we do omit
This reprobate till he were well inclined,
And satisfy the deputy with the visage
Of Ragozine, more like to Claudio?
    Duke.   O, 't is an accident that Heaven provides!
Despatch it presently: the hour draws on
Prefixed by Angelo.   See this be done,
And sent according to command, whiles I
Persuade this rude wretch willingly to die.
    Prov.   This shall be done, good father, presently.
But Barnardine must die this afternoon;
And how shall we continue Claudio,
To save me from the danger that might come
If he were known alive?
    Duke.   Let this be done,—put them in secret holds,
Both Barnardine and Claudio:
Ere twice the sun hath made his journal greeting
To the under generation, you shall find
Your safety manifested.
    Prov.   I am your free dependant.
    Duke.   Quick, despatch,
And send the head to Angelo.   [*Exit Provost*
Now will I write letters to Angelo—
The provost, he shall bear them—whose contents
Shall witness to him, I am near at home,
And that, by great injunctions, I am bound
To enter publicly: him I 'll desire
To meet me at the consecrated fount,
A league below the city; and from thence,
By cold gradation and well-balanced form,
We shall proceed with Angelo.

Re-enter PROVOST

    Prov.   Here is the head; I'll carry it myself.
    Duke.   Convenient is it.   Make a swift return;
For I would commune with you of such things
That want no ear but yours.
    Prov.   I'll make all speed.   [*Exit*
    Isab. [*Within*] Peace, ho, be here!
    Duke.   The tongue of Isabel.—She's come to know
If yet her brother's pardon be come hither:
But I will keep her ignorant of her good,
To make her heavenly comfort of despair,
When it is least expected.

Enter ISABELLA

    Isab.   Ho, by your leave!
    Duke.   Good morning to you, fair and gracious daughter.

Isab.   The better, given me by so holy a man.
Hath yet the deputy sent my brother's pardon?
Duke.   He hath released him, Isabel, from the world.
His head is off, and sent to Angelo.
Isab.   Nay, but it is not so.
Duke.   It is no other: show your wisdom, daughter,
In your close patience.
Isab.   O, I will to him, and pluck out his eyes!
Duke.   You shall not be admitted to his sight.
Isab.   Unhappy Claudio! Wretched Isabel!
Injurious world! Most damnéd Angelo!
Duke.   This nor hurts him, nor profits you a jot;
Forbear it therefore; give your cause to Heaven.
Mark what I say to you, which you shall find
By every syllable a faithful verity:
The duke comes home to-morrow;—nay, dry your eyes;
One of our convent, and his confessor,
Gives me this instance: already he hath carried
Notice to Escalus and Angelo,
Who do prepare to meet him at the gates,
There to give up their power. If you can, pace your wisdom
In that good path that I would wish it go;
And you shall have your bosom on this wretch,
Grace of the duke, revenges to your heart,
And general honour.
Isab.   I am directed by you.
Duke.   This letter then to Friar Peter give;
'T is that he sent me of the duke's return:
Say, by this token, I desire his company
At Mariana's house to-night. Her cause and yours,
I'll perfect him withal, and he shall bring you
Before the duke; and to the head of Angelo
Accuse him home, and home. For my poor self,
I am combinéd by a sacred vow,
And shall be absent. Wend you with this letter:
Command these fretting waters from your eyes
With a light heart: trust not my 's holy order,
If I pervert your course.—Who 's here?

Enter LUCIO

Lucio.   Good even, friar: where 's the provost?
Duke.   Not within, sir.
Lucio.   O pretty Isabella, I am pale at mine heart to
see thine eyes so red: thou must be patient. I am fain
to dine and sup with water and bran; I dare not for my
head fill my belly; one fruitful meal would set me to 't.
But they say, the duke will be here to-morrow. By my
troth, Isabel, I loved thy brother: if the old fantastical
duke of dark corners had been at home, he had lived.
                                      [Exit Isabella

Duke. Sir, the duke is marvellous little beholding to your reports; but the best is, he lives not in them.

Lucio. Friar, thou knowest not the duke so well as I do: he's a better woodman than thou takest him for.

Duke. Well, you'll answer this one day. Fare ye well.

Lucio. Nay, tarry; I'll go along with thee: I can tell thee pretty tales of the duke.

Duke. You have told me too many of him already, sir, if they be true; if not true, none were enough.

Lucio. I was once before him for getting a wench with child.

Duke. Did you such a thing?

Lucio. Yes, marry, did I; but I was fain to forswear it: they would else have married me to the rotten medlar.

Duke. Sir, your company is fairer than honest. Rest you well.

Lucio. By my troth, I'll go with thee to the lane's end. If bawdy talk offend you, we'll have very little of it. Nay, friar, I am a kind of burr; I shall stick.   [*Exeunt*

Scene IV.—A Room in Angelo's House

Enter Angelo *and* Escalus

Escal. Every letter he hath writ hath disvouched other.

Ang. In most uneven and distracted manner. His actions show much like to madness: pray Heaven, his wisdom be not tainted! and why meet him at the gates, and re-deliver our authorities there?

Escal. I guess not.

Ang. And why should we proclaim it in an hour before his entering, that if any crave redress of injustice they should exhibit their petitions in the street?

Escal. He shows his reason for that: to have a despatch of complaints and to deliver us from devices hereafter, which shall then have no power to stand against us.

Ang. Well, I beseech you, let it be proclaimed:
Betimes i' the morn, I'll call you at your house.
Give notice to such men of sort and suit
As are to meet him.

Escal.   I shall, sir: fare you well.

Ang. Good night.—   [*Exit Escalus*
This deed unshapes me quite, makes me unpregnant,
And dull to all proceedings. A deflowered maid,
And by an eminent body, that enforced
The law against it!—But that her tender shame
Will not proclaim against her maiden loss,
How might she tongue me! Yet reason dares her no:
For my authority bears a credent bulk
That no particular scandal once can touch

But it confounds the breather. He should have lived,
Save that his riotous youth, with dangerous sense,
Might in the times to come have ta'en revenge,
By so receiving a dishonoured life
With ransom of such shame. Would yet he had lived!
Alack, when once our grace we have forgot.
Nothing goes right,—we would, and we would not. [*Exit*

SCENE V.—Fields without the Town

Enter DUKE, *in his own habit, and* FRIAR PETER

Duke. These letters at fit time deliver me. [*Giving letters*
The provost knows our purpose and our plot.
The matter being afoot, keep your instruction,
And hold you ever to our special drift;
Though sometimes you do blench from this to that,
As cause doth minister. Go call at Flavius' house,
And tell him where I stay: give the like notice
To Valentinus, Rowland, and to Crassus,
And bid them bring the trumpets to the gate;
But send me Flavius first.
　　Fri. Pet. 　　　　　　　It shall be speeded well.
　　　　　　　　　　　　　　　　　　　　　　　[*Exit*

Enter VARRIUS

Duke. I thank thee, Varrius; thou hast made good
　　haste:
Come, we will walk. There's other of our friends
Will greet us here anon, my gentle Varrius. [*Exeunt*

SCENE VI.—Street near the City Gate

Enter ISABELLA *and* MARIANA

Isab. To speak so indirectly I am loth:
I would say the truth; but to accuse him so,
That is your part: yet I'm advised to do it,
He says, to 'vailful purpose.
　　Mari. 　　　　　　　　Be ruled by him.
　　Isab. Besides, he tells me, that, if peradventure
He speak against me on the adverse side,
I should not think it strange; for 't is a physic
That's bitter to sweet end.
　　Mari. I would, Friar Peter—
　　Isab. 　　　　　　　O, peace, the friar is come.

Enter FRIAR PETER

Fri. Pet. Come, I have found you out a stand most fit,
Where you may have such vantage on the duke,
He shall not pass you. Twice have the trumpets sounded:

329

The generous and gravest citizens
Have hent the gates, and very near upon
The duke is entering: therefore hence, away.   [*Exeunt*

ACT FIVE

SCENE I.—A Public Place near the City Gate

MARIANA, *veiled*, ISABELLA, *and* FRIAR PETER, *behind.*
Enter on one side, the DUKE, *in his own habit,* VARRIUS,
Lords ; from the other, ANGELO, ESCALUS, LUCIO,
Provost, Officers and Citizens, at several doors

Duke.   My very worthy cousin, fairly met:—
Our old and faithful friend, we are glad to see you.
Ang. and Escal.   Happy return be to your royal grace!
Duke.   Many and hearty thankings to you both.
We've made inquiry of you; and we hear
Such goodness of your justice, that our soul
Cannot but yield you forth to public thanks,
Forerunning more requital.
Ang.   You make my bonds still greater.
Duke.   O, your desert speaks loud; and I should
          wrong it,
To lock it in the wards of covert bosom,
When it deserves, with characters of brass,
A forted residence 'gainst the tooth of time
And razure of oblivion.   Give me your hand,
And let the subject see, to make them know
That outward courtesies would fain proclaim
Favours that keep within.—Come, Escalus;
You must walk by us on our other hand:—
And good supporters are you.

FRIAR PETER *and* ISABELLA *come forward*

Fri. Pet.   Now is your time.   Speak loud, and kneel
          before him.
Isab.   Justice, O royal duke!   Vail your regard
Upon a wronged, I'd fain have said, a maid!
O worthy prince, dishonour not your eye
By throwing it on any other object
Till you have heard me in my true complaint,
And given me justice, justice, justice, justice!
Duke.   Relate your wrongs; in what? by whom?   Be
          brief.
Here is Lord Angelo shall give you justice:
Reveal yourself to him.
Isab.   O worthy duke,
You bid me seek redemption of the devil.
Hear me yourself; for that which I must speak

Must either punish me, not being believed,
Or wring redress from you. Hear me, O, hear me, here!
   Ang. My lord, her wits, I fear me, are not firm:
She hath been a suitor to me for her brother,
Cut off by course of justice,—
   Isab.   By course of justice!
   Ang. And she will speak most bitterly and strange.
   Isab. Most strange, but yet most truly will I speak,
That Angelo 's forsworn; is it not strange?
That Angelo 's a murderer; is 't not strange?
That Angelo is an adulterous thief,
An hypocrite, a virgin-violator;
Is it not strange, and strange?
   Duke.   Nay, it is ten times strange.
   Isab. It is not truer he is Angelo,
Than this is all as true as it is strange;
Nay, it is ten times true; for truth is truth
To the end of reckoning.
   Duke.   Away with her.—Poor soul,
She speaks this in the infirmity of sense.
   Isab. O prince, I conjure thee, as thou believ'st
There is another comfort than this world,
That thou neglect me not, with that opinion
That I am touched with madness. Make not impossible
That which but seems unlike. 'T is not impossible
But one, the wicked'st caitiff on the ground,
May seem as shy, as grave, as just, as absolute,
As Angelo; even so may Angelo,
In all his dressings, characts, titles, forms,
Be an arch-villain; believe it, royal prince:
If he be less, he 's nothing; but he 's more,
Had I more name for badness.
   Duke.   By mine honesty,
If she be mad, as I believe no other,
Her madness hath the oddest frame of sense,
Such a dependency of thing on thing,
As e'er I heard in madness.
   Isab.   O gracious duke,
Harp not on that; nor do not banish reason
For inequality; but let your reason serve
To make the truth appear where it seems hid,
And hide the false, seems true.
   Duke.   Many that are not mad,
Have, sure, more lack of reason.—What would you say?
   Isab. I am the sister of one Claudio,
Condemned upon the act of fornication
To lose his head; condemned by Angelo.
I, in probation of a sisterhood,
Was sent to by my brother; one Lucio
As then the messenger—

Lucio.   That 's I, an 't like your grace.
I came to her from Claudio, and desired her
To try her gracious fortune with Lord Angelo,
For her poor brother's pardon.
    Isab.   That 's he, indeed.
    Duke.   You were not bid to speak.
    Lucio.   No, my good lord;
Nor wished to hold my peace.
    Duke.   I wish you now then:
Pray you, take note of it; and when you have
A business for yourself, pray Heaven, you then
Be perfect.
    Lucio.   I warrant your honour.
    Duke.   The warrant 's for yourself: take heed to it.
    Isab.   This gentleman told somewhat of my tale,—
    Lucio.   Right.
    Duke.   It may be right; but you are in the wrong
To speak before your time.—Proceed.
    Isab.   I went
To this pernicious caitiff deputy.
    Duke.   That 's somewhat madly spoken.
    Isab.   Pardon it:
The phrase is to the matter.
    Duke.   Mended again.   The matter;—proceed.
    Isab.   In brief,—to set the needless process by,
How I persuaded, how I prayed, and kneeled,
How he refelled me, and how I replied,—
For this was of much length,—the vile conclusion
I now begin with grief and shame to utter.
He would not, but by gift of my chaste body
To his concupiscible intemperate lust,
Release my brother; and, after much debatement,
My sisterly remorse confutes mine honour,
And I did yield to him: but the next morn betimes,
His purpose surfeiting, he sends a warrant
For my poor brother's head.
    Duke.   This is most likely!
    Isab.   O, that it were as like as it is true!
    Duke.   By Heaven, fond wretch! thou know'st not what
        thou speak'st,
Or else thou art suborned against his honour,
In hateful practice.   First, his integrity
Stands without blemish; next, it imports no reason,
That with such vehemency he should pursue
Faults proper to himself: if he had so offended,
He would have weighed thy brother by himself,
And not have cut him off.   Some one hath set you on:
Confess the truth, and say by whose advice
Thou cam'st here to complain.
    Isab.   And is this all?

Then, O, you blessed ministers above,
Keep me in patience; and, with ripened time,
Unfold the evil which is here wrapt up
In countenance!—Heaven shield your grace from woe,
As I, thus wronged, hence unbelievéd go!
    Duke.   I know, you'd fain be gone.—An officer!
To prison with her.—Shall we thus permit
A blasting and a scandalous breath to fall
On him so near us?   This needs must be practice.
Who knew of your intent, and coming hither?
    Isab.   One that I would were here, Friar Lodowick.
    Duke.   A ghostly father, belike.—Who knows that
       Lodowick?
    Lucio.   My lord, I know him: 't is a meddling friar;
I do not like the man: had he been lay, my lord,
For certain words he spake against your grace
In your retirement, I had swinged him soundly.
    Duke.   Words against me?   This—a good friar, belike!
And to set on this wretched woman here
Against our substitute!—Let this friar be found.
    Lucio.   But yesternight, my lord, she and that friar,
I saw them at the prison.   A saucy friar,
A very scurvy fellow.
    Fri. Pet.   Blessed be your royal grace!
I have stood by, my lord, and I have heard
Your royal ear abused.   First, hath this woman
Most wrongfully accused your substitute,
Who is as free from touch or soil with her,
As she from one ungot.
    Duke.   We did believe no less.
Know you that Friar Lodowick, that she speaks of?
    Fri. Pet.   I know him for a man divine and holy;
Not scurvy, nor a temporary meddler,
As he 's reported by this gentleman;
And, on my trust, a man that never yet
Did, as he vouches, misreport your grace.
    Lucio.   My lord, most villainously: believe it.
    Fri. Pet.   Well; he in time may come to clear himself,
But at this instant he is sick, my lord,
Of a strange fever.   Upon his mere request,
Being come to knowledge that there was complaint
Intended 'gainst Lord Angelo, came I hither,
To speak, as from his mouth, what he doth know
Is true, and false; and what he with his oath,
And all probation, will make up full clear,
Whensoever he 's convented.   First, for this woman,
To justify this worthy nobleman,
So vulgarly and personally accused,
Her shall you hear disprovéd to her eyes,
Till she herself confess it.

Duke.   Good friar, let's hear it.
    [Isabella is carried off guarded ; and Mariana
                                      comes forward

Do you not smile at this, Lord Angelo?—
O heaven, the vanity of wretched fools!—
Give us some seats.—Come, cousin Angelo;
In this I 'll be impartial: be you judge
Of your own cause.—Is this the witness, friar?
First, let her show her face, and after speak.
    Mari.   Pardon, my lord, I will not show my face
Until my husband bid me.
    Duke.   What, are you married?
    Mari.   No, my lord.
    Duke.   Are you a maid?
    Mari.   No, my lord.
    Duke.   A widow then?
    Mari.   Neither, my lord.
    Duke.   Why, you
Are nothing then: neither maid, widow, nor wife.
    Lucio.   My lord, she may be a punk; for many of them
are neither maid, widow, nor wife.
    Duke.   Silence that fellow: I would he had some cause
To prattle for himself.
    Lucio.   Well, my lord.
    Mari.   My lord, I do confess I ne'er was married;
And, I confess, besides, I am no maid:
I have known my husband, yet my husband knows not
That ever he knew me.
    Lucio.   He was drunk then, my lord: it can be no
better.
    Duke.   For the benefit of silence, would thou wert so too!
    Lucio.   Well, my lord.
    Duke.   This is no witness for Lord Angelo.
    Mari.   Now I come to 't, my lord.
She that accuses him of fornication,
In selfsame manner doth accuse my husband;
And charges him, my lord, with such a time,
When, I 'll depose, I had him in mine arms,
With all the effect of love.
    Ang.   Charges she more than me?
    Mari.   Not that I know.
    Duke.   No? you say, your husband.
    Mari.   Why, just, my lord, and that is Angelo,
Who thinks he knows that he ne'er knew my body,
But knows he thinks that he knows Isabel's.
    Ang.   This is a strange abuse.—Let's see thy face.
    Mari.   My husband bids me; now I will unmask.
                                              [Unveiling
This is that face, thou cruel Angelo,
Which once thou swor'st was worth the looking on:

This is the hand which, with a vowed contráct,
Was fast belocked in thine: this is the body
That took away the match from Isabel,
And did supply thee at thy garden-house
In her imagined person.
    Duke.   Know you this woman!
    Lucio. Carnally, she says.
    Duke.   Sirrah, no more.
    Lucio. Enough, my lord.
    Ang. My lord, I must confess, I know this woman;
And five years since there was some speech of marriage
Betwixt myself and her, which was broke off,
Partly, for that her promiséd proportions
Came short of composition; but, in chief,
For that her reputation was disvalued
In levity: since which time of five years
I never spake with her, saw her, nor heard from her,
Upon my faith and honour.
    Mari.   Noble prince,
As there comes light from heaven and words from breath,
As there is sense in truth and truth in virtue,
I am affianced this man's wife, as strongly
As words could make up vows: and, my good lord,
But Tuesday night last gone, in 's garden-house,
He knew me as a wife. As this is true,
Let me in safety raise me from my knees,
Or else for ever be confixéd here,
A marble monument.
    Ang.   I did but smile till now:
Now, good my lord, give me the scope of justice;
My patience here is touched. I do perceive,
These poor informal women are no more
But instruments of some more mightier member,
That sets them on. Let me have way, my lord,
To find this practice out.
    Duke.   Ay, with my heart;
And punish them to your height of pleasure.—
Thou foolish friar, and thou pernicious woman,
Compact with her that 's gone, think'st thou, thy oaths,
Though they would swear down each particular saint,
Were testimonies 'gainst his worth and credit,
That 's sealed in approbation?—You, Lord Escalus,
Sit with my cousin: lend him your kind pains
To find out this abuse, whence 't is derived.—
There is another friar that set them on;
Let him be sent for.
    Fri. Pet. 'Would he were here, my lord; for he, indeed,
Hath set the women on to this complaint.
Your provost knows the place where he abides,
And he may fetch him.

Duke.   Go, do it instantly.—[*Exit Provost*
And you, my noble and well-warranted cousin,
Whom it concerns to hear this matter forth,
Do with your injuries as seems you best,
In any chastisement: I for a while will leave you;
But stir not you, till you have well determined
Upon these slanderers.

Escal. My lord, we 'll do it thoroughly.   [*Exit Duke*]—
Signior Lucio, did not you say, you knew that Friar Lodowick to be a dishonest person?

Lucio. *Cucullus non facit monachum :* honest in nothing,
but in his clothes; and one that hath spoke most villainous
speeches of the duke.

Escal. We shall entreat you to abide here till he come,
and enforce them against him. We shall find this friar
a notable fellow.

Lucio. As any in Vienna, on my word.

Escal. Call that same Isabel here once again: I would
speak with her. [*Exit an Attendant*] Pray you, my lord,
give me leave to question; you shall see how I 'll handle
her.

Lucio. Not better than he, by her own report.

Escal. Say you?

Lucio. Marry, sir, I think, if you handled her privately,
she would sooner confess: perchance, publicly she 'll be
ashamed.

Escal. I will go darkly to work with her.

Lucio. That's the way; for women are light at midnight.

Re-enter Officers, with ISABELLA

Escal. [*To Isab.*] Come on, mistress. Here 's a gentlewoman denies all that you have said.

Lucio. My lord, here comes the rascal I spoke of; here,
with the provost.

Escal. In very good time:—speak not you to him,
till we call upon you.

Lucio. Mum.

Enter DUKE, *disguised as a friar, and Provost*

Escal. Come, sir: did you set these women on to
slander Lord Angelo? they have confessed you did.

Duke. 'T is false.

Escal. How! know you where you are?

Duke. Respect to your great place! and let the devil
Be sometime honoured for his burning throne.—
Where is the duke? 't is he should hear me speak.

Escal. The duke 's in us, and we will hear you speak:
Look you speak justly.

Duke.   Boldly at least.—But, O, poor souls!

336

Come you to seek the lamb here of the fox?
Good night to your redress. Is the duke gone?
Then is your cause gone too. The duke's unjust,
Thus to retort your manifest appeal,
And put your trial in the villain's mouth
Which here you come to accuse.
    Lucio. This is the rascal: this is he I spoke of.
    Escal. Why, thou unreverend and unhallowed friar,
Is 't not enough, thou hast suborned these women
To accuse this worthy man, but, in foul mouth,
And in the witness of his proper ear,
To call him villain?
And then to glance from him to the duke himself,
To tax him with injustice!—Take him hence;
To the rack with him:—we'll touse you joint by joint,
But we will know his purpose.—What, unjust?
    Duke. Be not so hot; the duke
Dare no more stretch this finger of mine, than he
Dare rack his own: his subject am I not,
Nor here provincial. My business in this state
Made me a looker-on here in Vienna,
Where I have seen corruption boil and bubble,
Till it o'er-run the stew: laws for all faults,
But faults so countenanced, that the strong statutes
Stand like the forfeits in a barber's shop,
As much in mock as mark.
    Escal. Slander to the state!—Away with him to prison.
    Ang. What can you vouch against him, Signior Lucio?
Is this the man that you did tell us of?
    Lucio. 'T is he, my lord.—Come hither, goodman
baldpate: do you know me?
    Duke. I remember you, sir, by the sound of your voice:
I met you at the prison, in the absence of the duke.
    Lucio. O, did you so? And do you remember what
you said of the duke?
    Duke. Most notedly, sir.
    Lucio. Do you so, sir? And was the duke a flesh-
monger, a fool, and a coward, as you then reported him
to be?
    Duke. You must, sir, change persons with me, ere
you make that my report: you, indeed, spoke so of him;
and much more, much worse.
    Lucio. O thou damnable fellow! Did not I pluck
thee by the nose, for thy speeches?
    Duke. I protest, I love the duke as I love myself.
    Ang. Hark, how the villain would close now, after
his treasonable abuses.
    Escal. Such a fellow is not to be talked withal:—Away
with him to prison. Where is the provost?—Away with
him to prison. Lay bolts enough upon him, let him speak

no more.—Away with those giglots too, and with the other confederate companion.

                              [The Provost lays hand on the Duke

Duke.   Stay, sir; stay awhile.

Ang.   What! resists he?   Help him, Lucio.

Lucio.   Come, sir; come, sir; come, sir; foh! sir. Why, you bald-pated, lying rascal! you must be hooded, must you? show your knave's visage, with a pox to you! show your sheep-biting face, and be hanged an hour. Will 't not off?

                    [Pulls off the friar's hood, and discovers the Duke

Duke.   Thou art the first knave that e'er made a duke.— First, provost, let me bail these gentle three.—

     [*To Lucio*]   Sneak not away, sir; for the friar and you Must have a word anon.—Lay hold on him.

Lucio.   This may prove worse than hanging.

Duke.   [*To Escal.*]   What you have spoke, I pardon; sit you down.
We'll borrow place of him.—[*To Ang.*]   Sir, by your leave:
Hast thou or word, or wit, or impudence,
That yet can do thee office?   If thou hast,
Rely upon it till my tale be heard,
And hold no longer out.

Ang.   O my dread lord,
I should be guiltier than my guiltiness,
To think I can be undiscernible,
When I perceive your grace, like power divine,
Hath looked upon my passes.   Then, good prince,
No longer session hold upon my shame,
But let my trial be mine own confession:
Immediate sentence then, and sequent death,
Is all the grace I beg.

Duke.   Come hither, Mariana.—
Say, wast thou e'er contracted to this woman?

Ang.   I was, my lord.

Duke.   Go take her hence, and marry her instantly.—
Do you the office, friar; which consummate,
Return him here again.—Go with him, provost.

          [Exeunt Angelo, Mariana, Friar Peter, and Provost

Escal.   My lord, I am more amazed at his dishonour,
Than at the strangeness of it.

Duke.   Come hither, Isabel.
Your friar is now your prince: as I was then
Advértising and holy to your business,
Not changing heart with habit, I am still
Attorneyed at your service.

Isab.   O, give me pardon,
That I, your vassal, have employed and pained
Your unknown sovereignty!

Duke.   You are pardoned, Isabel:
And now, dear maid, be you as free to us.
Your brother's death, I know, sits at your heart;
And you may marvel, why I obscured myself,
Labouring to save his life, and would not rather
Make rash remonstrance of my hidden power,
Than let him so be lost. O most kind maid,
It was the swift celerity of his death,
Which I did think with slower foot came on,
That brained my purpose: but now peace be with him!
That life is better life, past fearing death,
Than that which lives to fear: make it your comfort,
So happy is your brother.
    Isab.   I do, my lord.

Re-enter ANGELO, MARIANA, FRIAR PETER, *and* Provost

Duke. For this new-married man, approaching here,
Whose salt imagination yet hath wronged
Your well-defended honour, you must pardon
For Mariana's sake. But, as he adjudged your brother,—
Being criminal, in double violation
Of sacred chastity, and of promise-breach,
Thereon dependent, for your brother's life—
The very mercy of the law cries out
Most audible, even from his proper tongue,
"An Angelo for Claudio, death for death!"
Haste still pays haste, and leisure answers leisure,
Like doth quit like, and Measure still for Measure.
Then, Angelo, thy fault thus manifested,—
Which, though thou wouldst deny, denies thee vantage,—
We do condemn thee to the very block
Where Claudio stooped to death, and with like haste.—
Away with him.
    Mari.   O my most gracious lord,
I hope you will not mock me with a husband.
    Duke. It is your husband mocked you with a husband.
Consenting to the safeguard of your honour,
I thought your marriage fit; else imputation,
For that he knew you, might reproach your life,
And choke your good to come. For his possessions,
Although by confiscation they are ours,
We do instate and widow you withal,
To buy you a better husband.
    Mari.   O my dear lord,
I crave no other, nor no better man.
    Duke. Never crave him: we are definite.
    Mari. Gentle my liege,—   [*Kneeling*
    Duke.   You do but lose your labour.
Away with him to death.—[*To Lucio*] Now, sir, to you.
    Mari. O my good lord!—Sweet Isabel, take my part:

Lend me your knees, and all my life to come
I'll lend you all my life to do you service.
    Duke.   Against all sense you do importune her:
Should she kneel down in mercy of this fact;
Her brother's ghost his pavéd bed would break,
And take her hence in horror.
    Mari.   Isabel,
Sweet Isabel, do yet but kneel by me:
Hold up your hands, say nothing, I'll speak all.
They say, best men are moulded out of faults,
And, for the most, become much more the better
For being a little bad: so may my husband.
O Isabel, will you not lend a knee?
    Duke.   He dies for Claudio's death.
    Isab.   Most bounteous sir,   *[Kneeling*
Look, if it please you, on this man condemned,
As if my brother lived. I partly think,
A due sincerity governed his deeds,
Till he did look on me: since it is so,
Let him not die. My brother had but justice,
In that he did the thing for which he died:
For Angelo,
His act did not o'ertake his bad intent;
And must be buried but as an intent
That perished by the way. Thoughts are no subjects,
Intents but merely thoughts.
    Mari.   Merely, my lord.
    Duke.   Your suit 's unprofitable: stand up, I say.—
I have bethought me of another fault.—
Provost, how came it Claudio was beheaded
At an unusual hour?
    Prov.   It was commanded so.
    Duke.   Had you a special warrant for the deed?
    Prov.   No, my good lord: it was by private message.
    Duke.   For which I do discharge you of your office:
Give up your keys.
    Prov.   Pardon me, noble lord:
I thought it was a fault, but knew it not,
Yet did repent me, after more advice;
For testimony whereof, one in the prison,
That should by private order else have died,
I have reserved alive.
    Duke.   What 's he?
    Prov.   His name is Barnardine.
    Duke.   I would thou hadst done so by Claudio.—
Go fetch him hither: let me look upon him.
                         [Exit Provost
    Escal.   I am sorry, one so learned and so wise
As you, Lord Angelo, have still appeared,
Should slip so grossly, both in the heat of blood,

And lack of tempered judgment afterward.
    Ang.   I am sorry that such sorrow I procure;
And so deep sticks it in my penitent heart,
That I crave death more willingly than mercy:
'T is my deserving, and I do entreat it.

    Re-enter Provost, BARNARDINE, CLAUDIO, *muffled, and*
                   JULIET

    Duke.   Which is that Barnardine?
    Prov.   This, my lord.
    Duke.   There was a friar told me of this man.—
Sirrah, thou art said to have a stubborn soul,
That apprehends no further than this world,
And squar'st thy life according.   Thou 'rt condemned;
But, for those earthly faults, I quit them all,
And pray thee, take this mercy to provide
For better times to come.—Friar, advise him:
I leave him to your hand.—What muffled fellow 's that?
    Prov.   This is another prisoner that I saved,
That should have died when Claudio lost his head,
As like almost to Claudio as himself.   [*Unmuffles Claudio*
    Duke.   [*To Isab.*] If he be like your brother, for his
      sake
Then is he pardoned; and for your lovely sake
Give me your hand, and say you will be mine,
He is my brother too.   But fitter time for that.
By this Lord Angelo perceives he 's safe:
Methinks I see a quickening in his eye.—
Well, Angelo, your evil quits you well:
Look that you love your wife; her worth, worth yours.—
I find an apt remission in myself,
And yet here's one in place I cannot pardon.—
[*To Lucio*] You, sirrah, that knew me for a fool, a coward,
One all of luxury, an ass, a madman:
Wherein have I so deservéd of you,
That you extol me thus?
    Lucio.   Faith, my lord, I spoke it but according to the
trick.   If you will hang me for it, you may; but I had
rather it would please you, I might be whipped.
    Duke.   Whipped first, sir, and hanged after.—
Proclaim it, provost, round about the city,
If any woman's wronged by this lewd fellow—
As I have heard him swear himself there 's one
Whom he begot with child—let her appear,
And he shall marry her: the nuptial finished,
Let him be whipped and hanged.
    Lucio.   I beseech your highness, do not marry me to a
whore!   Your highness said even now, I made you a duke:
good my lord, do not recompense me in making me a
cuckold.

Duke.   Upon mine honour, thou shalt marry her.
Thy slanders I forgive; and therewithal
Remit thy other forfeits.—Take him to prison,
And see our pleasure herein executed.
   Lucio.   Marrying a punk, my lord, is pressing to death,
whipping and hanging.
   Duke.   Slandering a prince deserves it.—
                          [Exeunt officers with Lucio
She, Claudio, that you wronged, look you restore.
Joy to you, Mariana!—love her, Angelo:
I have confessed her, and I know her virtue.—
Thanks, good friend Escalus, for thy much goodness:
There's more behind that is more gratulate.
Thanks, provost, for thy care, and secrecy;
We shall employ thee in a worthier place.—
Forgive him, Angelo, that brought you home
The head of Ragozine for Claudio's:
The offence pardons itself.—Dear Isabel,
I have a motion much imports your good;
Whereto if you 'll a willing ear incline,
What 's mine is yours, and what is yours is mine.—
So, bring us to our palace; where we 'll show
What 's yet behind, that 's meet you all should know.
                                 [Exeunt

THE PEEBLES CLASSIC LIBRARY

BLACK BEAUTY

PRIDE AND PREJUDICE

AROUND THE WORLD IN 80 DAYS

THE VICAR OF WAKEFIELD

TREASURE ISLAND

KIDNAPPED

BARCHESTER TOWERS (2 VOLUMES)

JANE EYRE (2 VOLUMES)

GULLIVER'S TRAVELS

ROBINSON CRUSOE

A TALE OF TWO CITIES

SENSE AND SENSIBILITY

WUTHERING HEIGHTS